AF575459

Helen Chadwick

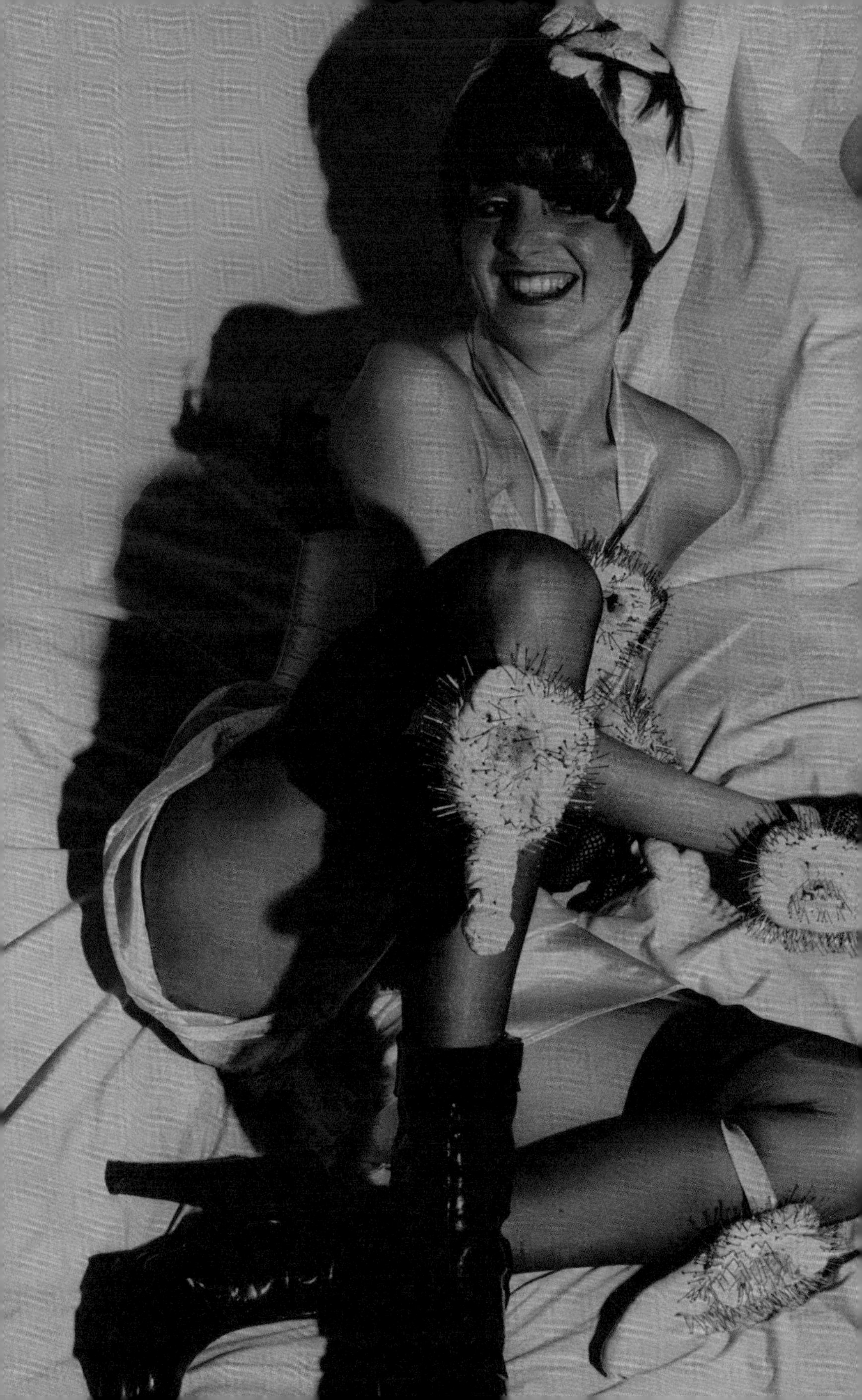

Helen Chadwick

Life Pleasures

Edited by **Laura Smith**
Foreword by **Marina Warner**

Essays by **Katrin Bucher Trantow, Maria Christoforidou, Philomena Epps and Laura Smith**
Interviews by **Laura Smith with Louisa Buck and David Notarius**

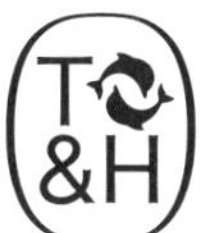

Frontispiece: Helen Chadwick, photographic print from *Fancy Dress and Sculptures Photograph Book*, 1974

First published in the United Kingdom in 2025 by Thames & Hudson Ltd, 6–24 Britannia Street, London WC1X 9JD

First published in the United States of America in 2025 by Thames & Hudson Inc., 500 Fifth Avenue, New York, New York 10110

Published on the occasion of the major exhibition 'Helen Chadwick: Life Pleasures' at The Hepworth Wakefield (7 May–27 October 2025); touring to Museo Novecento, Florence (November 2025–February 2026) and Kunsthaus Graz (March–August 2026)

Edited by Laura Smith
With assistance from Farah Dailami

Publication supported by:

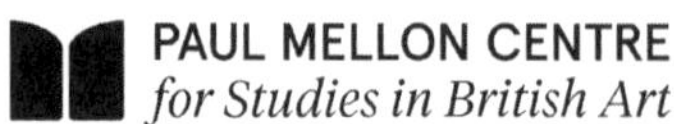

Exhibition supported by:

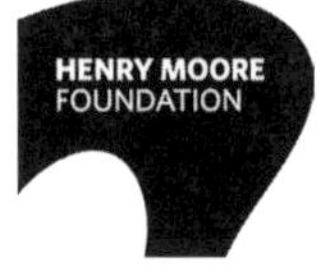

RICHARD SALTOUN
LONDON | ROME | NEW YORK

The Helen Chadwick Exhibition Circle

Leeds Museums & Galleries

In-kind supporters:

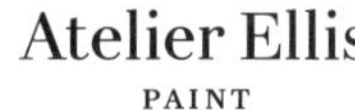

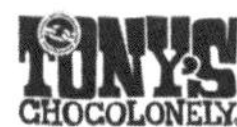

EU Authorized Representative:
Interart S.A.R.L.
19 rue Charles Auray, 93500 Pantin, Paris, France
productsafety@thameshudson.co.uk
www.interart.fr

A CIP catalogue record for this book is available from the British Library

Library of Congress Control Number 2024943720

ISBN 978-0-500-02888-9
01

Printed and bound in Bosnia and Herzegovina by GPS Group

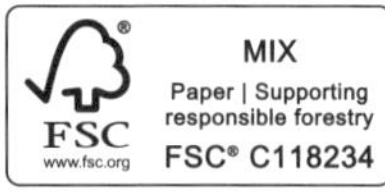

Foreword
Marina Warner

Ego Geometria Sum – 'I am Geometry', declared Helen Chadwick in the title of her 1982–83 installation. I saw the full spiral of ten geometrical solids laid out in the hangar-like space of Riverside Studios, London: it mapped out her life in objects, each one marking a certain phase, from the incubator in which she lay as a premature baby to the front door of her studio/home in Beck Road, Hackney, the symbol of her hard-won artist's independence. For this early magnum opus, Helen developed a printing technique – she was an irrepressible and canny technical experimenter with media – which allowed her to superimpose photographs of herself onto the sculptures, to float there in the wood, materialized spirits of memory, ghosts in the machine. Set against the walls all around were more naked Helens, bearing her Euclidian solids like a bodybuilder posing for a naturist calendar against pink (fleshy) studio drapes. The combination of self-fashioning and defiant assertion, parodic wit and consummate aesthetic precision would become defining aspects of Chadwick's art. 'I am Geometry' proclaims the central axiom of her imagination: she was 'turning the past, my body, into Form, Number, Divinity', and throughout her short life she continued to puzzle over the opposition between beauty and nature, the ideal and the organic, the permanent and the transitory, the bodily and the aesthetic, and to explore, reconfigure and invert conventions governing art and taste. 'Geometry' implies a Platonic eternal and absolute. By imbuing ideals of order, taking up occupation of abstract symbols of perfection with things that had served an ordinary female life, Helen was making a more general claim about women, their life experiences, their bodies, their destinies. She was Everywoman, and the forms she adapted could serve her ethical vision. In her performances of *In the Kitchen* (1977) for her MA degree show, she invested herself and

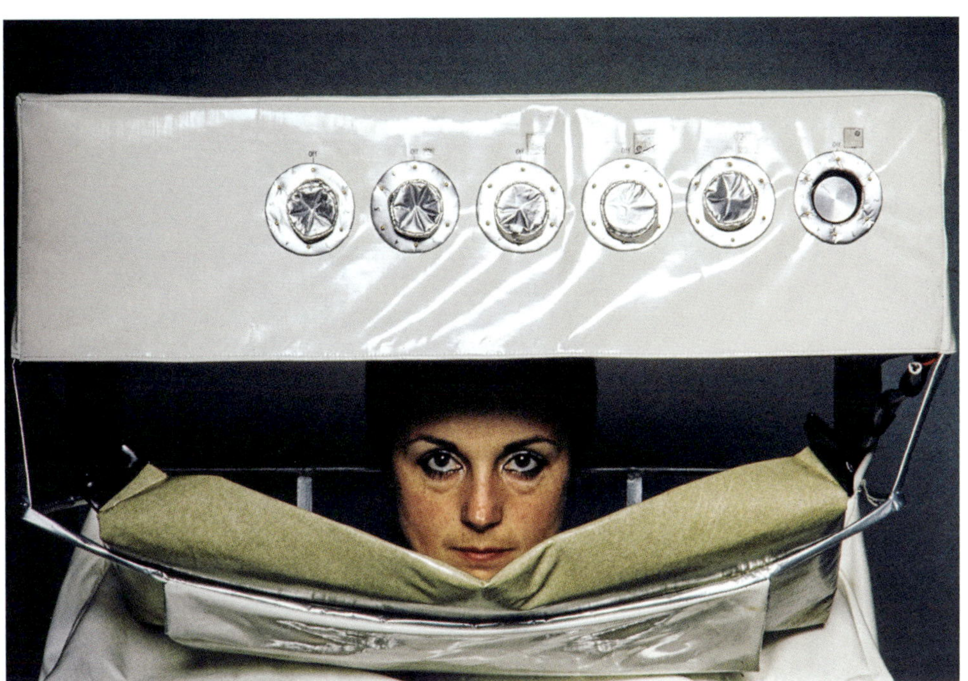

her fellow students in the appliances of domestic destiny, dressing up as a soft washing machine, a kitchen stove, a fridge. She was angry, she was edgy, she was witty; she was wicked.

It is difficult now to remember and revive the feelings that her startling originality aroused. From the punk rebel of the lovingly hand-sewn, provocative variations on lingerie (1973) and the autobiographical chronicler on display in *Ego Geometria Sum*, she became more flamboyant, more flagrant, with nods to Renaissance allegories, to Venus and vanitas and to rococo ornament, especially in *The Oval Court*, part of her installation *Of Mutability* at the Institute of Contemporary Art (ICA), London, in 1986 (this elegiac yet exuberant meditation on pleasure, desire and time, is now on display in full at The Hepworth Wakefield for the first time in forty years). The 1980s were a time of feminist agitprop rooted in anger and anxiety, and Helen came under criticism for giving the male gaze the chance to feast on her. But the full tableau of *Of Mutability* took further that questioning of the classical binary between nature and the ideal: here was a gorgeous, festive cornucopia climaxing in *Carcass*, a pillar

Helen Chadwick, *In the Kitchen (oven)*, 1977 (detail).
Photograph, 41 × 30.5 cm (16¼ × 12⅛ in.)

of bubbling smelly gunge. *Effluvia* and *Enfleshings* were titles Chadwick chose for her later work, as she searched for the sensory knowledge that comes through touch into sex, menstruation, childbirth (*One Flesh*, 1985), and micturition (*Piss Flowers*, 1991–92) and, later, in vitro fertilization, into deliquescence and rot, into genitalia. She became fascinated by the natural mimicry of flowers and orifices, by the rhymes between cocoa and caca, chocolate and poo, by the interchangeability of male and female organs when viewed from a certain angle, often in hallucinatory close-up. In short, for Helen, the profane haunted the sacred, and vice versa. Form was her goal, the reinvention of form the work of her studio-laboratory, and new forms were her achievement. In an era when the ambition to subvert often left the artist stranded in irony, Helen was on a mission to upturn conventional aesthetics, to transvalue the despised and disregarded, to tap delight from disgust: she was revolutionary in her constant rethinking of traditional aesthetic affect.

For *Imaginary Women*, a film I made with Gina Newson for Channel Four in 1985, Gina sat us round a table to talk while we ate. Alongside Helen, there were Susan Hiller (1940–2019), Gaby Agis (b. 1960), Rose Garrard (b. 1946) and others. The format was a tribute to *The Dinner Party* (1974–79) by Judy Chicago (b. 1939); now and then, however, feminist solidarity became strained, especially regarding Helen's approach to her body. Afterwards, Helen invited me to write for the *Of Mutability* exhibition catalogue. I went to see her many times in Beck Road, where we talked and talked and became friends. She was enthralling, a vivid presence, stylish and neat, with a dazzling wide smile that lit up her small face, her Louise Brooks helmet of a haircut gleaming, and always, her talismanic brooch of a fist grasping a dagger. She was Helen of Troy, Puck, Joan of Arc, Venus – Luciferian, angelic, spirited, ardent, eloquent, and a generous celebrant of all things erotic, while approaching them with sharpened intellectual tools. She once exclaimed: 'Triumph of pleasure – sublime desire.' Her articulacy was unusual, formal – you can hear it in the British Library's excellent recordings for the 'Oral History of British Photography' as she talks with Mark Haworth-Booth (b. 1944). He was then Curator of Photography at the Victoria and Albert Museum, London, and his collection of her work has preserved key pieces for us to enjoy now (she never could have afforded storage). On the recordings, Helen speaks in full, shapely, often elaborate sentences, drawing on a vast vocabulary gathered from wide reading. Her wordsmithery dazzles in 'Piss Posy', an ecstatic paean to all things bodily (see pages 162–3), as well as in so many of her works' titles. I remember her describing an Otto Dix reclining nude, *Nude Girl on a Fur* (1932), as a *telluric* goddess – the only time, then as now, that I have heard the word.

Helen asked me to write about her work again for the catalogue for *Piss Flowers* at the Serpentine, London; I've always kicked myself for passing up the chance – she could use a different pair of eyes on that adventurous work, I said, and I wasn't sure I would strike the right note. I couldn't have foreseen that there was little time left to work together.

Helen Chadwick mounted an enquiry into gender, sexuality and ecology from a subject position that embraced femininity in all its historical and cultural aspects and did not restrict the definition of a woman. Her independence of mind, her blazing, innovatory ideas and meticulous execution staked out the ground on which several women artists have become visible – and acclaimed; she was part of a larger movement, but she extended inherited boundaries and, in so doing, took traditional women's themes way out beyond the known horizon.

On the morning of 15 March 1996, Helen went to the V&A Print Room to look at the textile designs of Anna Maria Garthwaite (1688–1763), a Spitalfields silk weaver who had set up her own business and succeeded as an artist-craftworker, and an artist who had long inspired her. From South Kensington, she travelled to Bedford Square for a meeting at the Architectural Association; on arrival, she said she didn't feel well. It is still not known exactly what took her. She would have turned seventy in 2023; there would now be three more decades of work behind her and still years ahead to make more – think Leonora Carrington (1917–2011), Louise Bourgeois (1911–2010), Georgia O'Keeffe (1887–1986). This publication, the largest since her death twenty-eight years ago, at last reveals the full sweep, from the 1970s to the 1990s, of her unique and exhilarating artistry.

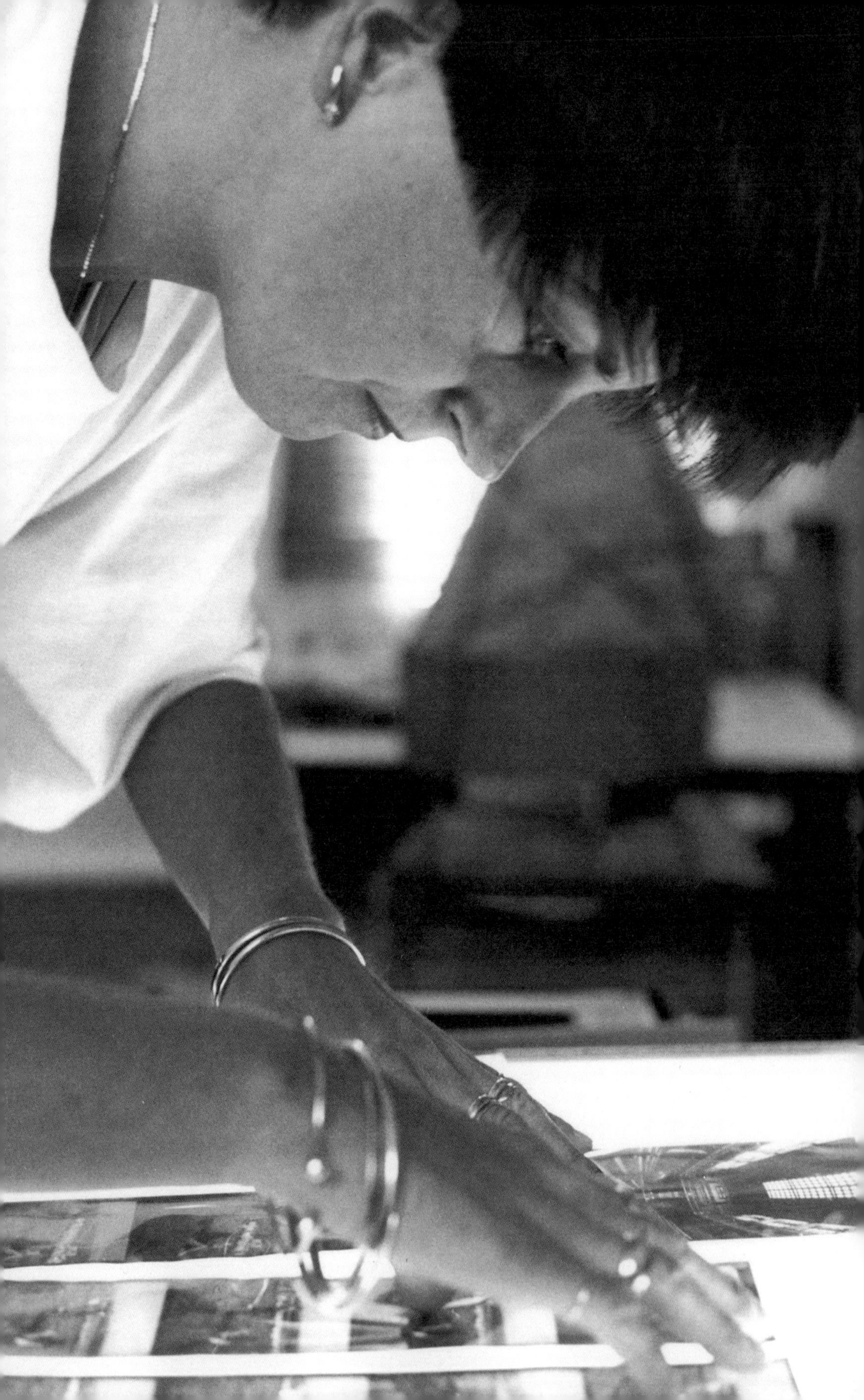

CHAPTER 1

Mortality, desire, all those kinds of words

Laura Smith

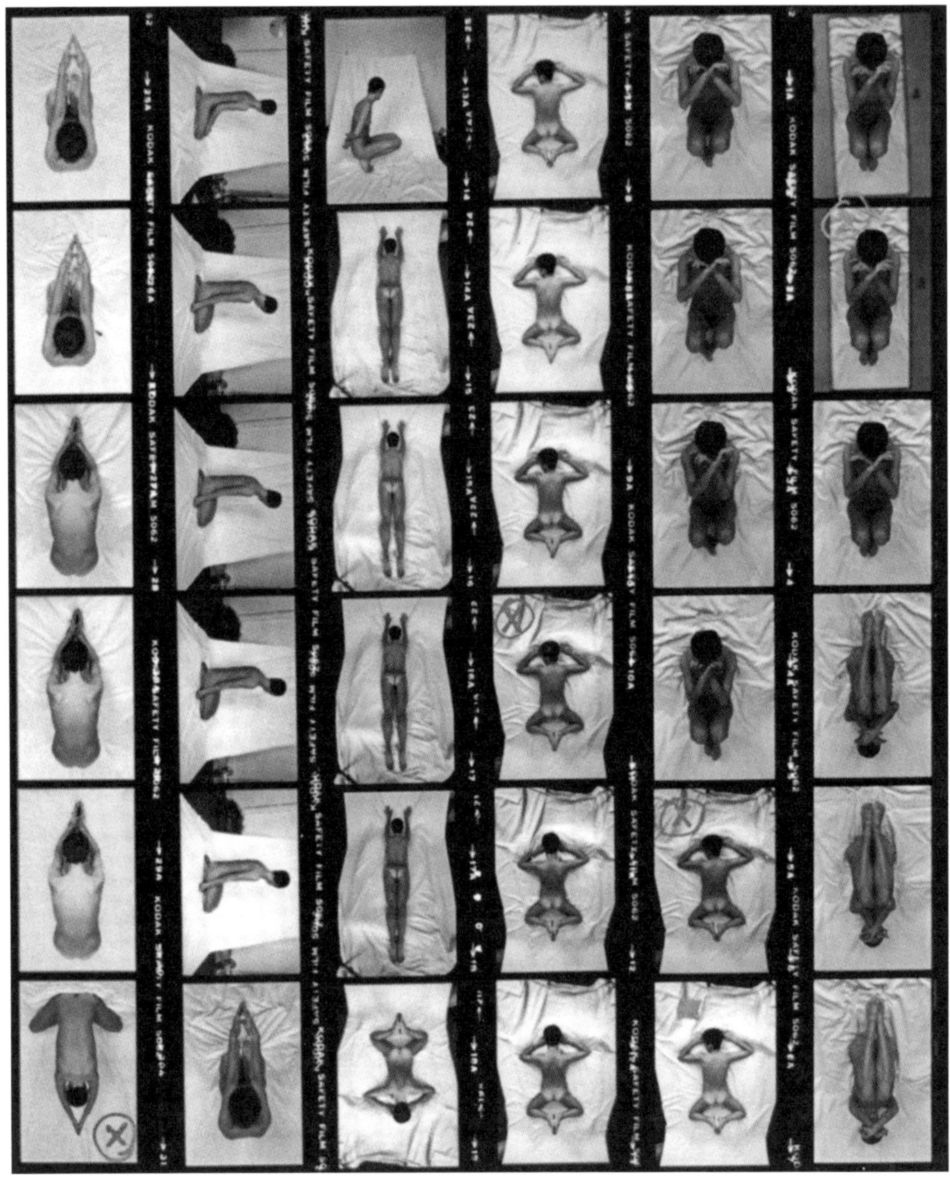

ABOVE **Contact prints of Helen Chadwick performing sequences for poses for *Ego Geometria Sum I: Incubator – Birth*, *II: Font – 3 months*, *IV: Boat – 2 years* and *IX: High School – 13 years*, 1983**

PAGE 10 **Helen Chadwick looking at slides for her work *Three Houses*, 1987**

> **If I have an intent, it is to open up a crease in language and look at what cannot be articulated – the phenomena of consciousness, the enigma and riddles of selfhood, the momenta of sexuality and emotionality.[1]**

> **All the mythic versions of women, from the myth of the redeeming purity of the virgin to that of the healing, reconciling mother, are consolatory nonsenses; and consolatory nonsense seems to me to be a fair definition of myth, anyway. Mother goddesses are just as silly a notion as father gods. If a revival of the myths of these cults gives women emotional satisfaction, it does so at the price of obscuring the real conditions of life. This is why they were invented in the first place.[2]**

Helen Chadwick has been described variously as wicked, raunchy, funny, clever, fierce, brilliant, tough, confronting, provocative, meticulous, a genius, ahead of her time....None of these descriptions are mythic. Despite the fact that she is no longer with us, her presence and influence on the history of art is real and multifaceted. And her attention to examining and dismantling the myth of the woman is enduring and powerful.

Chadwick was an artist who worked beyond boundaries, beyond the boundaries of the self, of gender, of the body and its skin, beyond what is polite or expected. Her art wittingly compounds numerous physical sensations: thrill, wonder, erotic desire, disgust, repulsion, tenderness, queasiness, awe. Her materials are affecting in both the simple fact of their application as artistic supplies and their unexpected combinations. She sought to multiply and sustain associations of bodily experience from sight to touch, and from smell to taste. To these ends she used flowers (in abundance; orchids, bluebells, buttercups, dandelions, narcissi, tulips, roses, daisies, honeysuckle), chocolate, fur, hair, bubble bath, bronze, blankets, mattresses, snow, milk, oysters, meat, window cleaner, engine oil, rotting vegetables, earthworms, pigs intestines, animal carcasses, urine, and the cells and form of her own body.

She made sculptures, installations, photography, performances, lightboxes and prints, working across the genres of portraiture, still life, landscape painting and the *memento mori* and *vanitas* traditions.[3] She approached these artistic categories with the same disregard for their established hierarchies as she did any hierarchies of medium. Her art was mischievously unruly and luxuriously disruptive; she was interested in confronting the idea of 'experience' to directly address issues around feminism, sexuality, classism and austerity, death, disease and beauty. As she comments:

> *a broad conception of my activities over the years is an involvement with female sexuality. I have felt that a conflict exists between a conditioned and an instinctive response. I have attempted to find a language to express this ambiguity and the complex feelings that this area of involvement generates. The work would seem to represent a fusion between a world of pre-defined archetypes and subjective flow of experience.*[4]

Chadwick's works make no attempt to provide a verdict on or conclusion to any of the issues that she approached. Her endeavour was to stimulate an individual's intuitive, involuntary reactions and sensations as a way of destabilizing the conditioned and constructed aspects of contemporary culture around sex, gender, death, beauty, class and power. As Chadwick's friend, the writer and art historian Marina Warner, asserts: 'she wanted to reorientate the tradition of aesthetics in order to shape a better fit between representation, sensation and knowledge.'[5]

An important feature across Chadwick's entire output was her meticulous approach to making; she was highly skilled across a vast number of materials and processes, and her abilities with construction and manufacture were enviably proficient. Chadwick was adept at photography, sewing, bookbinding, sculptural assembly, casting, printmaking and design. Her use of traditional fabrication methods and

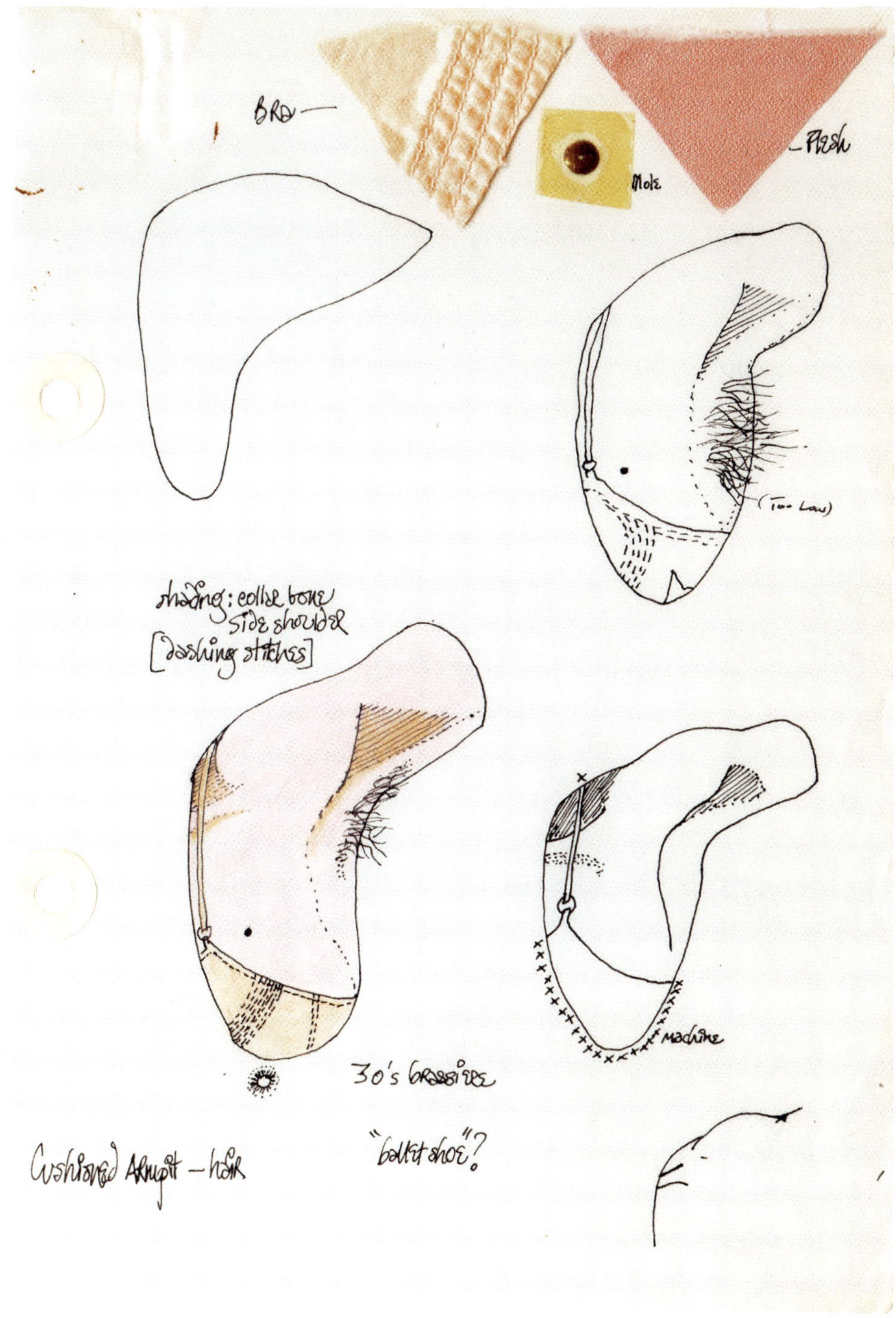

Helen Chadwick, Sketches, *c*. 1973–5

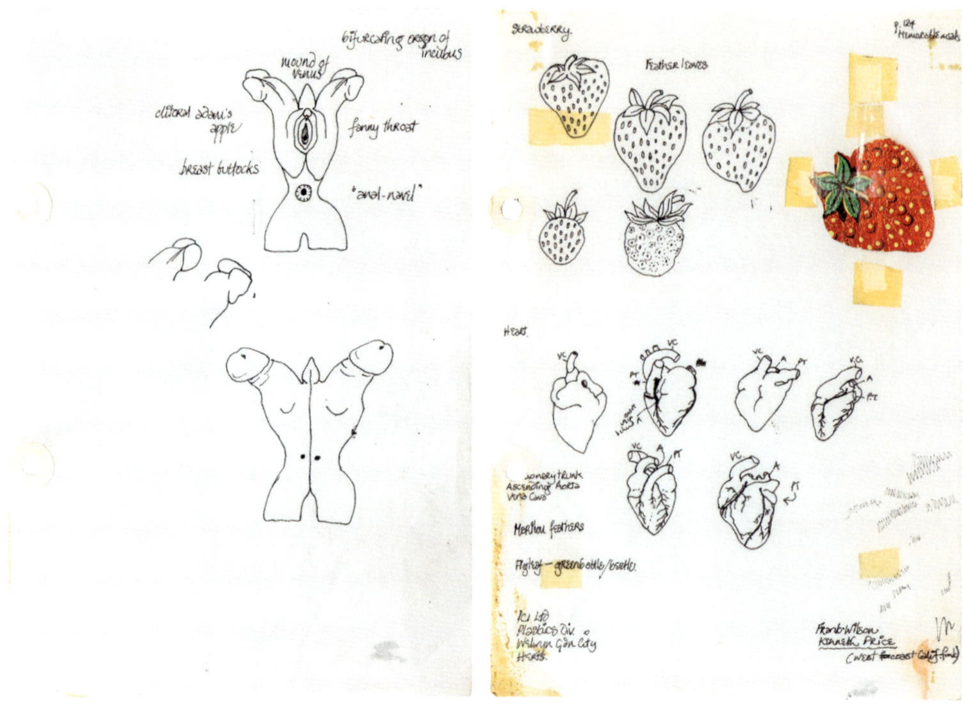

sophisticated technologies transformed the extraordinary materials she employed into installations that feel so unforced that there is no call to question why she used the materials that she used. The work is natural, effortless and genuine, and her 'immaculate craftsmanship helped her smuggle her ideas across the border of convention'.[6] Her handwriting was beautiful, her hand-stitching was pin-perfect; she retained painstaking records and archives, and she worked with steadfast tenacity to produce a delicate, vital, powerful and exquisitely crafted body of work that spans almost thirty years. To quote Warner again, she had 'astonishing standards of originality and versatility, determination and skill'.[7]

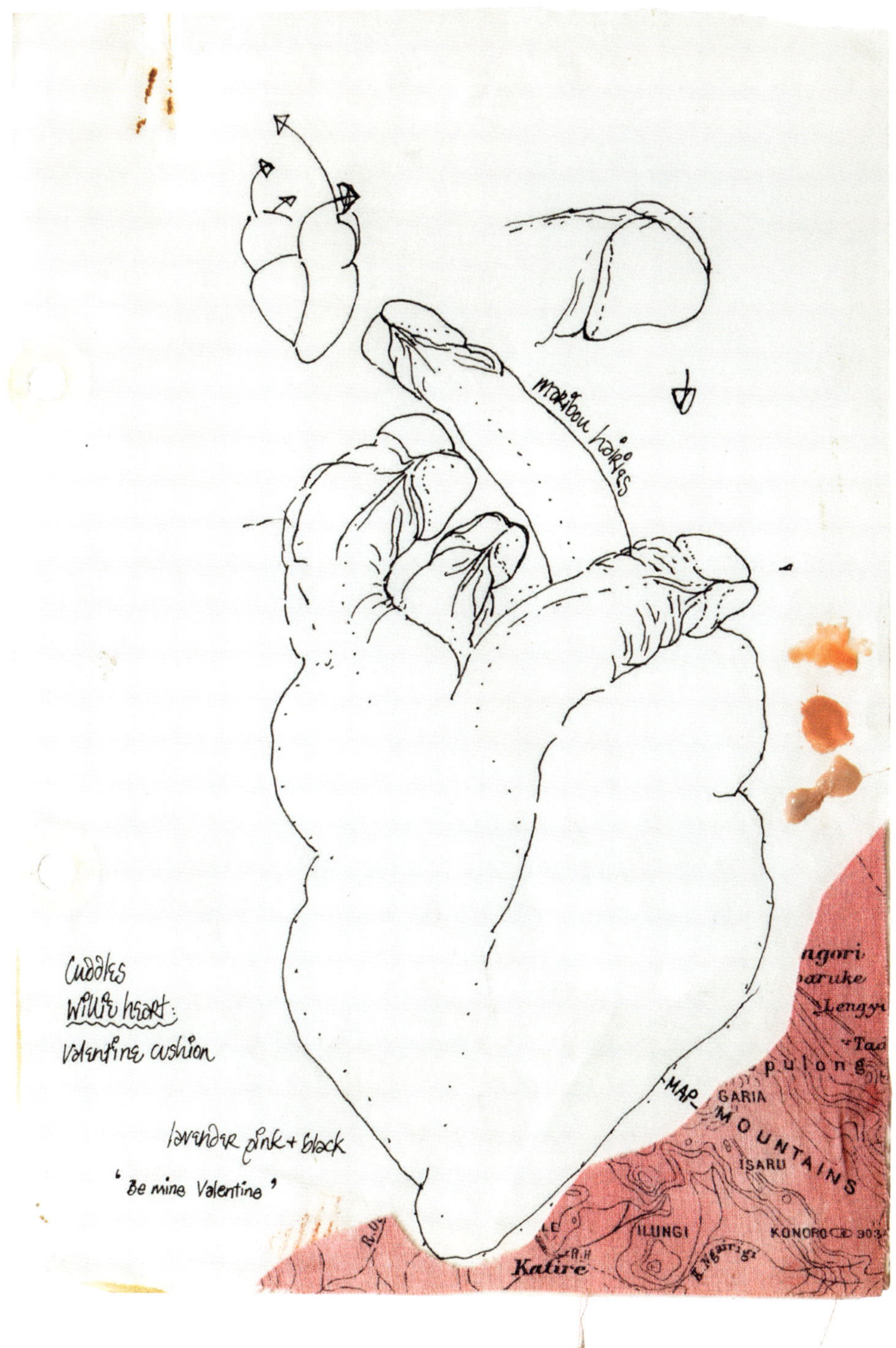

OPPOSITE AND ABOVE **Helen Chadwick, Sketches, *c.* 1973–5**

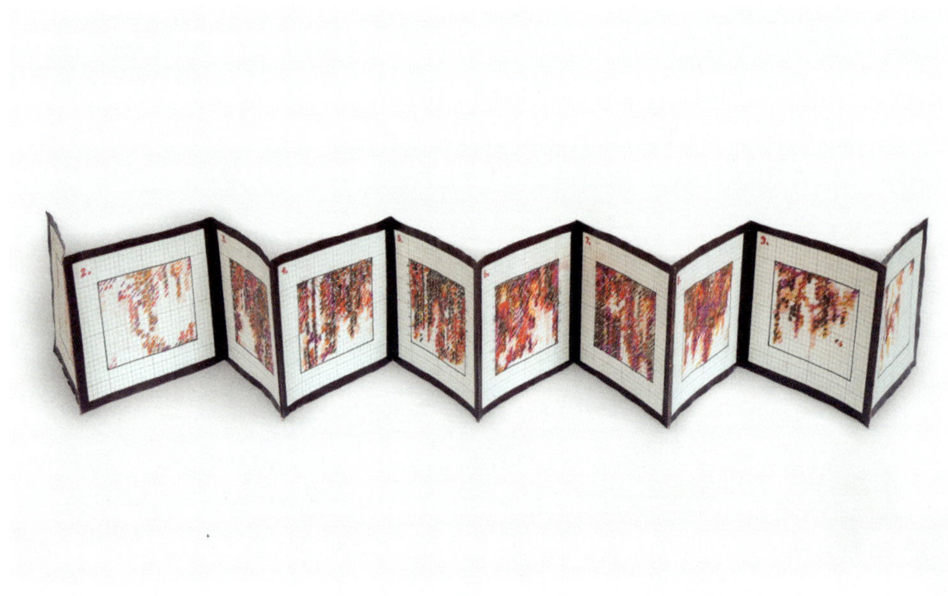

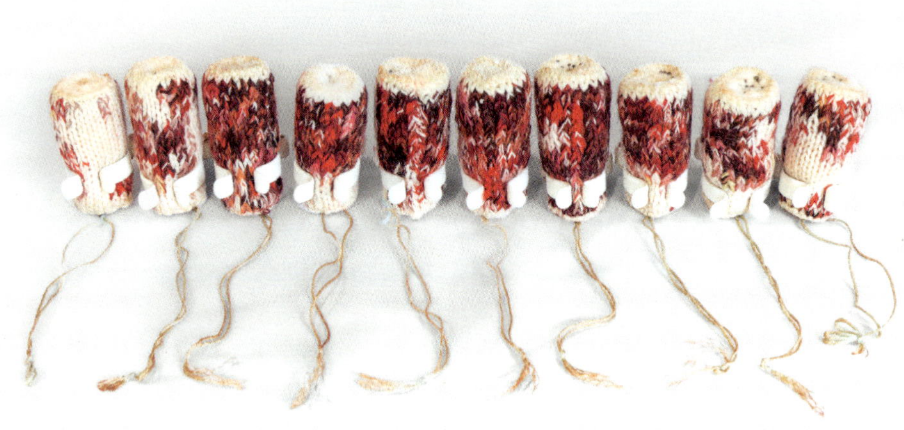

Helen Chadwick, *Lillet Pattern Fold-Out Book*, 1975. Artist book, graph paper mounted on black card, coloured pencil, length 40 cm (15¾ in.)

Helen Chadwick, *Knitted Lillet Blood Cycle*, 1975. Knitted tampons, wool, clips, cloth; tampons each 6 × 3 cm (2⅜ × 1⅛ in.)

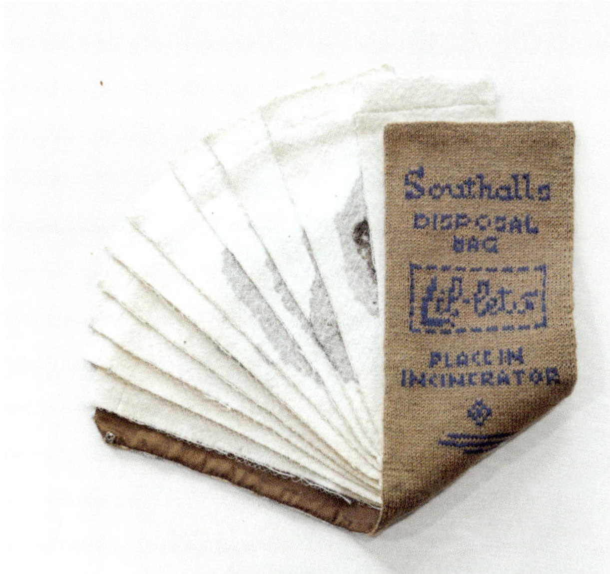

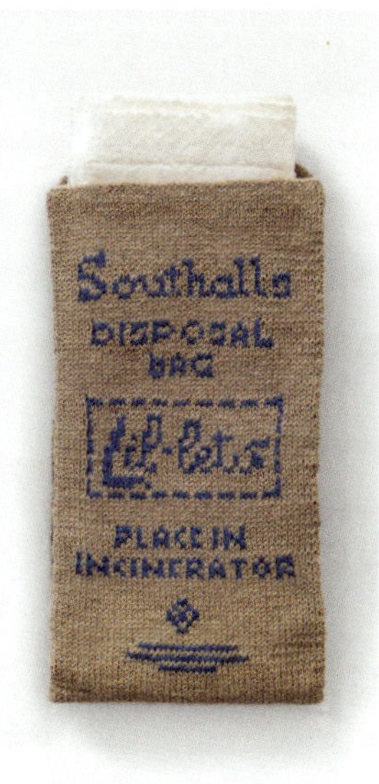

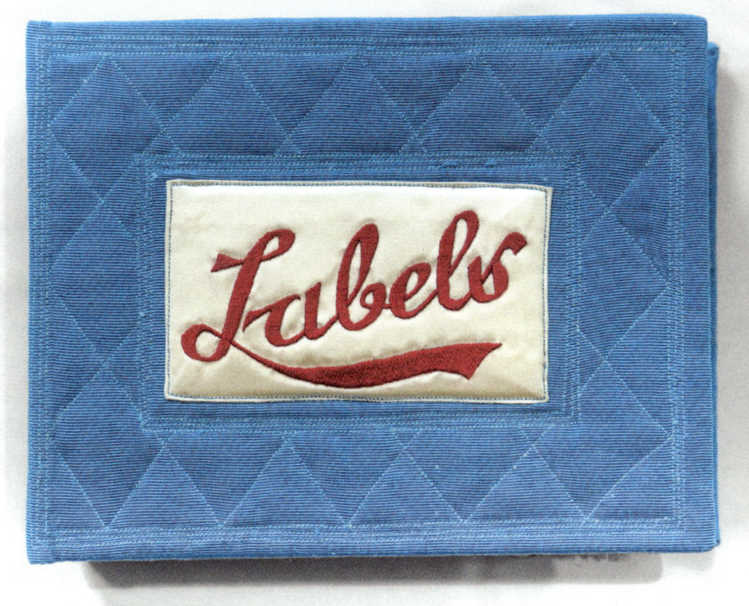

Helen Chadwick, *Knitted Disposal Bag*, 1975. Wool, lint, netting, dried blood, 31.2 × 25 cm ($12\frac{3}{8}$ × $9\frac{7}{8}$ in.)

Helen Chadwick, *Labels Book*, 1975. Assorted fabrics, needlework

The 1950s to the 1970s: Growing Up, Schooling, Working her Way

Chadwick was born prematurely in May 1953 in Croydon, London. Her mother was a Greek refugee from Athens and her father was an estate agent from east London (the two had met in Athens during the Second World War when her father was stationed there). In 1946, her mother immigrated to the UK, and the pair bought a home in the then new and aspirational London suburb of Croydon. Chadwick's father diligently began a new career as an estate agent and her mother committed herself to becoming a 'proper English housewife' - selecting soft furnishings for their immaculate middle-class bungalow and learning to play the piano. Chadwick grew up with a brother, who would later become a sheep farmer in Sussex, and from time to time they would all visit her mother's large and lively family in the Greek Peloponnese mountains, who would shower the children with loving attention. Back in Croydon, Littleheath Woods, an 'Area of Special Character', was just behind their home, and there Chadwick remembered making mudpies and rose petal perfumes as a small child. As she grew older she would walk in the woods and bring home injured animals; there are anecdotes of the neighbours complaining about the lame ferret and goose in the Chadwick's back garden. Chadwick passed her 11-plus exams with ease and began her secondary education at Croydon High School, where her inherent fascination with the natural world meant that she thrived in biology and geography. Surprisingly, she failed O-level art, with one art teacher commenting: 'Helen has an independent nature and has worked in her individual manner, but she needs to concentrate for longer periods.'[8]

Her mother had an interest in art, however, and together they regularly visited exhibitions. Chadwick recalls her curiosity when watching her mother look at (predominantly) paintings; she was engrossed by the myriad feelings that the works they viewed would engender - from delight and satisfaction to disgust and revulsion. Having secured a place to study archaeology and anthropology at Exeter University, Chadwick had a change of heart and declined her place in favour of a fine art foundation course at Croydon Art College. By this time, Helen's parents had separated, so continuing her education in Croydon allowed her to stay close to her mother. Once at art school, she soon discovered that she had little interest in drawing or painting but remembered making curious congregations of forms - many based on her own body - in materials such as jelly, chocolate and liquorice. These nascent works even attracted attention from the local press, who compared her work to that of artists in the Fluxus movement (who had, indeed, inspired some of Chadwick's ideas).

In 1973 Chadwick accepted a place to study for a BA in fine art at Brighton Polytechnic. Very quickly she developed an infamous reputation; frequently dressing head-to-toe in black leather, she travelled by motorbike and attracted a large group of friends and fans. Looking back on that time, Chadwick recalled: 'Traditional media were never dynamic enough... right from early on in art school, I wanted to use the body to create a set of inter-relationships with the audience.'[9] During her BA, Chadwick worked across film, sculpture and video, but the consistent anchor in her work was always an attention to the body, to her own body. One of her first documented works during this time was *Untitled (Eat Art)* (1973), for which she made individual jelly casts of her own face and then invited the public to eat them. She also made cushions shaped like body parts as a reference to the fractured bodies of surrealism, as well as another work

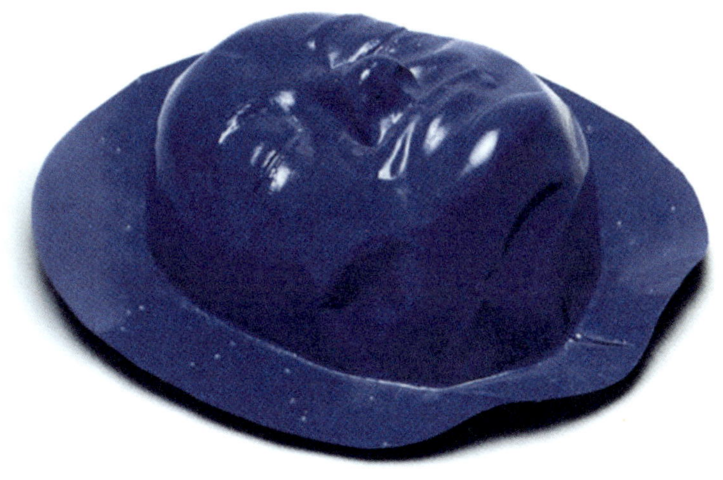

Helen Chadwick, *Untitled (Eat Art)*, 1973.
Plastic mould made from cast of the artist's face

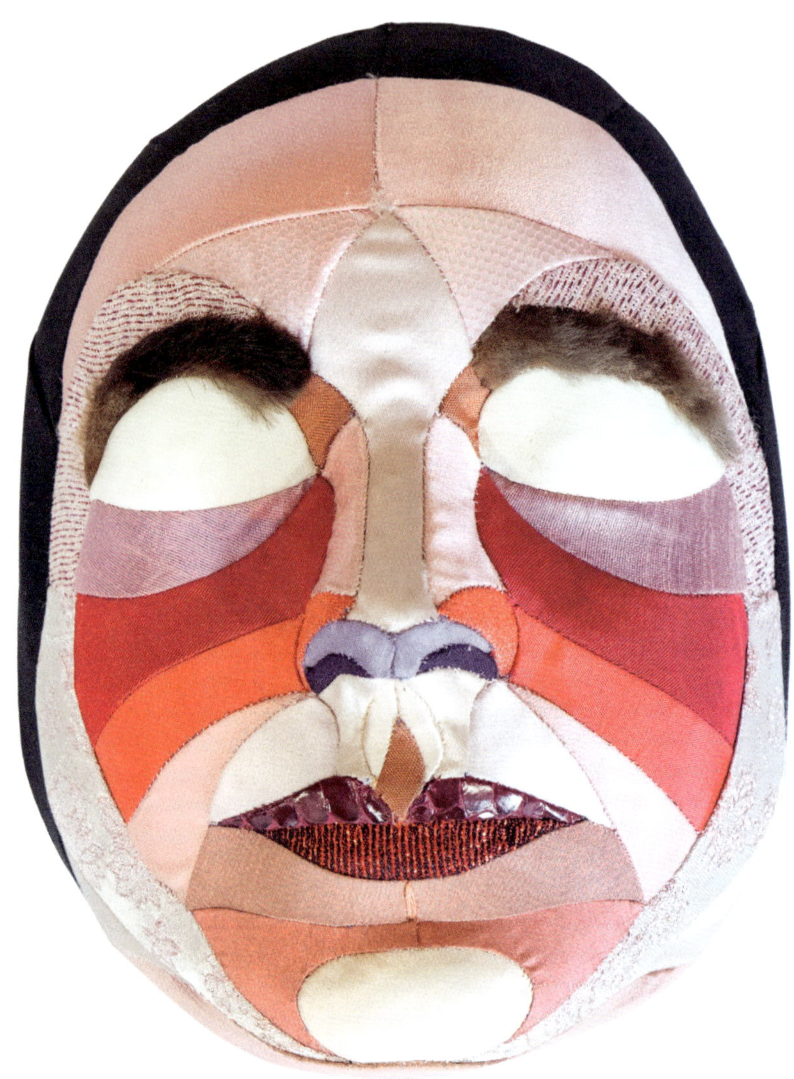

Helen Chadwick, *Face Mask*, 1974.
Assorted fabric, 20 × 13 × 4 cm ($7\frac{7}{8}$ × $5\frac{1}{8}$ × $1\frac{5}{8}$ in.)

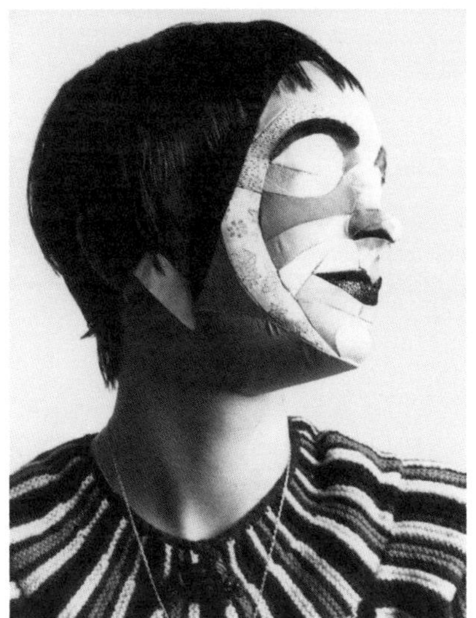
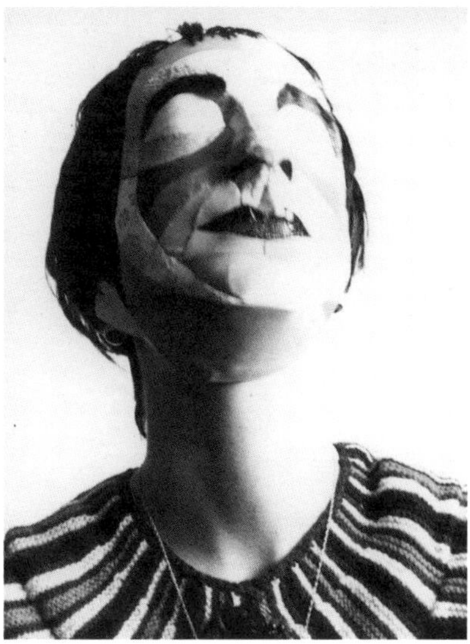

called *The Erotic Chocolate Box* (1973), in which the delicious chocolates inside were shaped like a range of erotic, titillating items: 'one of the first themes I became involved with was orality and its links to the sexual significance of food, particularly sweets'.[10]

For her degree show Chadwick created a work titled *Domestic Sanitation* (1976), which was a performance, an installation and a video. The performance included Chadwick herself as well as three other women, all wearing latex costumes (now lost) created by painting latex directly on to their skin, a method that produced 'clothing' that emphasized their breasts, buttocks and pubic hair but also played out ideas of nudity and nakedness, as the clothes indexically referred to their own naked skin. In these costumes the foursome engages in a bawdy, satirical and feminist play of cleaning and grooming one another. The first act of the work, *The Latex Glamour Rodeo*, takes place in a sort of stylized beauty salon: two of the women treat the third to something like a gynaecological examination, while the fourth woman, dressed in black latex, slinks along the walls like a cat, rubbing herself against the rubber membrane that protects the periphery. She then goes on to perform some frenzied, carnal gymnastics, all to a soundtrack of Donny Osmond and excerpts from American advertising voiceovers.

LEFT AND RIGHT **Helen Chadwick wearing *Face Mask*, 1974**

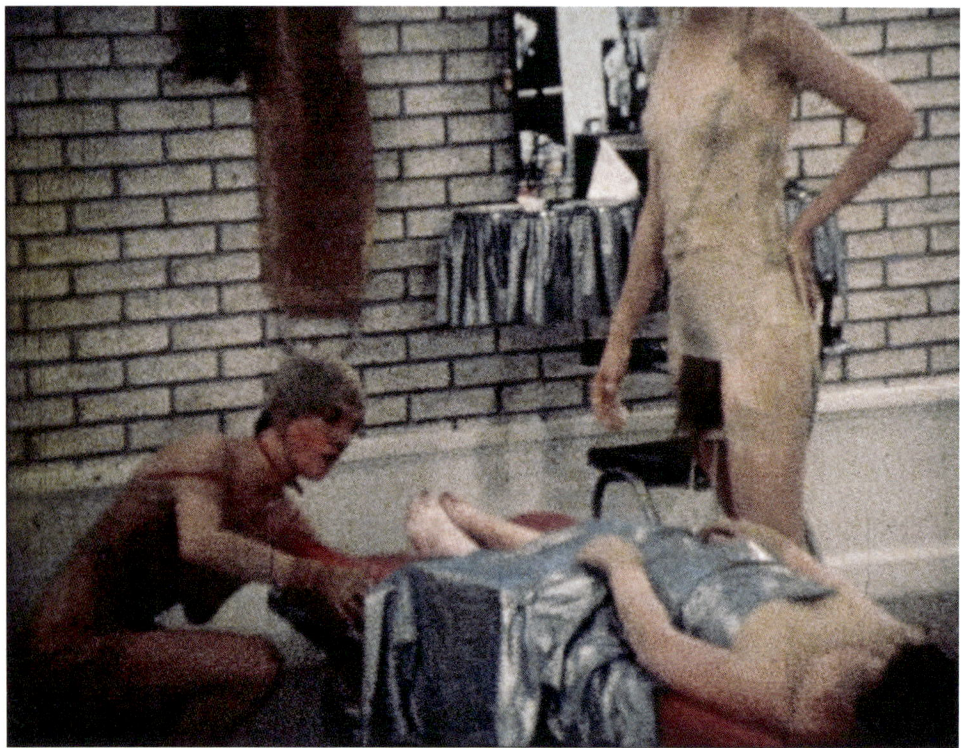

In the second act, *Bargain Bed Bonanza*, the same four women are dressed in costumes that are hybrids of beds, mattresses, blankets, women's bodies and lingerie - part clothing and part furniture. Each has a separate identity and colour: the 'Supermum Housewife' is yellow, 'Virgin Scandinavian' is white, the 'Tart Costume' is pink and the 'Rape Mattress' is blue-grey. The four take turns to enact farcical scenes that reflect the character of their costumes; cleaning, playing, and soliciting and suffering sexual encounters. The whole thing is partly humorous, partly dangerous, raunchy, disconcerting and taboo all at once. A video of the entire performance - both acts - exists in grainy footage, while only the 'bed' costumes survive, notable for their meticulous hand-stitching and exquisite attention to detail. At the same time as creating this remarkable work, Chadwick also researched and wrote her graduating dissertation 'Vulgarity in the Fashion of the 1960s', which scrutinized the relationship between fashion and society through the perspectives

Helen Chadwick, *Domestic Sanitation: The Latex Glamour Rodeo*, 1976. Film still

of taste, class, body politics and sexuality; her research for this thesis granted her feminism a social and collective perspective.

In 1976 Chadwick moved back to London, to Hackney, and enrolled on a Master of Fine Arts course at Chelsea College of Art. In 1977 she and over twenty other artists moved into Beck Road, squatting in a strip of semi-derelict Victorian terrace houses that was destined for demolition. The houses had been compulsorily purchased by the Inner London Education Authority, so that an extension and car park for Hackney Technical College could be built where they stood. After Chadwick and her fellow artists had been squatting in the houses for two years, the ILEA licensed the houses to Acme, an organization that delivers affordable and secure artist studio provision and residencies. Acme then leased the houses to the artists, plus an additional grant of £750 per house for necessary renovation work. Artist Deborah Duffin (b. 1953) recalls: 'We spent months knocking down walls, getting basic plumbing in, plastering and decorating, with help and advice from Acme and other artists. But we had space to live and work at a nominal rent.'[11] In saving the street

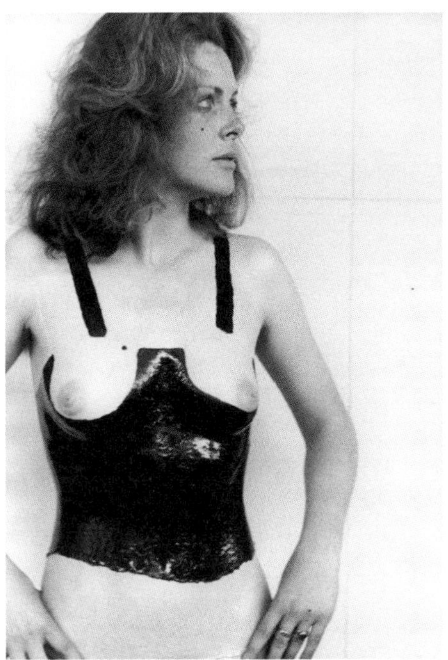

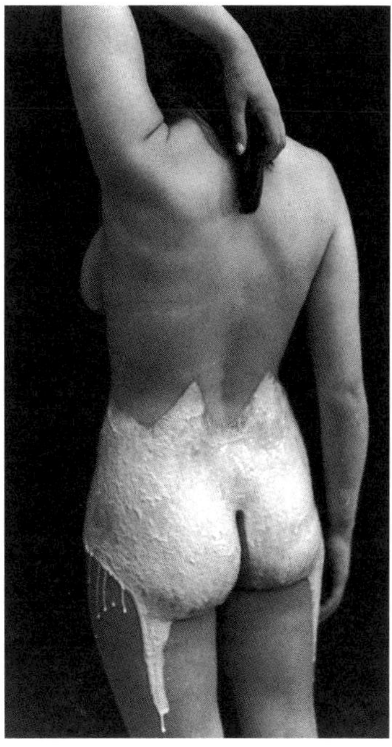

LEFT AND RIGHT **Helen Chadwick, latex costumes for *Domestic Sanitation*, 1976**

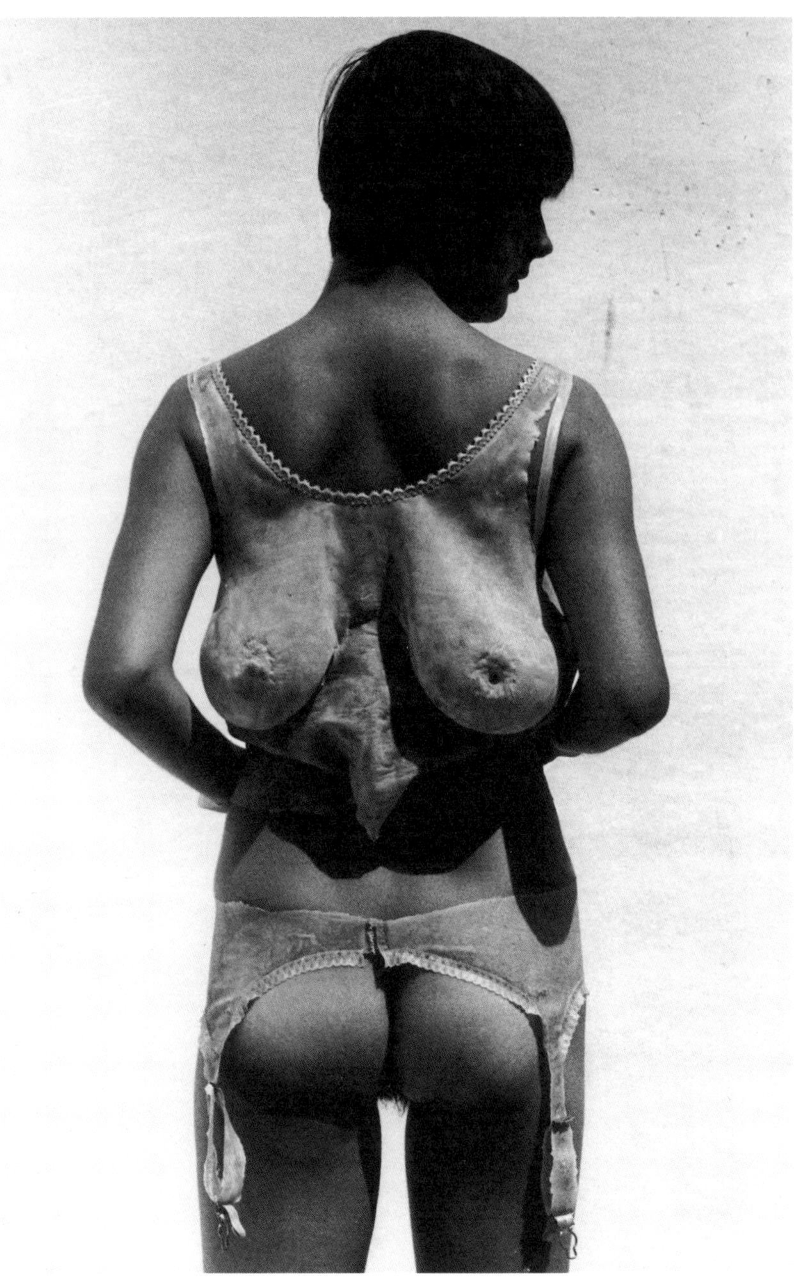

Helen Chadwick, latex costume for *Domestic Sanitation*, 1976

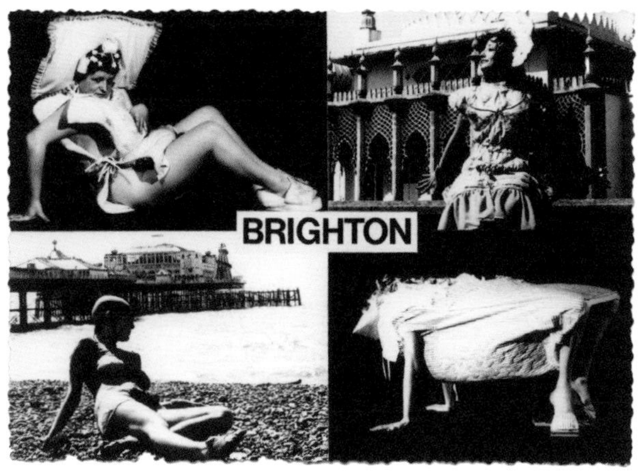

Studio Girl
(BRIGHTON)
presents
Domestic Sanitation
a special summer event featuring
The Latex Glamor Rodeo
and for a short season only
Bargain Bed Bonanza
Thursday 17th June at 6 pm
We hope you will come – this card is your passport to a whole new world of beauty
Our showrooms are open daily from 10 until 1 and 2 until 5 June 14th to 19th 1976
Your Brighton Representative:
Miss Helen Chadwick
opp. Pavilion: corner Edward St.

from demolition, Chadwick and her fellow artists were instrumental in creating a community of creative individuals able to thrive and flourish. Beck Road became a hive of home studios whose residents included Maureen Paley, Ray Walker and Genesis P-Orridge. Residents would exchange materials and offer each other assistance, socialize and learn from one another. Later, in 1984, the artists formed a residents' association to address areas of concern to all residents, including maintenance, council services and the future of the street. Acme supported this group in negotiations with the Greater London Council to secure permanent tenure of the street, which would allow for restoration of the buildings. Then in 1988 Acme and the resident's association formed the Beck Road

ABOVE **Invitation card for the performance *Studio Girls (Domestic Sanitation: The Latex Glamour Rodeo and Bargain Bed Bonanza)*, 1976**

AN AGREEMENT FOR A LICENCE made this 28th day of February ONE THOUSAND NINE HUNDRED AND 77 BETWEEN ACME HOUSING ASSOCIATION LIMITED OF 117 Devons Road Bow London E3 (herein after called "The Licensor") of the one part and Philip Stanley of 45 Beck Road London E8 (herein after called "The Licensee") of the other part.

WHEREBY IT IS AGREED AS FOLLOWS:-

1 The Licensor agrees to let the Licensee occupy and the Licensee agrees to occupy the property situated at and being 45 Beck Road London E8 with the land held therewith (herein after called "the Premises") for the term of one week from the 17th day of February 19 and thereafter from week to week until determined by either party giving to the other not less than four weeks notice to determine the licence created at the licence fee of £4.96 per week payable in advance on the Monday of each week.

2 THE LICENSEE HEREBY AGREES with the LICENSOR as follows:-

a To pay the licence fee at the times and in the manner aforesaid.

b To pay all rates taxes duties assessments impositions and outgoings which are now or which may at any time hereafter be assessed charged or imposed upon the premises or on the owner or occupier in respect thereof.

c To use the premises in a licensee-like manner.

d To keep in repair the structure and exterior of the premises (including the drains gutters and external pipes).

e To keep in repair and proper working order the installations in the premises for the supply of water gas and electricity and for sanitary conveniences.

f To keep in good and complete repair order and condition (damage by accidental fire only accepted) the interior of the premises and the painting papering and decoration thereof and the fixtures and appliances therein.

g Not to use or permit to be used the premises for any purpose other than that of artists studio and living accommodation.

h Not to do or permit to be done upon the premises any act or thing which may be a nuisance damage or annoyance to the licensor or the licensees or occupiers of any of the adjoining premises.

i Not to part with the possession of assign charge or let the premises or any part thereof.

j That the licensor or any person authorised by the licensor in writing may at reasonable times of the day on giving 24 hours notice in writing to the occupier enter the premises for the purpose of viewing their condition and the state of their repair.

k At the expiration or sooner determination of the licence to deliver up to the licensor in such order condition and state as shall be consistent with the due performance of the obligations of the licensee herein contained.

l That there is no rehousing liability at the expiration or sooner determination of the license.

Tenancy agreement for Beck Road, 1997

Arts Trust as a formal fundraising appeal to enable the artists to afford to purchase their own homes under the then new 'right to buy' initiative that had been implemented by the Conservative government.

Throughout her campaign to save - and live in - Beck Road, Chadwick was also studying for her Masters. In 1977 her graduating degree show brought both attention and acclaim. Titled *In the Kitchen*, for this performance and installation Chadwick created a series of wearable sculptures that resembled various household whitegoods: a fridge, an oven, a washing machine...These 'costumes' - again part clothing, part furniture - were constructed from metal frames with soft white PVC outers. As in her previous performance work, Chadwick, alongside several of her classmates, wore the costumes in a series of live and videoed performances in which they presented choreographed movements and sang and spoke. The performance opened with a speech, while a soundtrack of collaged daytime radio segments aimed at housewives played in the background:

> *Ladies and Gentlemen, I am so happy to be here today. Let me welcome you to the dream world of kitchen beauty....Here sumptuous models of unparallel loveliness can be yours today instead of tomorrow. - Ladies, if I may address myself to you and you alone for a moment: We all know that historically a woman's place was in the kitchen and that a kitchen's place was out of sight. Well, here is 'kitchen-lib', where a woman can do time in her kitchen and actually enjoy herself....Because let's face facts...you are going to be living in your kitchen for quite a while.*[12]

Through combining women's bodies with kitchen appliances, Chadwick stressed the stereotypes of domesticity that women were expected to inhabit. The structures naturally restricted the women's movements, forcing them to become mechanical and at times involuntary, while the appliances softened, anthropomorphized - the hob rings resembling breasts and the washing machine door looking like a pregnant tummy. Chadwick's efforts in this work to connect the physical, social and representational realms of women would go on to demarcate her practice for years to come.

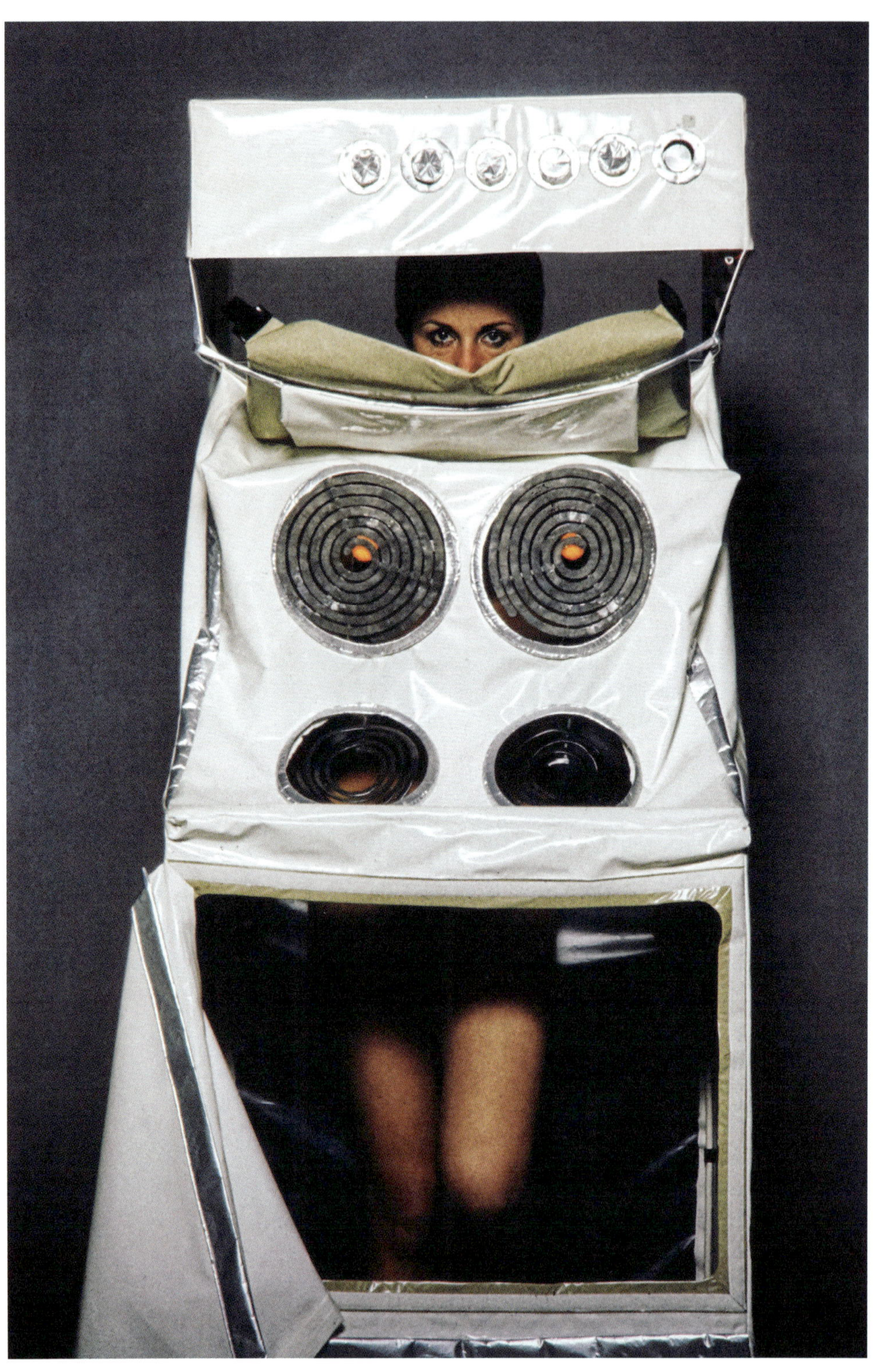

Helen Chadwick, *In the Kitchen (oven)*, 1977.
Photograph, 41 × 30.5 cm (16¼ × 12⅛ in.)

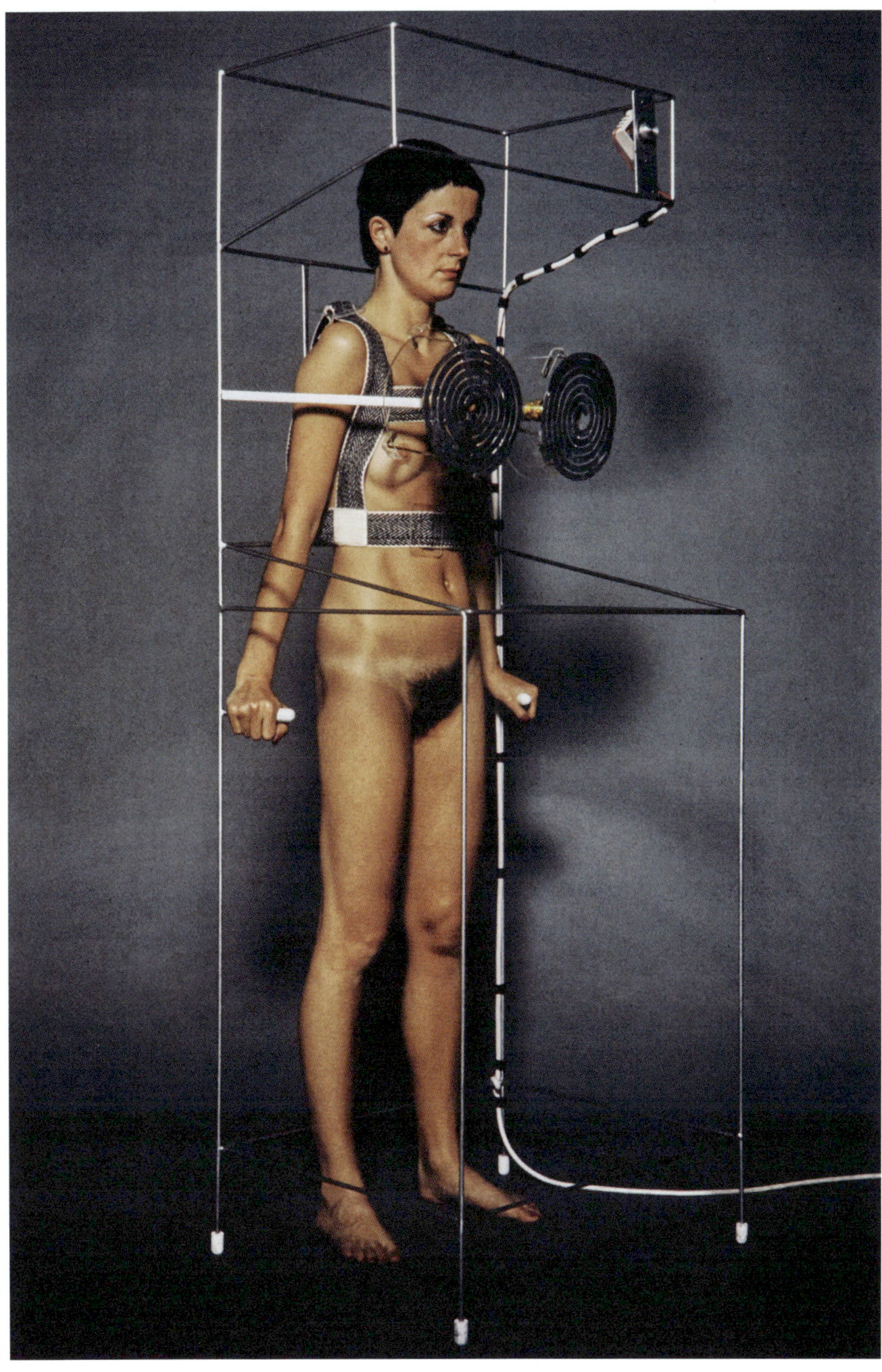

Helen Chadwick, *In the Kitchen (oven)*, 1977.
Photograph, 41 × 30.5 cm (16 ¼ × 12 ⅛ in.)

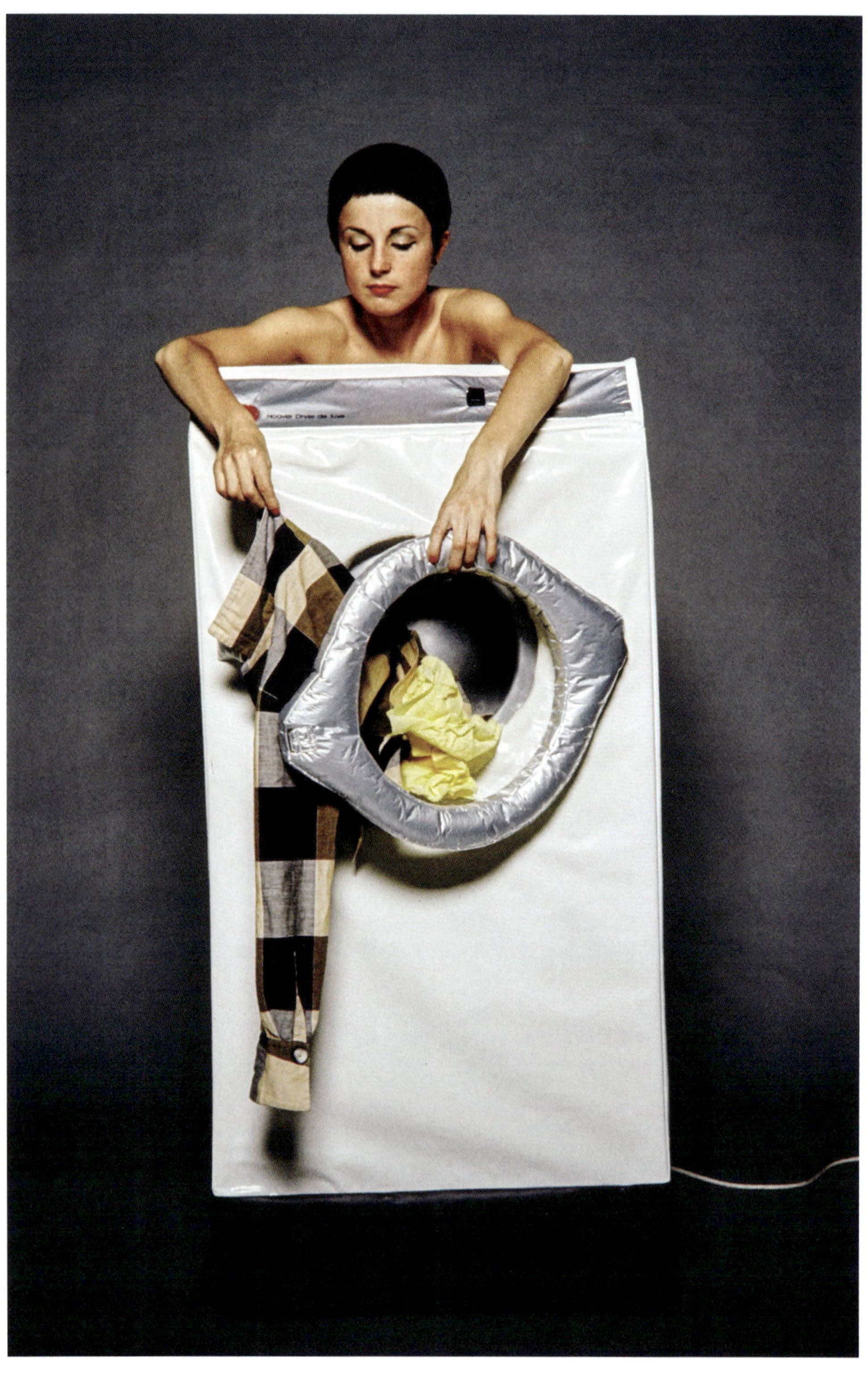

Helen Chadwick, *In the Kitchen (washing machine)*, 1977.
Photograph, 41 × 30.5 cm (16 1/4 × 12 1/8 in.)

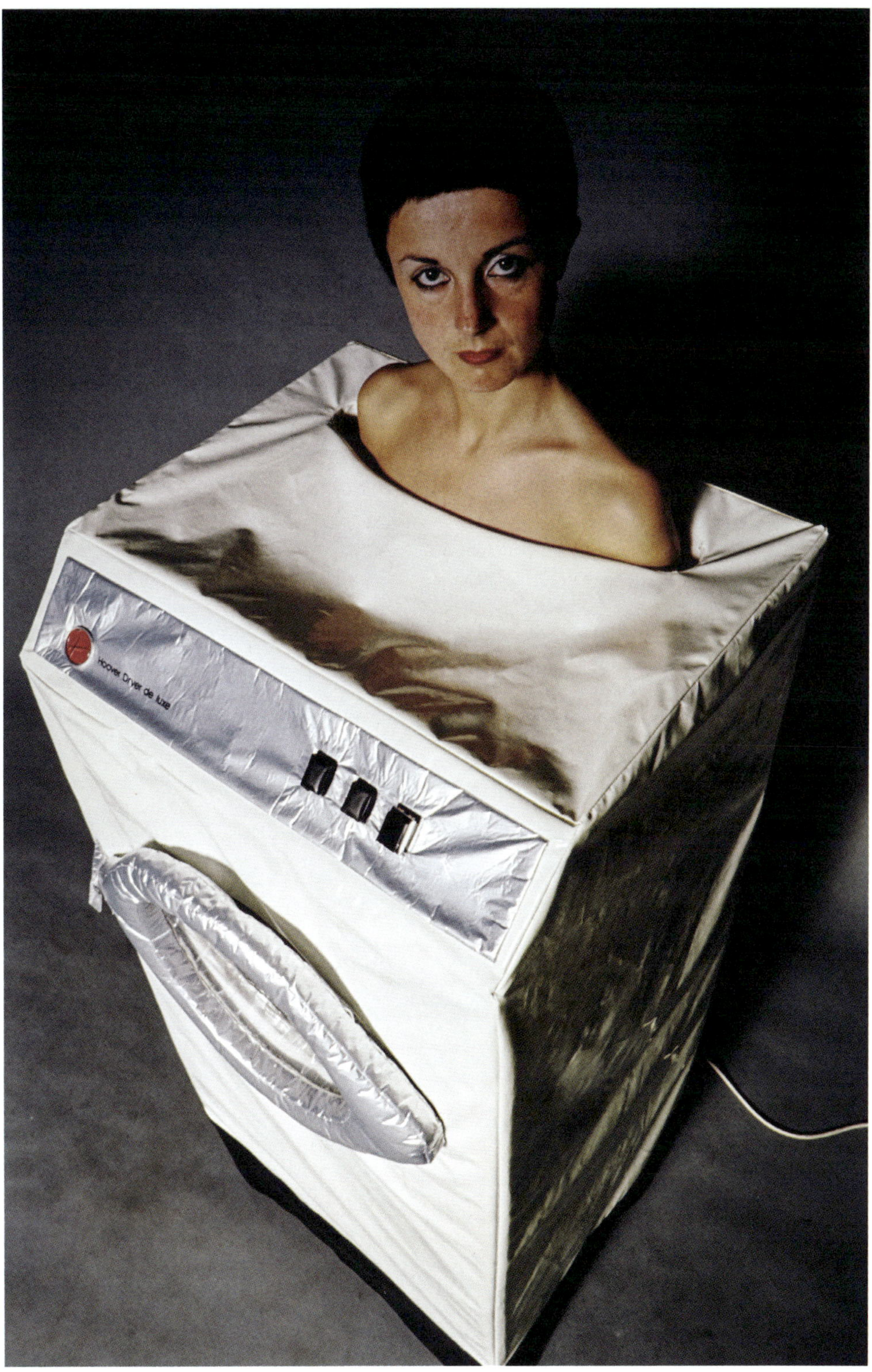

Helen Chadwick, *In the Kitchen (washing machine)*, 1977.
Photograph, 41 × 30.5 cm ($16\frac{1}{4} \times 12\frac{1}{8}$ in.)

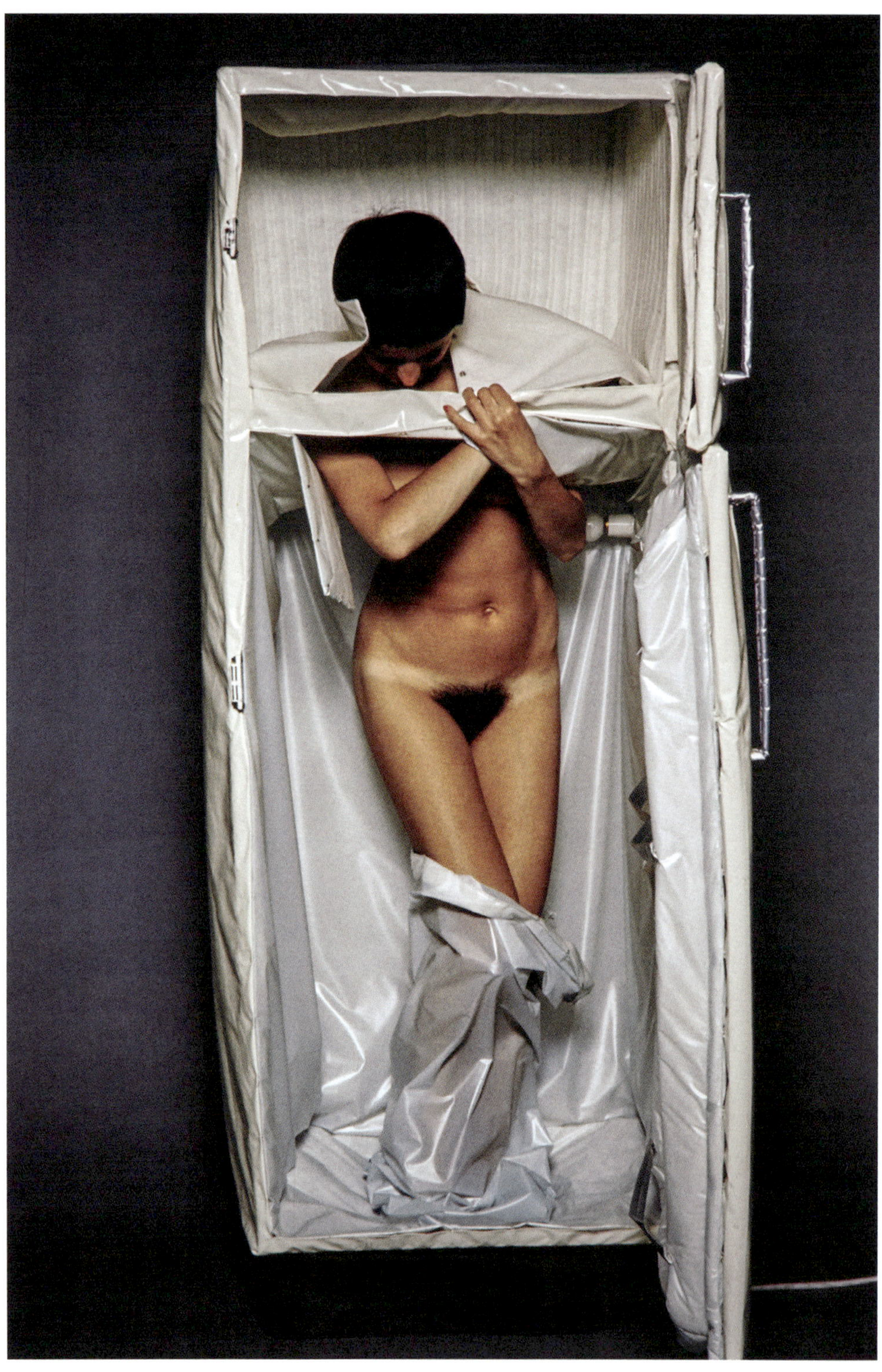

**Helen Chadwick, *In the Kitchen (fridge)*, 1977.
Photograph, 41 × 30.5 cm (16¼ × 12⅛ in.)**

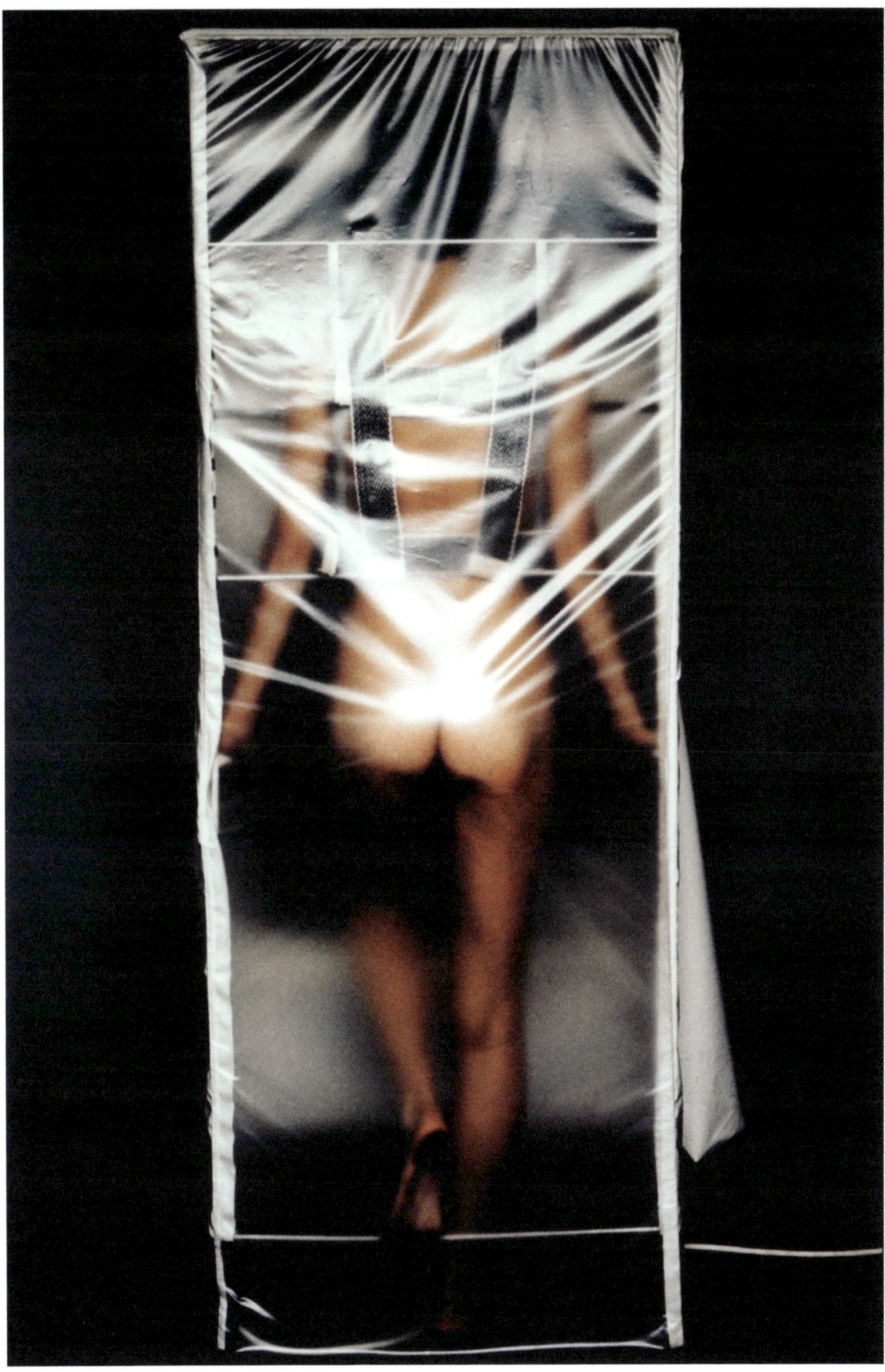

Helen Chadwick, *In the Kitchen (fridge)*, 1977.
Photograph, 41 × 30.5 cm (16¼ × 12⅛ in.)

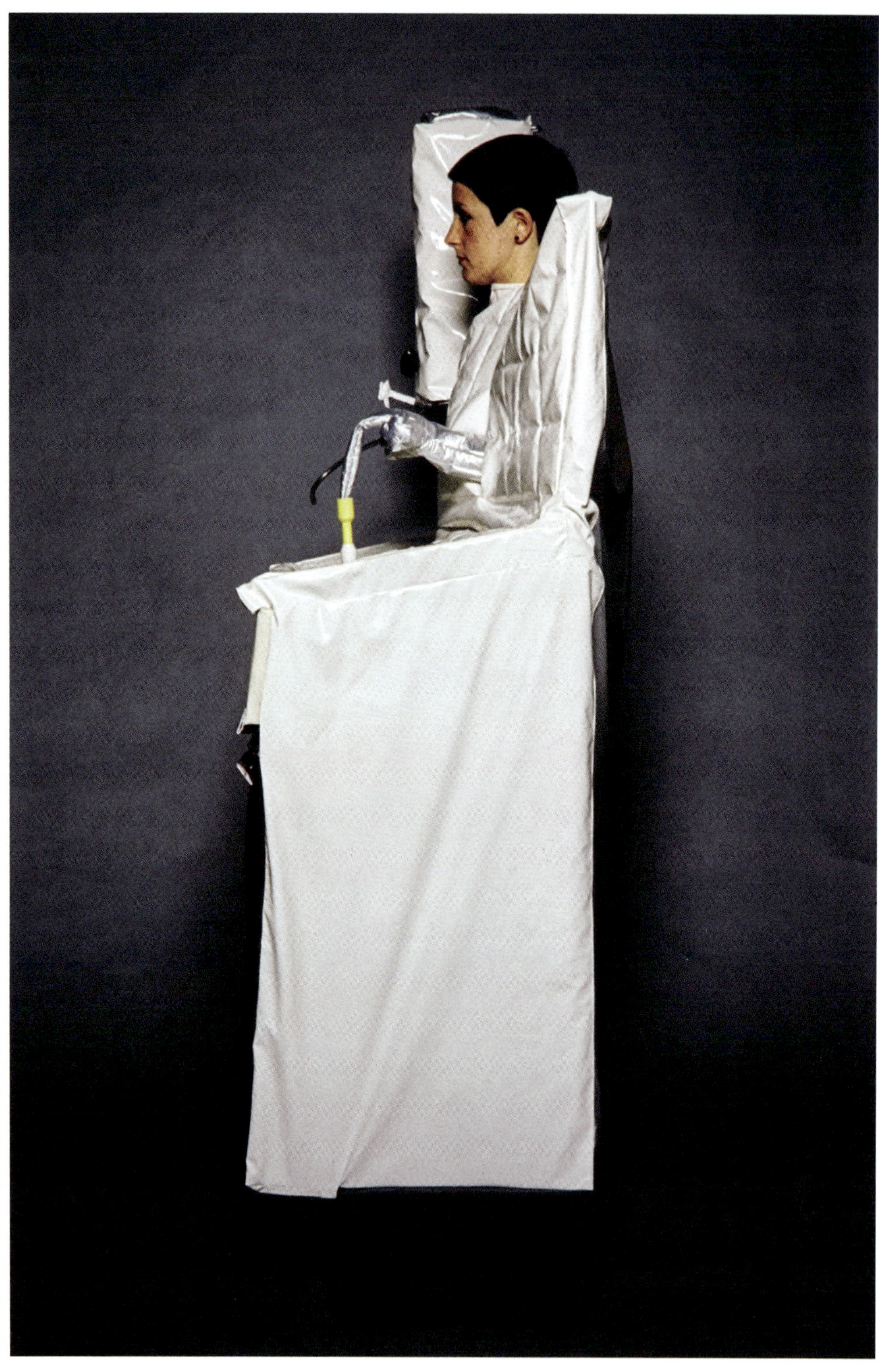

Helen Chadwick, *In the Kitchen (sink)*, 1977.
Photograph, 41 × 30.5 cm (16¼ × 12⅛ in.)

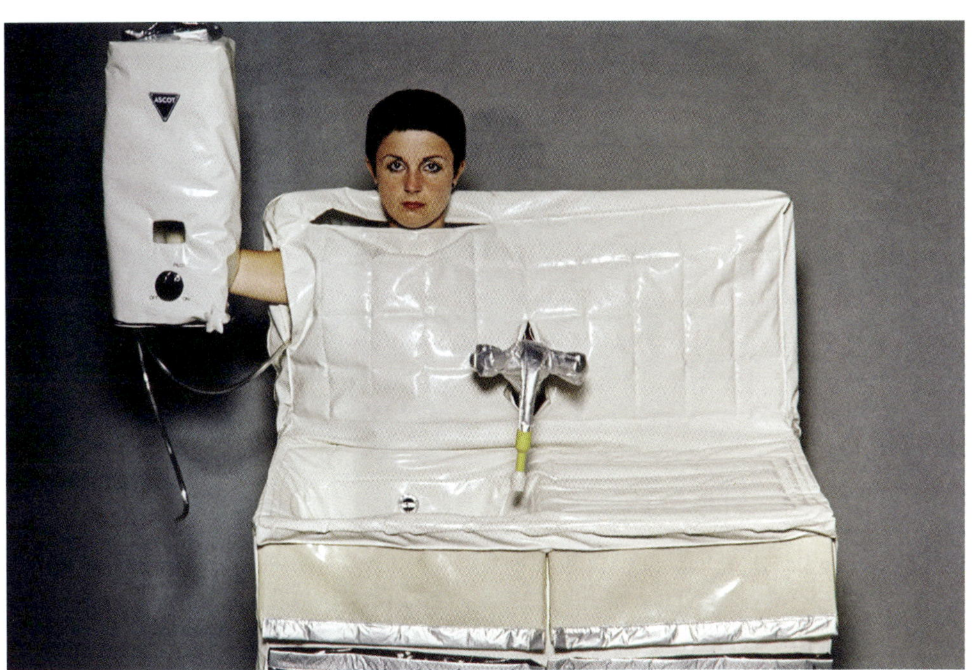

Helen Chadwick, *In the Kitchen (sink)*, 1977.
Photograph, 30.5 × 41 cm ($12\frac{1}{8}$ × $16\frac{1}{4}$ in.)

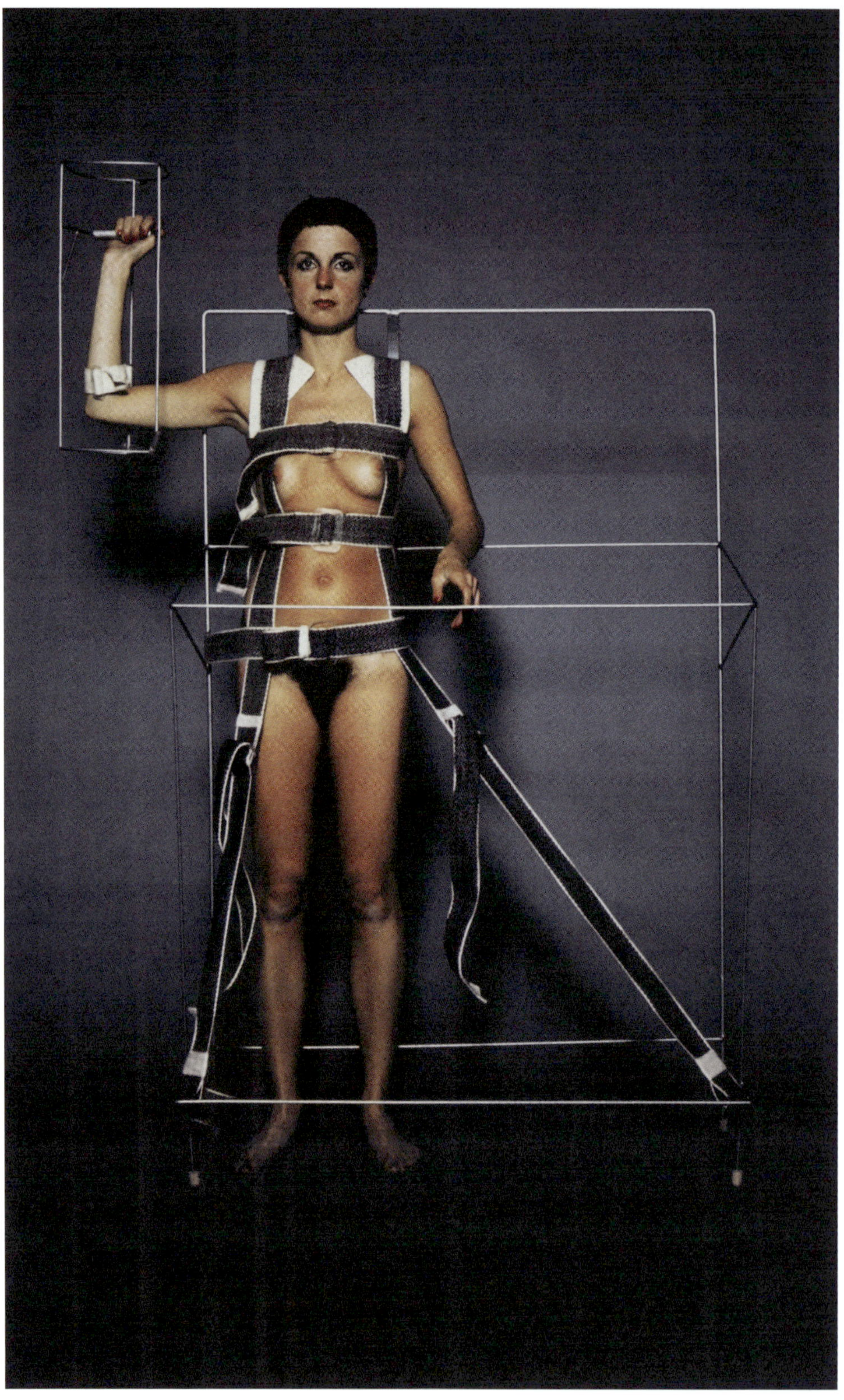

Chadwick began exhibiting regularly from 1977 onwards, however, she quickly became the target of some heavy criticism from a generation of feminists who objected to her use of her own naked body in her work and accused her of regressive female narcissism. Their denigration centred around the idea that Chadwick's use of her body was actively perpetuating the objectification of women and reinforcing the very stereotypes that she sought to subvert. But from Chadwick's perspective, she was interested in complicating the idea of the objectification of women: 'I was looking at a vocabulary for desire where I was the subject and the object and the author....I felt by directly taking all these roles, the normal situation in which the viewer operated as a kind of voyeur broke down.'[13] Her endeavour was to both expose and exploit the conventional modes of feminine display and to challenge the idea of the female body as a site of spectacle. Her retort was: 'I'm disappointed that a false rationalism is used as a stick with which to measure what I'm doing when I am looking to cross the taboos that have been instigated. I hate being hauled up as an example of negative women's work.'[14]

Nonetheless, Chadwick's work of the late 1970s took a different turn and led her to create a series of works that were more overtly socially focused and did not include imagery of her naked body - or those of any of her peers. These works generally took the form of installations with an unyielding political focus, in which she would select one aspect of life in Britain and use it to examine an issue such as sexism or class. The first of these, *Train of Thought* (1978), was essentially about conflict (imagined or real) between men and women. The work consisted of an exact replica of a London Underground train carriage in which Chadwick installed two audio tracks on either side of the seating. The audio tracks played the internal monologues of two strangers, one male, one female, as they assessed the imaginary stranger sitting opposite them, the female voice revealing how precarious and vulnerable she felt to be a woman on her own in a train carriage with an unknown man. Chadwick explained that the work was about 'the way a female might react inwardly to a male on the tube. It was very much a sexual arena then - harassment a-gogo. The way a kind of formal public place like a tube train can suddenly precipitate into a very intimate, disturbing contest.'[15]

Helen Chadwick, *In the Kitchen (oven)*, 1977.
Photograph, 41 × 35 cm (16¼ × 12⅛ in.)

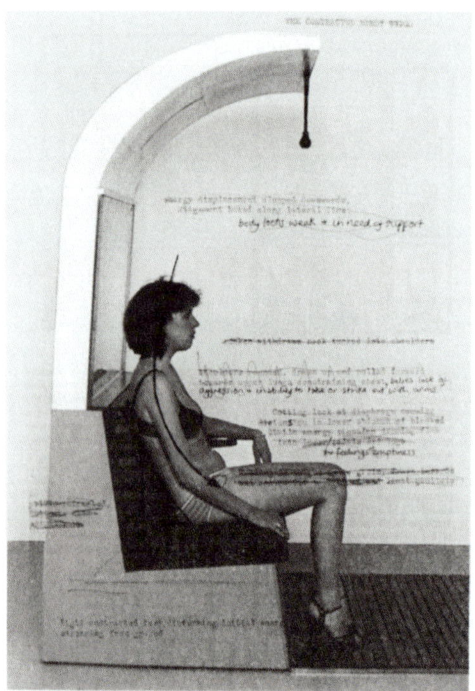

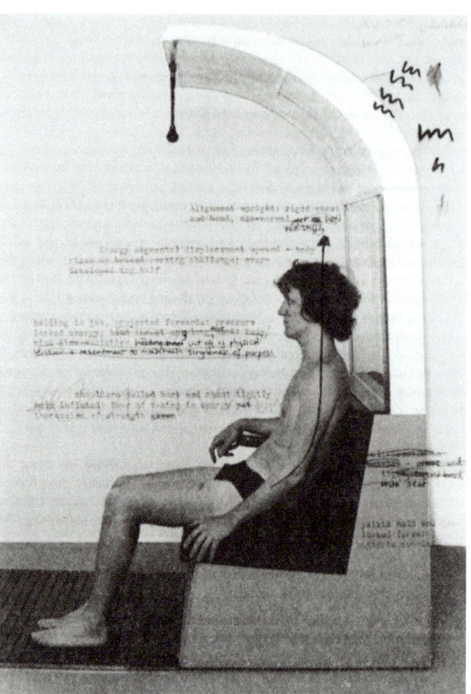

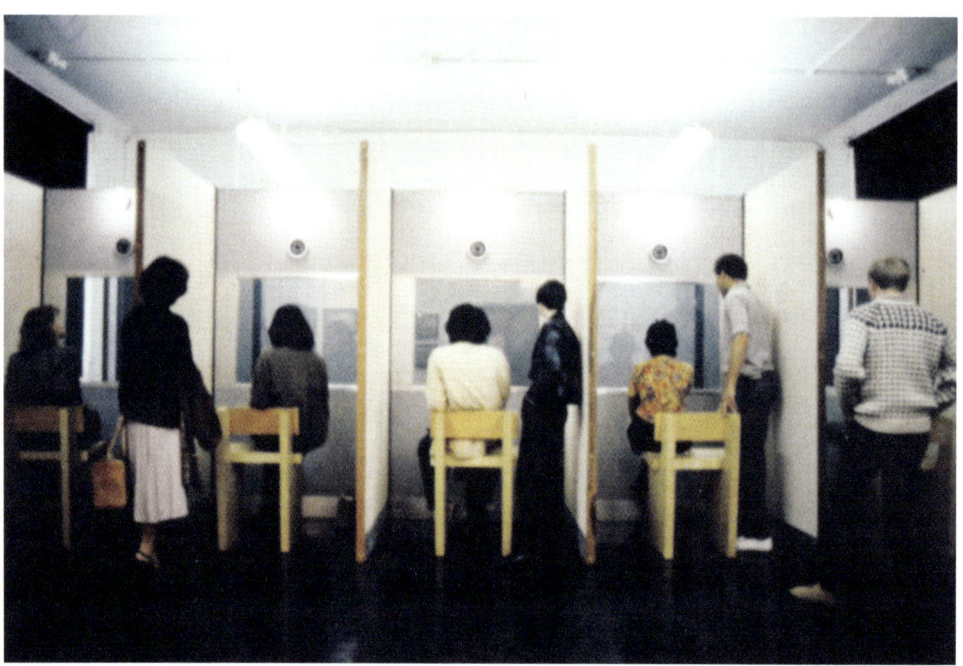

Helen Chadwick, preparatory sketches for *Train of Thought*, 1978

Helen Chadwick, *Model Institution*, 1981

Another work from this era, *Model Institution* (1981), was an installation - again with sound - that examined the effects of unemployment and austerity in 1980s Britain. The installation was an exact replica of a dole office, including five cubicles playing five voiceovers. These voiceovers came from real-life interviews that Chadwick had conducted with recipients of welfare benefits; they exposed feelings of frustration, anger, regret and guilt, and in order to listen to them, a visitor had to sit in the seat of the individual on benefits. The installation revealed how the architecture of these offices and institutional spaces enacted a hierarchical positioning of surveillance and domination rather than support and encouragement.

Despite the fact that these works do not include imagery of the human body, Chadwick's enduring line of enquiry, to use materiality in an indexical way - in that there is a physical and aesthetic correlation in their manifestation - clearly exists through her use of her own live body (and that of her friends) and her use of real-life architecture and infrastructures. This indexicality endures across Chadwick's career. It challenges the notion of art as a purely representational form of expression and instead highlights the materiality and physicality of art, emphasizing the connection between artists, artworks and audiences and distorting the boundary between art and life.

The 1980s: A Return to Herself

Throughout the 1980s Chadwick continued to live on Beck Road, and also began teaching across the country - a part of her life and career that would come to define her influence on contemporary art in Britain, almost as much as her work. In 1983, as part of a placement she was undertaking across three schools in Newcastle, Chadwick proposed a project for her pupils in which she asked them to produce life-size self-portraits using painting and collage. While working with her pupils on this brief, Chadwick also started working on her own kind of self-portrait, a work that would signal her rise into the public sphere through its inclusion in the summer exhibition at the Serpentine, London, in 1983. The work is *Ego Geometria Sum* (1983), made the year that Chadwick turned thirty.

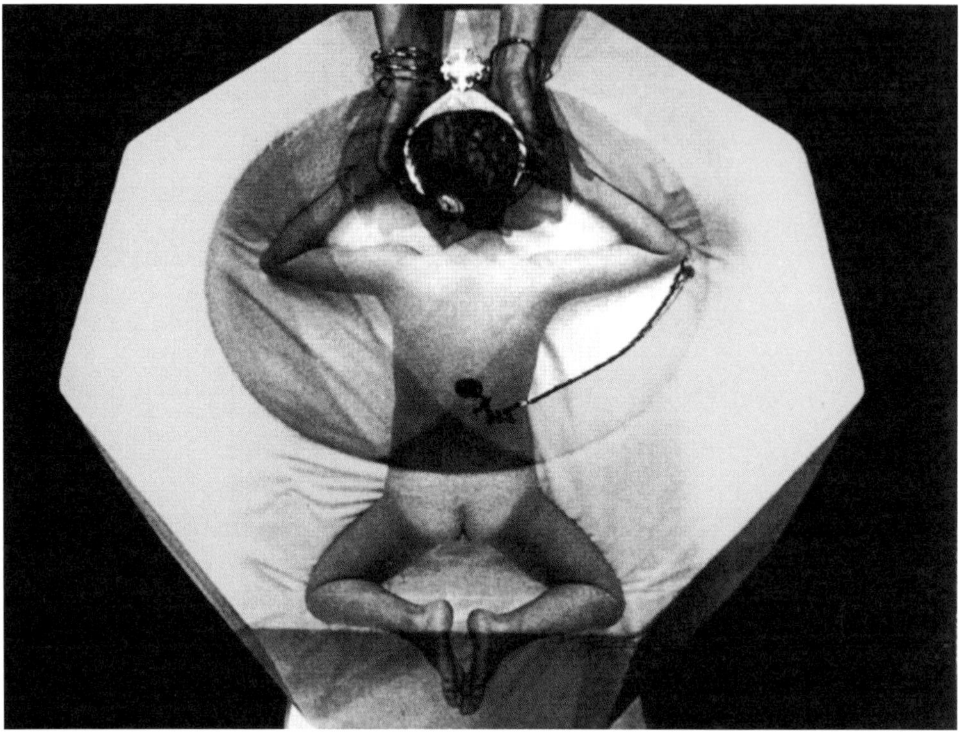

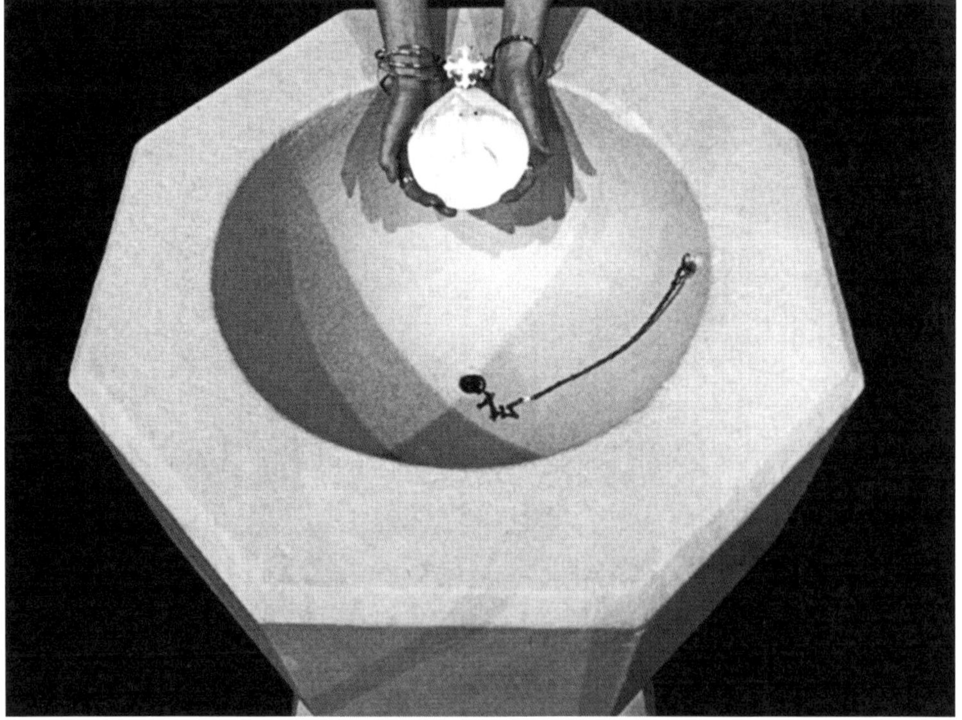

THIS PAGE AND OPPOSITE, TOP **Two-dimensional model and black and white tests prints for *Ego Geometria Sum II: Font – 3 Months*, 1982**

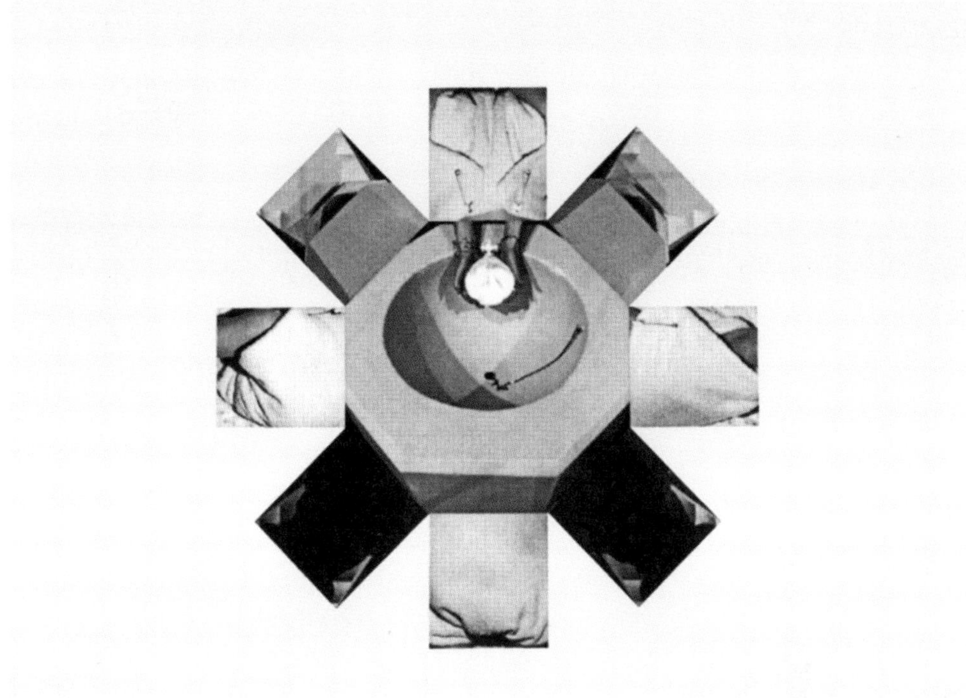

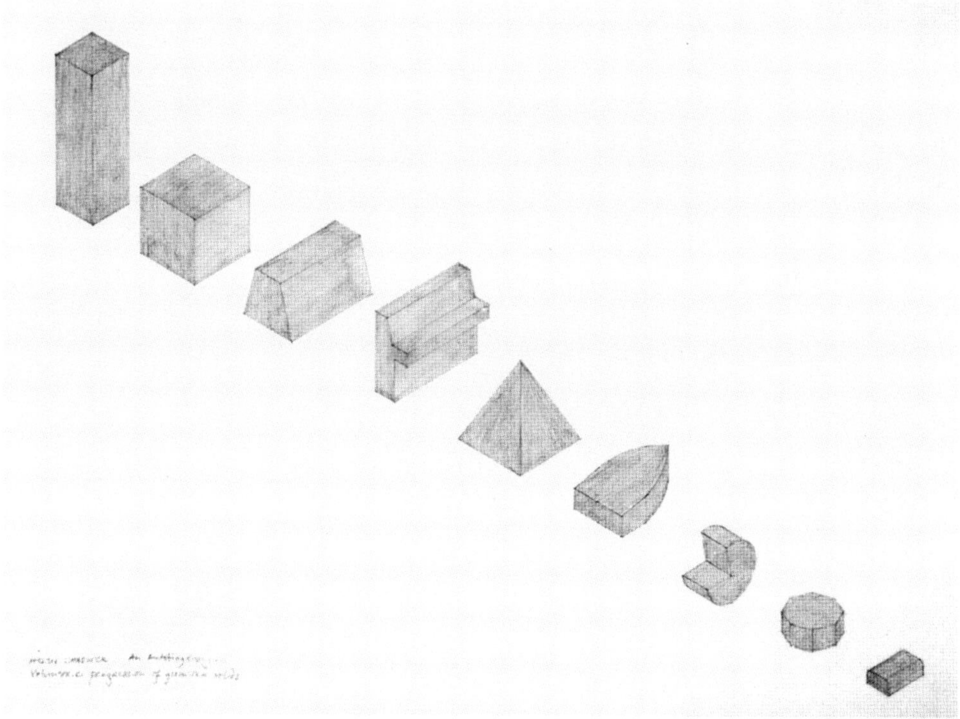

ABOVE **Pencil drawing of the ten geometric objects used in *Ego Geometria Sum*, depicting the gradual increase in scale from *Incubator – Birth* (bottom right) to *Statue – 15–30 Years* (top left), 1982**

Ego Geometria Sum, or 'I am Geometry', consists of ten plywood geometrical forms each representing a symbolic moment in Chadwick's life to date: the exact model of Oxygenaire incubator in which she was treated after her premature birth, a font, the pram in which her parents transported her, a toy boat, the garden tent that she shared with her brother, her bed from the age of six, a vaulting horse used in school gymnastics, a piano, a cube (which to her represented high school, as well as church) and finally a door, as a symbol of her adulthood, all arranged in a spiral on the floor. In the notes in Chadwick's archive, she describes the ten forms as 'objects that a) contained me b) (re)oriented me c) moulded / shaped me'.[16] The size of the sculptures reflects the exact mass of her body at each applicable age, and their surfaces are adorned with black-and-white images of Chadwick's naked body interacting with the objects that the sculptures represent - her fingers flicker on the keys of the piano, her arm reaches to write her name across a blackboard on the cube, she curls a diminished (in scale) version of herself into her tiny incubator, or around the rocking form of her pram, and she straddles the gymnastics horse. Other significant elements - bows, toys, childhood shoes, musical instruments - from specific moments in her life also feature in these highly personal, though frequently collective, experiences. In order to make these images appear embedded in the plywood surfaces of the sculptures, Chadwick developed a new technique, won through much trial and error, in which she first painted photographic emulsion onto the wood and then exposed it to her monochromatic images, heating it gently with a collection of hairdryers to achieve the exact effect that she wanted.

This was a period of evolution in Chadwick's practice, marking a transition from her previous, explicitly feminist work towards a more poetic and autobiographical application of imagery, as well as a return to using her own body and self as a material to be examined, reappropriated and explored. In *Ego Geometria Sum* she sought to 'poke about in the dimly charted corners of the id where sex drive, childhood memory, sense of place, the appetite for security, fear of dying and a host of other subcutaneous human motor forces squelch around the subconscious like mud wrestlers'.[17] The form of each sculpture refers to the next

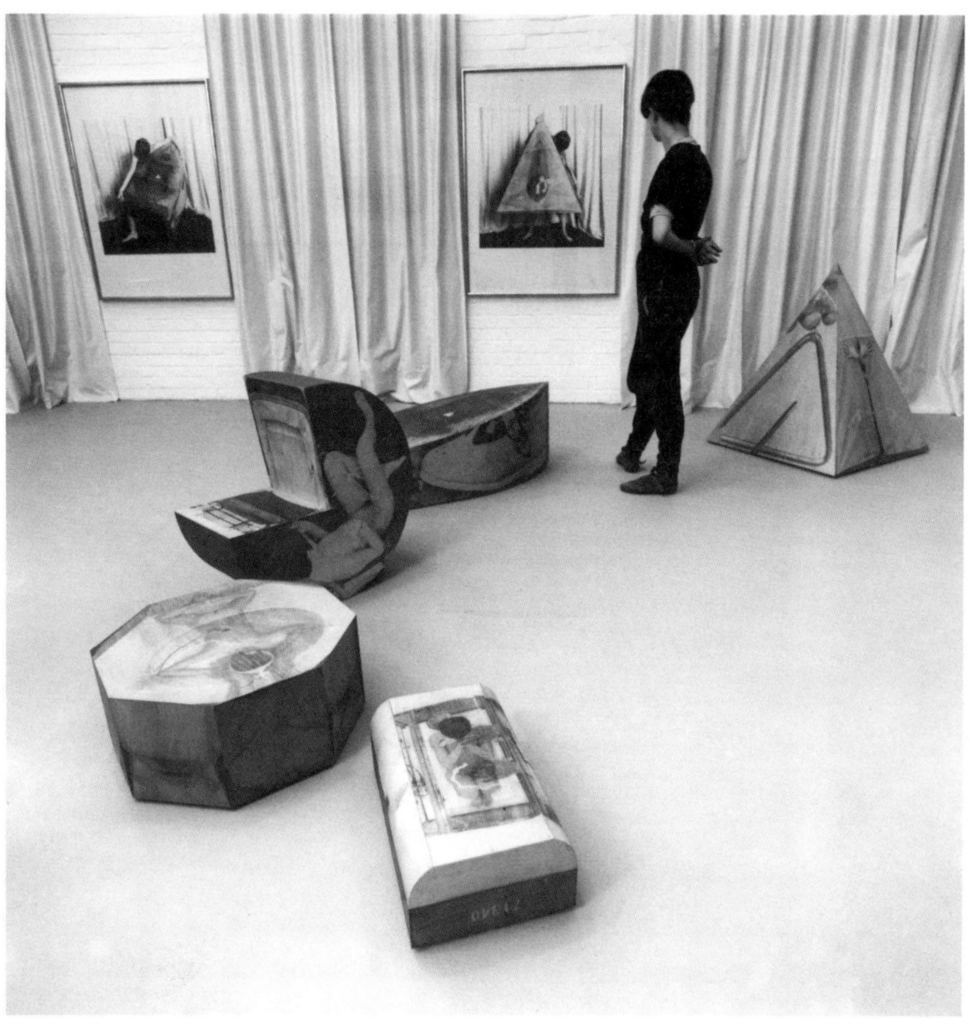

Helen Chadwick with *Ego Geometria Sum*, 1983.
Installed at Riverside Studios, London, 1985

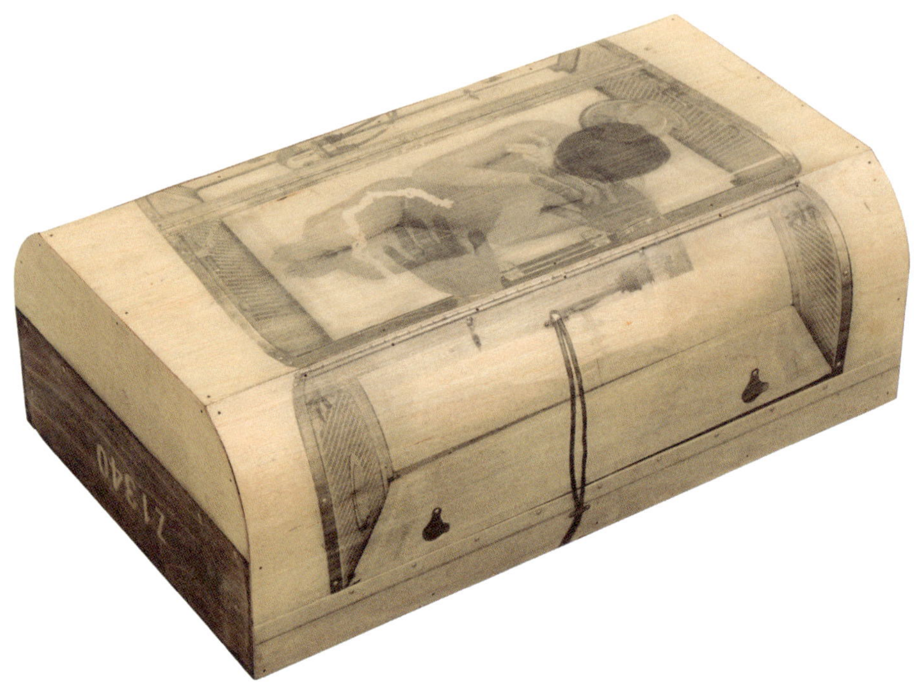

Helen Chadwick, *Ego Geometria Sum I: Incubator – Birth*, 1983.
Photographic emulsion on plywood, 15 × 27 × 45 cm (5 ⅞ × 10 ⅝ × 17 ¾ in.)

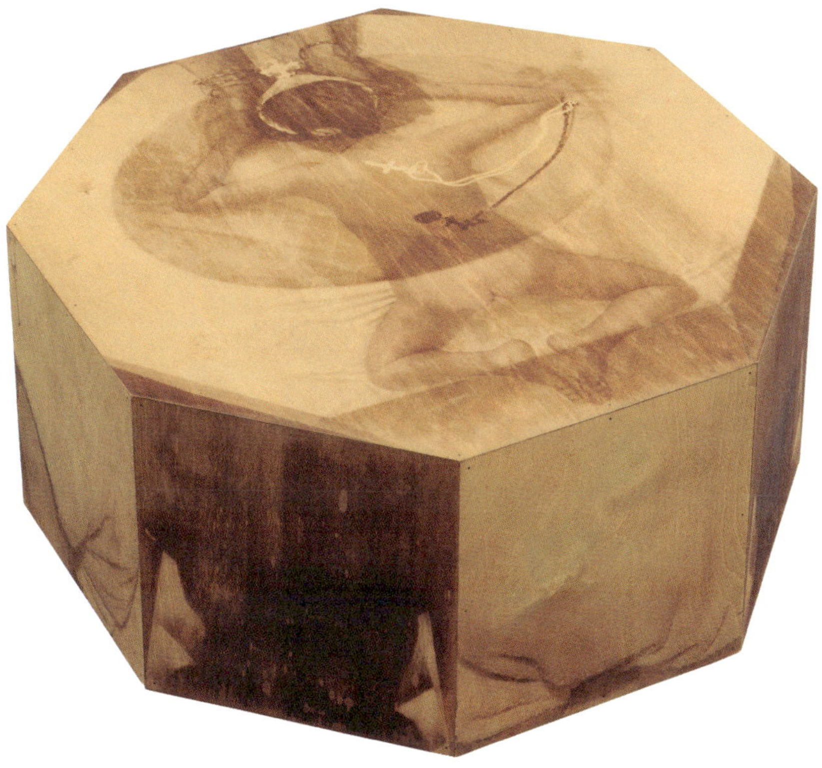

Helen Chadwick, *Ego Geometria Sum II: Font – Age 3 Months*, 1983.
Photographic emulsion on plywood, 23 × 50 × 50 cm (9 × 19⅝ × 19⅝ in.)

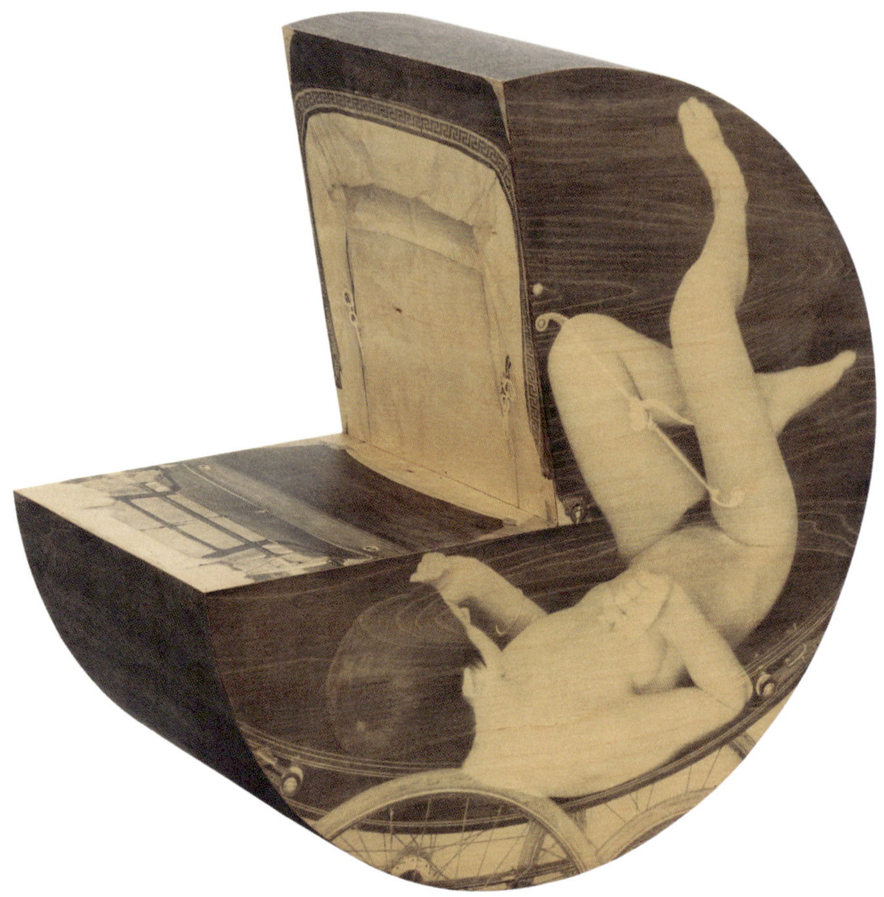

Helen Chadwick, *Ego Geometria Sum III: Pram – Age 10 Months*, 1983.
Photographic emulsion on plywood, 64 × 32 × 64 cm (25¼ × 12⅝ × 25¼ in.)

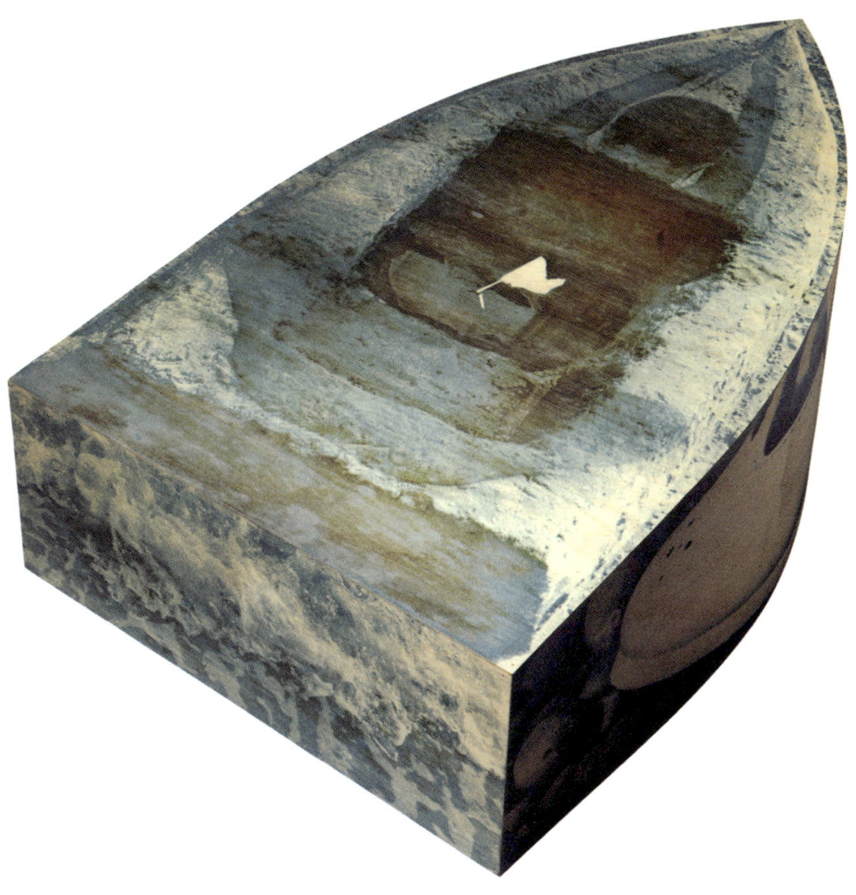

Helen Chadwick, *Ego Geometria Sum IV: Boat – Age 2 Years*, 1983. Photographic emulsion on plywood, 38 × 24 × 91 cm (15 × 9½ × 35⅞ in.)

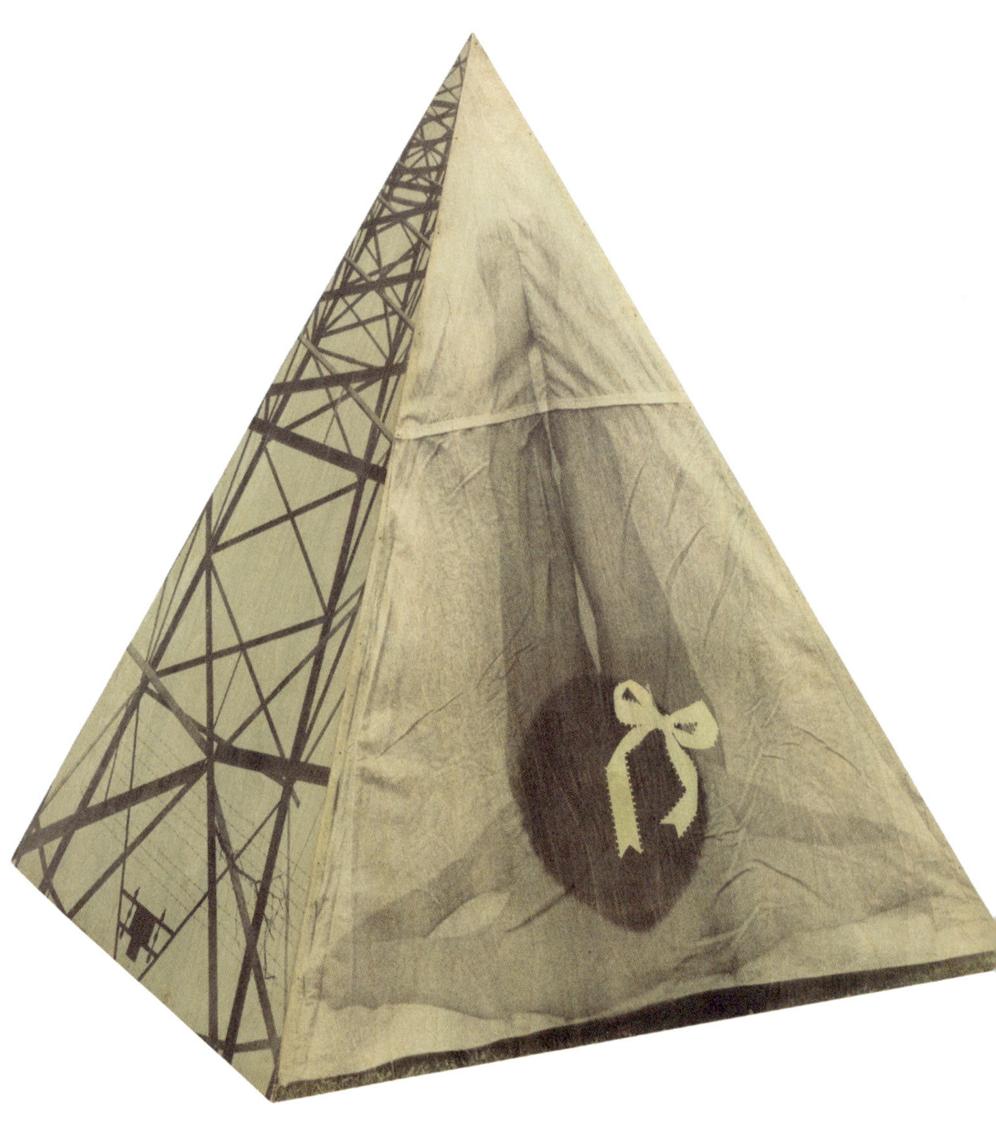

Helen Chadwick, *Ego Geometria Sum V: Wigwam – Age 5 Years*, 1983.
Photographic emulsion on plywood, 89 × 79 × 79 cm (35⅛ × 31⅛ × 31⅛ in.)

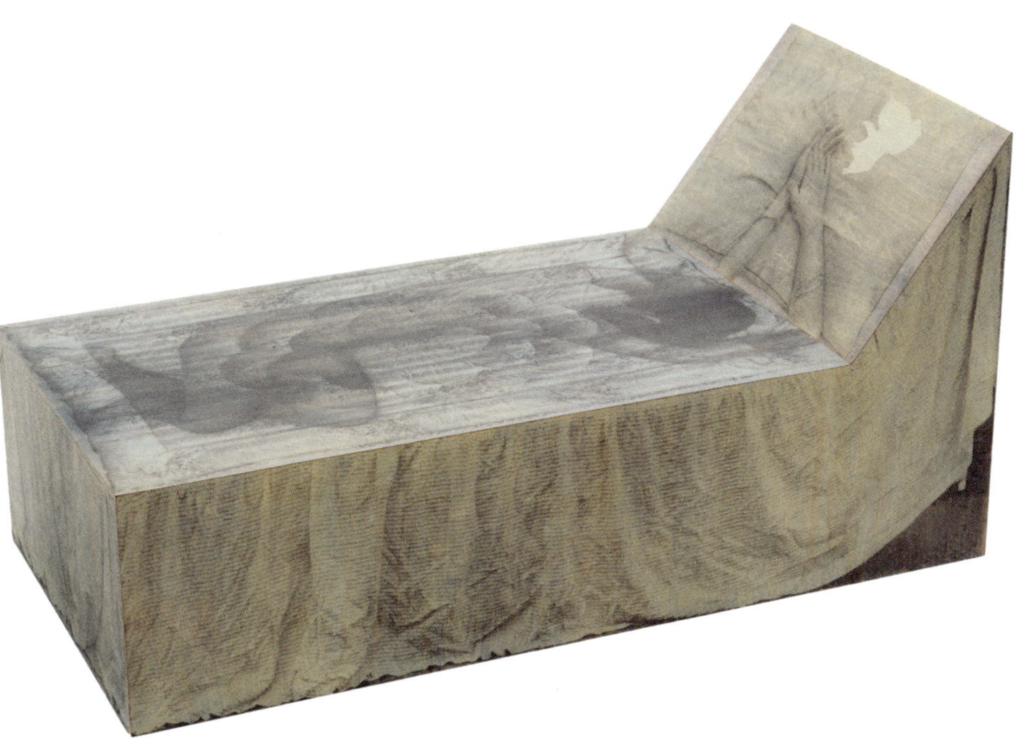

**Helen Chadwick, *Ego Geometria Sum VI: Bed – Age 6½ Years*, 1983.
Photographic emulsion on plywood, 54 × 56 × 115 cm (21¼ × 22 × 45¼ in.)**

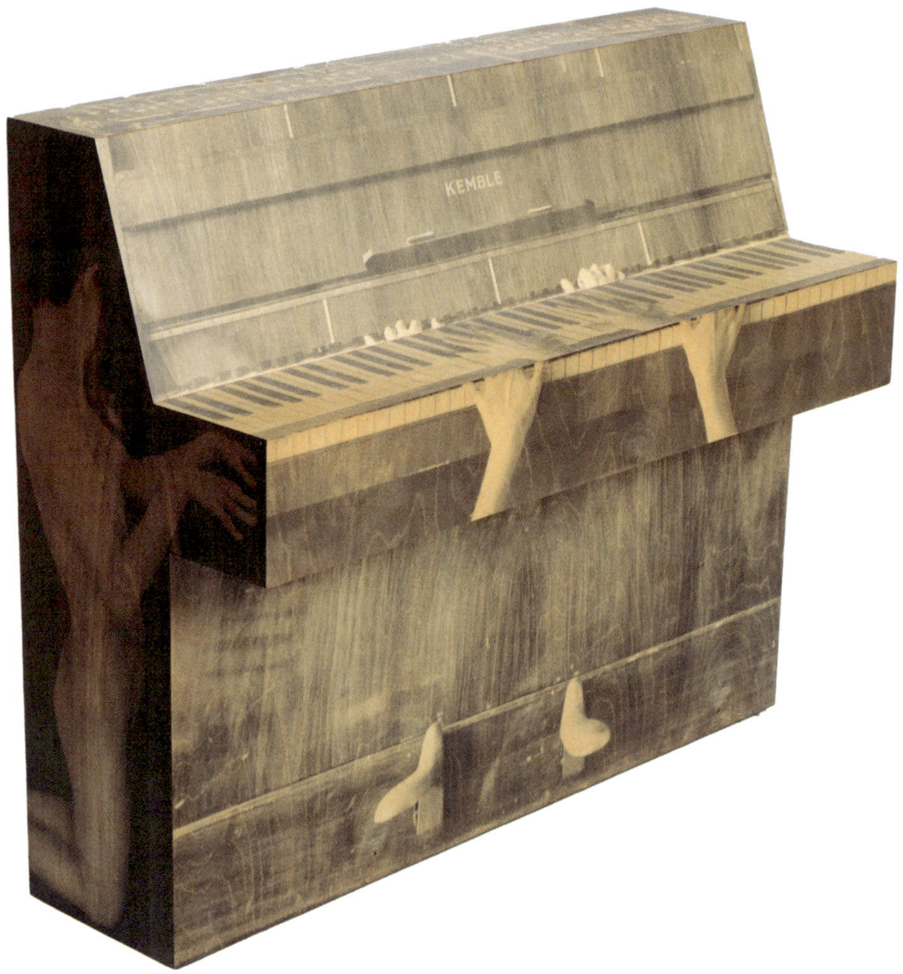

**Helen Chadwick, *Ego Geometria Sum VII: Piano – Age 9 Years*, 1983.
Photographic emulsion on plywood, 86 × 105 × 42 cm (33 7/8 × 41 3/8 × 16 1/2 in.)**

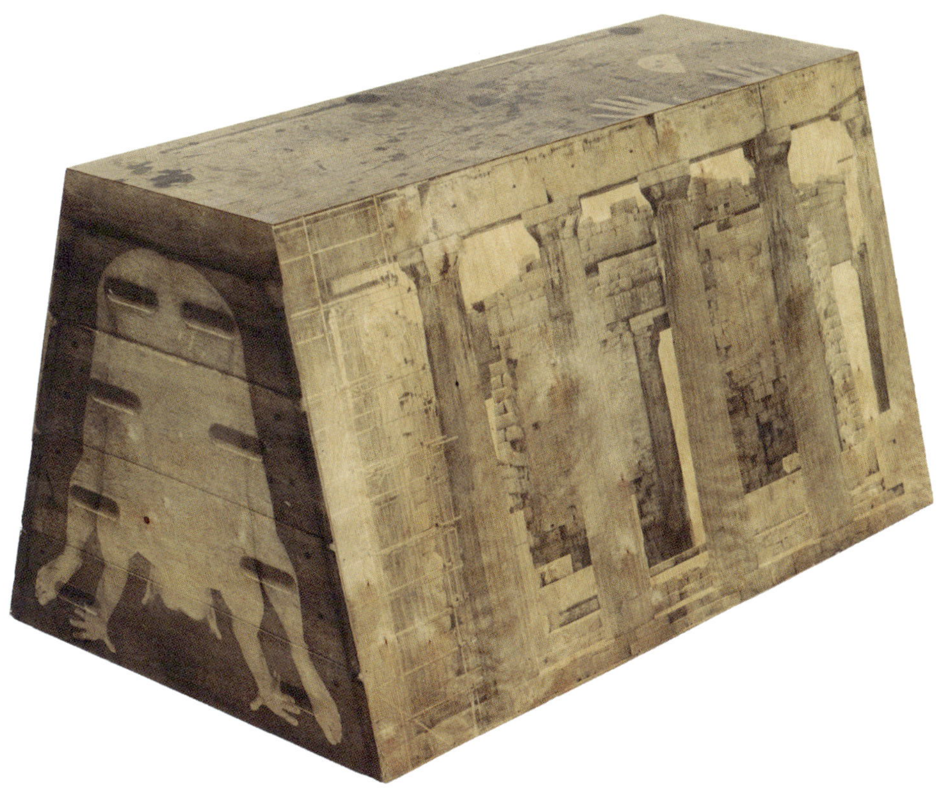

Helen Chadwick, *Ego Geometria Sum VIII: The Horse – Age 11 Years*, 1983.
Photographic emulsion on plywood, 57.5 × 101.9 × 61.9 cm (22 $\frac{5}{8}$ × 40 $\frac{1}{8}$ × 24 $\frac{3}{8}$ in.)

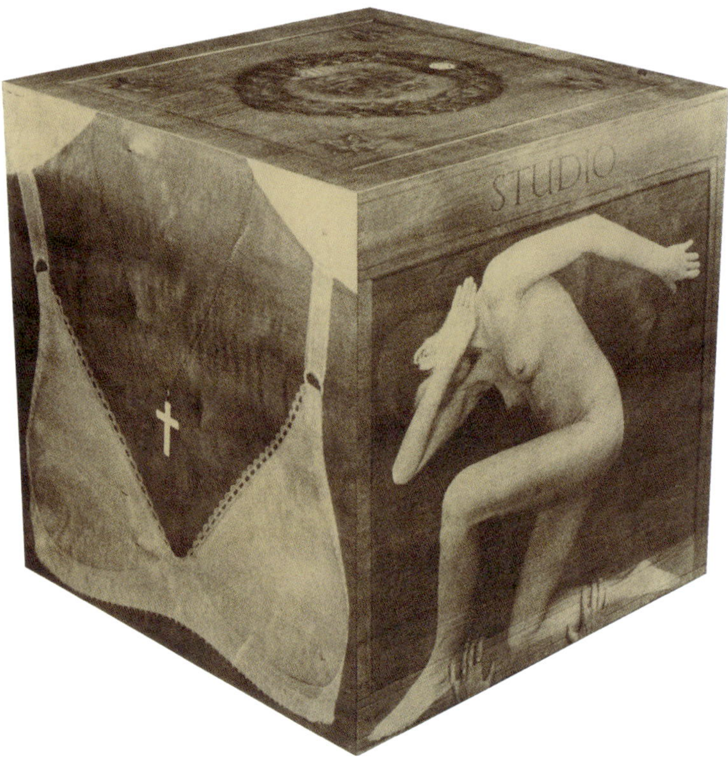

Helen Chadwick, *Ego Geometria Sum IX: High School – Age 13 Years*, 1983. Photographic emulsion on plywood, 70 × 70 × 70 cm (27⅝ × 27⅝ × 27⅝ in.)

within the geometric pattern of a spiral. In the shape of the installation Chadwick sought to represent the notion of evolution, as well as to give the complicated and irrational process of memory, growth and change a sense of structure: 'I had to make *Ego Geometria Sum* as a way of trying to define the past, so that I could then use this as a springboard into something else. So *Ego Geometria Sum* is very classical in its philosophy in that self is reduced to ten supposedly immutable forms which represent the pattern of growth...'[18]

Across her entire output, this is Chadwick's most autobiographical work. And yet she makes a conscious decision not to reveal her face at any point in any of the photographs. This grants her anonymity, and the work a universality, allowing viewers to project their own experiences of childhood and memory onto the works. Chadwick's naked body becomes a body for anyone, for anyone to look to and discover the affinities between the past, the self and the present world. As she explains, the work was an attempt to 'go back in memory to the origin of symptoms...and to free the ego from the traumas of the past'.[19] *Ego Geometria Sum* is a bid to trace one's body back 'through a succession of geometric solids...and if geometry is an expression of eternal and exact truths...then let this model of mathematical harmony be infused with a poetry of feeling and memory to sublimate the discord of past passion and desire in a recomposed neutrality of being'.[20]

To follow, in a multifaceted and profound act of re-representation, Chadwick created a sister-work to *Ego Geometria Sum* titled *The Labours I-X* (1983-84). Here - working with the photographer Mark Pilkington - she photographed herself again, posing naked with the already photographically printed sculptures, lifting, heaving, examining and holding each form with what looks like Herculean strength. In these images Chadwick also appears to be trying to re-enter some of the sculptures, to climb inside their forms (just as in her previous works in which she very much did inhabit her textile sculptures as costumes). Now it feels like she is trying to re-enter her past as a way of puzzling it out.

The title of *The Labours* refers to the Greek myth 'The Twelve Labours of Hercules', in which the Greek demi-god was ordered by King Eurystheus to perform twelve perilous tasks as penance for a treacherous crime. Hercules' labours are traditionally thought of as requiring great strength and courage, although a feminist reinterpretation of them might recognize the foundational patriarchal performativity of solving problems through murder, theft and destruction. In Chadwick's labours, she elevates and scrutinizes her past selves, and in so doing suggests that the effort to continue evolving, reconciling and reconstructing the self as we grow requires great strength and courage. Chadwick's reference to classical Greece in this work alludes to her Greek heritage. But moreover, her depiction of physical strength in lifting her own sculptures is reminiscent of the Caryatides, the six female statues that supported the roof of the Erechtheion, a temple dedicated to Athena (goddess of wisdom and strategy) in the Acropolis in Athens, Greece. This is an important and deliberate reference that symbolizes the strength, intelligence and fearlessness of women.

In 1985 Chadwick took up a teaching post in London at Goldsmiths College of Art, where she taught until 1990. At the same time, Chadwick also taught at Chelsea College of Arts from 1985 to 1996 and Central St Martins from 1986 to 1996. In addition, she maintained a post at the Royal College of Art from 1989 to 1996. Across these posts, Chadwick taught a significant group of artists including Tracey Emin (b. 1963), Sarah Lucas (b. 1962), Anya Gallaccio (b. 1963), Fiona Rae (b. 1963), Damien Hirst (b. 1965), Angus Fairhurst (1966-2008) and Angela Bulloch (b. 1988). As a result, Chadwick's impact on the British art scene as both an artist and a teacher throughout the 1980s and 1990s, helped pave the way for the next generation, specifically the group that would become known as the Young British Artists.

In 1986 Chadwick opened her first major solo exhibition, titled 'Of Mutability', at the Institute of Contemporary Arts (ICA), London. This exhibition explored the natural order of life, death and regeneration, as is always happening all around us. It toured several institutions across England, Scotland and Switzerland and in 1987 resulted in Chadwick being the first woman to be nominated for the Turner Prize. The title for the exhibition was: 'the cue for a concept of the self as being infinitely subject to change'.[21]

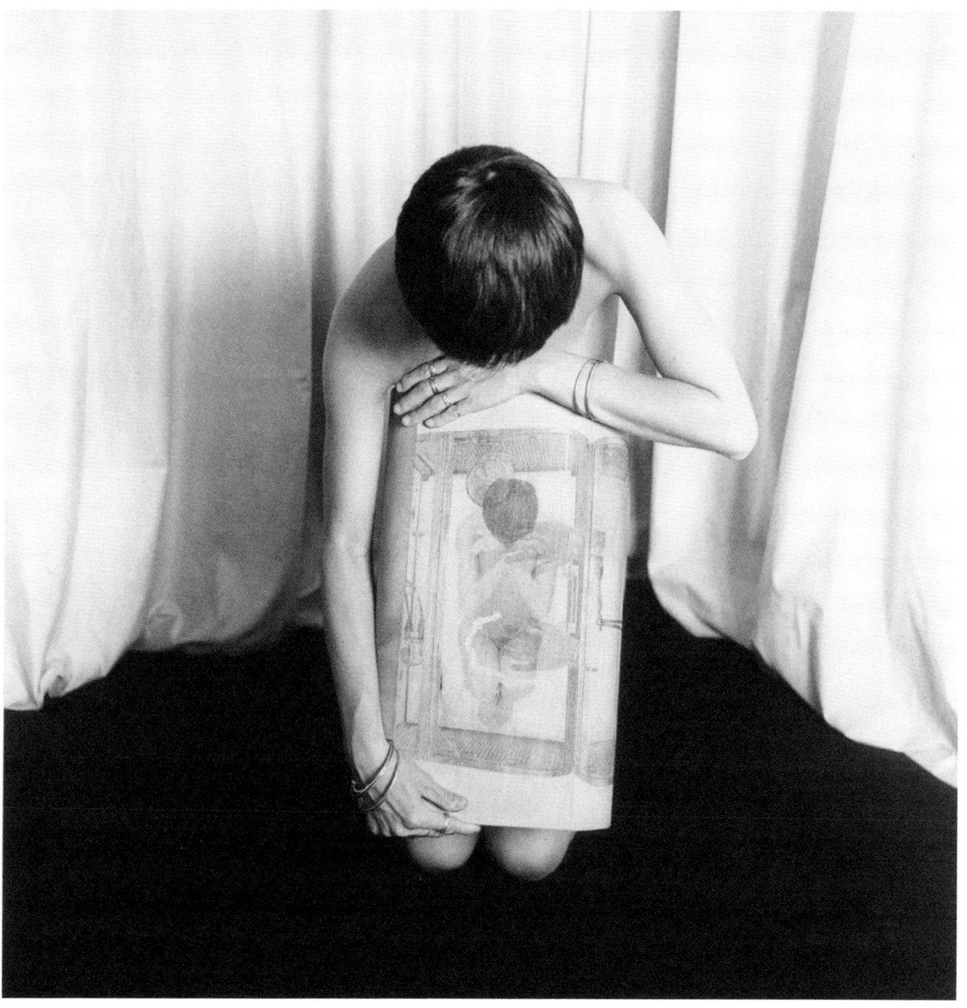

Helen Chadwick in collaboration with Mark Pilkington, *The Labours I: Incubator – Birth*, 1983–84. Dyed silver gelatin photograph, 122 × 91 cm (48 × 35⅞ in.)

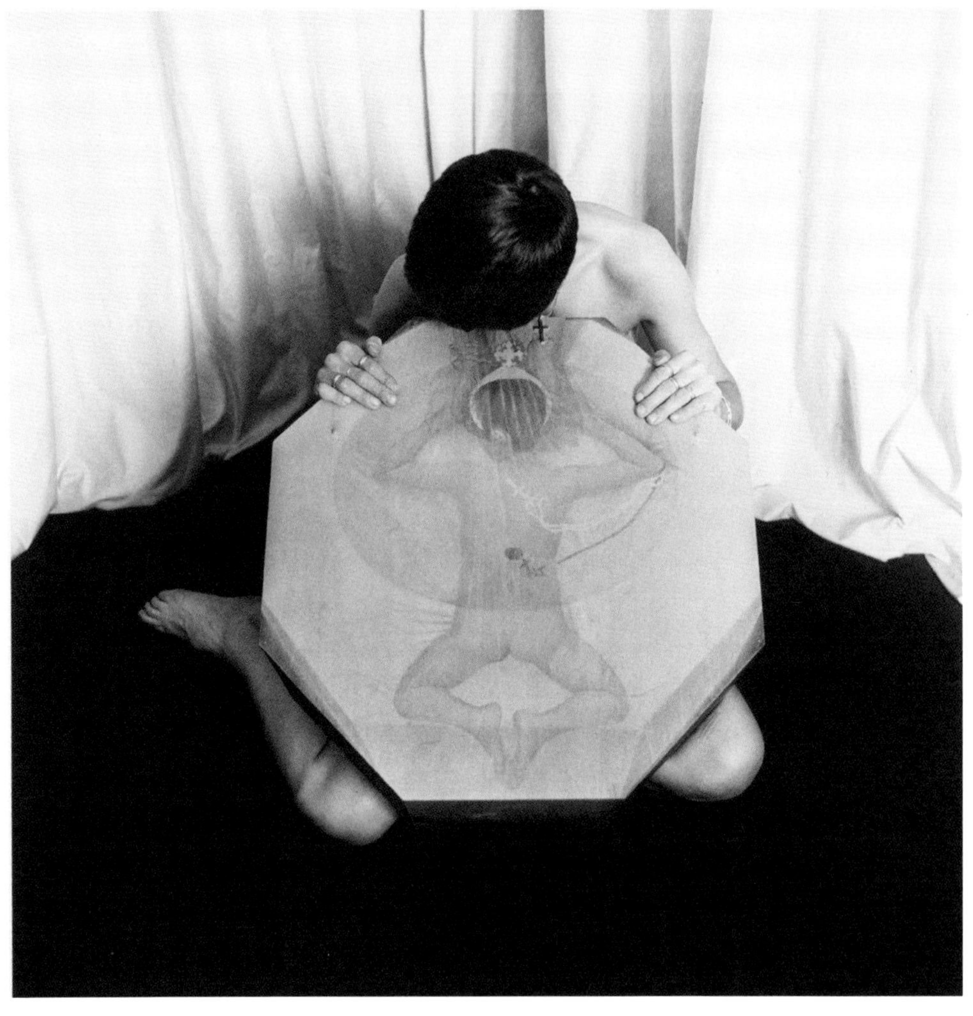

Helen Chadwick in collaboration with Mark Pilkington, *The Labours II: Font – 3 Months*, 1983–84. Dyed silver gelatin photograph, 123 × 91 cm (48 3/8 × 35 7/8 in.)

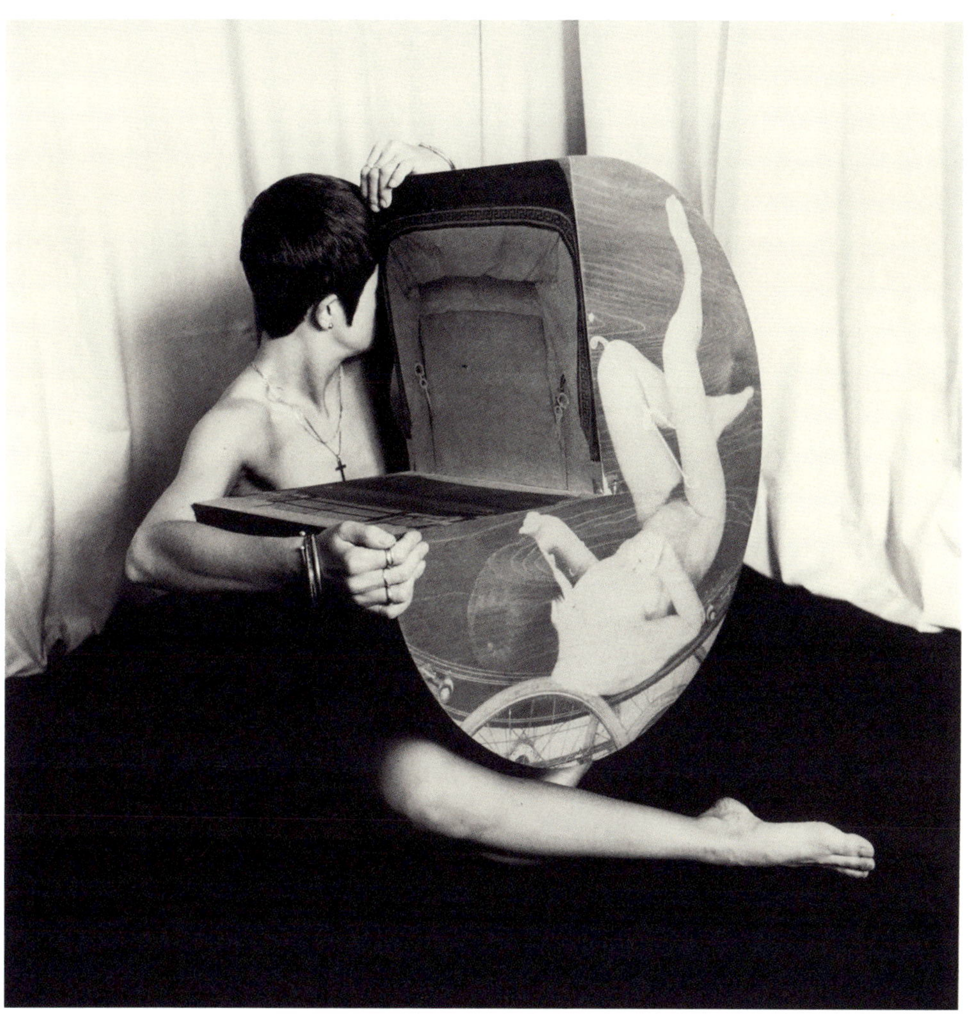

Helen Chadwick in collaboration with Mark Pilkington, *The Labours III: Pram – 10 Months*, 1983–84. Dyed silver gelatin photograph, 124 × 91 cm (48 7/8 × 35 7/8 in.)

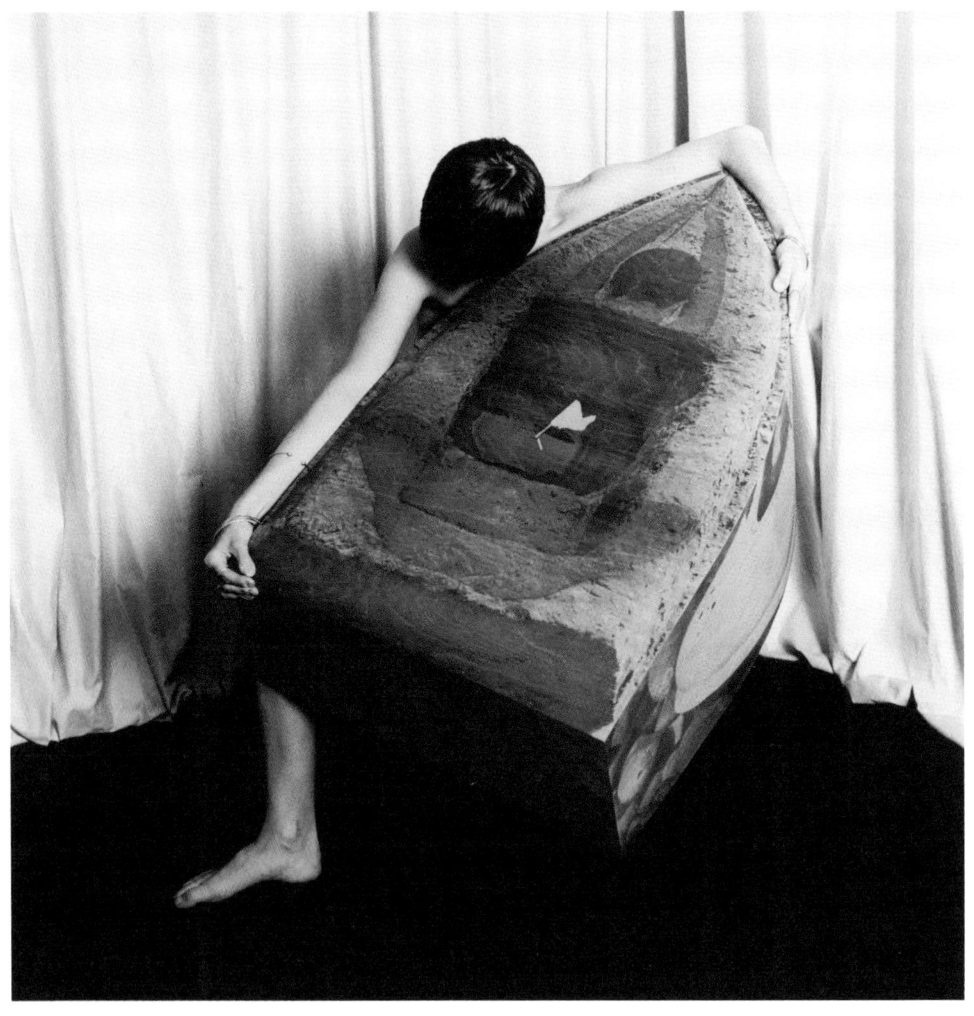

Helen Chadwick in collaboration with Mark Pilkington, *The Labours IV: Boat – 2 Years*, 1983–84. Dyed silver gelatin photograph, 125 × 91 cm (49 1/4 × 35 7/8 in.)

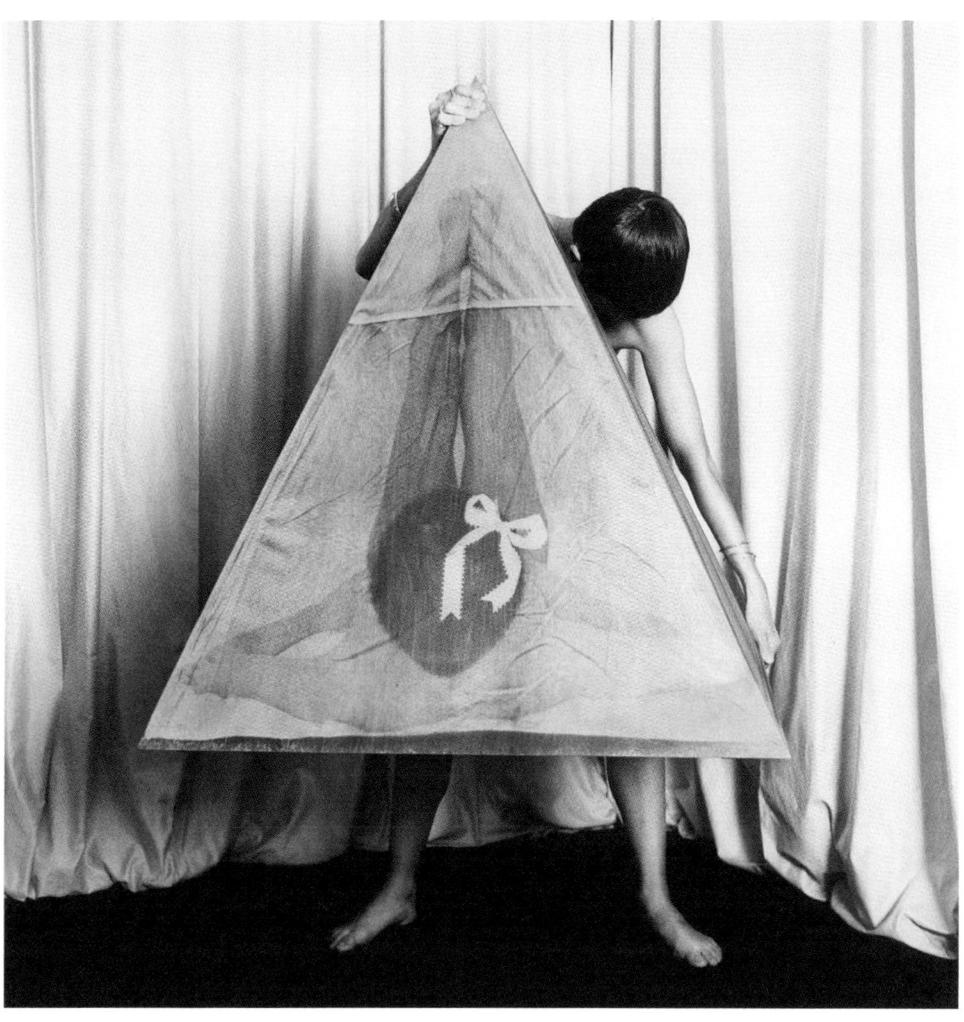

Helen Chadwick in collaboration with Mark Pilkington, *The Labours V: Wigwam – 5 Years*, 1983–84. Dyed silver gelatin photograph, 126 × 91 cm (49⅝ × 35⅞ in.)

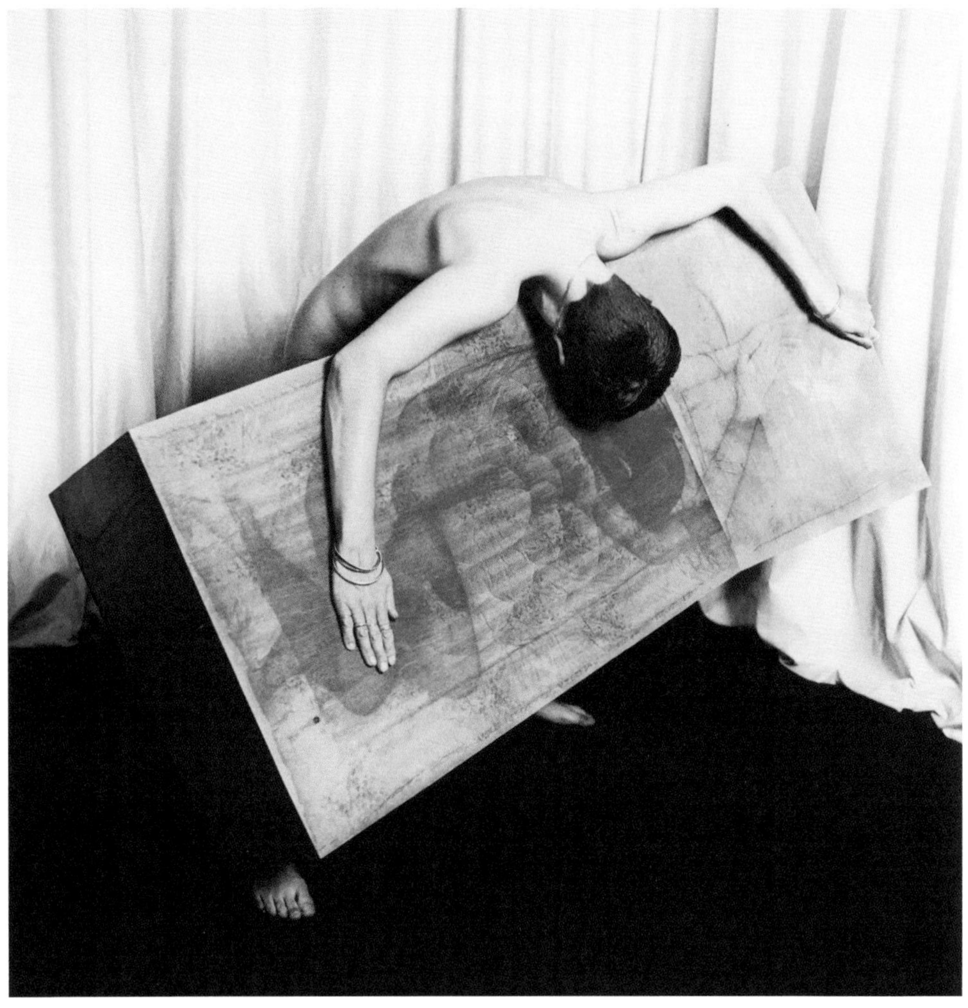

Helen Chadwick in collaboration with Mark Pilkington, *The Labours VI: Bed – 6½ Years*, 1983–84. Dyed silver gelatin photograph, 127 × 91 cm (50 × 35⅞ in.)

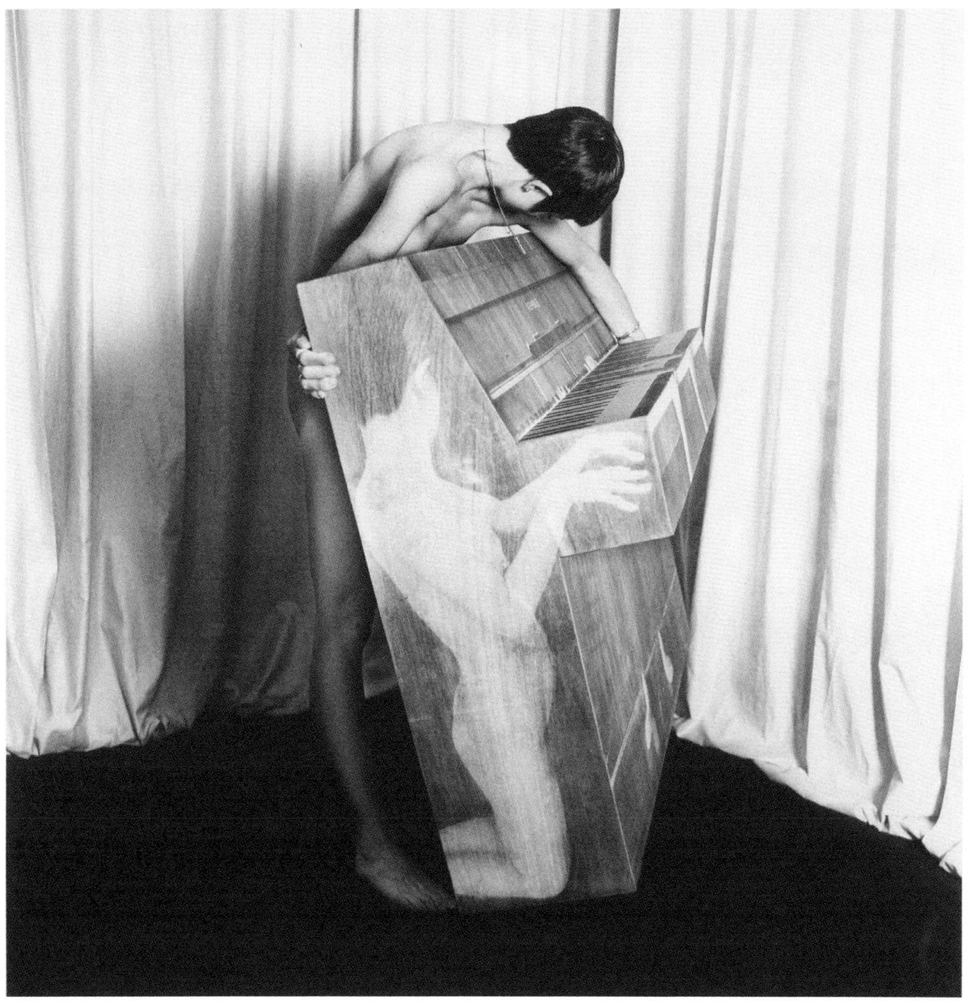

Helen Chadwick in collaboration with Mark Pilkington, *The Labours VII: Piano – 9 Years*, 1983–84. Dyed silver gelatin photograph, 128 × 91 cm ($50\frac{3}{8}$ × $35\frac{7}{8}$ in.)

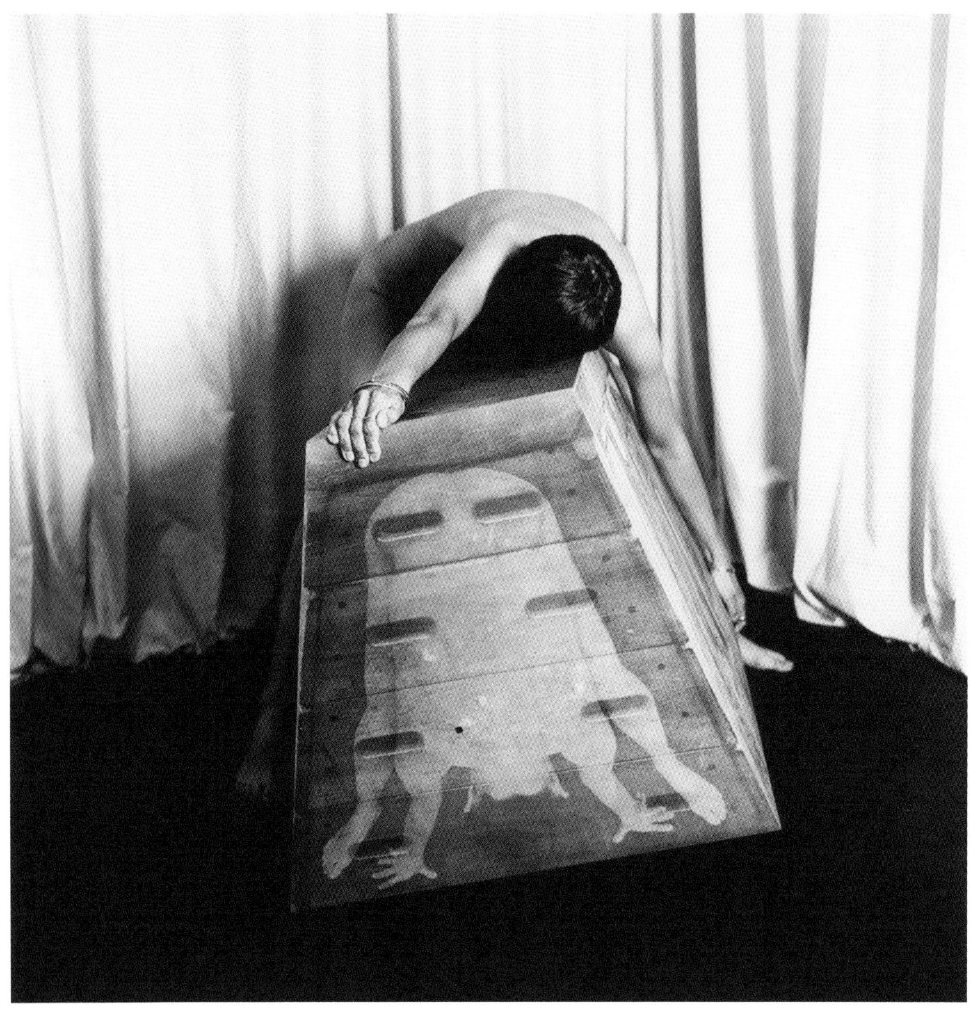

Helen Chadwick in collaboration with Mark Pilkington, *The Labours VIII: Horse – 11 Years*, 1983–84. Dyed silver gelatin photograph, 129 × 91 cm (50$\frac{3}{4}$ × 35$\frac{7}{8}$ in.)

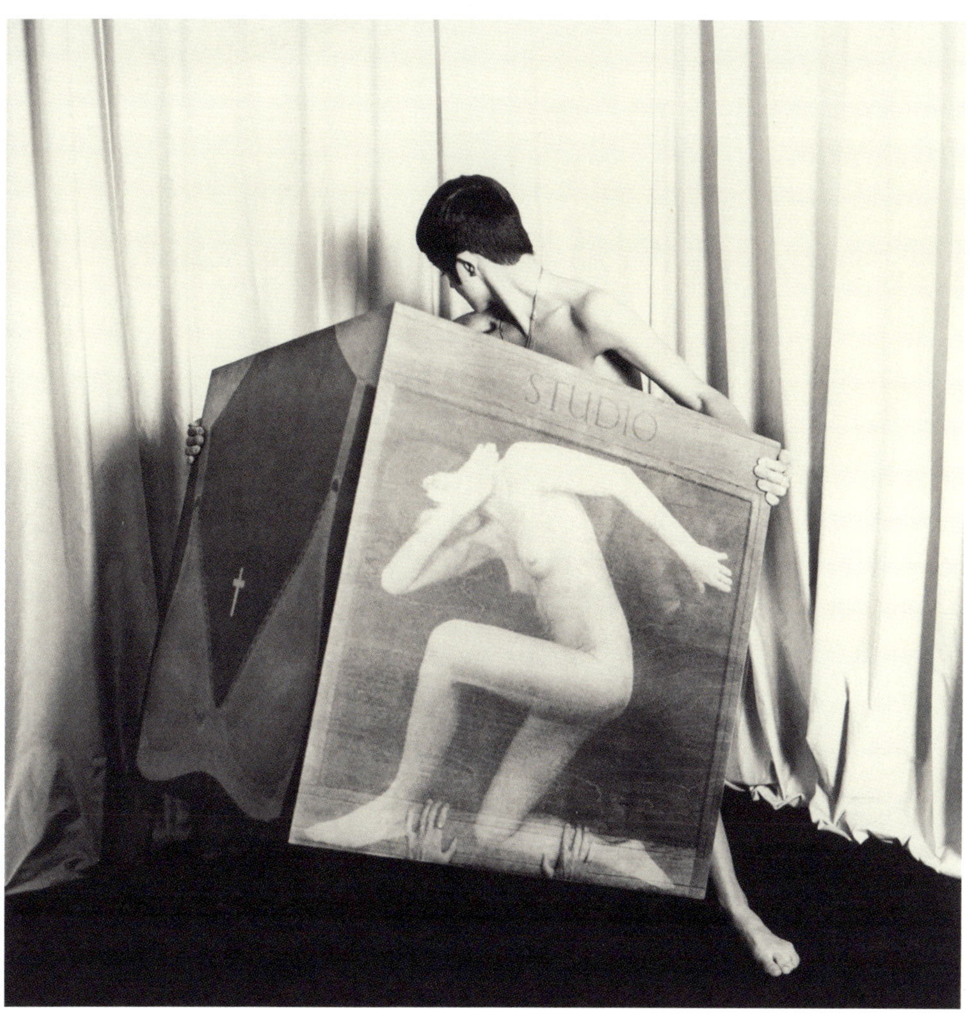

Helen Chadwick in collaboration with Mark Pilkington, *The Labours IX: High School – 13 Years*, 1983–84. Dyed silver gelatin photograph, 130 × 91 cm ($51\frac{1}{8} \times 35\frac{7}{8}$ in.)

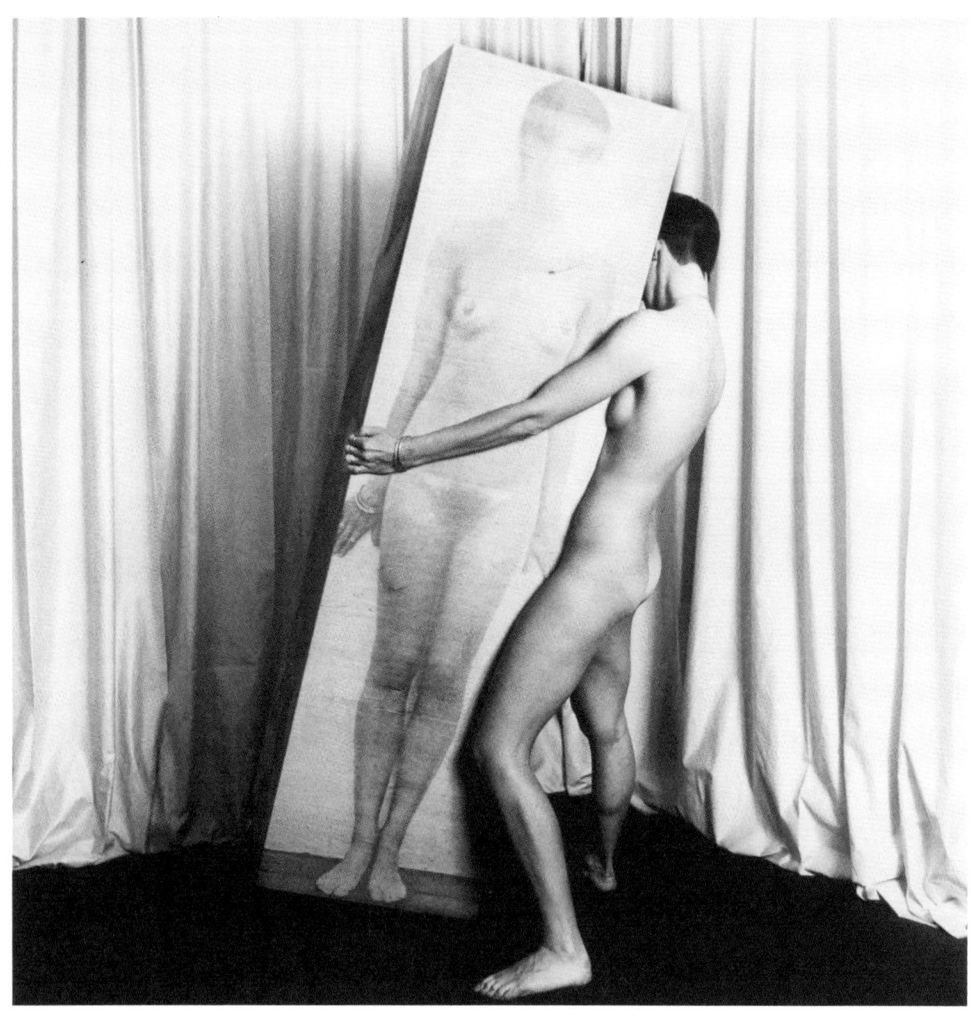

Helen Chadwick in collaboration with Mark Pilkington, *The Labours X: Statue – 15–30 Years*, 1983–84. Dyed silver gelatin photograph, 131 × 91 cm (51 $\frac{5}{8}$ × 35 $\frac{7}{8}$ in.)

For the exhibition, Chadwick took inspiration from the ceremonial character of the ICA's upper galleries' neo-classical architecture to create an installation that consisted of a number of autonomous but connected artworks. The largest of these works was *The Oval Court* (1984–86). Consisting of a low, ovoid-shaped platform on which she placed a twelve-part collage of cyan-toned photocopies of her own naked body posed, swimming, frolicking, amidst a fantasia of photocopied images of animals, plants, botanicals, drapery, fruit, ribbons and ornaments all swirling around her. The result is a deep aquamarine pool, within which Chadwick's body appears twelve times. The twelve figures – according to the artist's notes – represent the 'twelve gates to paradise, the twelve paths to self-knowledge through the power of love', where Chadwick will achieve 'oneness with all living things'.[22] Sitting on top of the platform are five large gold spheres suggesting the touch of five divine fingers, while on the surrounding walls hang images of twisting barley sugar columns (created from drawings of the baroque columns from the baldacchino of St Peter's Basilica, Vatican City) that reach down to the floor, atop which are images of Chadwick's own face, weeping and crying, the tears falling down the columns into the 'pool' below: 'art, like crying, is an act of self-repair, to shed the natural tears that free us, make us strong'.[23] Though tear-filled, this pool could be seen as the pool of Narcissus (from the Greek myth in which Narcissus dies by a pool after gazing at his own reflection for so long that he falls in love with himself), however, here Chadwick is 'looking through herself to search out something on the other side'.[24] *The Oval Court* exploits the *vanitas* tradition within the genre of still life. *Vanitas* in this context refers to pointlessness or futility, and employs symbolism to show the transience of life, the futility of pleasure and the certainty of death, and thus the vanity of ambition and pursuit of worldly desires. Through her use of dead animals (for the skate, lamb, rabbit, goose, monkfish and starfish, as well as the other animals, bugs and beings that she choreographs herself alongside, are all dead specimens), maggots, flora and fauna, and her signals to seventeenth- and eighteenth-century still life (fruits, beads, drapes and decadence), Chadwick both refers to and subverts the *vanitas* tradition, her naked body delighting in the transient bounty surrounding her.

The Oval Court was made with a Xerox machine, which Chadwick received as sponsorship from Xerox themselves. Chadwick claimed to enjoy the photocopier as a medium, describing it as 'extraordinarily direct and efficient'; she also liked that there was no conscious framing of the image. She described this work as 'a stitching together of so many different references, ultimately post-modern, a kind of bowerbird theft of facets from everywhere, from architecture, from painting'. Chadwick recalled that she was heavily influenced by the rococo and baroque eras during the creation of this work. She visited churches, palaces, cathedrals and citadels from this era during her research, flipping their highly detailed and heavenly ceiling paintings upside down and pulling them into an earthly realm of desire. She also took her facial expressions and the poses of her body directly from paintings and sculpture of this period, such as *The Ecstasy of Saint Teresa* (1647–52) by Gian Lorenzo Bernini (1598–1680), *The Raised Chemise* (c. 1770) by Jean-Honoré Fragonard (1732–1806) and *The Brunette* and *The Blonde Odalisque* (both 1775) by François Boucher (1703–1770).

The work has a deeply sensual quality; it appears almost as an earthly paradise occupied by an unashamed Eve. Each of Chadwick's twelve poses deals with a different sensation stimulated, for example, through kissing, licking, orgasming....And several of the accoutrements floating around the pool – a noose, an axe, a hood – lend a sado-masochistic edge. As Marina Warner describes: 'we see the artist as the one who leaps and gluts and feels and gorges and makes herself over to pleasure in a deliberately provocative display of the female nude'.[25] This is one of art history's most extensive exercises in self-imaging. It is a joyous, uninhibited celebration of the union of Chadwick's own body with nature. However, once again, she faced considerable hostility due to her use of nudity and, this time, was even accused of encouraging rape. In response to this criticism, Chadwick began to question the use of her own body in her art once more, stating that 'I made a conscious decision in 1988 not to represent my body. It immediately declares female gender and I wanted to be more deft.'[26] *The Oval Court* is the last work by Chadwick to use her own body as an image; her work still surveyed the notion of the self, and indeed the body as a material, but through more indirect methods.

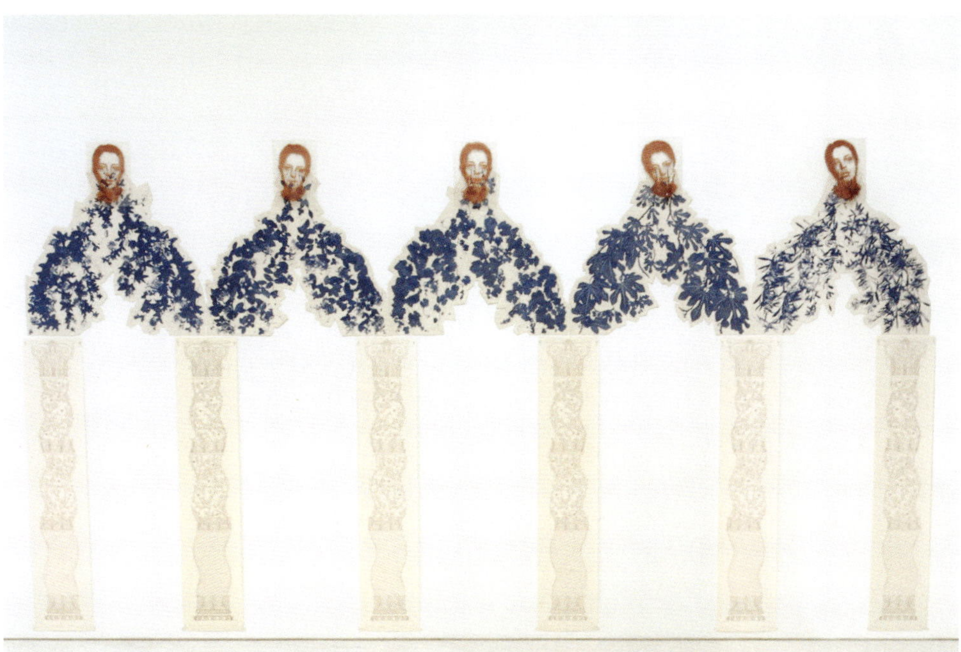

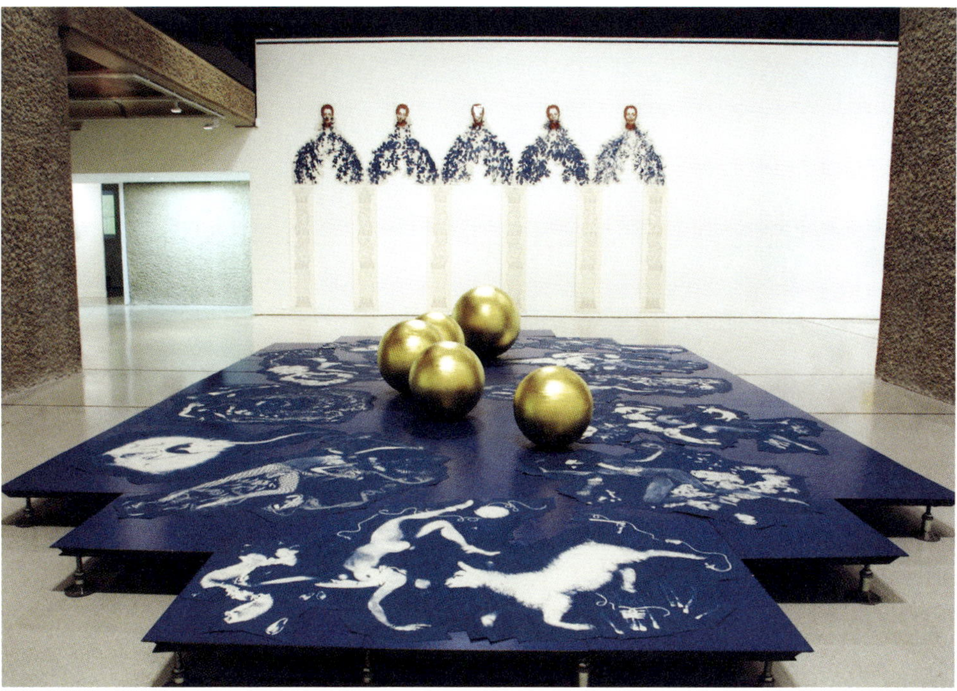

Helen Chadwick, *The Oval Court*, 1984–86. Photocopies on paper and board with blue pigment, acetate, plywood, gesso, gold leaf, laminated metal and concrete tiles, in twelve collaged parts, 427 × 792 cm (168$\frac{1}{8}$ × 311$\frac{3}{4}$ in.) overall

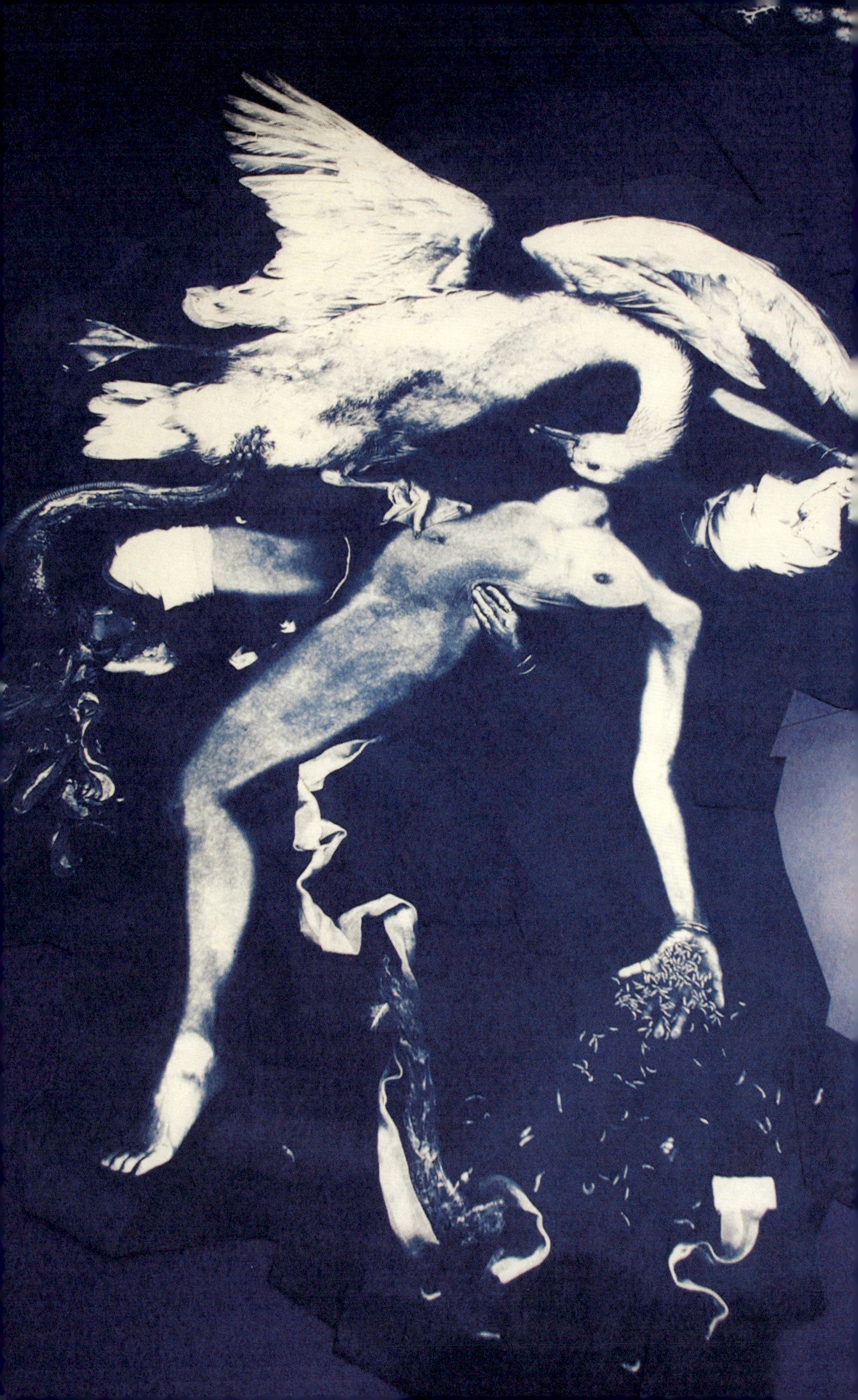

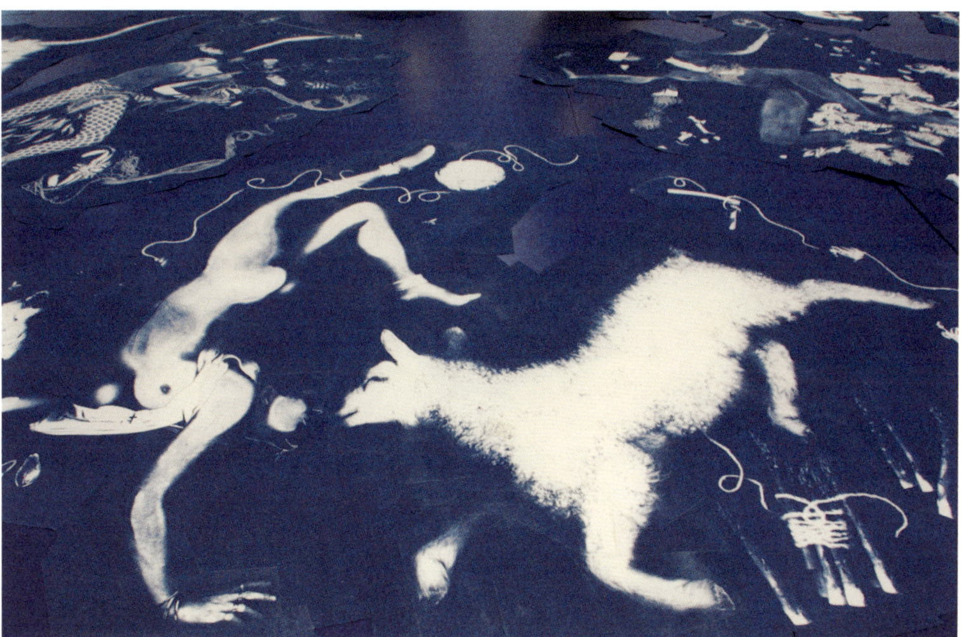

The second room of 'Of Mutability' housed *Carcass* (1986), a huge 2-metre-high (6½ ft) glass cuboid tower into which Chadwick poured the objects (fruits, flowers, meats) that she'd used in *The Oval Court*, as well as the food waste of her neighbours on Beck Road, regularly topping it up over the course of the exhibition. Like a giant digestive system or compost machine, the layers of rotting food initially formed stripes and strata that then dissolved as the organic material broke down. Playing with the relationship between repugnance – the notion of the 'abject' – and captivation, it elevated that which is usually disregarded to a far higher status. The rotting tower of compost generated new organisms and forms of life through the processes of decay, and thus took on an extraordinary life of its own, as Chadwick describes: 'what I hadn't anticipated was the fact that there would be this fermentation process, particularly with the weight compacting the lower, older material down, and it was constantly percolating bubbles, which you could watch kind of fizzing up. So...it became more a metaphor for life.'[27]

This notion of the abject is a complicated psychological, philosophical and linguistic concept that was developed in depth by writer Julia Kristeva

OPPOSITE AND ABOVE **Helen Chadwick, *The Oval Court*, 1984–86 (details)**

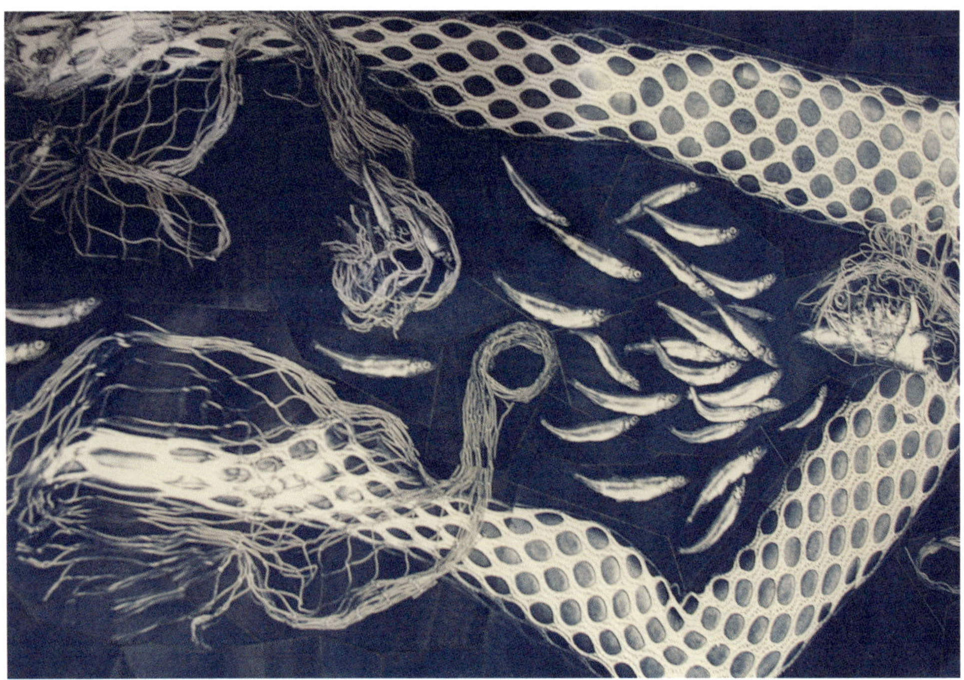

in her book *Powers of Horror* (1980). Herein she describes the abject as that which is rejected by, or disturbs, social reason. However, Kristeva then evolves this meaning: 'it is not the lack of cleanliness or health that causes abjection but what disturbs identity, system, and order. What does not respect borders, positions, rules. The in-between, the ambiguous, the composite.'[28] This way of thinking about the abject is highly relevant to Chadwick's work as she sought to intentionally disrupt systems of order, beauty and conventional identity concepts. The abject also has a strong feminist context, in that female bodily functions and reactions are so often 'abjected' by a patriarchal social order. In both *Carcass* and *The Oval Court*, Chadwick celebrates life, death, (female) desire, pain, excretion, decay, all at once, pulling the abject back into the throes of the everyday with a jolt. The fact too that she is still utilizing the indexical – the direct imprint of her own body, rather than a mediated image of it – makes this jolt all the more tangible.

Some time into the exhibition's run, the glass of *Carcass* cracked and, in a panic, the gallery staff tried to remove it from public view, tipping

ABOVE AND OPPOSITE **Helen Chadwick, *The Oval Court*, 1984–86 (details)**

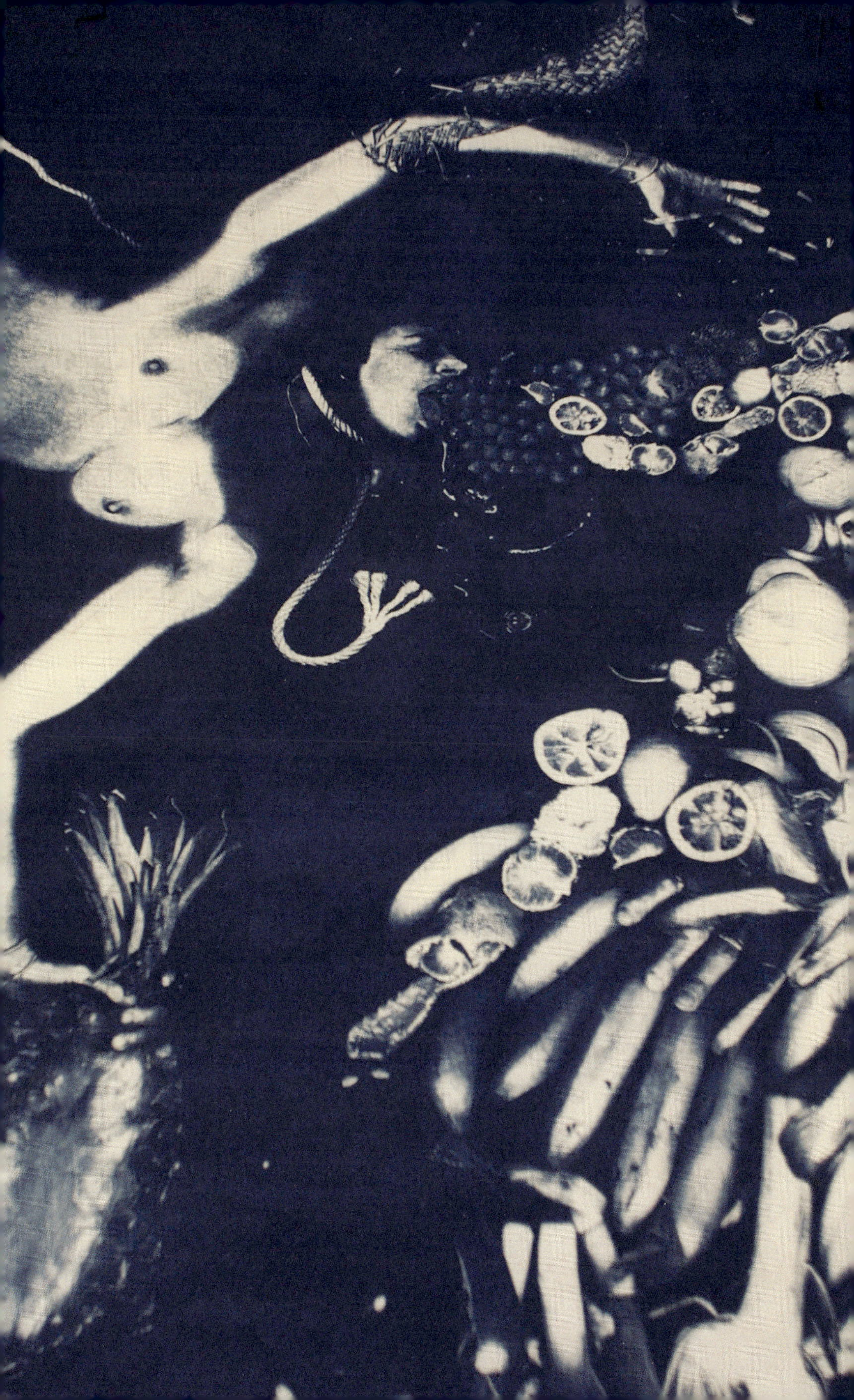

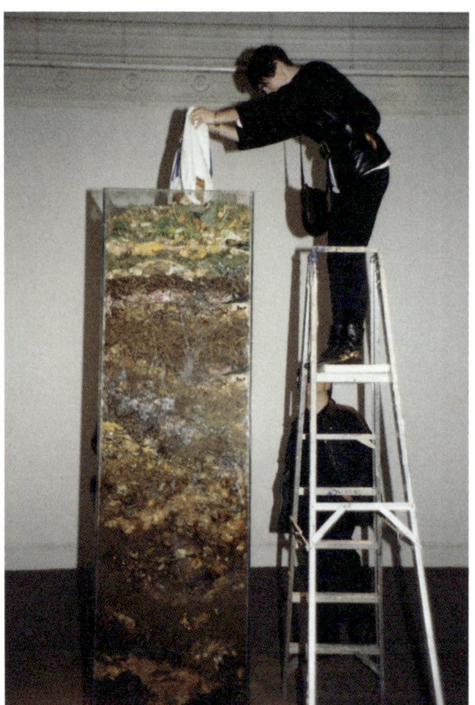

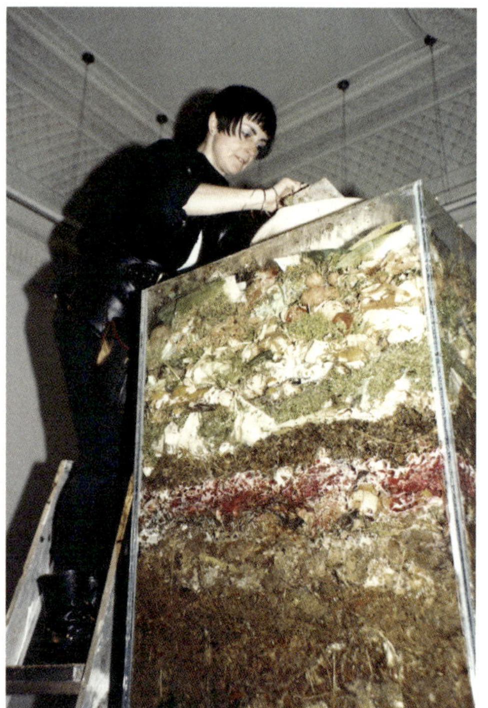

it onto its side to carry it more easily. As they did, the lid blew off (gas had built up inside and the effect was similar to shaking a bottle of fizzy drink), spraying fermented waste across the galleries of the ICA. It seems that the work had, indeed, developed a life of its own. This exposure granted Chadwick profile-raising notoriety, and the following year, in 1987, she became one of the first women to be nominated for the Turner Prize for her exhibition.

Following her avowal in 1988 not to represent her own naked body in her work any longer, Chadwick turned her attention inside the body to look at flesh, meat, blood and cells: 'I felt compelled to use materials that were still bodily, that were still a kind of self-portrait, but did not rely on representation of my own body.'[29] *Blood Hyphen* (1988) was an important transitional piece in this regard. Created for the Woodbridge Chapel, London (which for a time had been allocated to the Clerkenwell Medical Mission), Chadwick made use of the building's historic architectural alterations and history as both a religious institution and a former NHS

Helen Chadwick installing *Carcass*, 1986

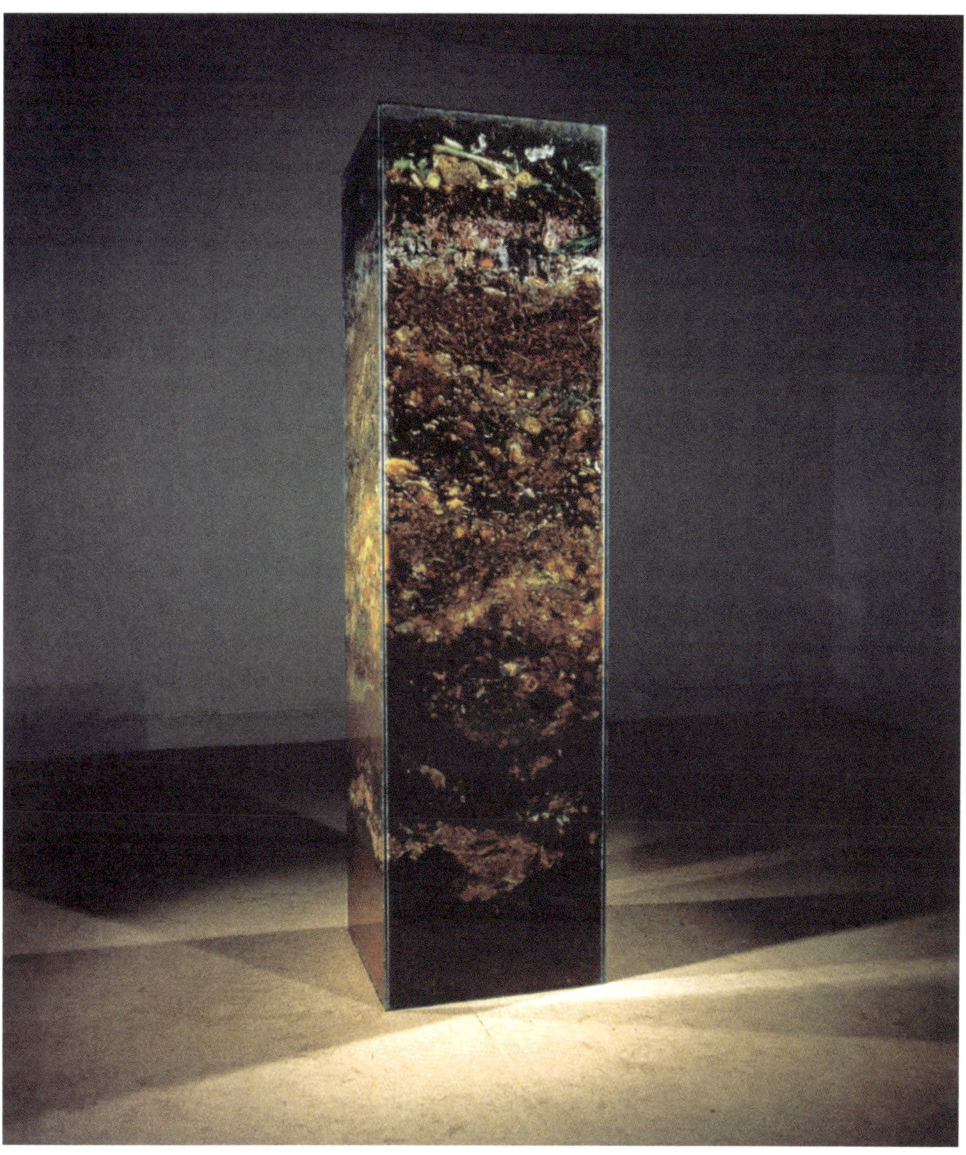

Helen Chadwick, *Carcass*, 1986. Organic material contained within a glass and Perspex tower, 229 × 61 × 61 cm (90¼ × 24 × 24 in.). Installed as part of Chadwick's exhibition 'Of Mutability' at the Institute of Contemporary Arts, London, 1986

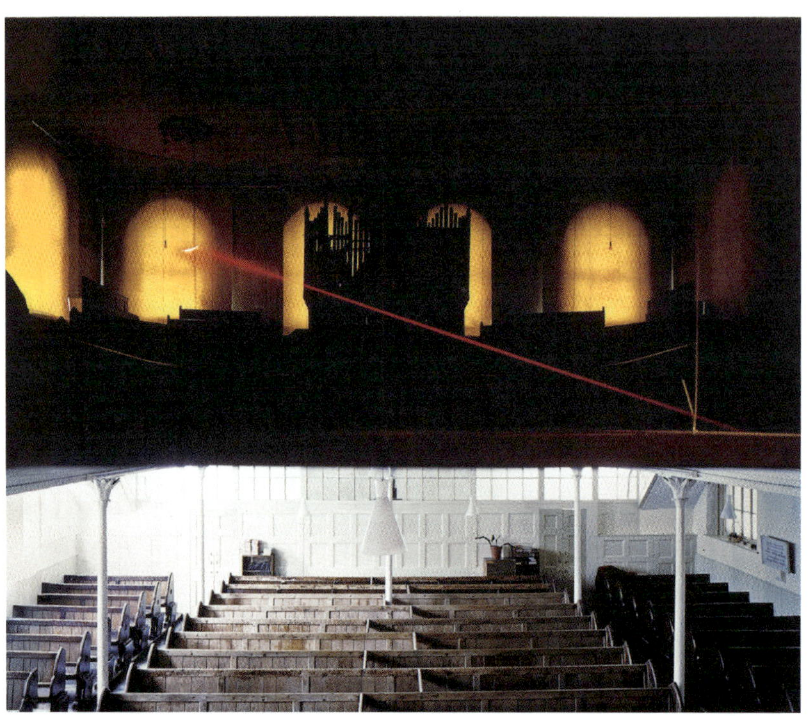

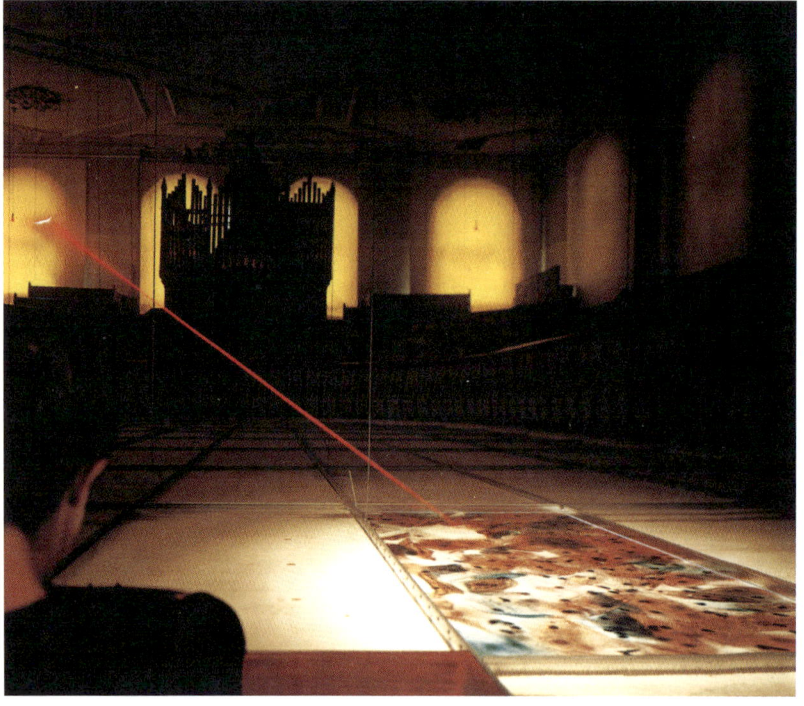

treatment centre. In the 1970s a false ceiling had been added to the venue, removing the top of the church hall from public view. Chadwick created an installation in this concealed space, which she kept dark and filled with smoke. A laser beam then cut through the gloom, directed at an enlarged photographic transparency of cells from a cervical smear test. To view the work, visitors were asked to climb a ladder and peep - one by one - through a hole in the ceiling. Chadwick's hope was that the space would be experienced like a bodily cavity, and she described it as a sort of 'divine gynaecology'.[30]

In his book *On the Strange Place of Religion in Contemporary Art* (2004), James Elkins writes:

> *the laser is reminiscent of the straight line painted in Renaissance depictions of the Annunciation: the Holy Spirit travels down the line from God to the Virgin. The blood is reminiscent of Christ's blood, and the brilliant upper floor contrasted against the spectral lower as the light of heaven to the unilluminated Earth. Even the title,* Blood Hyphen, *echoes the line, called a hyphen, between Christ's first and last wounds - between the circumcision and the wound in his side.*[31]

The work used the technology of medical science (the laser and microscopic cellular photography) to mimic historic representations of divine authority in a recognizably religious setting. As such, *Blood Hyphen* references and converges two powerful methodologies of being in and understanding the world, religion and medicine, while also encouraging a more primal, corporeal way of experiencing the work.

Travelling deeper inside the body, in 1989 Chadwick produced a series of photographic works titled *Meat Abstracts*, made with a large-format Polaroid camera. In these pieces, she created compositions with medleys of fresh meat; steak, tripe, offal, liver, hearts and kidneys, lovingly arranged à la seventeenth-century still lifes on sheets of coloured silk, velvet, leather or fur, occasionally accompanied by golden spheres or shining cutlery. In all the images a glowing light bulb illuminates the scene, sometimes buried inside the lumps of meat, sometimes silhouetting them from behind, and sometimes pointing directly at them so that they

OPPOSITE Helen Chadwick, *Blood Hyphen*, 1988. Site-specific installation with laser, smoke and photographic transparencies at Woodbridge Chapel, Clerkenwell, London

glisten wetly. The images are shot directly from above to create a shallow depth of field and single plane of focus. The resultant works resemble the sort of images associated with luxury fashion accessories: bags, jewellery, scarves etc. At the time of making the *Meat Abstracts*, Chadwick was deeply influenced by the films of David Cronenberg (b. 1943) and the body horror genre, as well as by the story of Frankenstein and his monster. She was keen to find a way reanimating the inanimate. To bring the meat to life with electricity and light, but in a way that was beautiful, sexy even, not monstrous. Chadwick's print *Anatoli* (1989), made for the King's Fund Hospital Project, was named after a town in Greece that held emotional significance to her. *Anatoli* appears to be an image of the sun over a rugged mountain-scape, but at the same time it is visually reminiscent of her *Meat Abstract No. 1* (1989). As such, this work combines the bodily with thinking about landscape and place, an approach that would become of great significance to her in her last major work of the 1980s.

In 1989 Chadwick was invited to participate in the 'Artists in National Parks' scheme, a government and oil-industry-sponsored programme of artists producing new work in response to the protected landscapes of England and Wales. Undertaking a placement in Pembrokeshire National Park in west Wales, Chadwick used her time to examine the relationship between the natural landscape and human beings, thinking about this from the perspective of host and virus and exploring the crossover between ecological pollution and human sickness: 'we have become a viral condition in the landscape'.[32] At the same time, the five enormous prints that comprise the *Viral Landscapes* (1988–89) series also seek to balance the evocation of the individual subject within a description of place and their impact thereon. For Chadwick, the coastline represented the uncertainty of boundaries – between land and sea, between body and disease and between individual and society. Deeply affected by the trauma of the AIDS crisis during the 1980s and its impact on communities all over the world, Chadwick's *Viral Landscapes* make visible the anxieties of the time. Her coastal landscapes could be interpreted as metaphors for the body as a site with frontiers, ingresses and openings, which may be vulnerable to infection and disease.

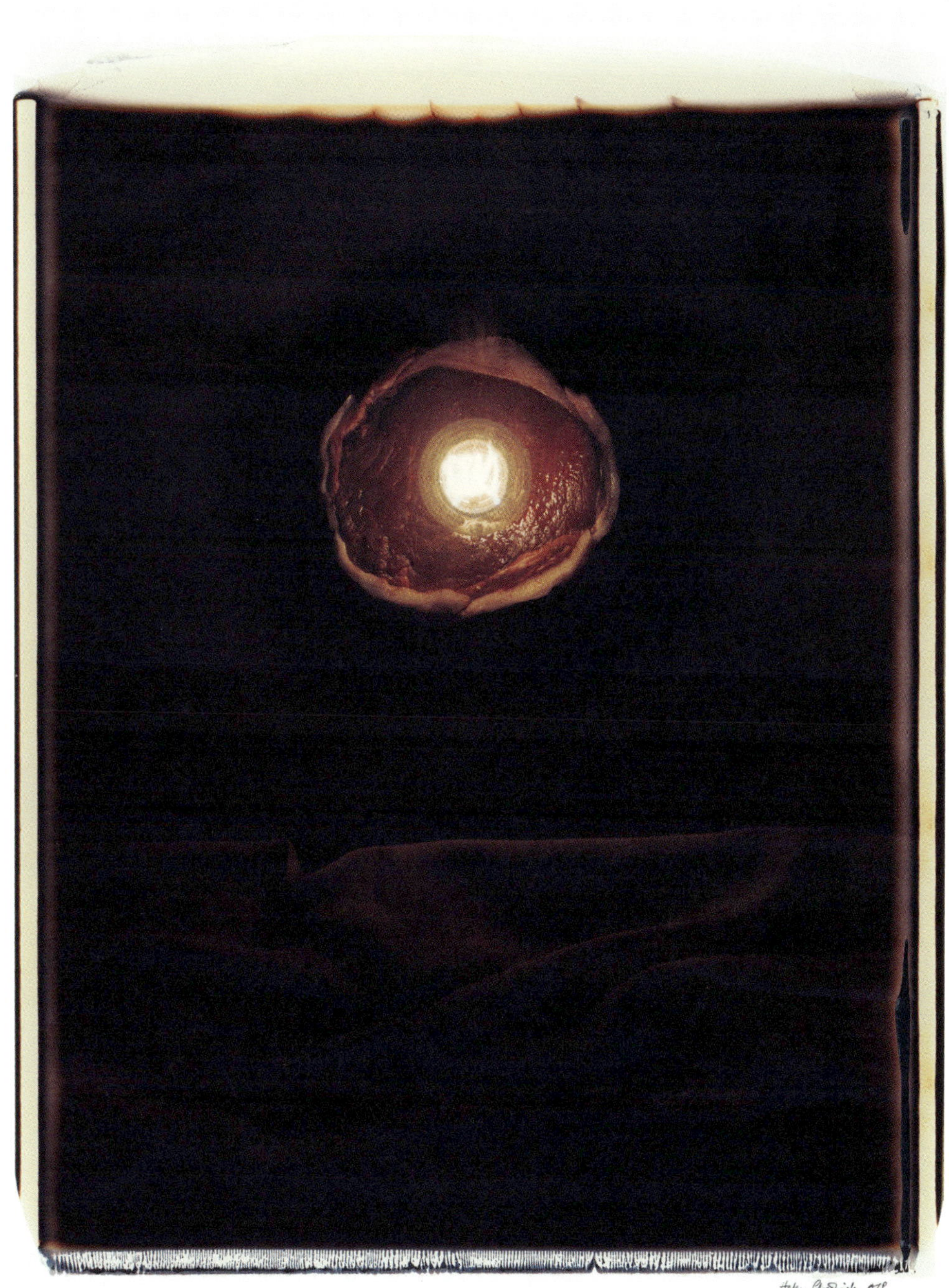

Helen Chadwick, ***Meat Abstract No. 1: Black Sun***, 1989.
Polaroid on silk mat, 81 × 71 cm (31 $\frac{7}{8}$ × 28 in.)

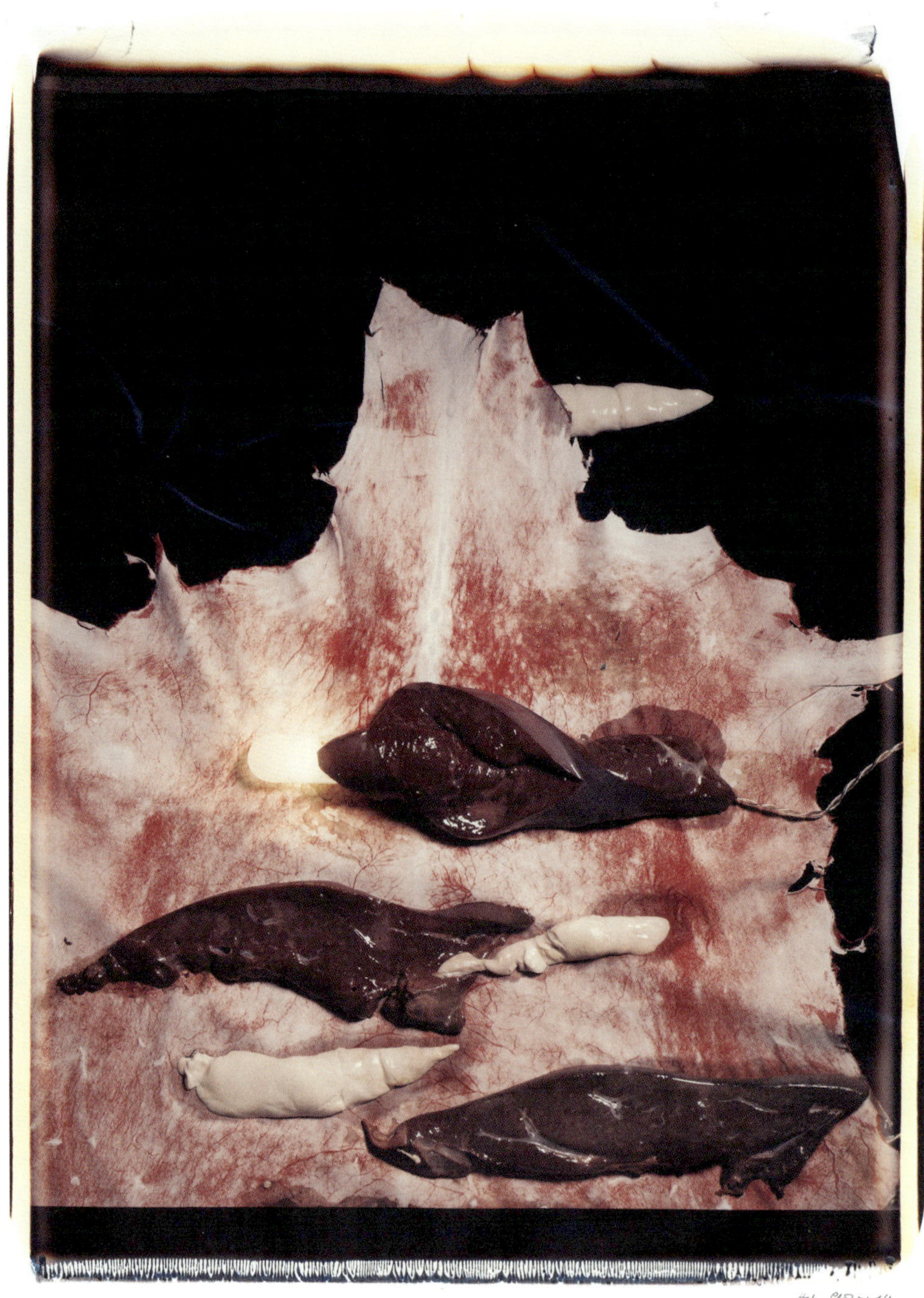

Helen Chadwick, *Meat Abstract No. 3: Liver*, 1989.
Polaroid on silk mat, 81 × 71 cm (31 7/8 × 28 in.)

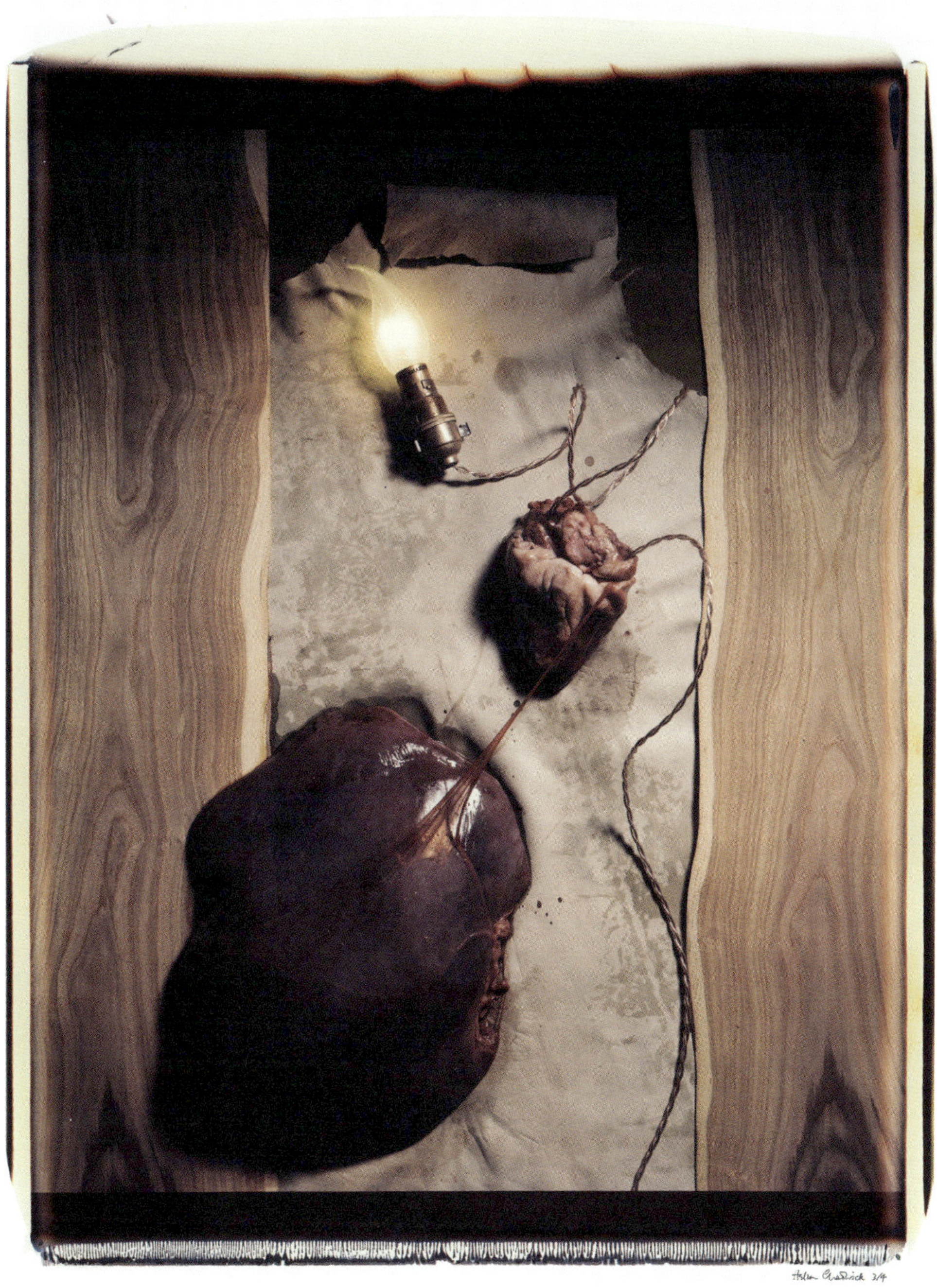

Helen Chadwick, ***Meat Abstract No. 5: Heart of Liver***, 1989.
Polaroid on silk mat, 81 × 71 cm (31 7/8 × 28 in.)

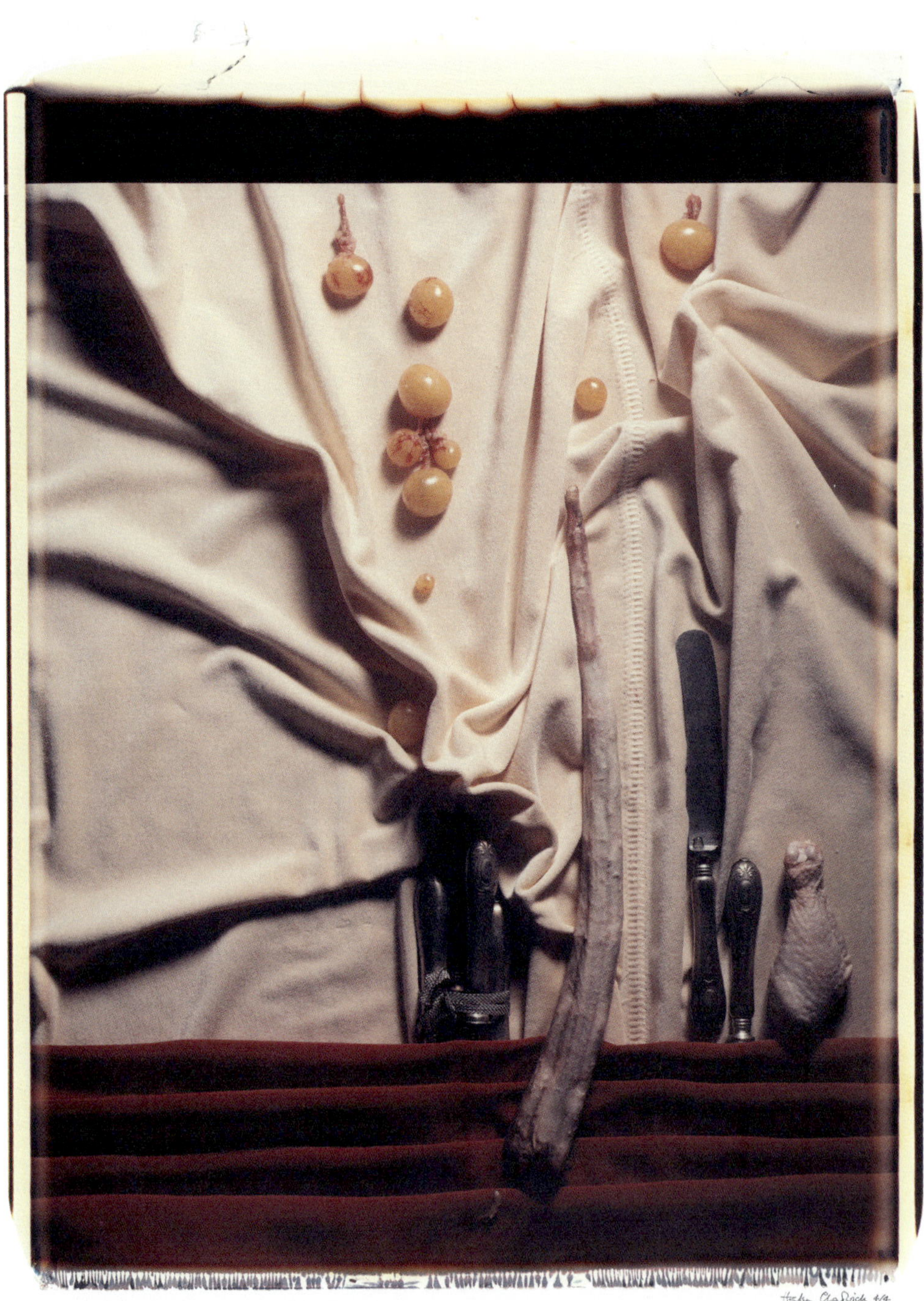

Helen Chadwick, *Meat Abstract No. 6: Cutlery*, 1989.
Polaroid on silk mat, 81 × 71 cm (31 $\frac{7}{8}$ × 28 in.)

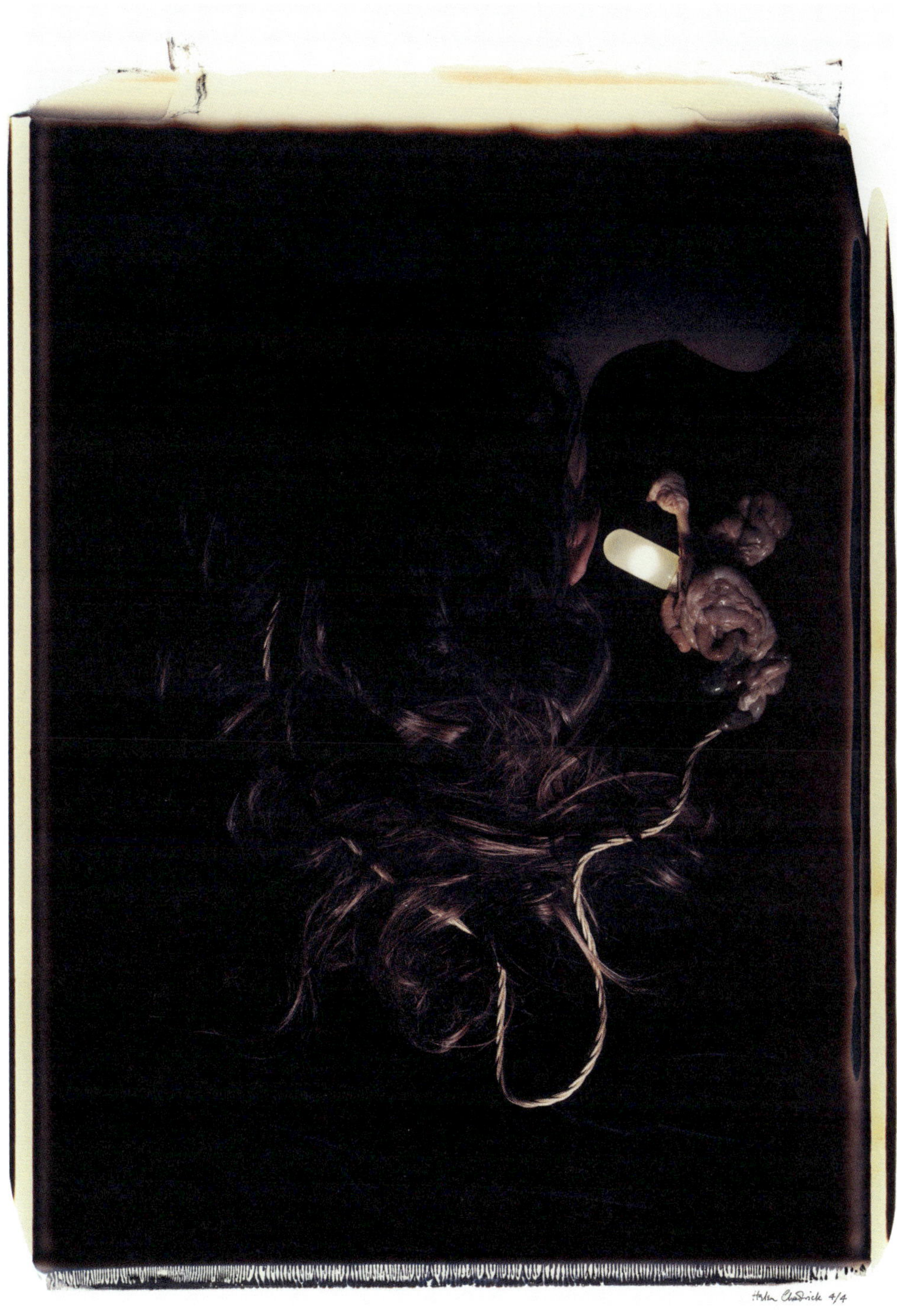

Helen Chadwick, *Meat Abstract No. 7: Hair and Entrails*, 1989.
Polaroid on silk mat, 81 × 71 cm ($31\frac{7}{8}$ × 28 in.)

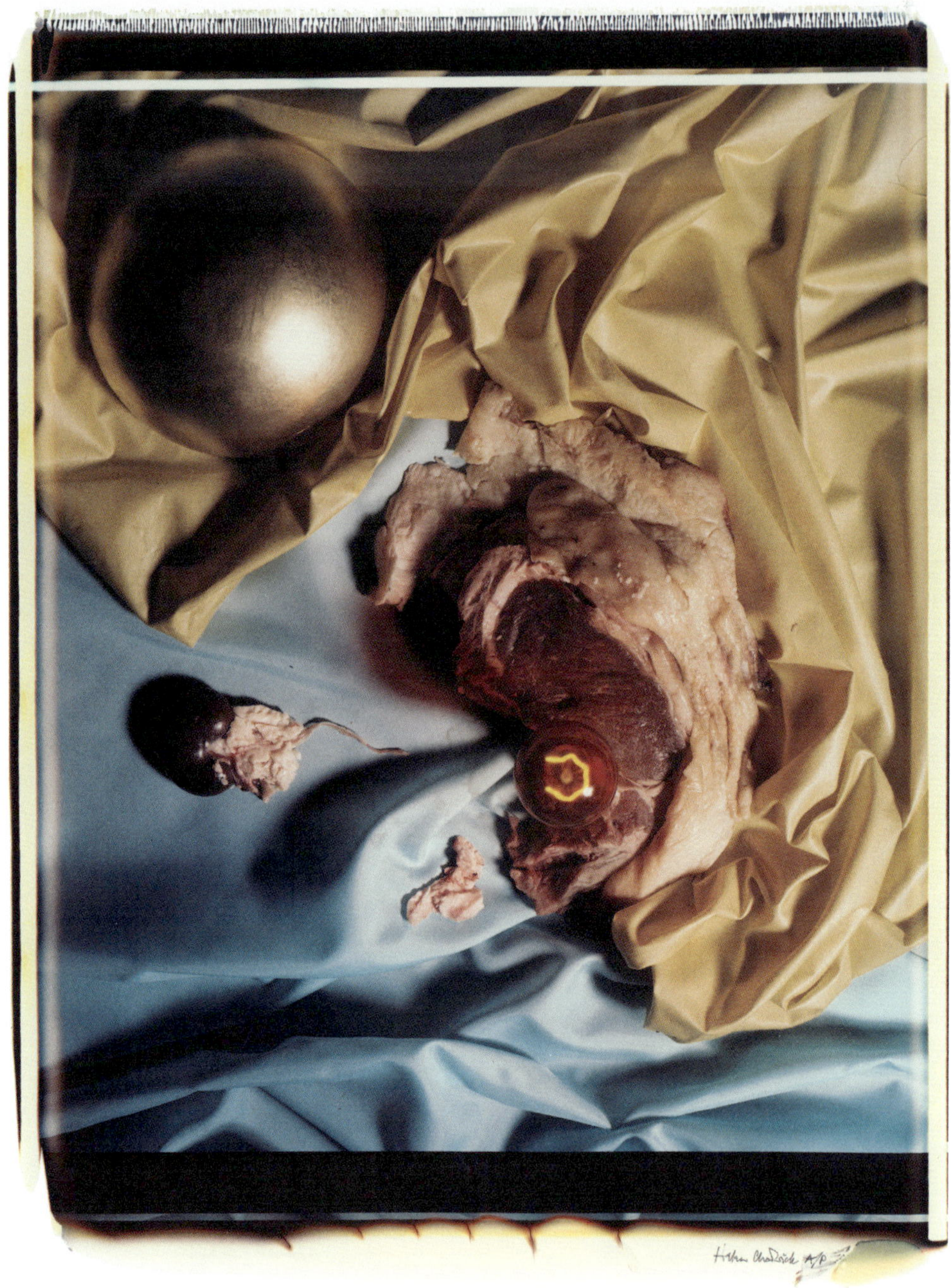

Helen Chadwick, *Meat Abstract No. 8: Gold Ball/Streak*, 1989.
Polaroid on silk mat, 81 × 71 cm (31$\frac{7}{8}$ × 28 in.)

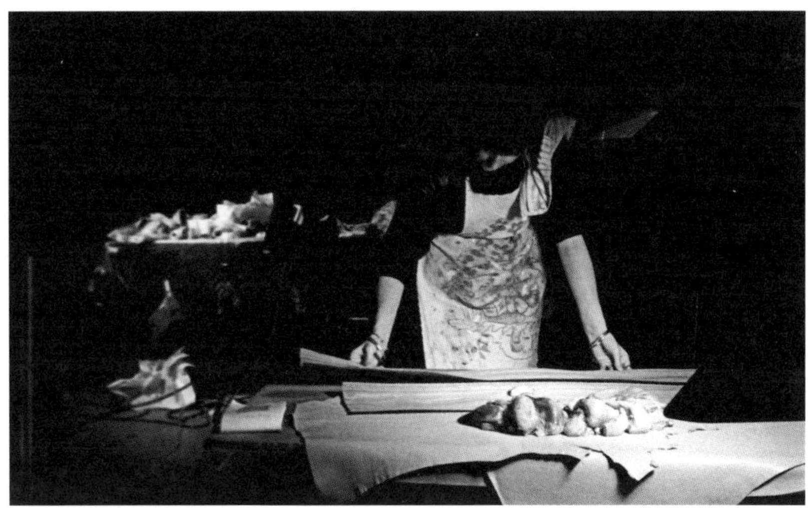

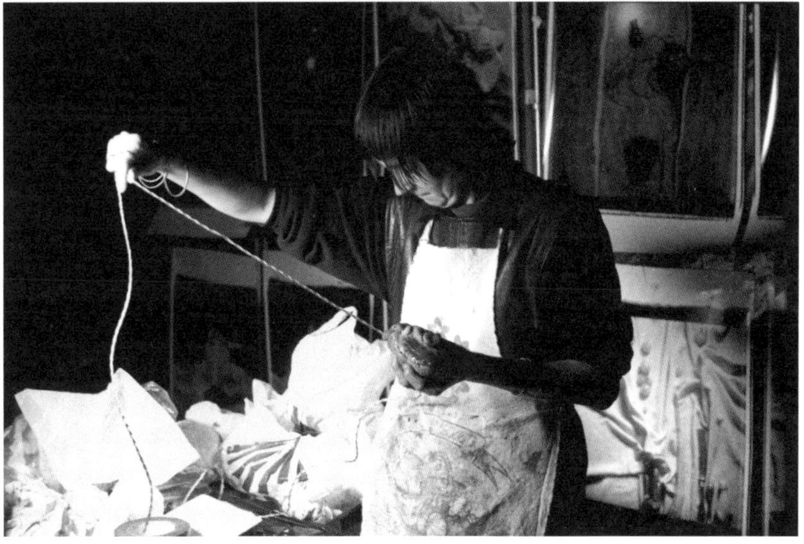

Helen Chadwick making *Meat Abstracts*, 1989

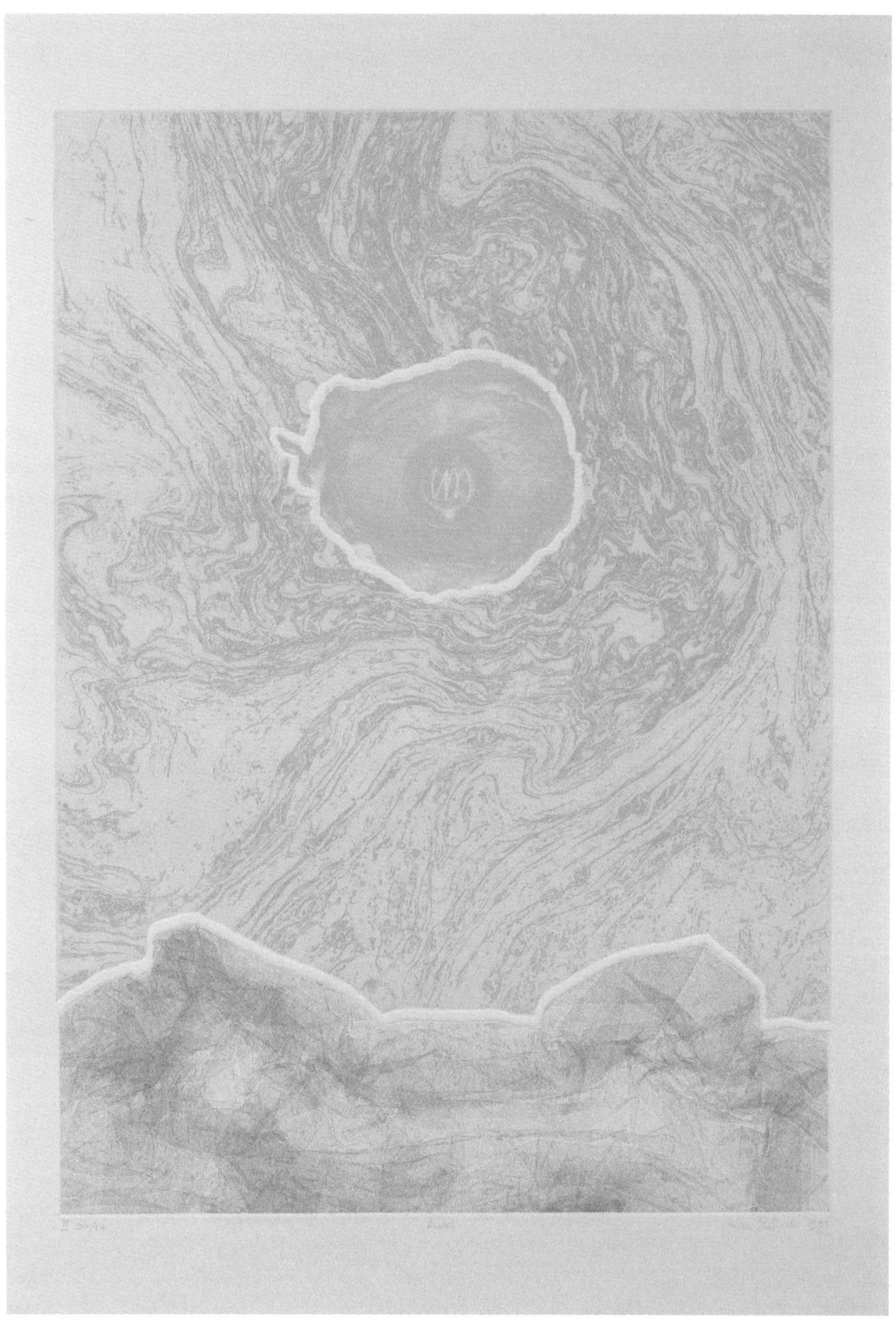

Helen Chadwick, *Anatoli*, 1989. Etching and aquatint with relief on wove paper, 95 × 67 cm (37 3/8 × 26 3/8 in.)

The works consist of panoramic photographs of coastlines in Pembrokeshire, which Chadwick then printed onto huge horizontal canvases. She then took these canvases to the coast and submerged them in the waves along with coloured pigments, allowing the sea to engage in the painting process as the movement of the water distributed and settled the colour. She then rephotographed the sea-painted canvases, and on top of these images, she printed photomicrographs of the cells of her own body (her blood, her ear, her mouth, her cervix and her urine). The format of the five resulting works was very deliberately made to echo the shape of a microscope slide. Through fusing nature and the body in a simultaneous depiction of interior and exterior, Chadwick pulls the metaphor of virus and host onto a comparison between the individual and the world. The work speaks, on an immediate level, to the angst of the time and the torment that AIDS wrought, but it also speaks on an allegorical level to the responsibilities of the subject within the world - both natural and cultural.

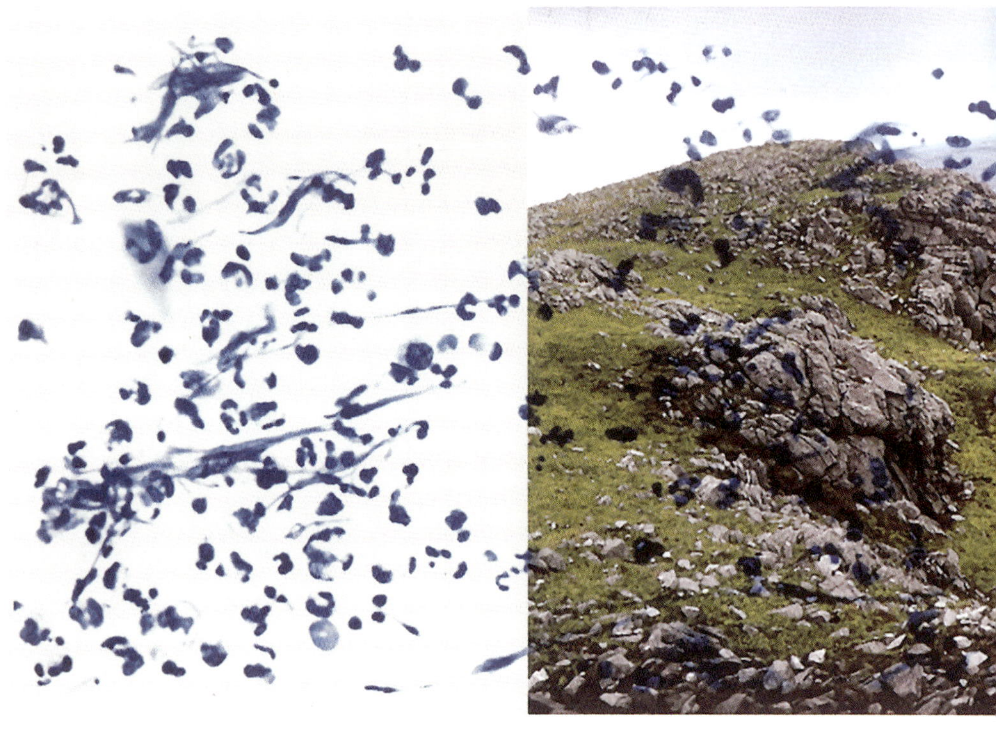

Helen Chadwick, *Viral Landscape No. 5*, 1988–89. C-print photograph, powder-coated steel, aluminium-faced plywood, Perspex, 120 × 300 × 5 cm (47¼ × 118⅛ × 2 in.)

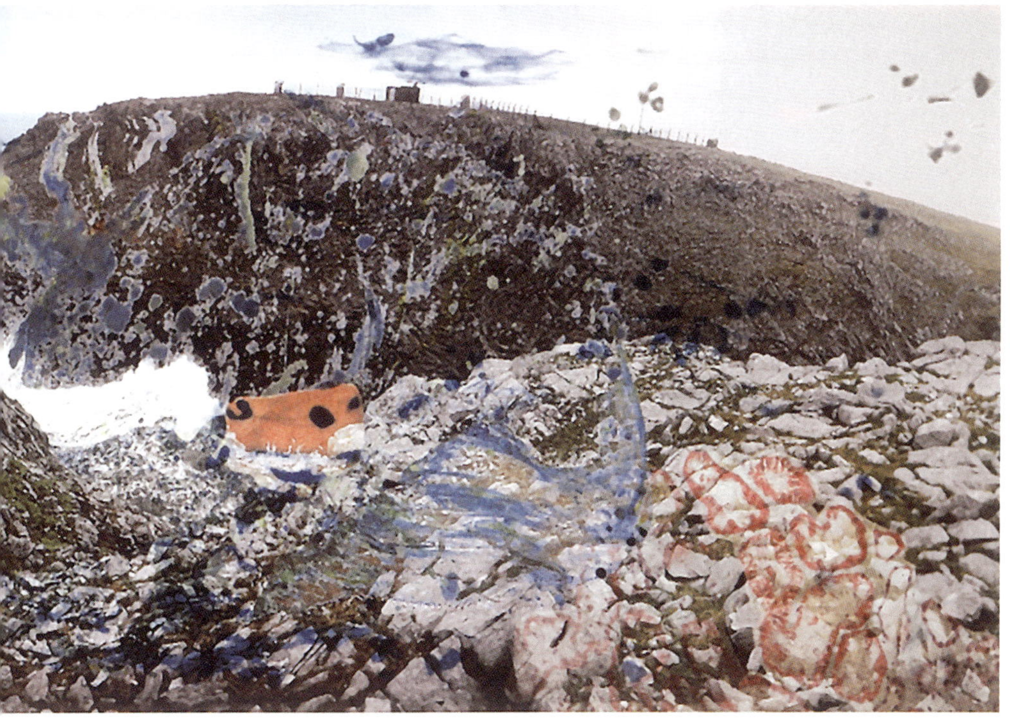

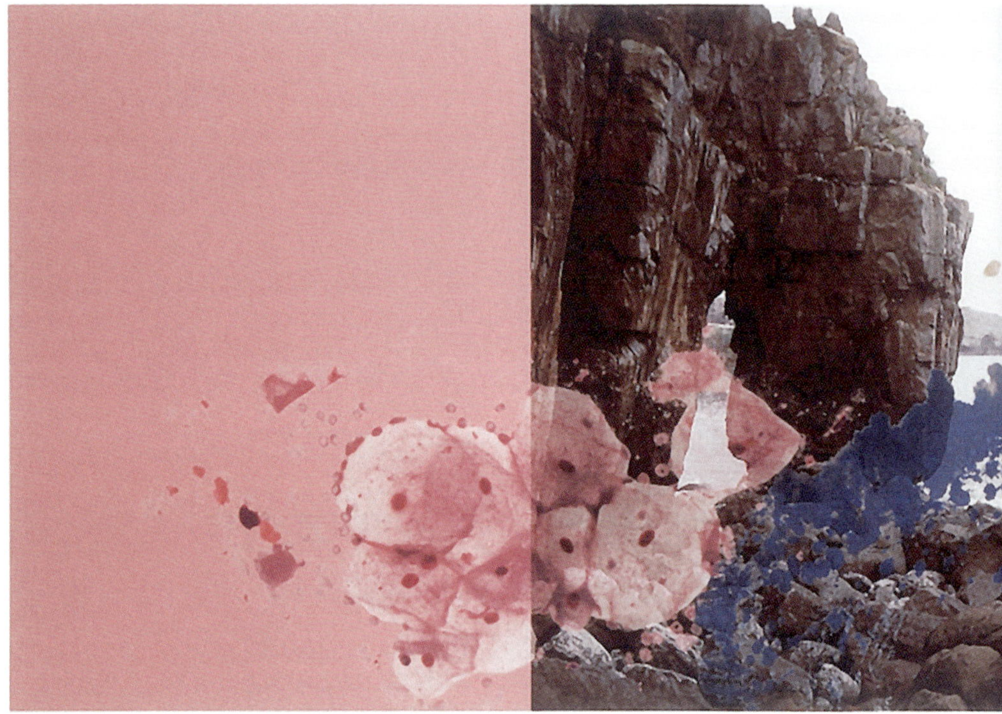

Helen Chadwick, *Viral Landscape No. 1*, 1988–89. C-print photograph, powder-coated steel, aluminium-faced plywood, Perspex, 120 × 300 × 5 cm (47 ¼ × 118 ⅛ × 2 in.)

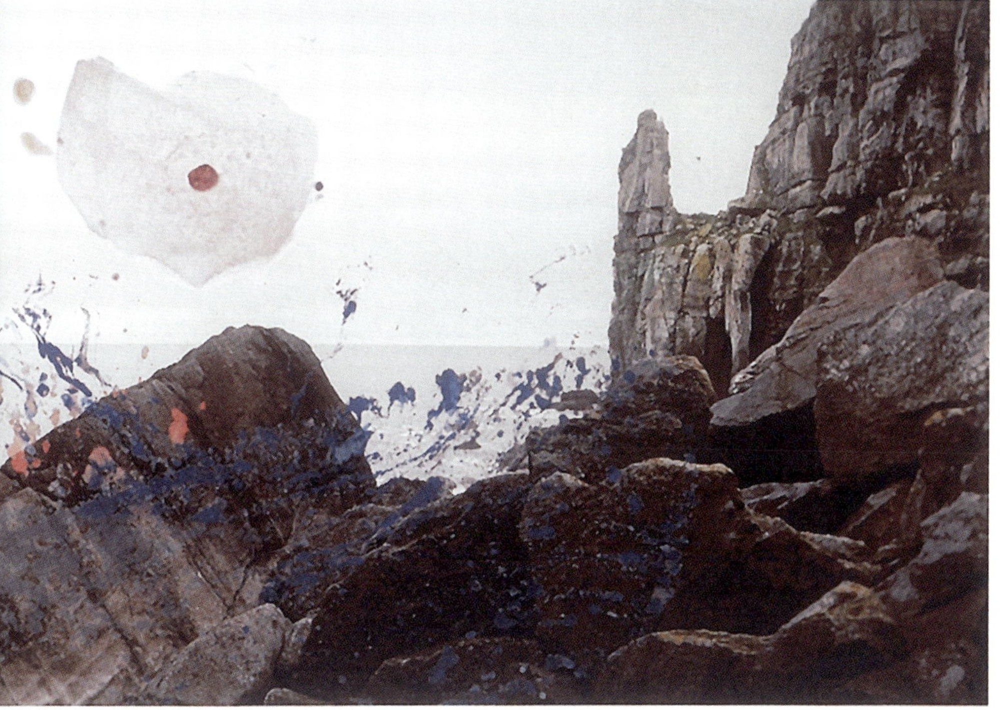

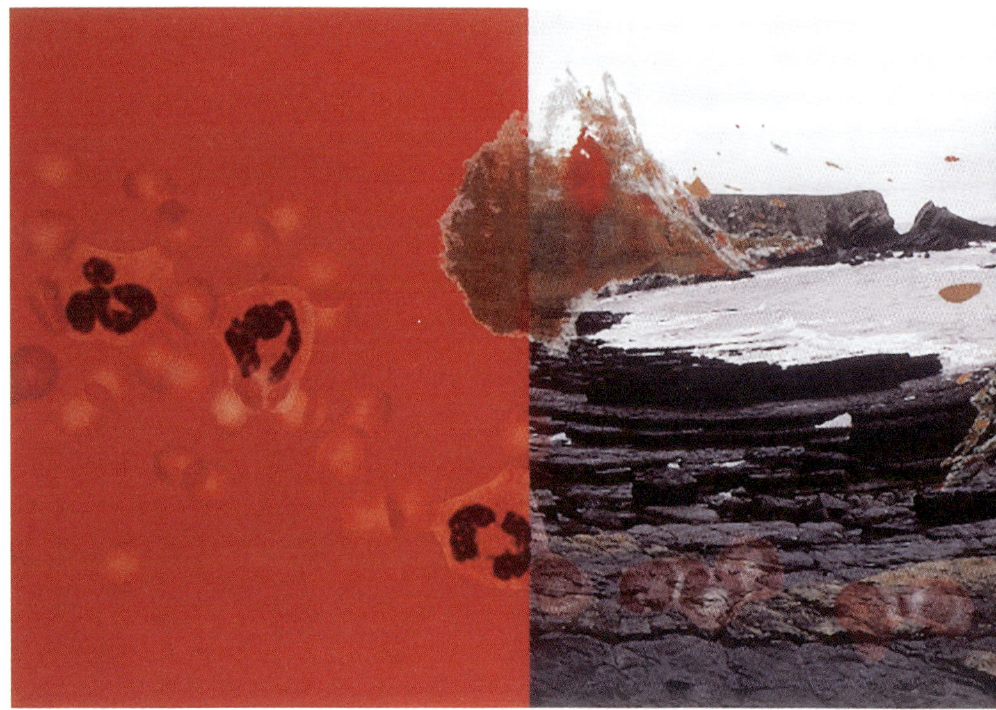

Helen Chadwick, *Viral Landscape No. 3*, 1988–89. C-print photograph, powder-coated steel, aluminium-faced plywood, Perspex, 120 × 300 × 5 cm (47¼ × 118⅛ × 2 in.)

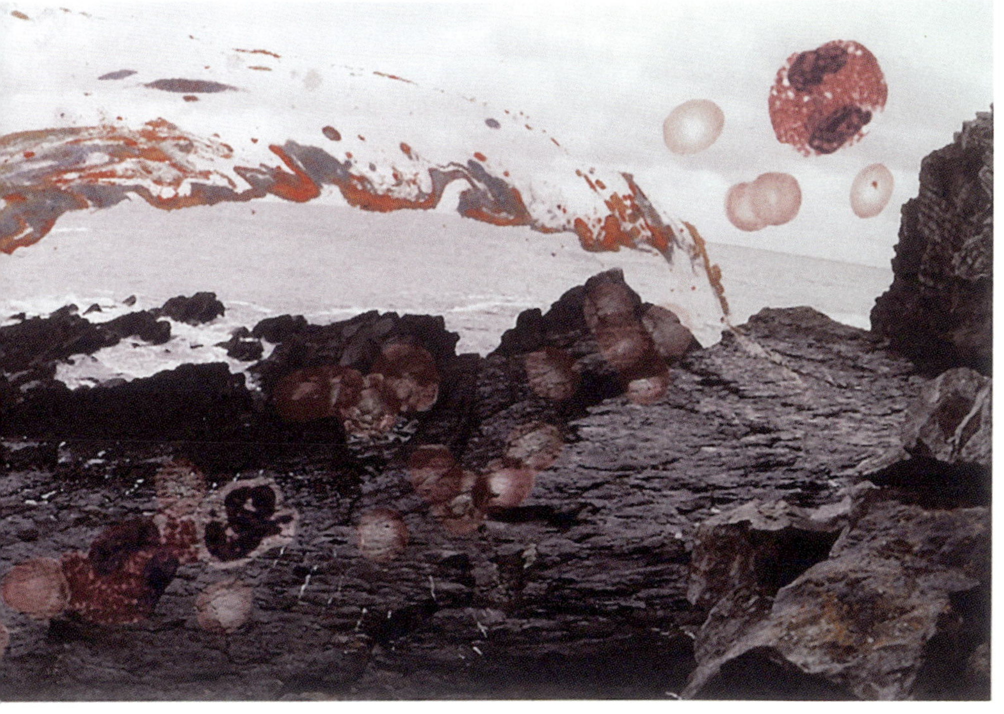

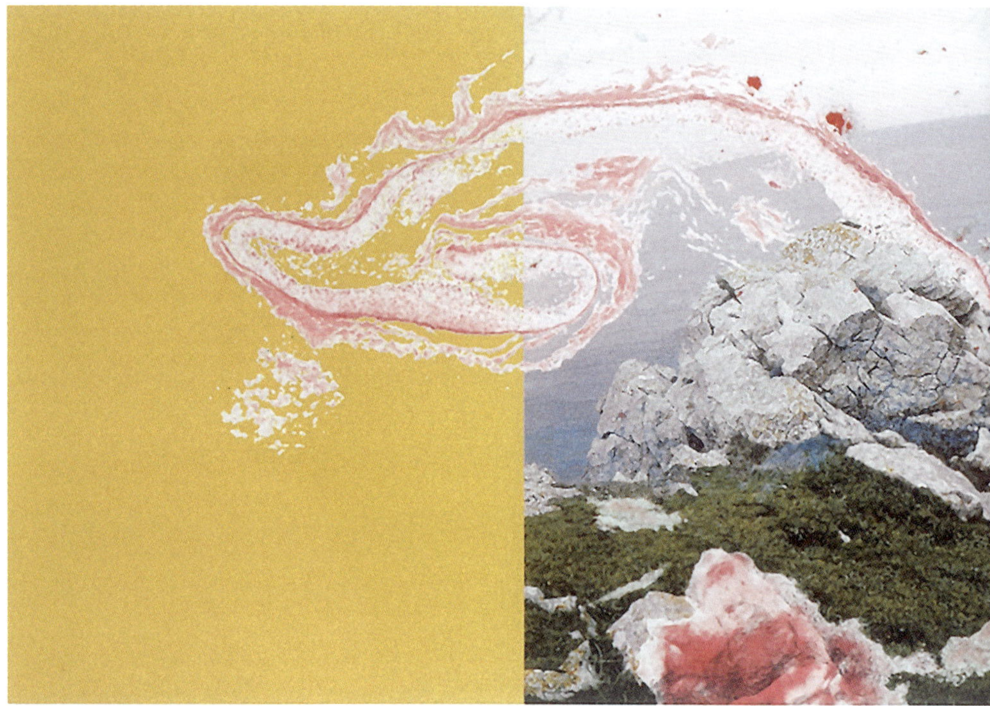

Helen Chadwick, *Viral Landscape No. 2*, 1988–89. C-print photograph, powder-coated steel, aluminium-faced plywood, Perspex, 120 × 300 × 5 cm (47¼ × 118⅛ × 2 in.)

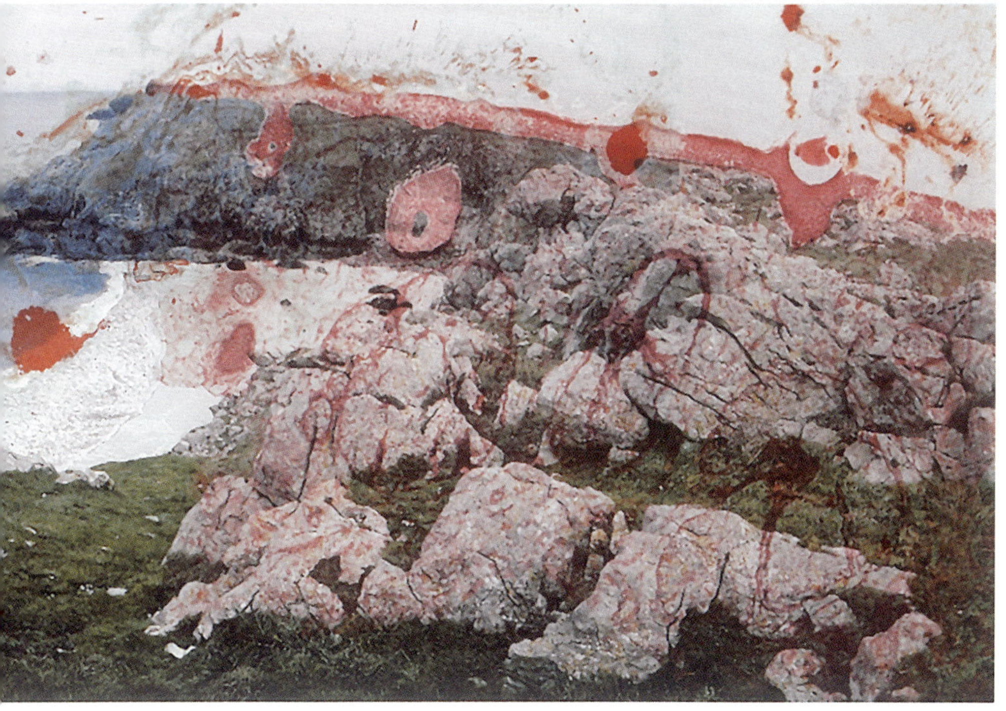

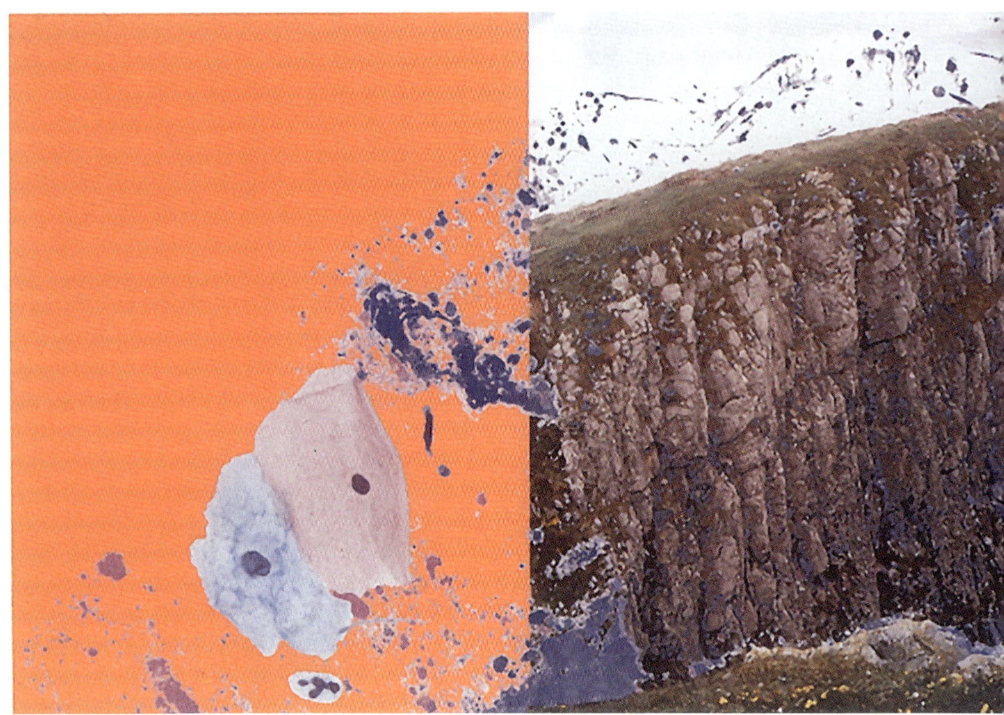

Helen Chadwick, *Viral Landscape No. 4*, 1988–89. C-print photograph, powder-coated steel, aluminium-faced plywood, Perspex, 120 × 300 × 5 cm (47 1/4 × 118 1/8 × 2 in.)

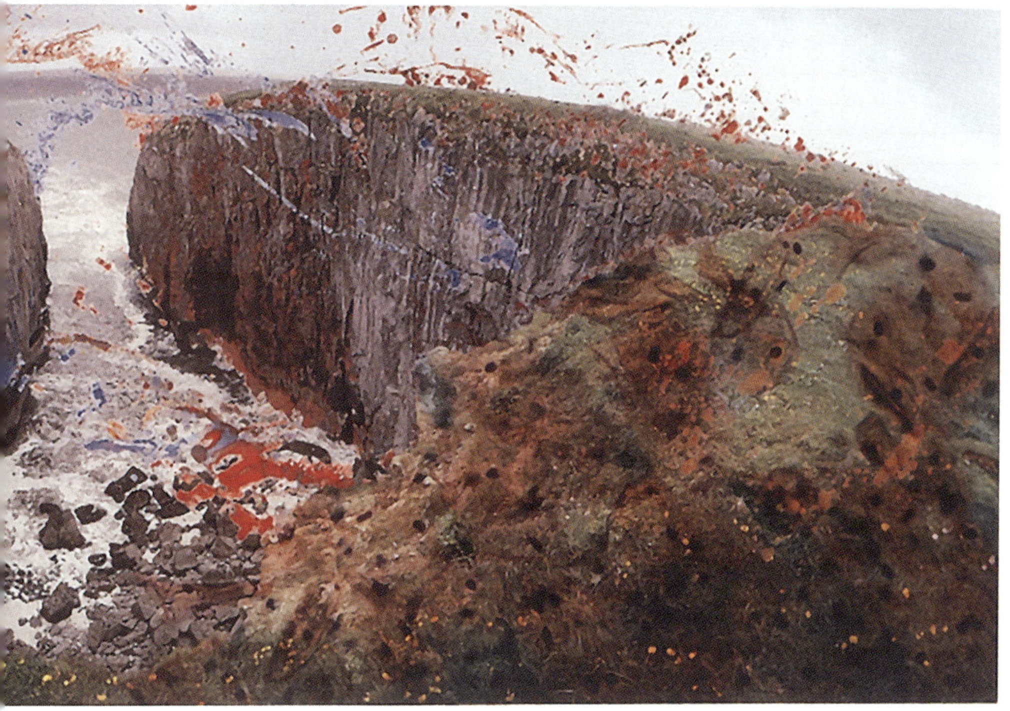

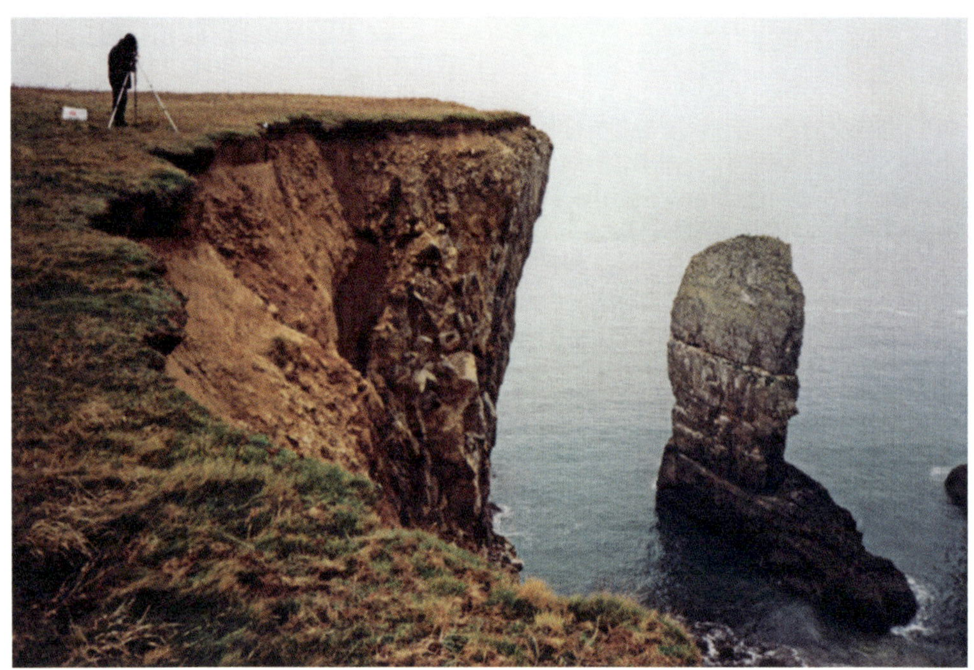

Helen Chadwick making paintings and photographs for the series *Viral Landscapes*, 1988–89

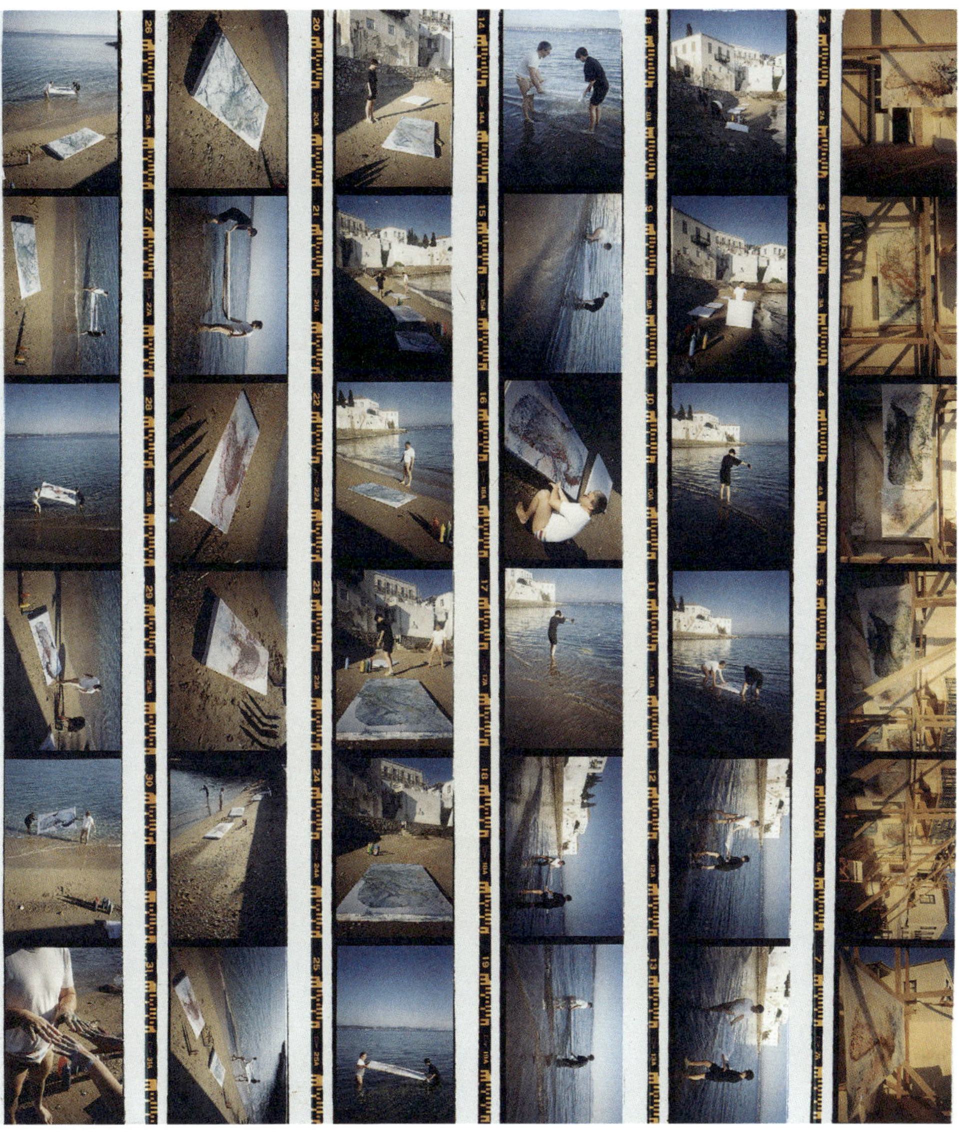

Contact sheet photographs of Helen Chadwick making paintings in the sea for the series *Viral Landscapes*, 1988–89

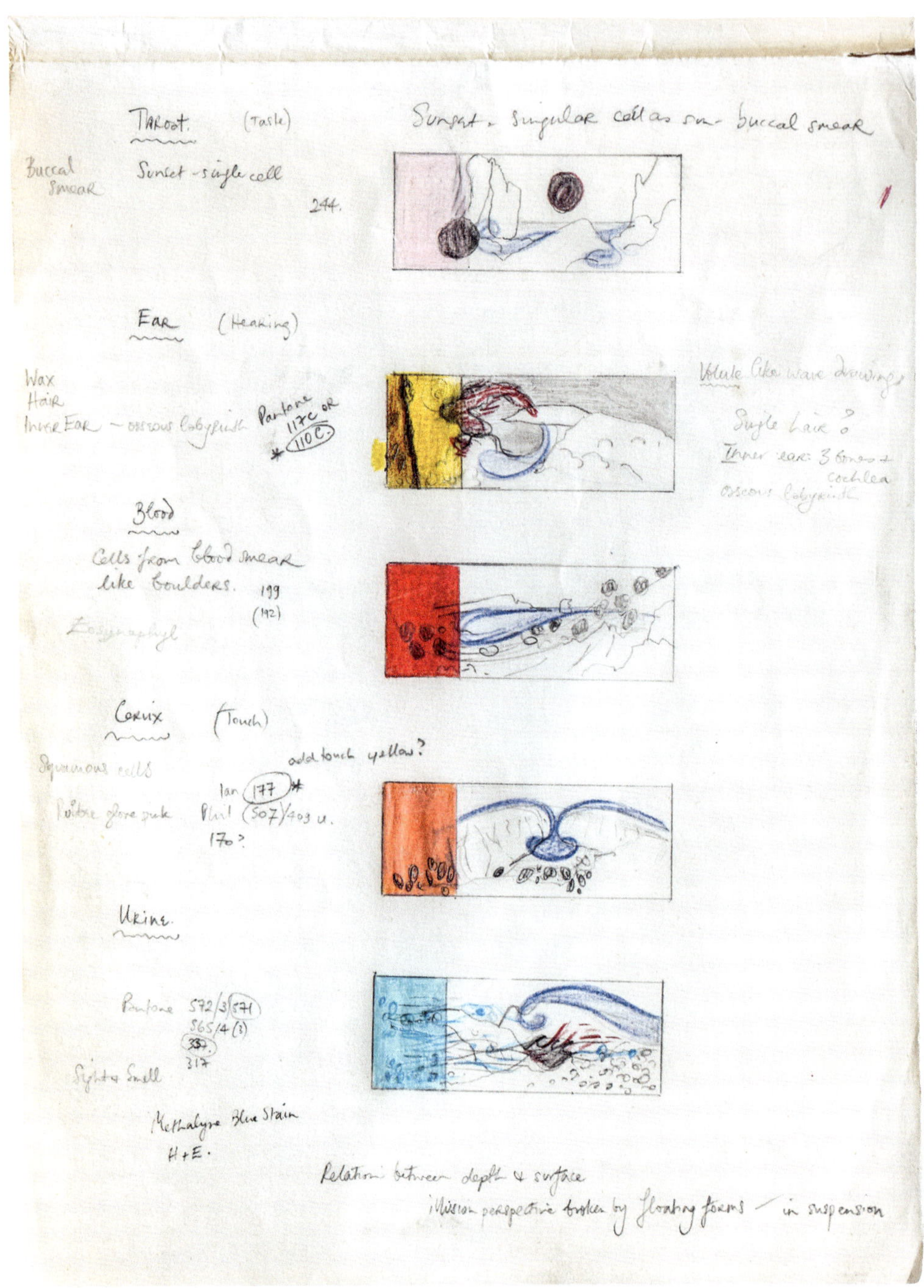

Helen Chadwick's sketchbook: *Viral Landscapes*, c. 1988–89

The 1990s: The Final Decade

In 1990 Chadwick was invited to exhibit a sister work to her *Meat Abstracts, Enfleshings* (1989), at Fotofest in Houston, Texas. These lightbox works comprised large Cibachrome transparencies lit from behind, and depicted enlarged, starkly composed images of vivid red meat, in which she had embedded from behind a light bulb - the actual light source becoming analogous with the depicted light source. This moment became a pivotal one for Chadwick for two reasons. It marked a newfound interest and confidence in creating and showing works that utilized lightboxes or real sources of light in their installation, a series of works that she would come to describe as 'Lumina'. And it was also a moment when she fell in love.

The 'Lumina' - or light works - were originally inspired by her viewing, by lamplight, of the prehistoric paintings in the caves of Perigord, France, an encounter in which her experience of the artworks was bodily as well as visual, and led her to want to create a series of works that pulled photographic imagery into space:

> *the shapes of these pieces are all curvilinear, and although they are photographs, they also have depth. They all use light, whether the light spills around them as an aura or whether the light is contained in a box. These things put them into the ambiguous position of being not exactly a sculpture and not exactly an image, and for me this is the space of the body.*[33]

These works also reveal Chadwick's abiding interest in combining - through staged photographic juxtapositions - body and mind, textures, touches, diseases, accidents, with desire and repulsion, sex and food, beauty and disgust:

> *A lot of my work relates to sex.... How to describe sexual pleasure in retrospect - and I want to - is an amazing problem. It would be farcical to try to express those states where the mind and senses are all scrambled up together - that you can also feel when eating or going to the loo - in spoken language. Art is one way to explore that synaesthesia of experience.*[34]

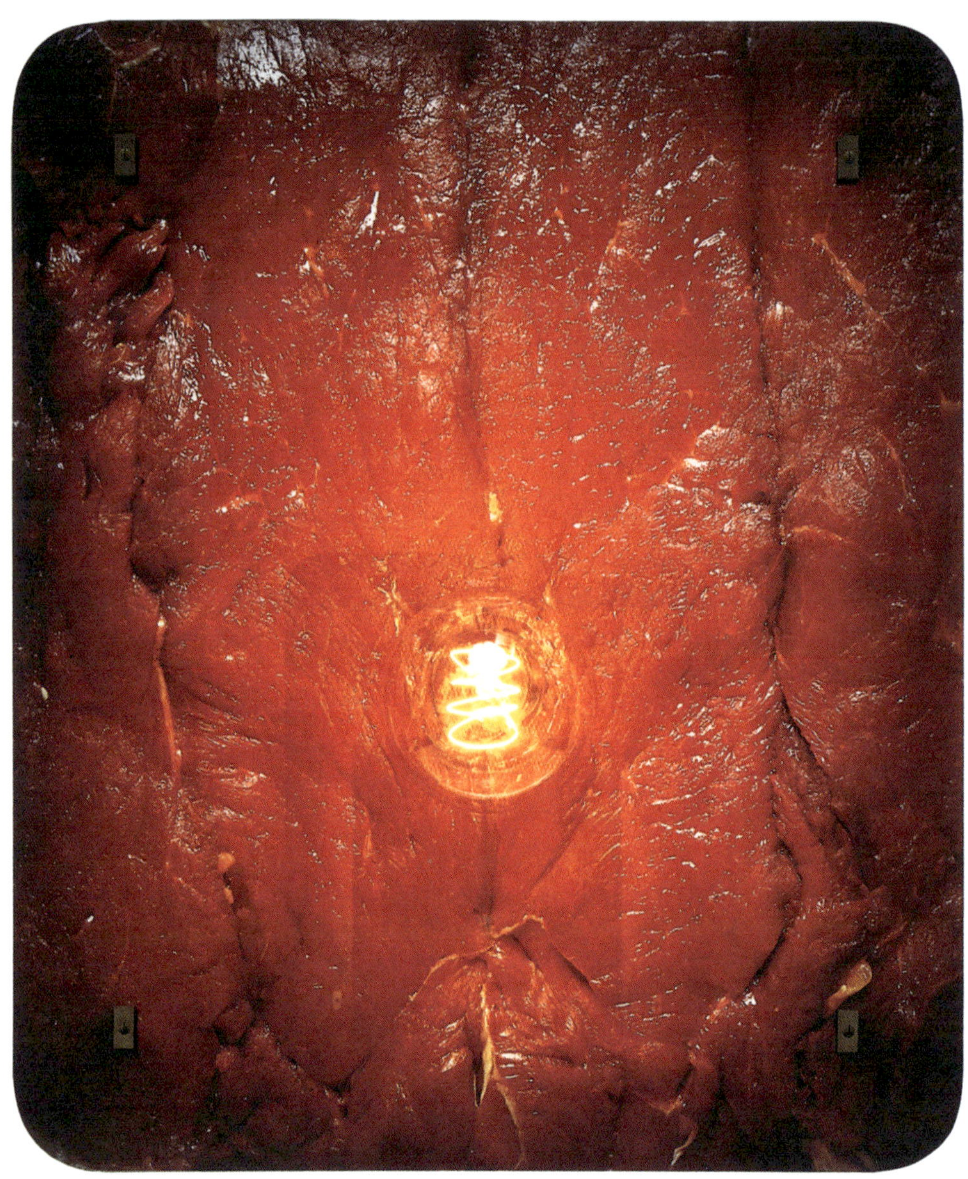

Helen Chadwick, *Enfleshings I*, 1989. Cibachrome transparency, glass, steel, electrical apparatus, 107 × 92 × 15 cm ($42\frac{1}{4}$ × $36\frac{1}{4}$ × 6 in.)

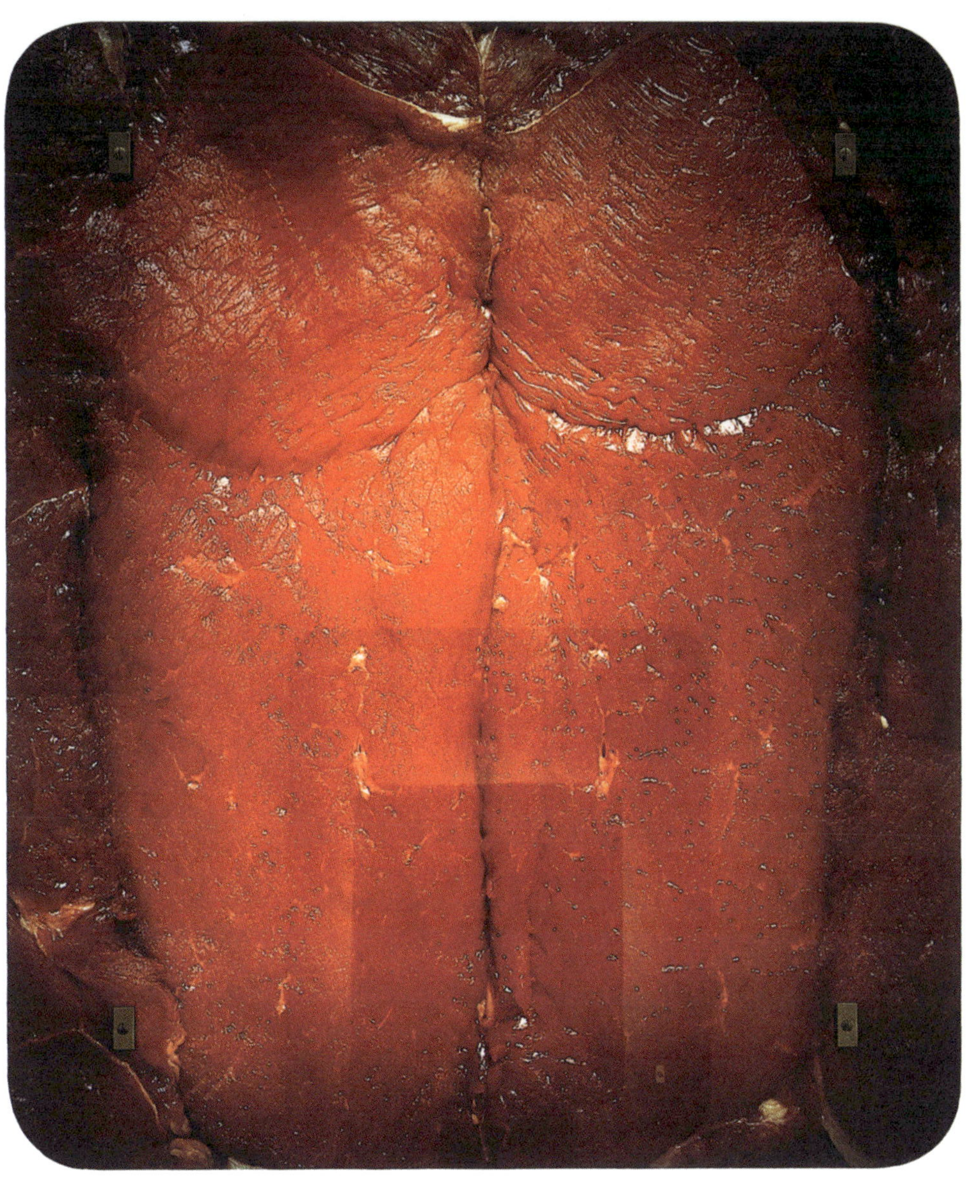

Helen Chadwick, *Enfleshings II*, 1989. Cibachrome transparency, glass, steel, electrical apparatus, 107 × 92 × 15 cm ($42\frac{1}{4}$ × $36\frac{1}{4}$ × 6 in.)

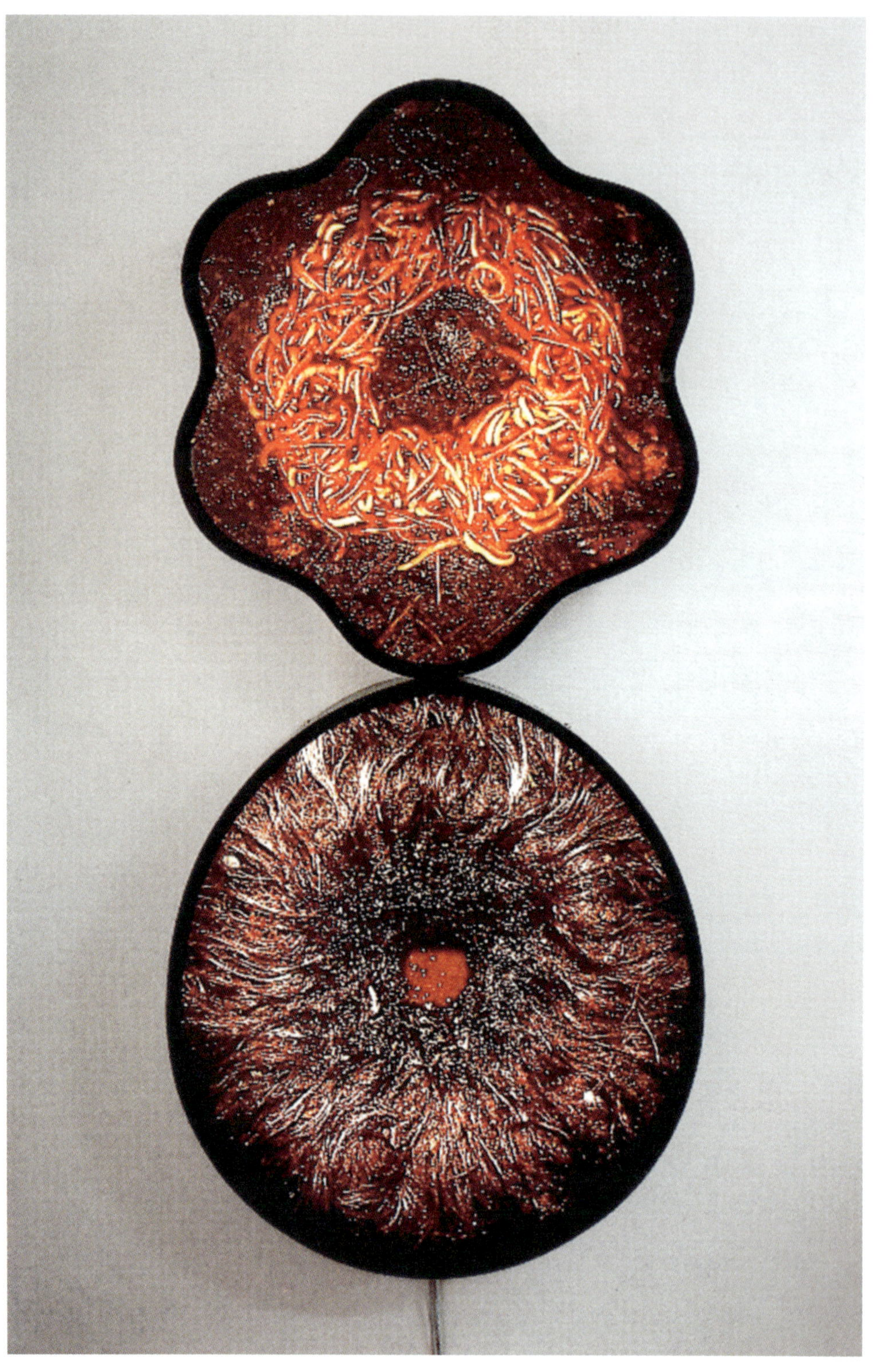

Helen Chadwick, *Nostalgie de la Boue*, 1990. Cibachrome transparency, rosewood, plywood, electrical apparatus, in two parts: 147 × 68 × 14 cm (57 ⅞ × 26 ⅞ × 5 ⅝ in.)

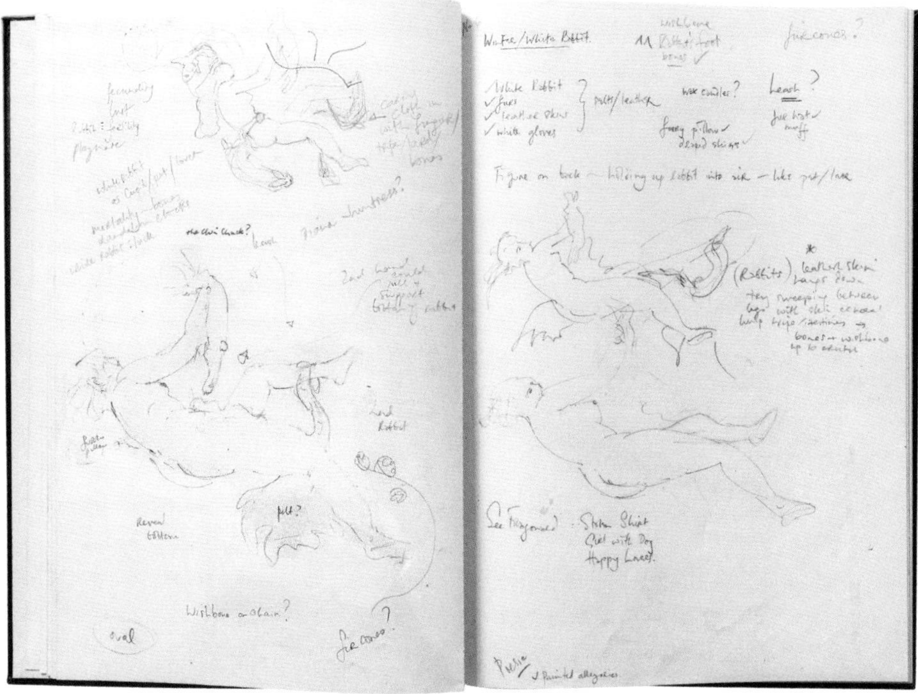

Nostalgie de la Boue (1990) comprises an infinity sign of two rounded cibachrome transparencies hung one above the other. The top contains an image of a circle of earthworms writhing in the dirt, while the bottom depicts a human scalp with the crown collapsing. Equally jarring, *Loop my Loop* (1991–92) juxtaposes a beautiful lock of (fake) blonde hair intertwined tenderly with a pale pink twist of pig intestines, both glistening in the photographic light. Here the lock of hair (a traditional Victorian keepsake from a sweetheart) signifies love, while the pig intestines imply a more primal, animalistic side to human relationships. As writer and curator David Hopkins points out: 'distinctions upholding the human above the animal no longer held. However Chadwick made such transgressions playful, celebratory...'.[35]

Transgressions abound in other 'Lumina' works. In *Agape* (1989) an enormous mouth, wide open, almost shouts at us to climb inside. For *Self-Portrait* (1991), Chadwick's own hands cradle the walnut-like form of

Helen Chadwick's sketchbook: *Kissing Chancre*, n.d.

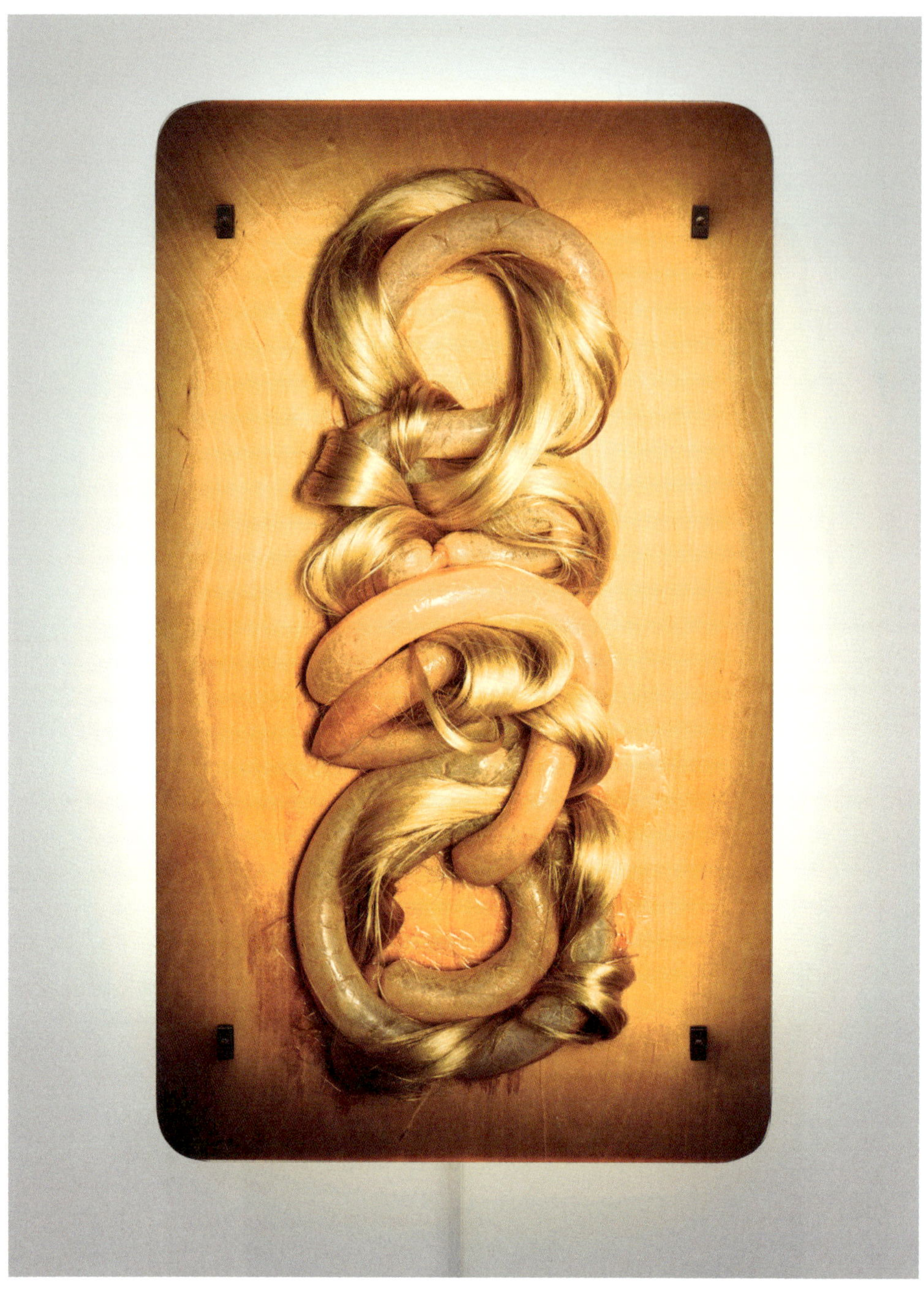

Helen Chadwick, *Loop my Loop*, 1991–92. Cibachrome transparency, glass, steel, electrical apparatus, 127 × 76 × 15 cm (50 × 30 × 6 in.)

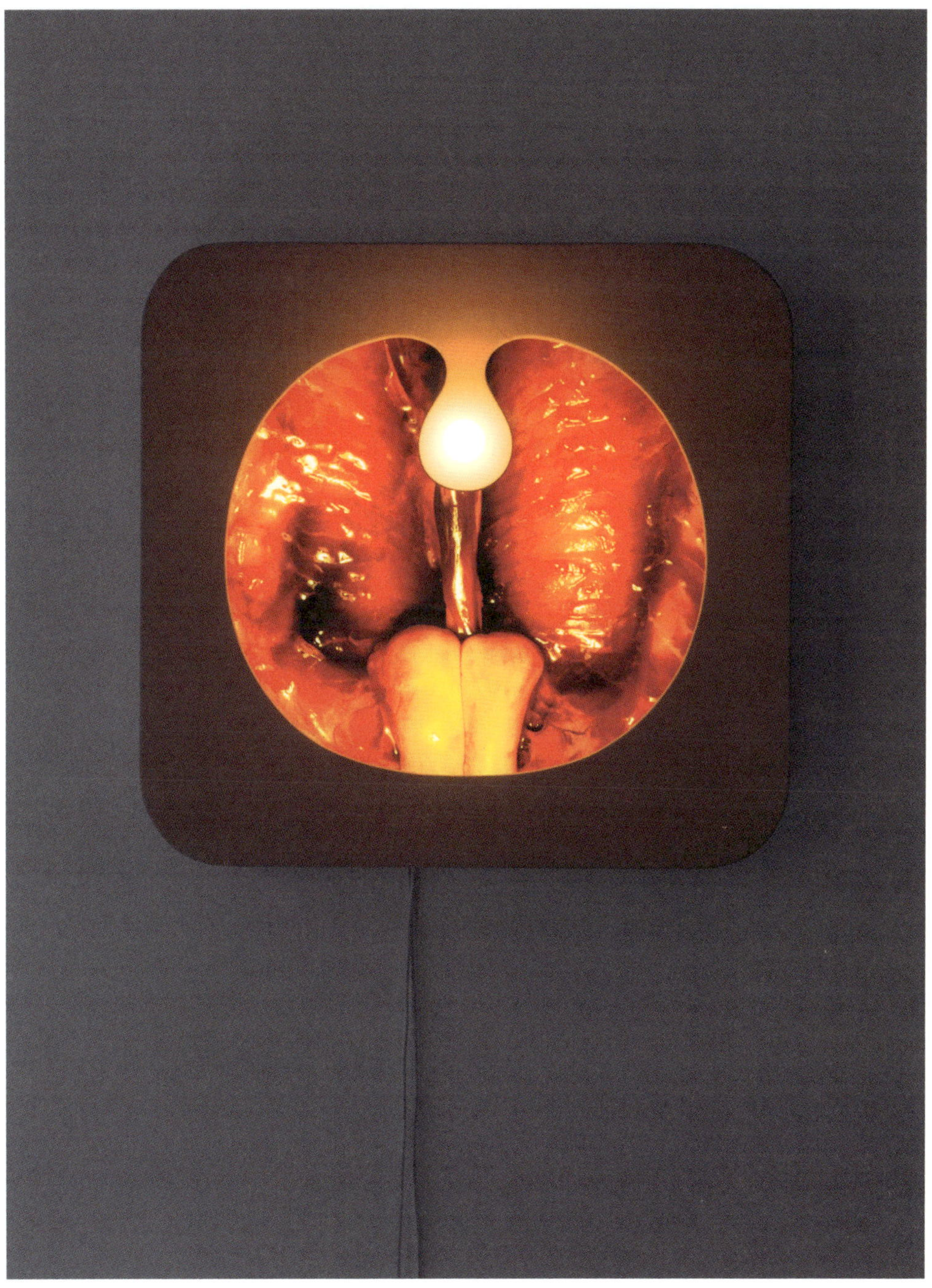

Helen Chadwick, *Agape*, 1989. Cibachrome transparency, bird's-eye maple, plywood, glass, electrical apparatus, 68 × 76 × 13 cm (26 $\frac{7}{8}$ × 30 × 5 $\frac{1}{8}$ in.)

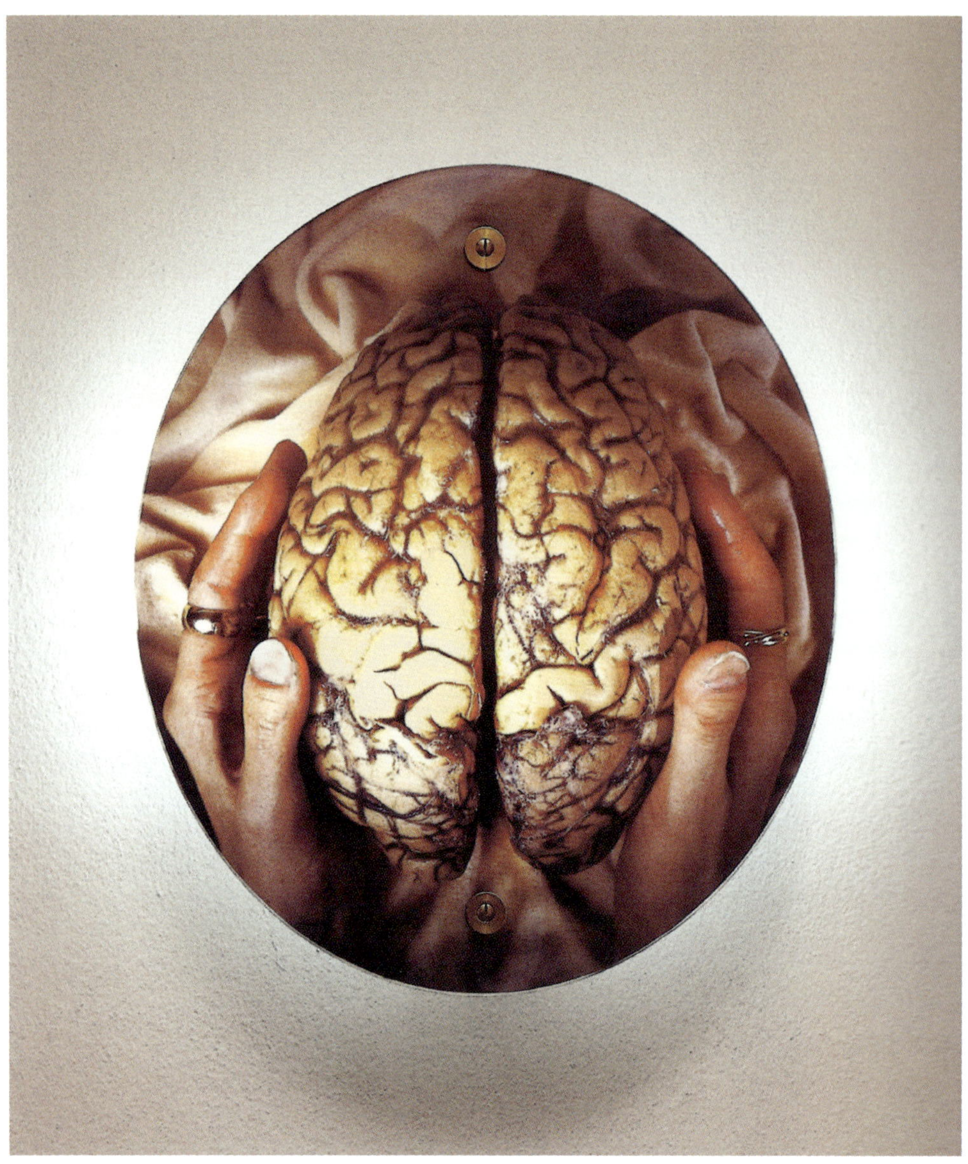

Helen Chadwick, *Self-Portrait*, 1991. Cibachrome transparency, aluminium frame, glass and electrics, 50.9 × 44.6 × 11.8 cm (20⅛ × 17⅝ × 4¾ in.)

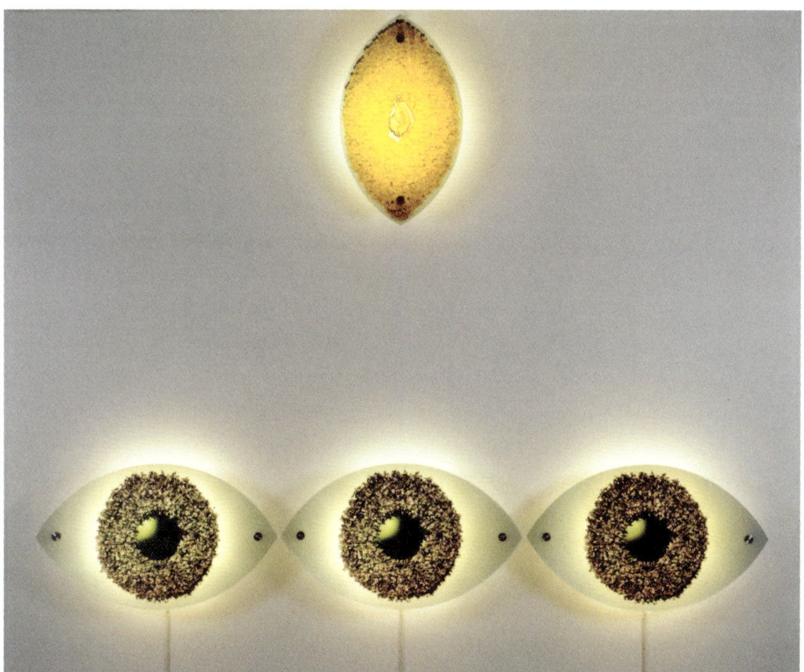

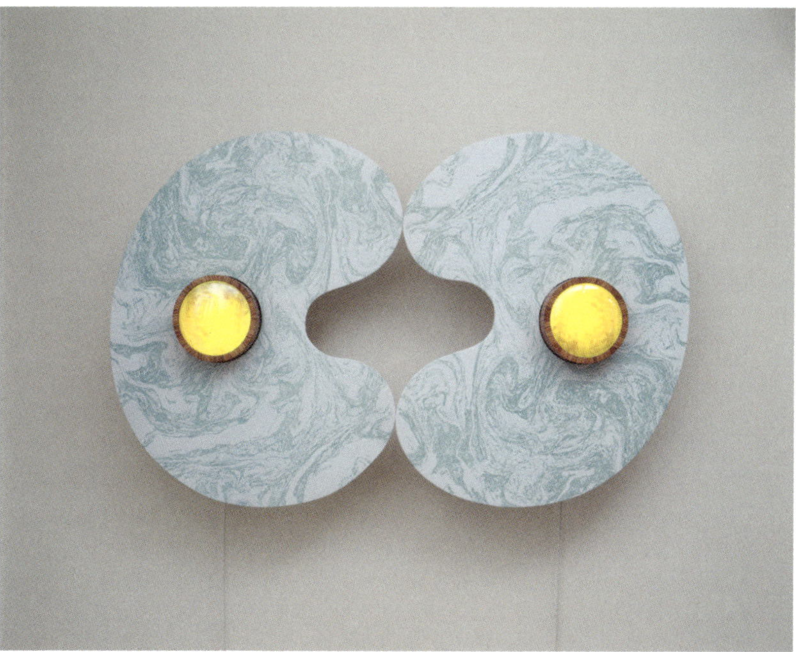

Helen Chadwick, *Eat Me*, 1991. Cibachrome transparency, glass, aluminium, electrical apparatus, in four parts: (i) 76 × 47 × 15 cm (30 × 18 5/8 × 6 in.), (ii–iv) 53 × 90 × 15 cm (20 7/8 × 35 1/2 × 6 in.)

Helen Chadwick, *Kissing Chancre*, 1989. Cibachrome transparency, leather, tulipwood, plywood, electrical apparatus, in two parts: 70 × 122 × 25.4 cm (27 5/8 × 48 1/8 × 10 in.)

a (clearly deceased) human brain in a collective, though uncomfortable, self-portrait, since – regardless of gender, age or race – everybody's brain looks the same, and all of us will one day die. *Billy Budd* (1994, page 200) shows us a beautiful close-up portrait of a Tiger Tulip with its stamens replaced by an intimate image of male genitals, thus framing the male sex organ inside a (traditionally feminine) flower, heightening its vulnerability as well as its sexual potency. Finally, *Eat Me* (1991) consists of a row of three eye-shaped lightboxes in which clusters of bluebells represent the iris of the eye, around a dark pool of liquid that imitates a pupil. Above them, a fourth eye shape, positioned vertically (like a lemon), is filled with an abundance of buttercups surrounding a small, squelchy oyster. In combination, these images blur depictions of the real and the artificial, and play with sensations of desire, satiability, sexual transgression, death, self-knowing and excess – the profusion of flowers and the implication of their heady scent becoming almost suffocating. As Chadwick explains:

> *I'm trying to make images of a kind of physical identification of the self through exploring physical matter – and by implication mortality, desire, all those kinds of words, all that kind of vague region – because it's a kind of space that none of us can really know for ourselves and because, for many people, it's a troubled terrain. It may be that individuals are projecting their difficulties into the work and thereby on to me.*[36]

While she was in Texas, exhibiting at Fotofest, Chadwick – meticulous as ever – was hanging her own works and needed a screwdriver; in requesting one from a technician who was installing the exhibition, she met local artist David Notarius (b. 1959); a year later (after a long-distance relationship), Notarius moved to Beck Road, and the pair married. Of his time living on Beck Road with Chadwick, Notarius says: 'there was life out of the house, and there was life in here....We had a different life.'[37] Together, the couple developed the ground floor of the house on Beck Road into a home studio where they could both live and work cheaply. They were not wealthy: despite the international respect for Chadwick's work, her collector base was not wide; she taught regularly to retain a reliable income while Notarius worked for an oil company. In 1993 the Serpentine agreed to give Chadwick a solo exhibition, to open in the summer of 1994.

This exhibition, titled 'Effluvia', sky-rocketed Chadwick's public profile, receiving critical acclaim and huge amounts of press coverage, and breaking the Serpentine's visitor record at 54,000 across its six-week run. 'Effluvia' contained several of Chadwick's most seminal works, from her hermaphroditic *Piss Flowers* (1991–92) to the sickly sweet *Cacao* (1994). The show's success brought Chadwick a level of international recognition that she wasn't ready for (she was offered a tour of South America with the British Council, and invited to co-produce a CD-ROM with the musician Peter Gabriel, among other ventures). Chadwick found the new levels of attention overwhelming and, occasionally, oppressive. Notarius remembers a time when a film crew (working on a production of Thomas Hardy's *Jude the Obscure*, 1895) on Beck Road damaged the phone lines, meaning that their home telephone didn't ring for days – which Chadwick relished. Most of the time, though, he remembers her longing to 'drop all this and go to Greece...'.[38] True to this wish, Chadwick purchased a small, dilapidated home in the Greek Peloponnese, where her mother's family came from, with views out to the sea, and they would stay there regularly over the summer months.

Responding to the Serpentine's surrounding environment, Hyde Park, 'Effluvia' was conceived as a garden, consisting of flowers (*Piss Flowers* and *Wreaths to Pleasure*, 1992–93) and a fountain (*Cacao*), as well as some older works such as *Viral Landscapes*, *Meat Abstracts* and some new works made with fur: *Glossolalia* and *I Thee Wed* (both 1993). *Piss Flowers* is now arguably Chadwick's most famous work. Described as 'a metaphysical conceit for the union of two people expressing themselves bodily',[39] it is a work made up of twelve sculptures that Chadwick made while on a residency at the Banff Centre for the Arts in Alberta, Canada, in February 1991. During their stay, she and Notarius travelled into the Rocky Mountains to create the works. In order to do this, Chadwick had a large cookie-cutter-like mould made out of sheet metal. She and Notarius would densely pack mounds of snow before inserting the mould into the mound and taking turns to piss into it. Chadwick squatting to pee in one central place and Notarius spraying his urine into and onto the entire mould. They then poured liquid plaster into the cavities, which, in turn, was cast in bronze, enamelled white and inverted so that the shapes and forms made by the hot urine rose into the air, creating a garden of gleaming stalactites and spread petals. Each flower has a flat surface, with one central pilaster surrounded by bumpy, uneven petals, the whole thing mounted onto a base shaped like a hyacinth bulb.

These works are a result of Chadwick's physical contact with a specific location. The process is indexical, a direct imprint of her own body (and Notarius's), exactly the same as photocopying her own naked form. Here, her urine produces a large, phallic form (due to the fact that female urine is hotter on expulsion than men's, as well as being expressed with more speed), while Notarius's has a more decorative, subtle effect, creating the texture of the petals or the labial circumference. Chadwick called the work a 'penis-envy-farce', and claimed that

> *to me the surprise was that I would want to show anything that was made by pissing in the snow. Sometimes I look at them and I think 'gosh they're amazing, they're fabulous' and they're truly fabulous in that you just can't really account for how they could be like that. I guess because they are not devised in the conventional way, they are not things made, they are the product of things that happen, chance things, even if there was a kind of premeditated script or choreography for how they were made. They're as implausible as the delicacy of an elephant, or the way a bumblebee can fly; it shouldn't be, but they are, and it does.*[40]

Chadwick's choice to use a flower as her form for these sculptures is significant. Flowers are the reproductive organs of plants, and they often contain both male and female sex organs – just as these bronze flowers do. In an accompanying poem written for the works, she describes them as 'vaginal towers with male skirt'. Through their mischievous inversion of traditional gender roles, they deliberately play on sexual difference and even muddy the whole notion of singularity or specificity of gender: '*Piss Flowers* synthesise sexual difference through the erotic play both

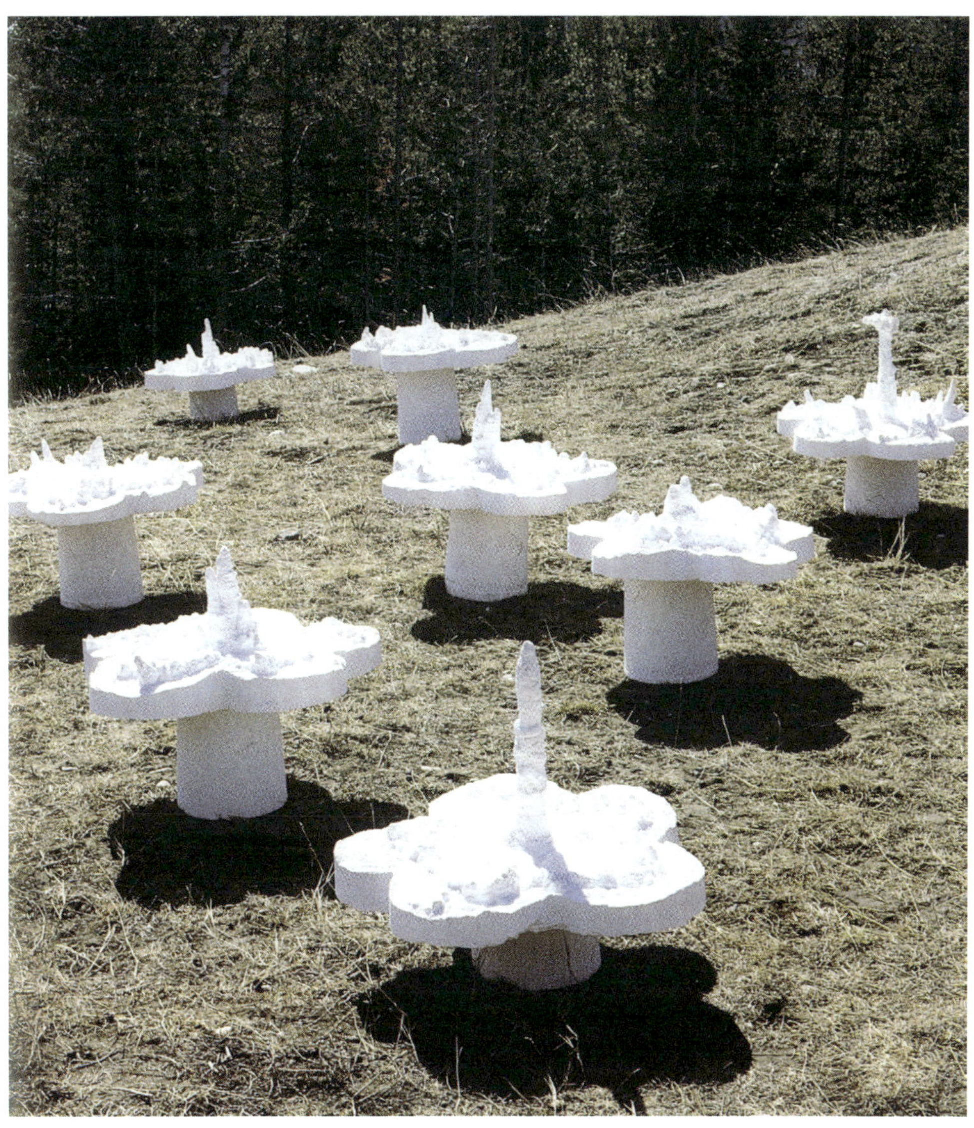

Helen Chadwick, *Piss Flowers*, 1991–2. Bronze, cellulose lacquer, in twelve parts: 70 × 65 × 65 cm (27⅝ × 25⅝ × 25⅝ in.). Installed at Banff National Park, Canada, 1991–92

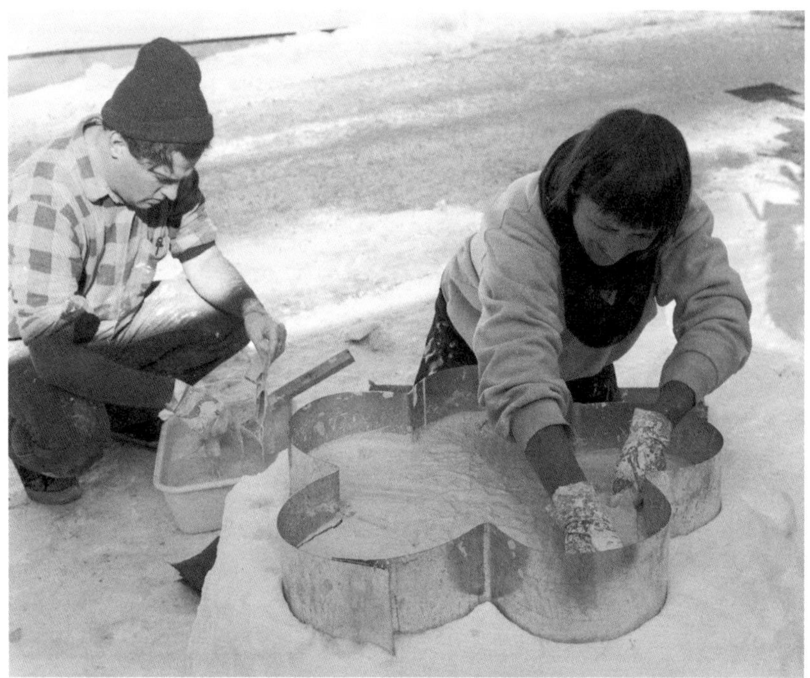

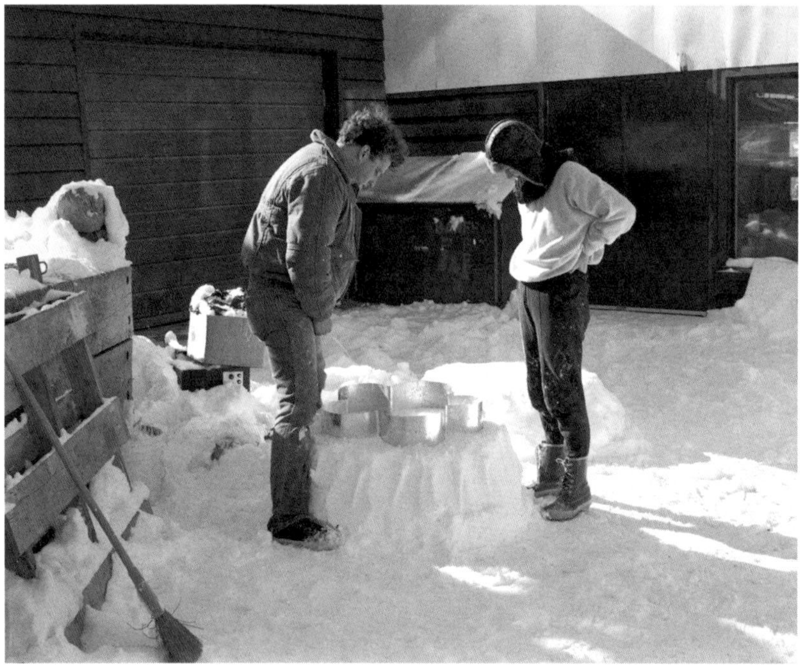

ABOVE AND OPPOSITE **Helen Chadwick and David Notarius urine casting for *Piss Flowers* in Banff National Park, Canada, 1991**

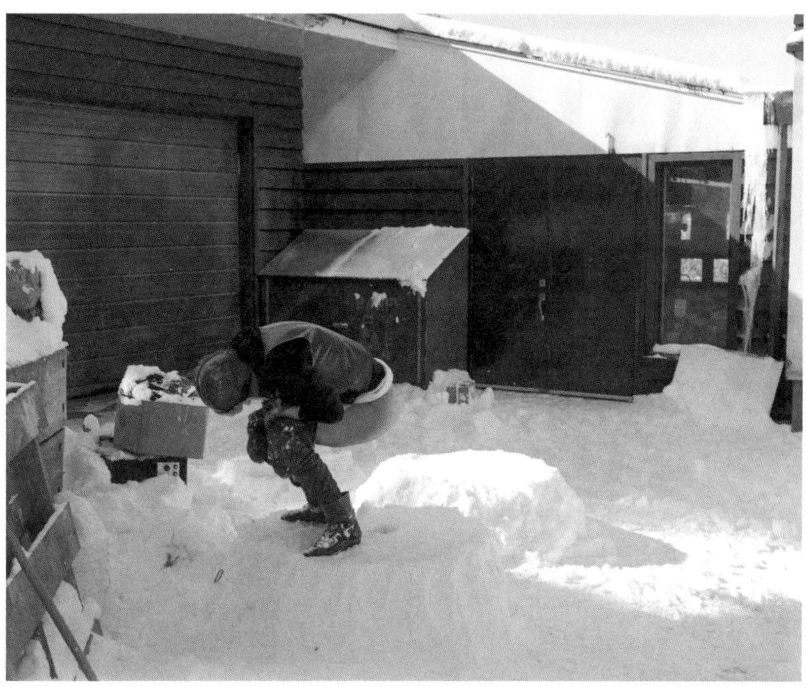

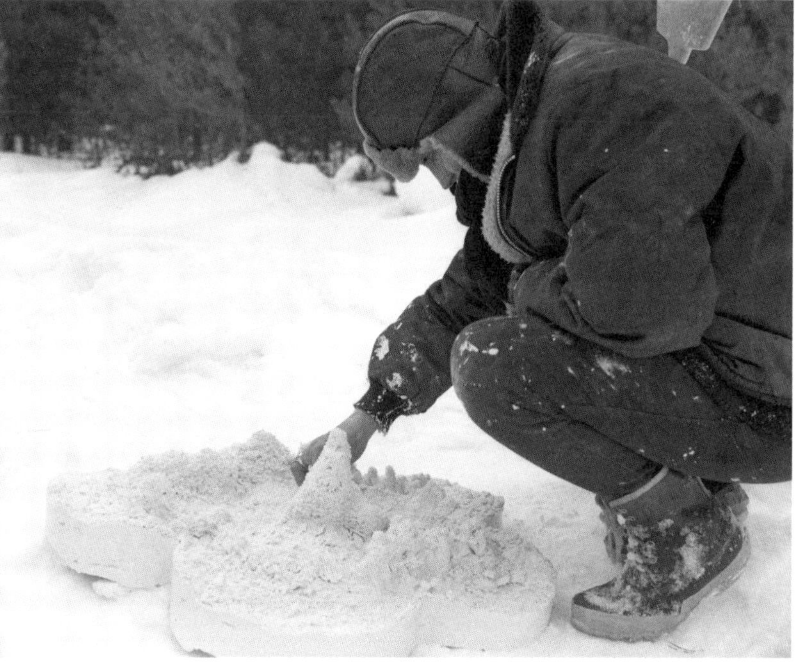

of their making and their forms'.[41] Throughout her career Chadwick expressed concerns with gender representation, moving from her early explorations into the objectification of women to a much more involved consideration of what gender is and can be. After reading the memoirs of Herculine Barbin, a nineteenth-century hermaphrodite whose writing was discovered and published by Michel Foucault in 1980, she asked: 'why do we feel compelled to read gender, and automatically wish to sex the body before us so we can orientate our desire and thus gain pleasure or reject what we see?'[42]

In a similar exploration of the symbolism of flowers and gender representation, Chadwick's *Wreaths to Pleasure* (1992–93) consists of thirteen circular photographic works exploring sexual pleasure, deviance, materiality and excess. These images are sumptuous and luminous; they depict different arrangements of flowers, petals and blossoms in ever-so-slightly suggestive shapes: vaginas, penises, breasts, etc., or often both – a duality of genders in one form – all suspended in a range of different liquids, some pleasurable, some toxic. Chadwick uses orchids, bluebells, buttercups, dandelions, narcissi, tulips, roses, daisies, honeysuckle and so on suspended in Windolene, Fairy Liquid, Swarfega, bubble bath, Germolene, hair gel, tomato juice, milk, molten chocolate....The fluidity of the liquid jars with the stillness of the arranged flowers and the results are heady, they fizz and effervesce. Almost scented, these works speak to desire and eroticism in a multisensory way.

The circular frames resemble biological or cellular forms, the building blocks of life. While their titular 'wreaths' make a clear connection to themes of death and mourning, Chadwick also nicknamed them 'bad blooms'. They are both seductive and dangerous, recognizable and disconcerting, combining wet and dry, sustenance and poison. In these pieces, 'Chadwick examines the notions of desire and repulsion, life and death, beauty and ugliness by analysing – almost with a scientific approach – the fluidity of our existence and the matter that constitutes it'.[43] The works held a central position in 'Effluvia', so much so that Chadwick was invited to present them at the Museum of Modern Art (MoMA), New York, in 1995 – an exhibition which she titled 'Bad Blooms'.

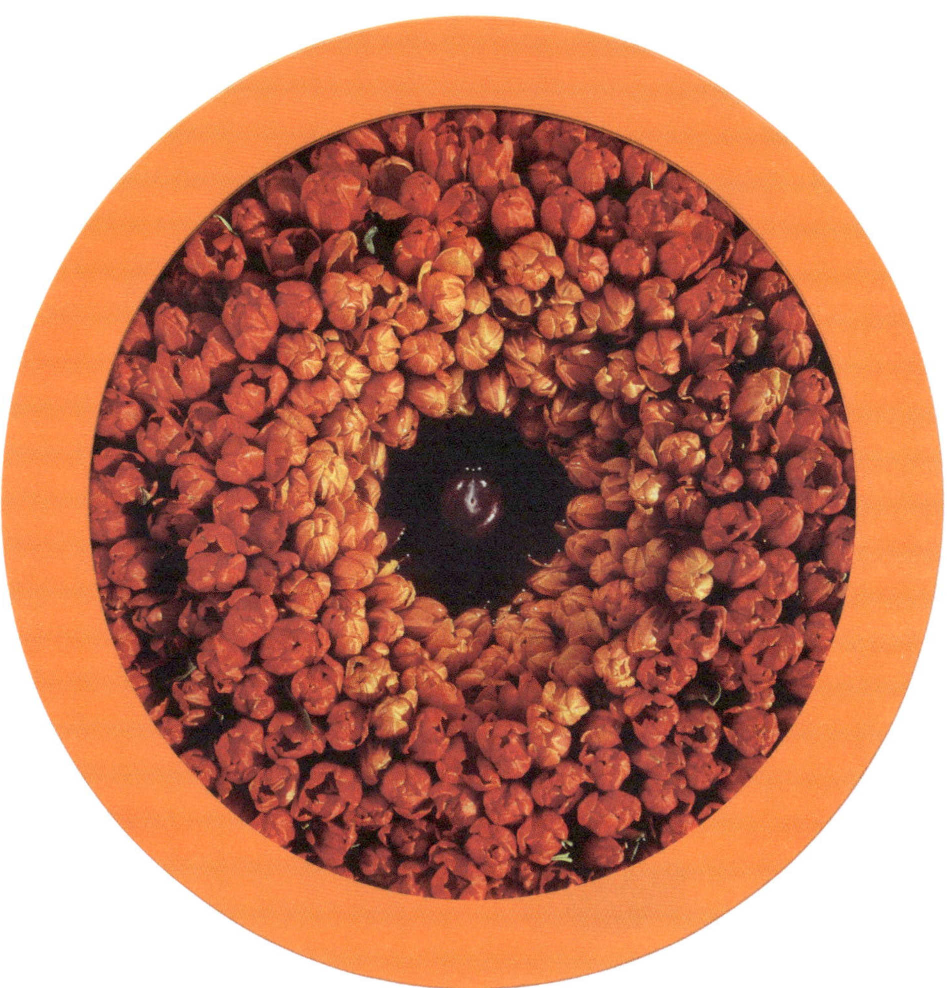

Helen Chadwick, *Wreath to Pleasure, No. 1 (Orange Tulips, Plum)*, 1992–93. Cibachrome prints, aluminium-faced MDF, glazed and powder-coated steel frame, 110 cm (43⅜ in.) diameter

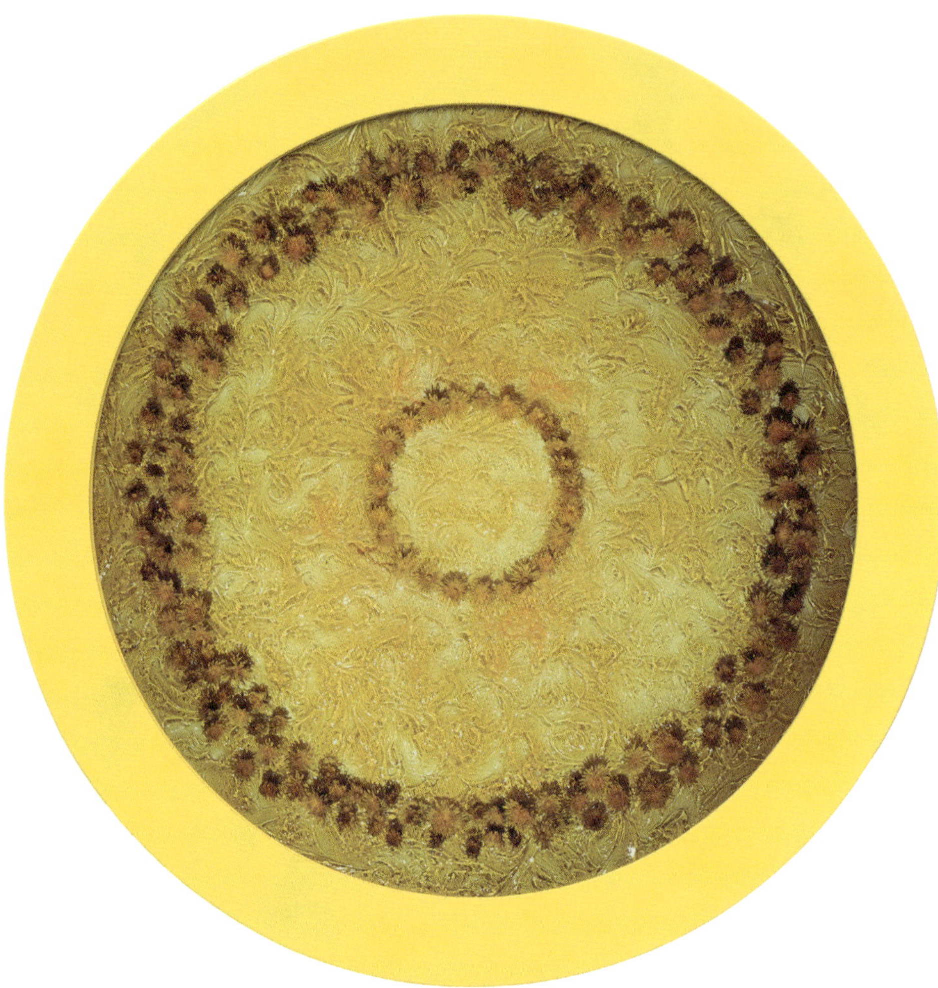

Helen Chadwick, *Wreath to Pleasure, No. 2 (Dandelions, Yellow Gel)*, 1992–93. Cibachrome prints, aluminium-faced MDF, glazed and powder-coated steel frame, 110 cm (43⅜ in.) diameter

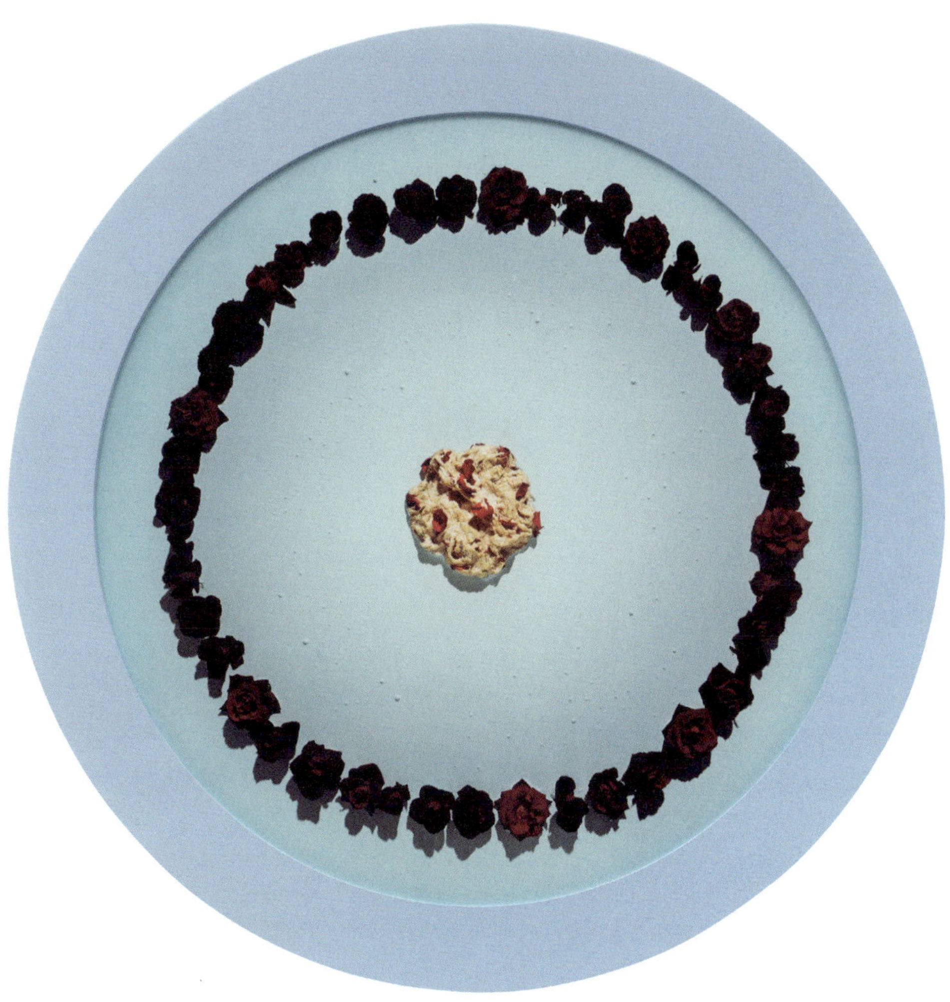

Helen Chadwick, *Wreath to Pleasure, No. 3 (Black Roses, Blue Paint)*, 1992–93. Cibachrome prints, aluminium-faced MDF, glazed and powder-coated steel frame, 110 cm (43⅜ in.) diameter

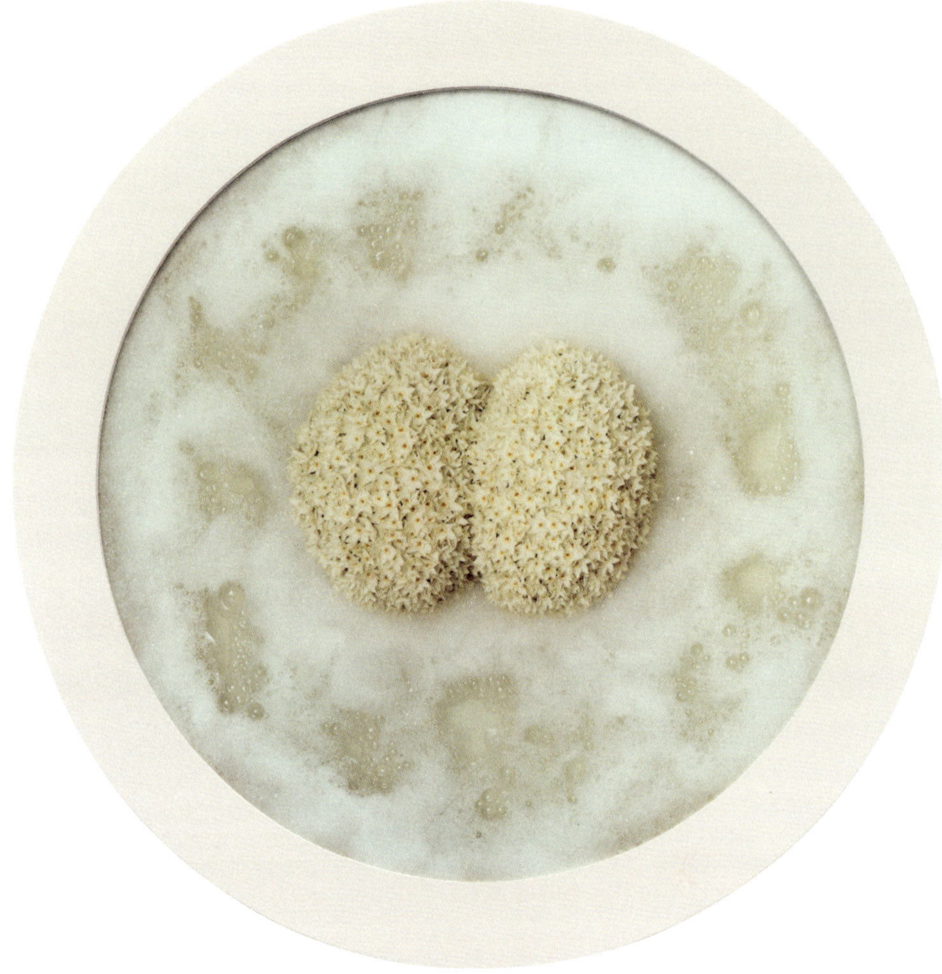

Helen Chadwick, *Wreath to Pleasure, No. 4 (White Narcissi, Soapsuds)*, 1992–93. Cibachrome prints, aluminium-faced MDF, glazed and powder-coated steel frame, 110 cm (43⅜ in.) diameter

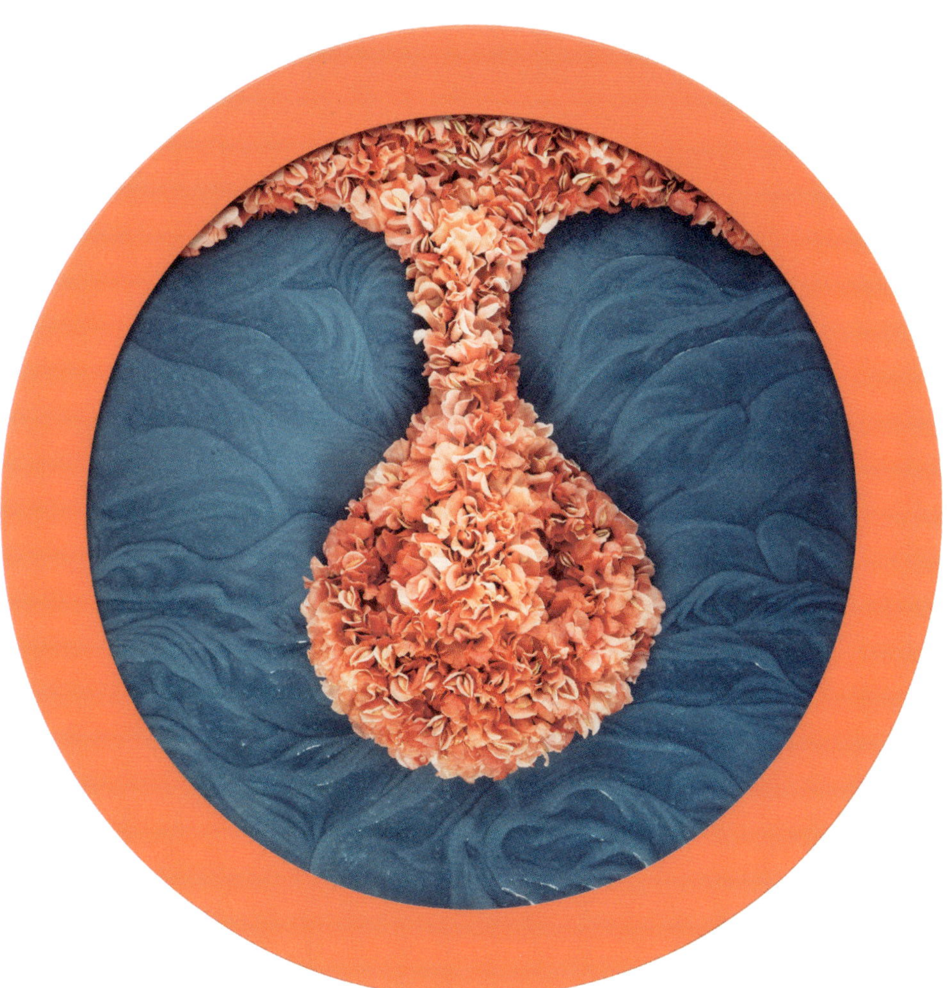

Helen Chadwick, *Wreath to Pleasure, No. 5 (Sweet Peas, Ariel)*, 1992–93. Cibachrome prints, aluminium-faced MDF, glazed and powder-coated steel frame, 110 cm (43$\frac{3}{8}$ in.) diameter

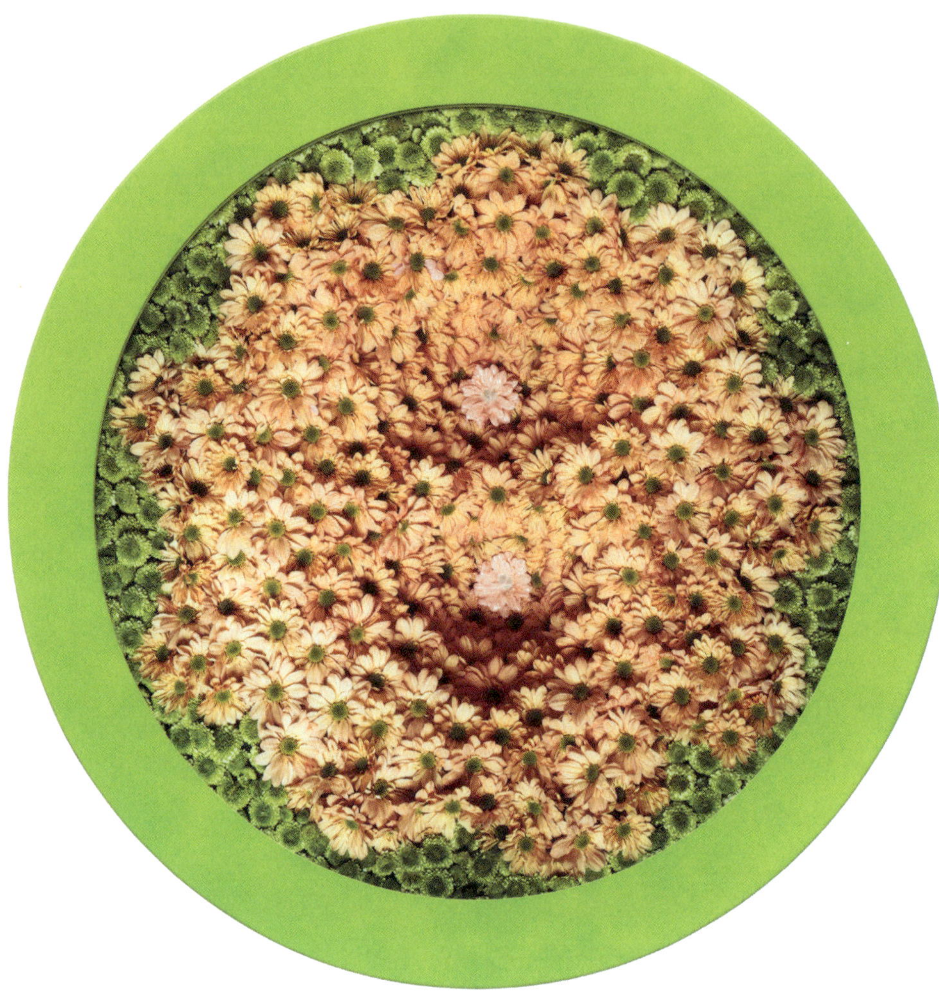

Helen Chadwick, *Wreath to Pleasure, No. 6 (Chrysanthemums, Angel Delight)*, 1992–93. Cibachrome prints, aluminium-faced MDF, glazed and powder-coated steel frame, 110 cm (43 3/8 in.) diameter

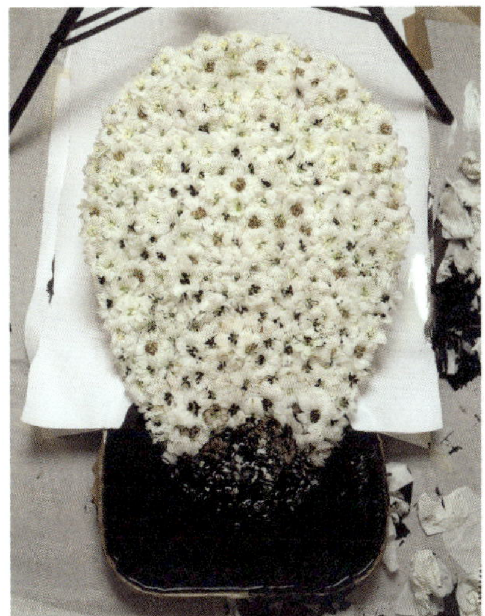

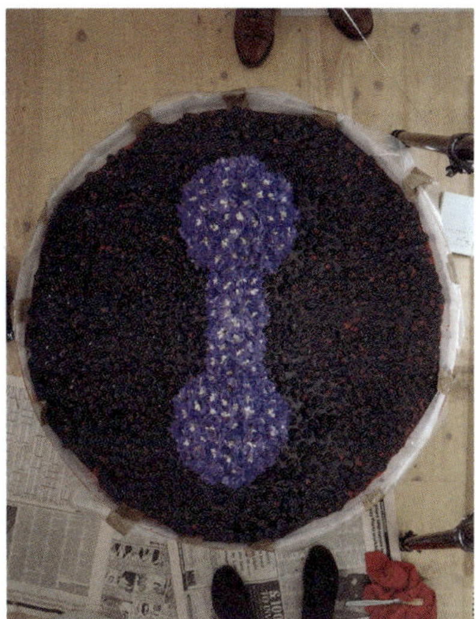

The *Wreaths to Pleasure* were shown alongside *Cacao*, a monumental fountain of liquid chocolate whose fragrance pervaded the gallery and whose form, once again, evoked both a phallus and a flower. The title is suggestive of chocolate - obviously - but also of earth, of faeces, of base matter. Chadwick described it as: 'a pool of primal matter, sexually indeterminate, in a perpetual state of flux'.[44] The work is very much 'alive': it bubbles and gloops audibly like a swamp or sewer, gloriously spurting molten chocolate out of its central pole in a continuous cycle that has frequently been described as a reference to the overwhelming powers of libido and desire. Chadwick originally conceived this work as a fountain of flowers but eventually settled on it as one giant chocolate bloom. Sensory and immersive, the work sparks a joy that is quickly drowned out by the nausea of excess as the sickly sweet chocolate becomes overpowering, inducing feelings of indulgence, greediness and other decadent inclinations.

The final series of works included in 'Effluvia' was a group of new pieces made with fur, a medium that Chadwick had started experimenting with in 1993. These explorations began when a friend of Notarius's was clearing out an old tannery in London and - knowing how Chadwick was interested in materials with a luxurious or repulsive effect - Notarius brought home a bag of furs for her to play with. From these scraps,

Helen Chadwick making *Wreath to Pleasure*. LEFT ***No. 10 (Pink Roses, Germolene)*** **and** RIGHT ***No. 9 (Blue Delphiniums, Blackberries)*****, 1992–93**

Chadwick was inspired to create several works. Displayed in 'Effluvia' were *Glossolalia*, *I Thee Wed* and *Adore/Abhor* (1994). For *Adore/Abhor*, Chadwick created two vagina-shaped fur plaques to be displayed on a wall around a corner, almost mirroring one another, though with slightly different shapes and shades of fur. Both panels have a shaven rectangle in their centre: one is painted lime green with the word 'abhor' scripted in white swirls, the other is forget-me-not blue and holds the word 'adore', thus directly referencing Chadwick's interest in the interplay between desire and repulsion, sex and loathing. *I Thee Wed* refers more directly to the body - specifically the fingers. It consists of five hyper-realistic bronze casts of bitter melons (a phallic-like vegetable), each fitted with a 'ring' of fur. The fur for the fourth finger, in Western wedding ceremonies the traditional 'ring finger', remains off to the side, resting nearby on the ovoid plinth. Deliberately teasing the systems and customs of marriage, Chadwick's use of the phallic form also alludes to sex, and the fur to condoms or cock rings, in an assured and yet rascally unification of eroticism and matrimony. *Glossolalia* comprises a large circular oak table, atop which fox pelts are arranged in a circle like the petals of a flower, sewn side-to-side around a large bronze stamen or phallus (again) cast from an accumulation of lambs' tongues. Materially disquieting and sexually intriguing, this work feels like a perilous Tower of Babel that confronts cultural difference, thoughts around comfort (the soft fur ground) and desire, as well as language and speech: who speaks and who does not? Who decides what desire is, and what or who is desirable...?

Together the works in 'Effluvia' enacted some of the most vital questions of Chadwick's career, bringing to the fore issue(s) that she had been interrogating for years around gender specificity, sex, communication, desire and deviance, luxury, excess and death. They use noises, odours, flavours, textures...they are slimy, spikey, sharp, oozing, sticky, slinky, sexy, savoury and sickly sweet. To quote Marina Warner again: 'she defied the *Western* emphasis on optics as the first of the instruments of enquiry and sense. She often spoke of wanting to create through her images "the discharge of energy that occurs in touch"; to find a material vehicle, which would arrest the passing character of such intense bodily responses.'[45]

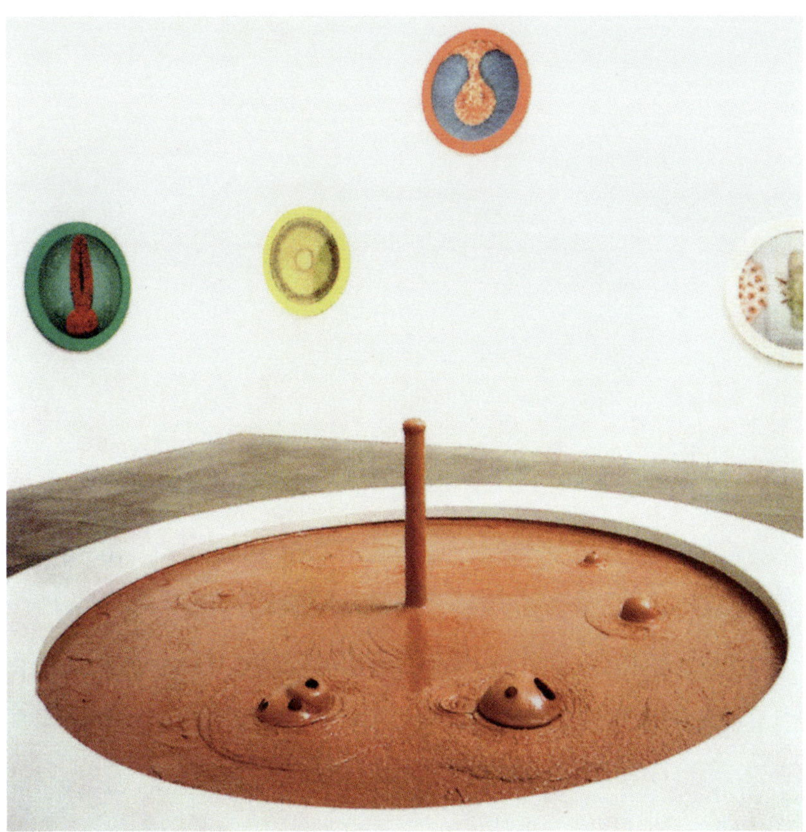

Helen Chadwick's *Cacao*, 1994 (foreground) with *Wreaths to Pleasure*, 1992–93 (background), in the exhibition 'Helen Chadwick: Effluvia', Serpentine Gallery, London, 1994

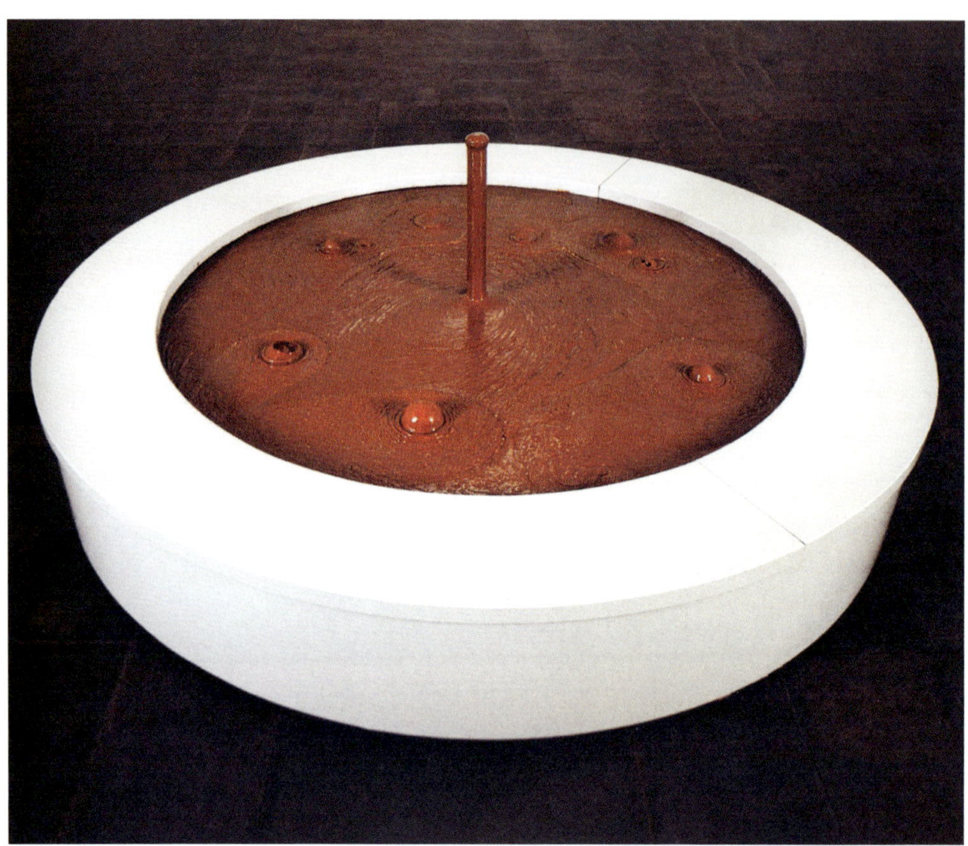

Helen Chadwick, *Cacao*, 1994. Chocolate, aluminium, steel, electrical apparatus, 85 × 300 × 300 cm (33½ × 118⅛ × 118⅛ in.)

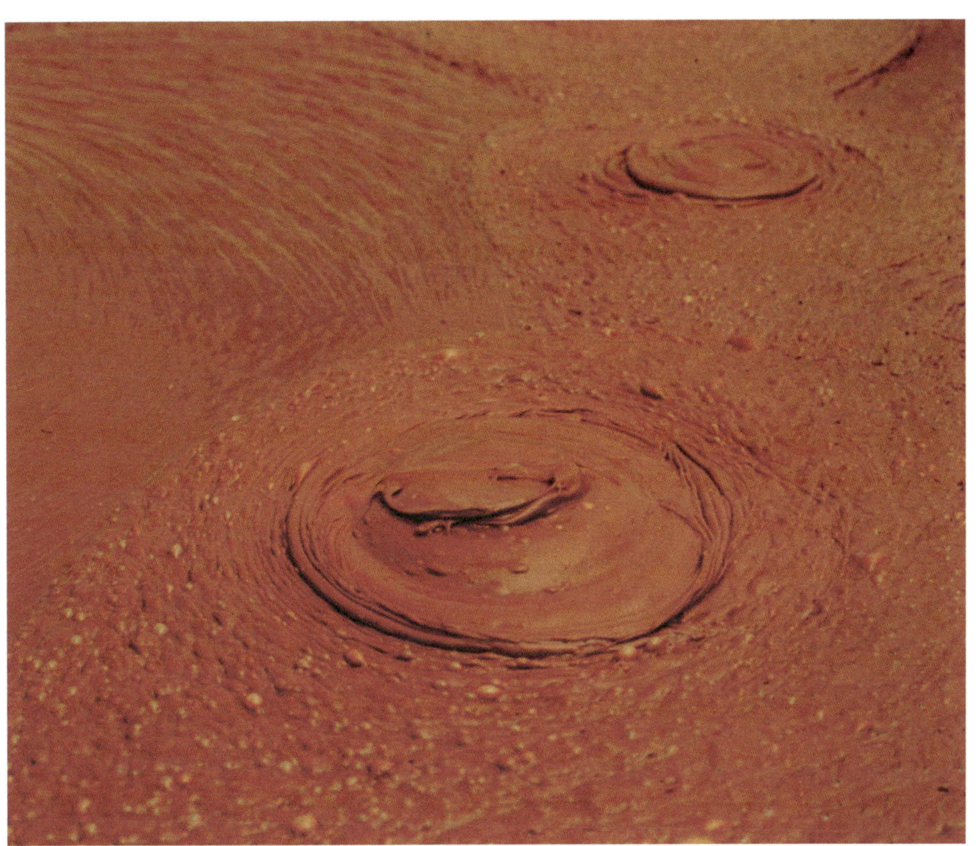

Helen Chadwick, *Cacao*, 1994 (detail)

When Chadwick died in 1996, her career was rising. Her solo exhibition at MoMA led to invitations for ten exhibitions across the world, from Uppsala, Sweden, to Indianapolis, USA. She was excitedly working on a residency in the Assisted Conception unit at Kings College Hospital, London, photographing IVF embryos that had been rejected for implantation in an attempt to create new work from this most delicate and sensitive subject matter and to truly explore the interstice between life, death and medical technology. On the day of her death, she had visited the Print Room at the Victoria and Albert Museum, London, to research and study the rococo fabric pattern-book of Anna Maria Garthwaite, a designer from the weaving community of eighteenth-century Spitalfields, London. It is impossible to speculate where these new directions of research would have taken her ever-inquiring mind and industrious hands. At the end of a documentary she presented for the BBC in 1992 about the pioneering Mexican painter Frida Kahlo (1907–1954), she comments, 'I don't think you can come up with some culminating verdict or understanding....Experience passes through you and you have to try and digest it in some way, assimilate it – and then let it pass.'

Chadwick is known now for her formal extravagance, her material literacy, her technological savvy, her incredible skill in making and

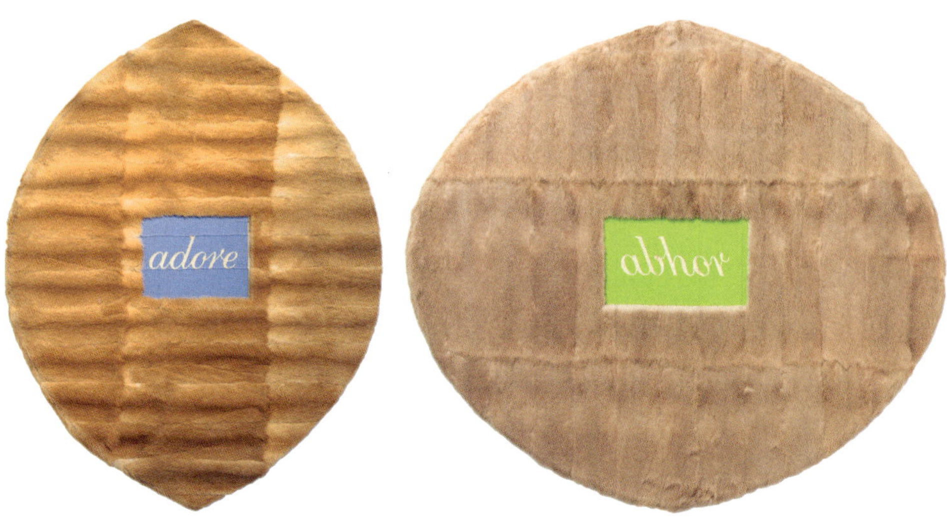

Helen Chadwick, *Adore/Abhor*, 1994. Oil on fur, plywood, MDF, on two panels: (i) 110 × 100 cm (33 ½ × 118 in.), (ii) 116 × 93 cm (45 ¾ × 36 ⅝ in.)

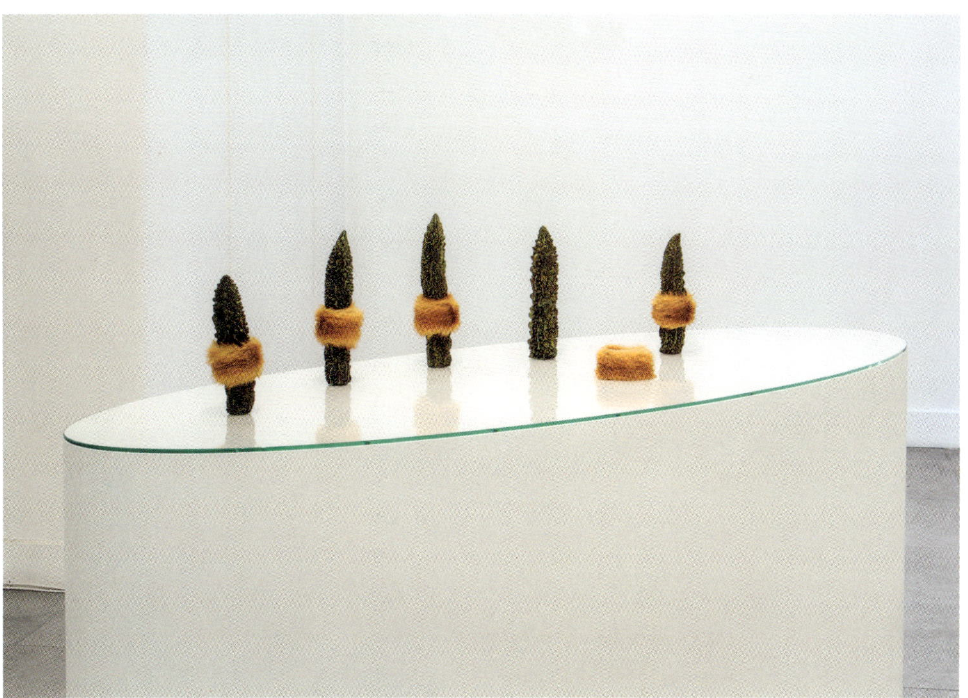

learning, and her enthusiasm for all that is base, bawdy, sexy and messy: 'She travelled to the very limits of the visible in pursuit of sexuality, pleasure and the sublime.'[46] Her unwillingness to accept any binary hierarchization of the world, from the conditions around male and female gender specificity to the separation of body and mind, to the distinction between human, animal and plant forms, allowed her to radically explore the mechanisms of the body, physically, emotionally, sensually, sexually and sensorially. In so doing, she produced a body of work that is generous, beautiful, complicated, confusing and compelling, 'she was a mischievous mistress at delivering funny feelings'.[47] Read as a whole, her output examines what it means to be a corporeal being in a mediated world and grants permission to subjective desire and individual craving, simultaneously nourishing body, mind and soul. Her work and teaching have had a palpable influence on the picture of contemporary art in Britain (and the Western world), as well as providing a guiding light for future generations of feminist thinkers.

Helen Chadwick, *I Thee Wed*, 1993. Painted bronze vegetables and fur on a glass-top painted plywood plinth, in five parts: 85 × 152 × 60 cm (33½ × 59⅞ × 23⅝ in.)

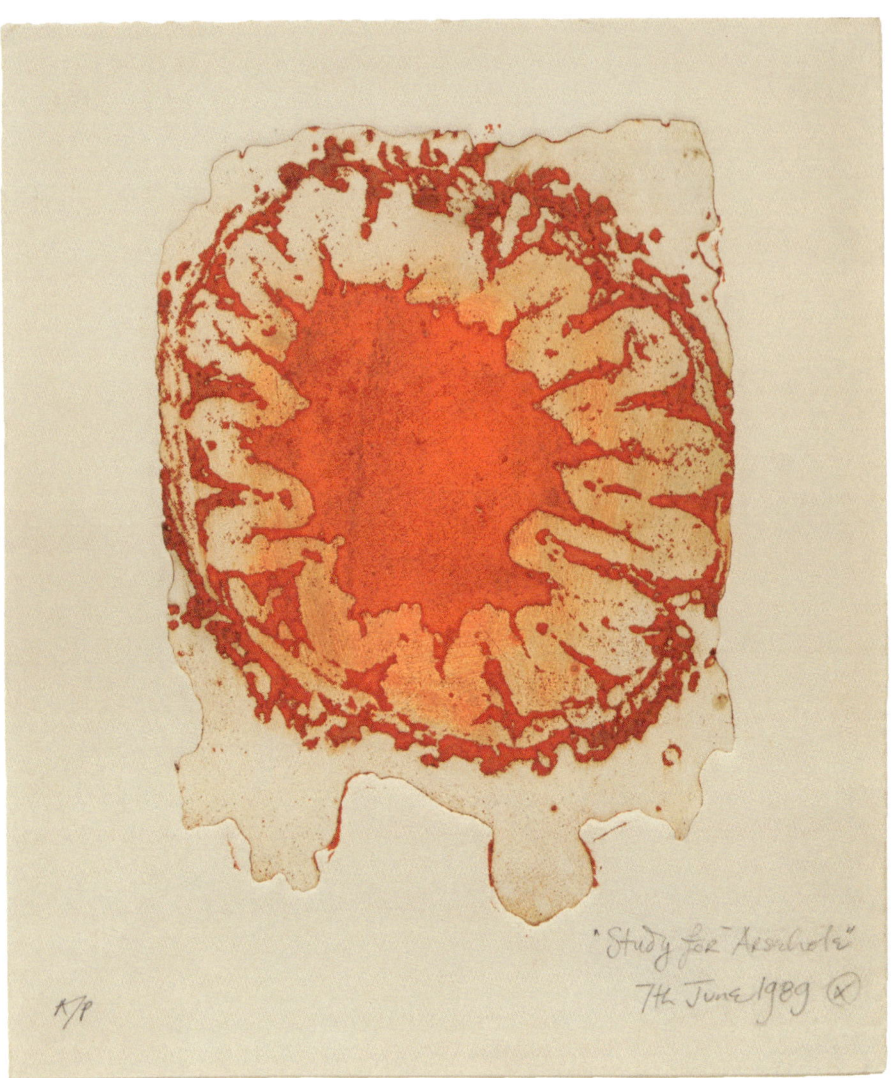

Helen Chadwick, *Study for Arsehole*, *c*. 1989. Colour lithograph on BFK Rives paper, 27.5 × 26 cm (10 7/8 × 10 1/4 in.)

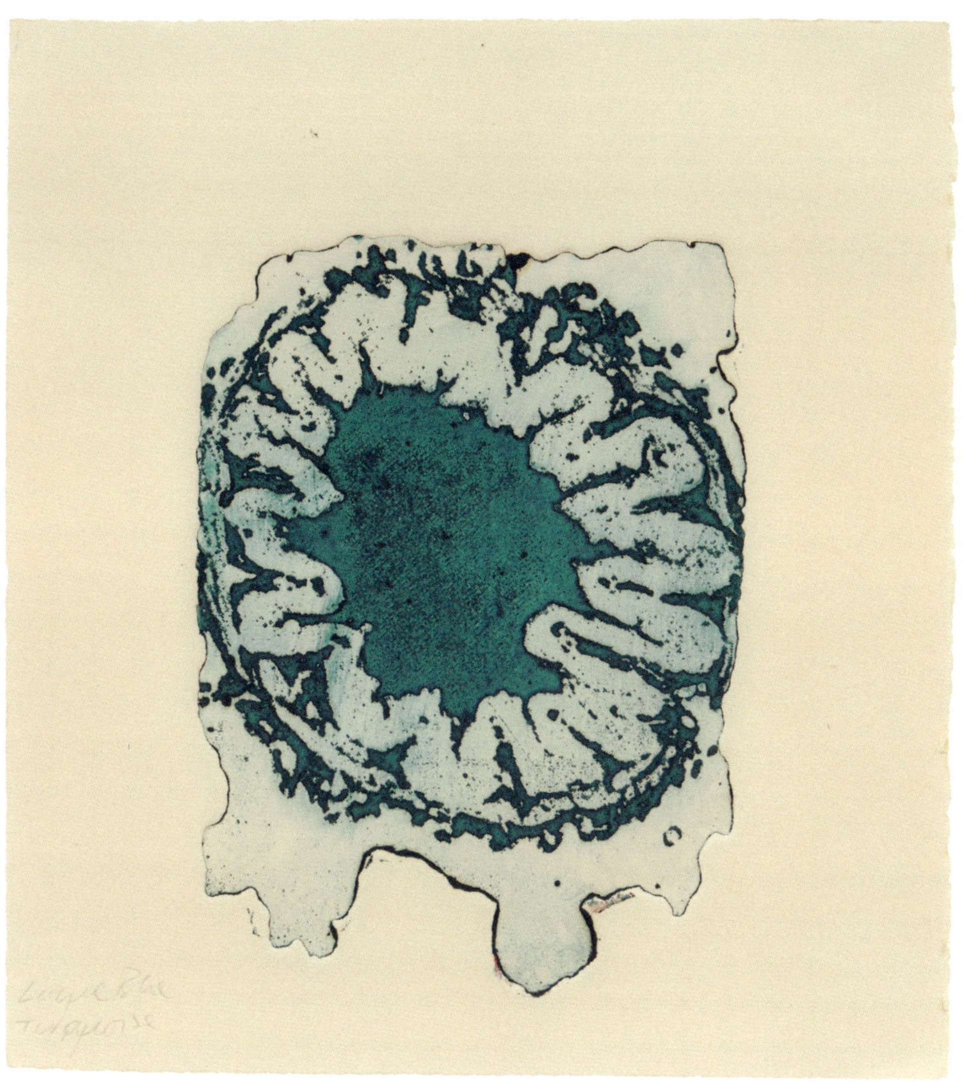

Helen Chadwick, *Untitled (Lacquer Blue Turquoise)*, *c.* 1989. Colour lithograph on BFK Rives paper, 27.5 × 26 cm ($10\frac{7}{8} \times 10\frac{1}{4}$ in.)

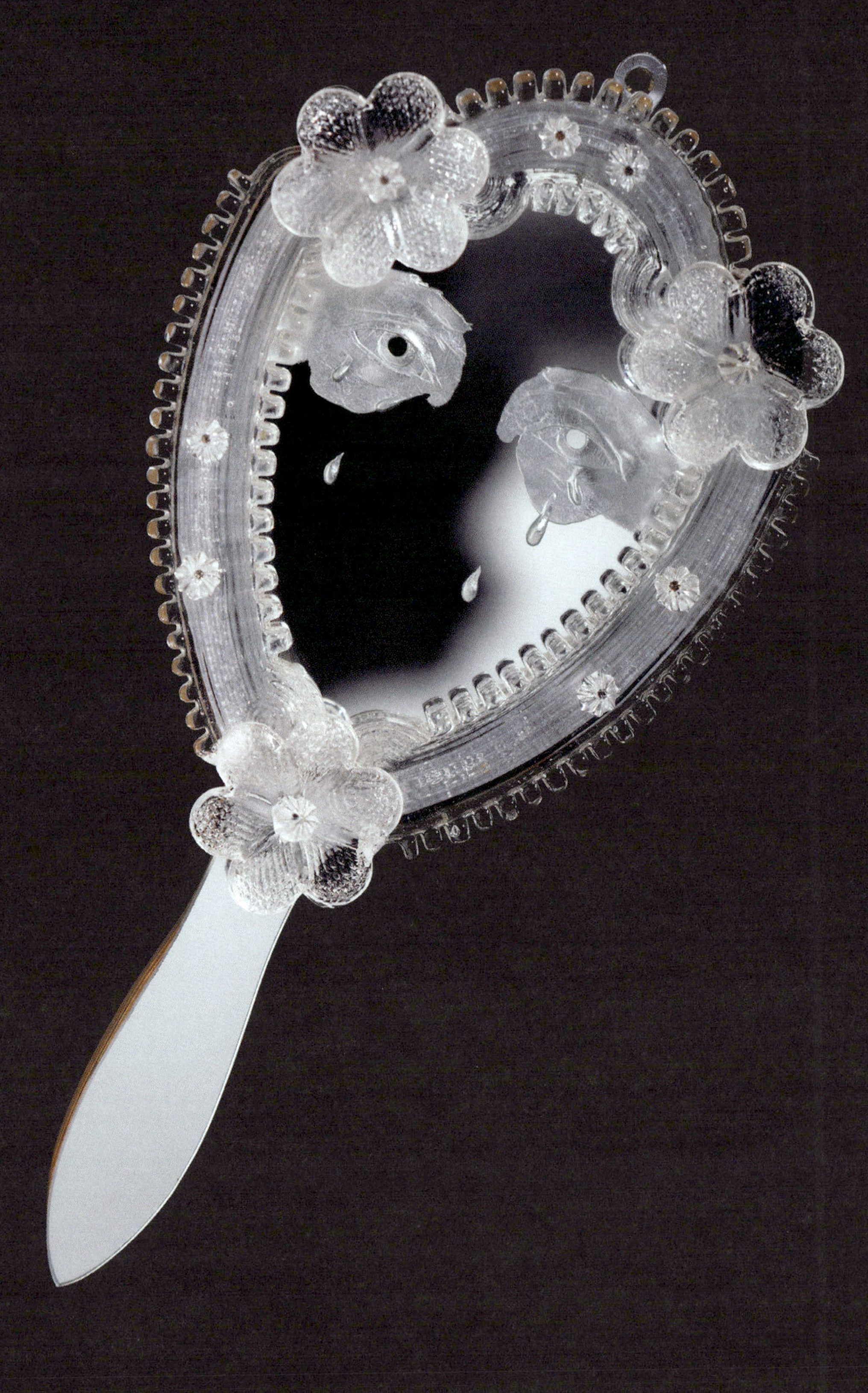

CHAPTER 2

Fetishistic, quite exquisite, quite troubling

Philomena Epps

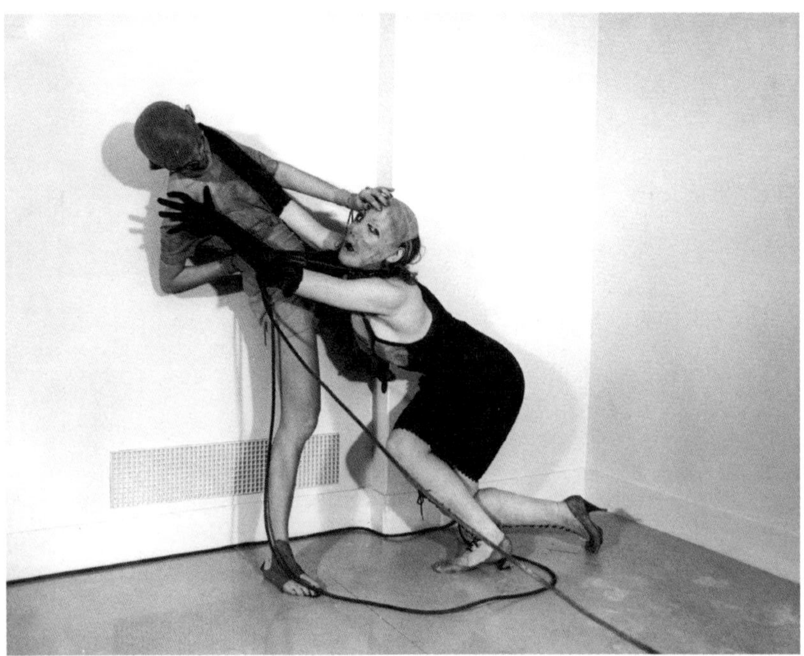

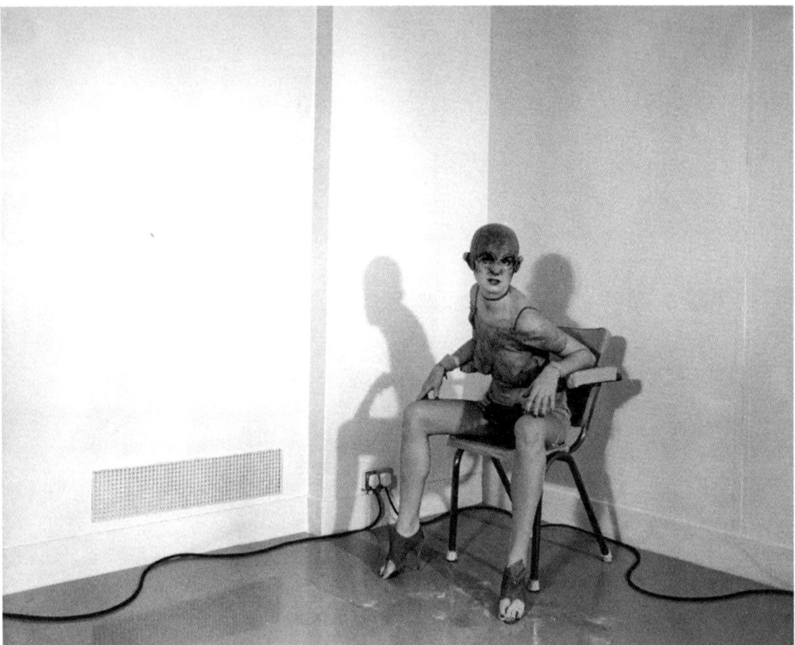

ABOVE **Helen Chadwick, *Domestic Sanitation: The Latex Glamour Rodeo*, 1976. Performance**

PAGE 132 **Helen Chadwick, *Vanitas*, 1985–86. Installation comprising photocopies on board and engraved Venetian glass mirror, in two parts: 240 × 290 cm (94½ × 114⅛ in.)**

> **I foraged around in woods and collected animal droppings and nibblings and kept them in little boxes....There are congruencies [to my professional work], there is a sort of perverse biological ikebana about it all, then and now. I would store little follies, such as fingernail parings....They were my childhood treasures.[1]**

In June 1976, Helen Chadwick staged *Domestic Sanitation* at the Brighton School of Art, an installation and performance she had devised as part of her undergraduate degree show. The event was broken into two acts: *The Latex Glamour Rodeo* and *Bargain Bed Bonanza*. Chadwick fabricated the eccentric, sculptural costumes worn by the performers, in an overtly sexualized and subversive send-up of haute couture. For the *Rodeo*, five performers wore a series of 'Latex Body Garments', bizarre, bondage-like coverings constructed from skin-tight latex and rubber in the style of lingerie. The scenography converged the mise-en-scène of a brick-walled gymnasium with the setting of a dressing room or boudoir, and the participants enacted a series of ritualistic exercises and parodic beauty routines. In addition to a leather couch in the style of a treatment bed, a dressing table and a trolley piled up with various aesthetician instruments, Chadwick fabricated a latex trampoline and installed a horizontal exercise bar. The domestic tableaux of *Bargain Bed Bonanza* was separated from *The Latex Glamour Rodeo* by barrier ropes. Here, a cradle swinging chair and polythene-wrapped armchair had been installed, alongside a vacuum cleaner, a feather duster and a mattress base. The four performers participating in the *Bonanza* wore the 'Bed Costumes': 'Supermum Housewife', 'Tart Duvet', 'Rape Mattress' and 'Virgin Scandinavian'. These were far more fanciful and exaggerated garments than those in the *Rodeo*, with Chadwick highlighting or exposing

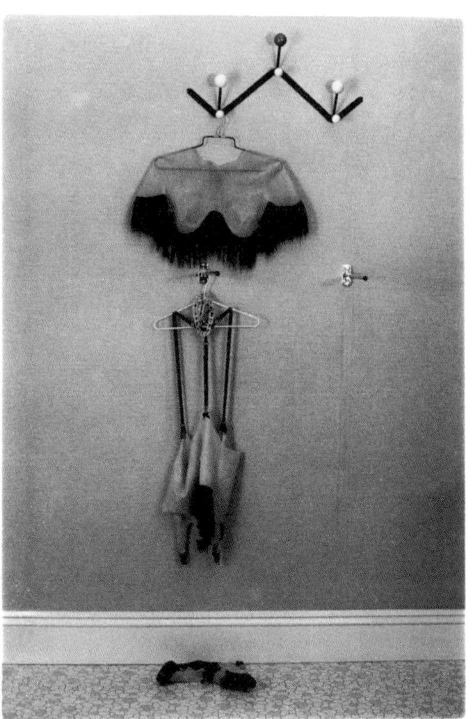

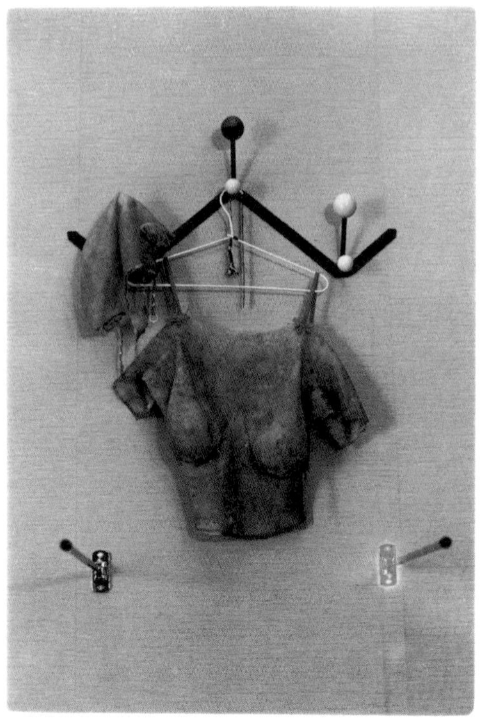

the commonly sexualized aspects of the female body (breasts, hips, buttocks etc.) and making them absurdly pneumatic through the use of soft furnishings, bedding and upholstery, assembling tunics, elaborate headpieces and even high-heeled shoes from foam, mattress springs, ticking, duvets, towelling, eiderdowns and electric blankets. Each costume had its own idiosyncrasies. The 'Supermum Housewife' had swatches of fake pubic and armpit hair, while the body of the model wearing 'Virgin Scandinavian' had been additionally wrapped in clingfilm. The photographs that Chadwick staged and shot to promote the show deployed a kitsch pastiche of the British - specifically Brighton - seaside postcard: one of the models languidly poses on the pebble beach in front of the Palace Pier in a full latex look, while the performer in the 'Tart Duvet' eiderdown costume basks in the sun outside the Royal Pavilion. These two specific sites, the seafront and the pleasure palace, can be framed as clearly alluding to Brighton's history as a liminal site of entertainment and the carnivalesque due to its burgeoning popularity as a resort in the

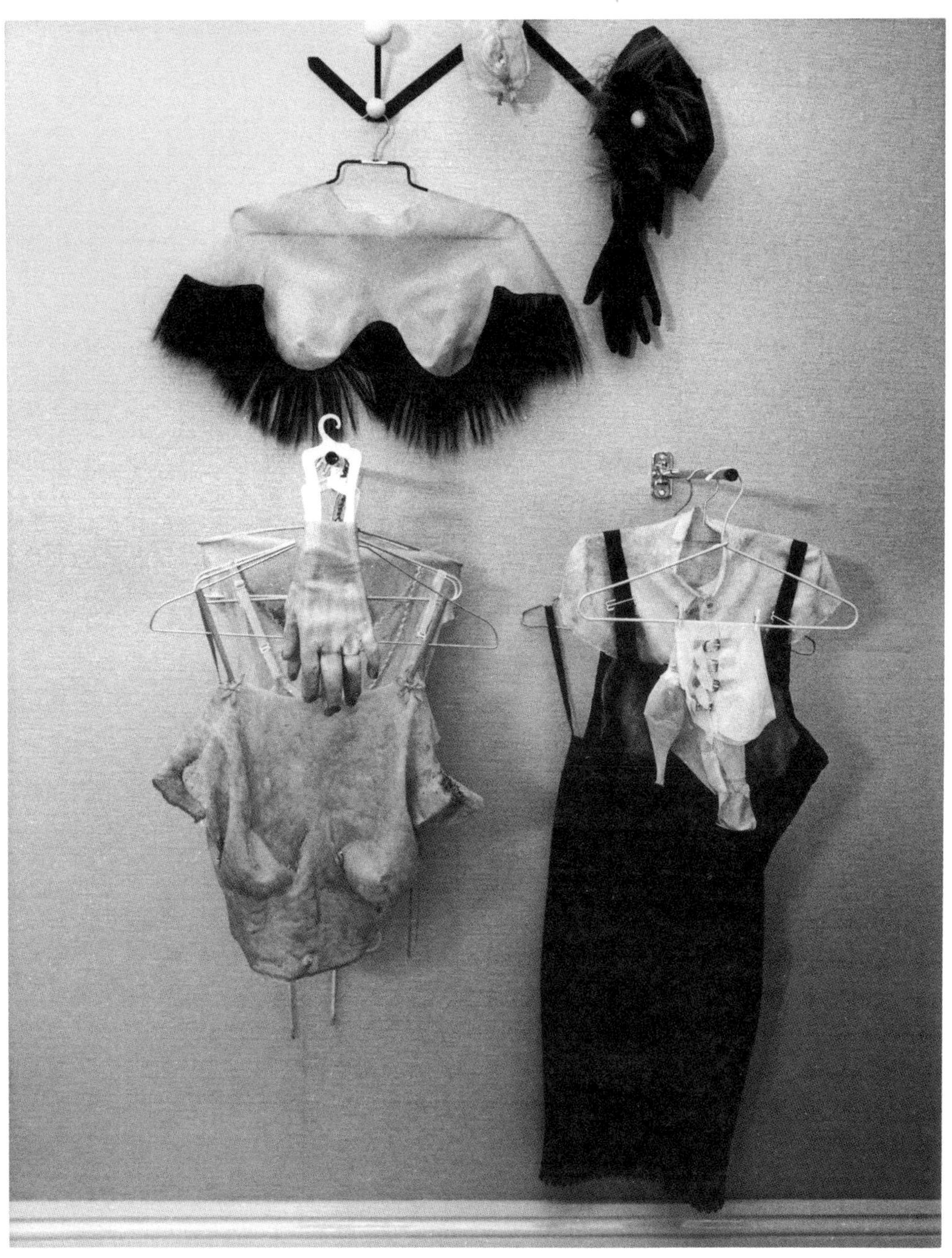

OPPOSITE AND ABOVE **Helen Chadwick, latex costumes for *Domestic Sanitation: The Latex Glamour Rodeo*, 1976**

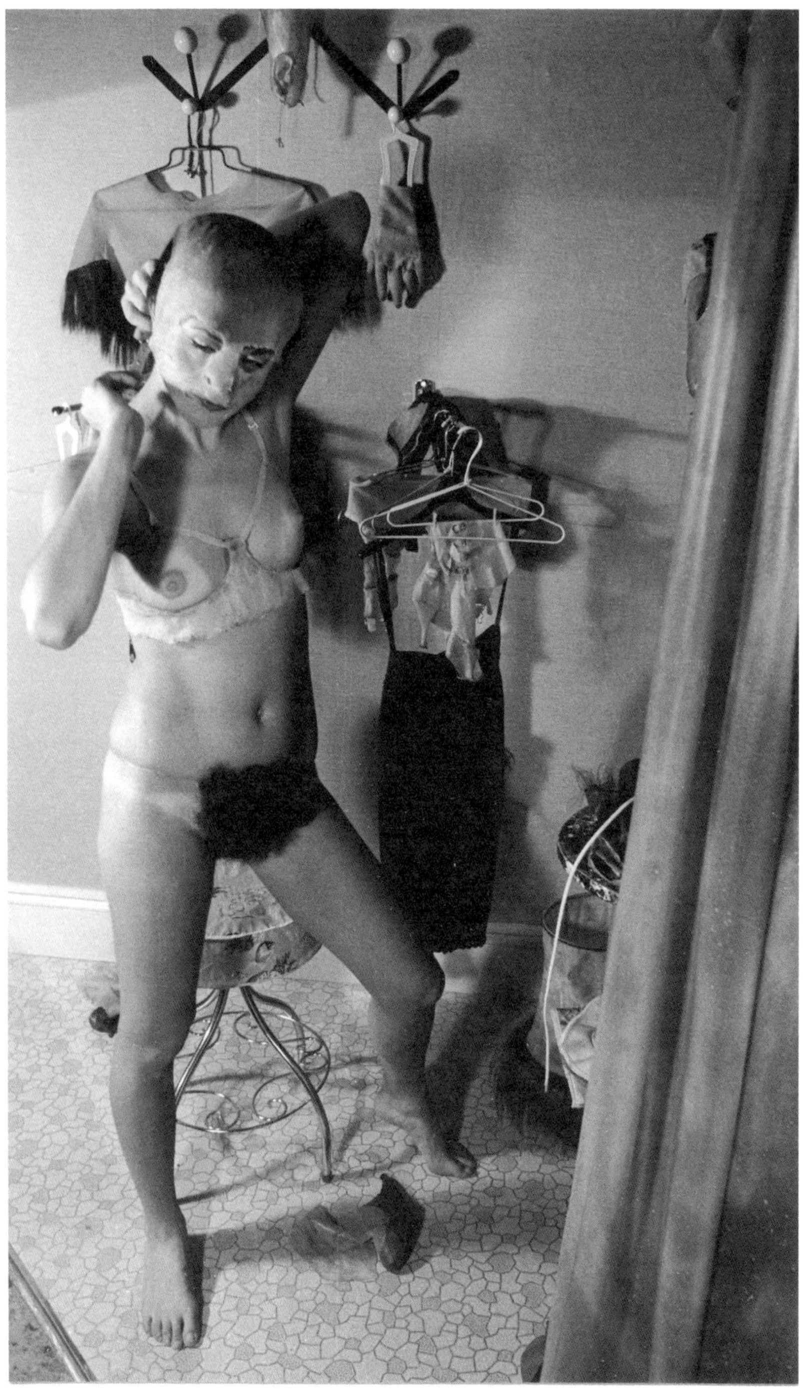

Helen Chadwick, *Domestic Sanitation: The Latex Glamour Rodeo*, 1976. Performance

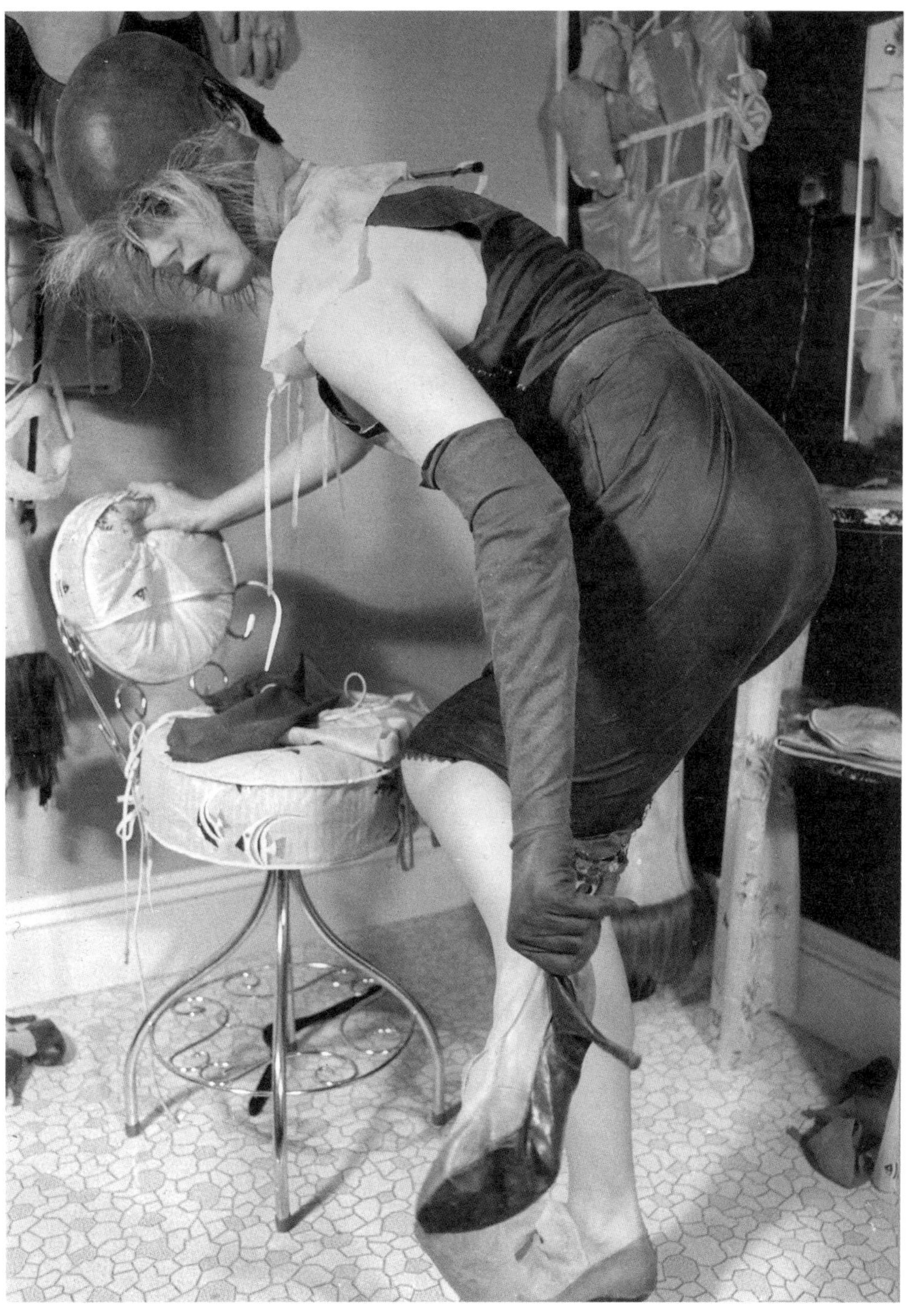

Helen Chadwick, *Domestic Sanitation: The Latex Glamour Rodeo*, 1976. Performance

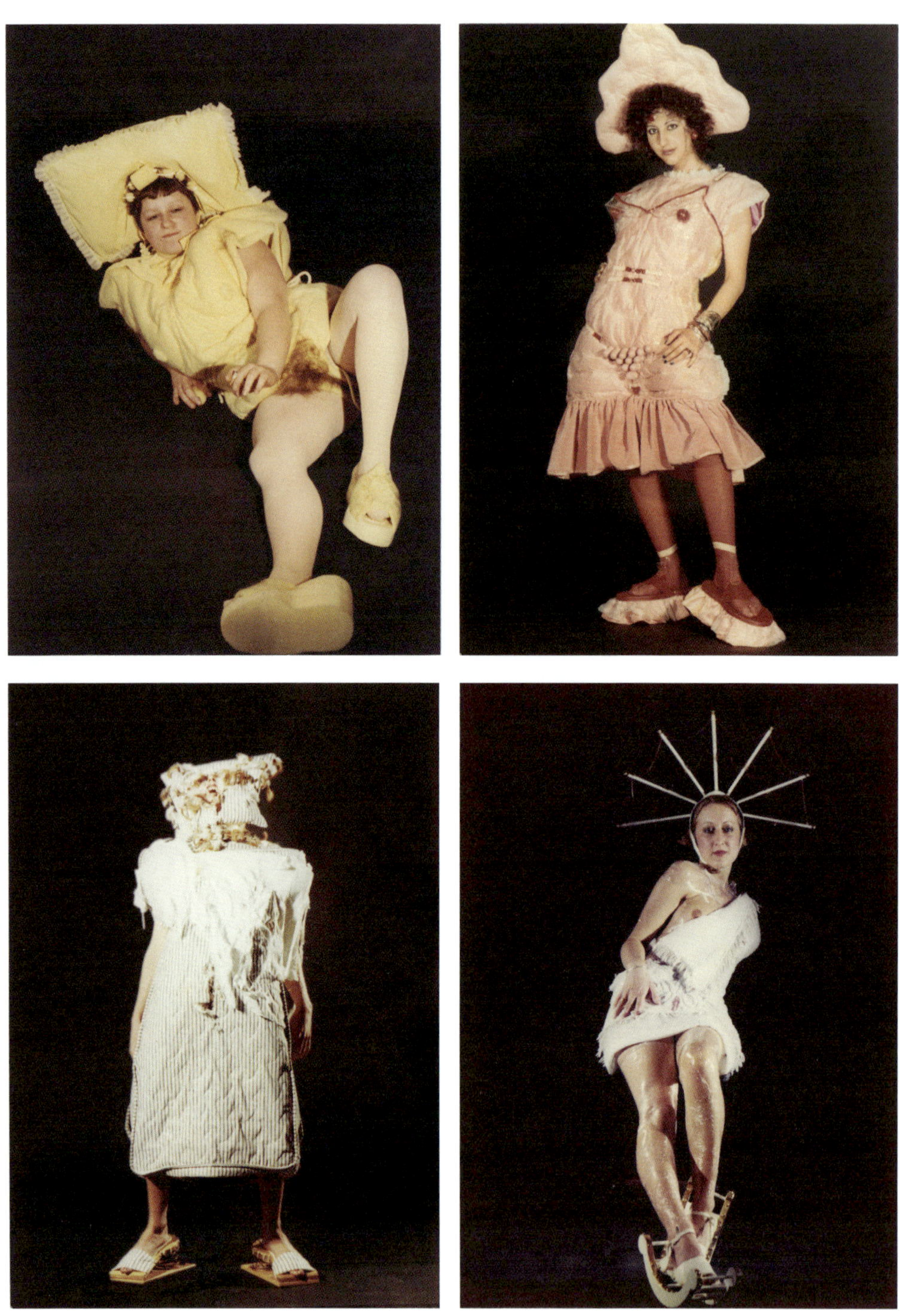

Costumes for Helen Chadwick's *Bargain Bed Bonanza,* 1976.

CLOCKWISE FROM LEFT ***Supermum Housewife*, 1976. Fleece fabric, padding, hair, electric switch, 110 × 30 cm (43 3/8 × 11 7/8 in.); *Tart Costume*, 1976. Velvet, satin, lining fabric, netting, PVC, battery operated lights, padding and rubber thimbles, 110 × 30 cm (43 3/8 × 11 7/8 in.); *Virgin Scandinavian*, 1976. Fabric, metal and plastic, 110 × 30 cm (43 3/8 × 11 7/8 in.); *Rape Mattress*, 1976. Cotton, padding, wool, felt and springs, 110 × 30 cm (43 3/8 × 11 7/8 in.)**

late eighteenth century. The playful licentiousness of the carnival spirit similarly simmers in Chadwick's own polymorphous interest in notions of the body, fetishism and the grotesque, demonstrating how formative these early experiments were for her rapidly advancing practice.

Two decades later, in an interview with Mark Haworth-Booth, Chadwick described the *Domestic Sanitation* garments as 'pre-Punk, erotic artefacts, quite glamorous, but with a disturbing edge....Fetishistic, quite exquisite, quite troubling.'[2] This dichotomy between glamorous and disturbing, exquisite and troubling, is a tension that runs throughout her oeuvre. To paraphrase the title of a series of later works from the 1990s, they provoke the viewer to both adore and abhor. While comparisons have been previously made between the 1976 Brighton production and Louise Bourgeois's protuberant and draped costumes for *A Banquet: A Fashion Show of Body Parts*, a performance that took place at New York's Hamilton Gallery of Contemporary Art in 1978, there is also an interesting parallel with the Spring/Summer 1997 collection by Rei Kawakubo (b. 1942) for Comme des Garçons, 'Body Meets Dress, Dress Meets Body'. Infamously coined as the 'lumps and bumps' collection by fashion critics and buyers unsettled by the distorted and asymmetric silhouettes, these garments saw Kawakubo utilize surplus mounds of padded stuffing to inflate and amplify the wearer's abdomen, hips and shoulders. Chadwick constructed her taut latex garments by making life casts of her own body and those of her willing participants, painting latex onto their shaved bodies and then peeling it off once dried. The resulting body skins were then given buttons, zips, straps and thongs, to be worn as skin on skin. The fluidity and malleability of latex, its association with the residues of the body and its ability to render a visceral simulacrum of flesh has appealed to numerous artists wanting to exploit skin-like effects. However, the instability of the material has meant that it is often associated with dissolution and degradation. Unlike the 'Bed Costumes', which are available to view in the Helen Chadwick Archive, maintained by the Henry Moore Institute, Leeds, the 'Latex Body Garments' have deteriorated and are therefore housed in specialist preservation storage. Chadwick documented the production of her costumes through detailed and extensive photography. The contact sheet photographs cut and pasted into her sketchbooks

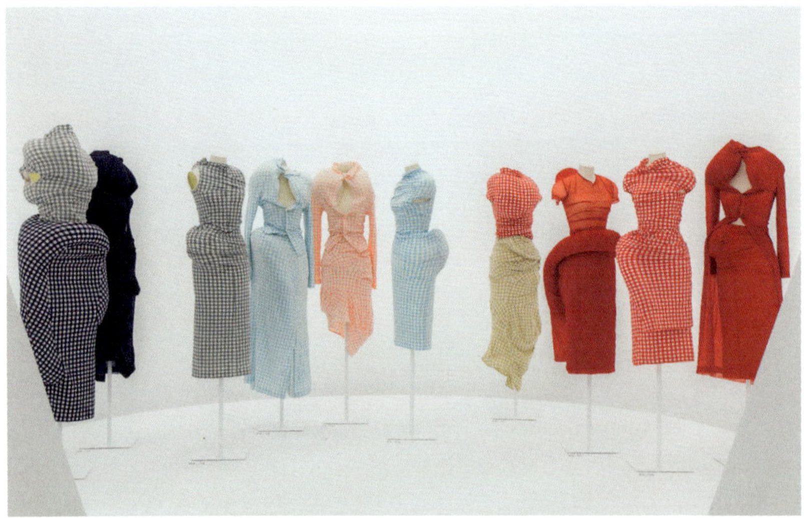

show feet and shoes dipped into latex, long gloves being peeled off arms and various casts made from maternity bras and corsets. Her focus on feet, shoes, gloves and underwear approximates the quintessential objects of desire in scenarios of sexual fetishism. In 1905, influenced by developing contemporary sexology, Freud theorized how fetishism was the 'model perversion' due to the sexual object being replaced by an unsuitable substitute: 'the substitute for the sexual object is some part of the body (such as the foot or hair)...or it is some inanimate object in some demonstrable relation to the person whom it replaces, and preferably to that person's sexuality (e.g. items of clothing, or underwear)'.[3] Chadwick's exploitation of material pliability can additionally be aligned with Freud's adjacent theory of polymorphous perversity and the bisexuality of the infantile drives, which perceive the whole body as a landscape of multiple, unfixed sensing zones: 'any part of the skin and any sense organ could probably function as an erogenous zone'.[4]

Through studying her notebooks and various drawings made between 1972 and 1975, Chadwick can be seen to continually rework multiple recurring motifs, with sexual organs often conflated with aphrodisiacs, flowers, sweets and fruit (particularly strawberries, raspberries, figs and pomegranates), alongside making detailed notes on various topics, including anatomy, divination, mythology and fairy tales. Her design for

Rei Kawakubo, *Body Meets Dress, Dress Meets Body*, 1997. Installation view of 'Rei Kawakubo/Comme des Garçons: Art of the In-Between', The Metropolitan Museum of Art, New York, 2017

a heart-shaped tasting box of chocolates titled 'erotic exotica' comprised a menu where each saccharine bon-bon was fused with a different part of the body. From butterscotch bottoms and Turk's tit delight, to whipped walnut wombs, vaginal vermicelli and lips liqueur, Chadwick's sexy pick-n-mix demonstrated her Bataillean flair for perverse forms of transgression. Her taste for the carnivalesque was also reflected in her 'Magic Jelly Circus' collages, constructing a miniature striped marque tent and populating it with decorated Jelly Babies sweets. In additional drawings, sexual and vital organs are shown converged in unique ways. A sketch titled 'love organ' shows the heart's aorta and artery valves replaced with erect phalluses, whereas in 'incubus' a woman's torso sprouts a constellation of phallic protrusions, which in turn part to reveal an intricately drawn vulva at its centre. Other sketches include renderings of hands, gloves, brassieres, corsets and chimerical winged figures, accompanied by annotated diagrams, articles and advertisements ripped from newspapers or magazines, with swatches of fabrics and textiles, marabou feathers and clusters of hair habitually taped to the pages.

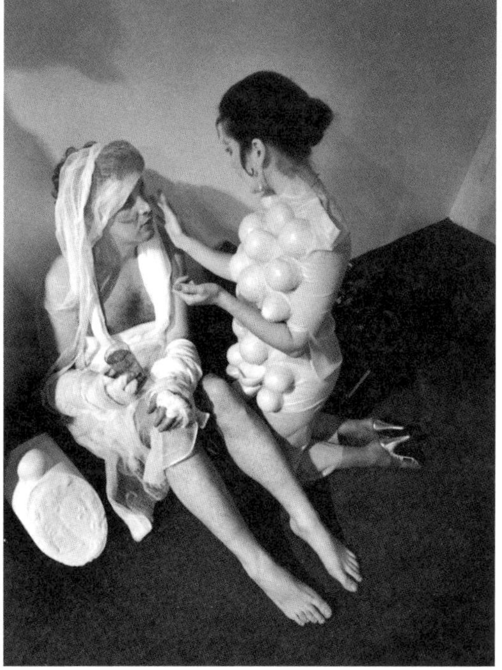

Gert Schiff, a professor at the Institute of Fine Arts in NYC, wearing a latex costume created by Louise Bourgeois during her performance *A Banquet/ A Fashion Show of Body Parts* at the Hamilton Gallery of Contemporary Art, New York, 1978

In 1973, during her undergraduate degree, Chadwick constructed a trio of 'Body Cushions' out of satin and kapok stuffing: *Fanny*, *Armpit* and *Buttocks/Thigh*. These were later exhibited in the 1976 degree show, arranged on a sofa in an area of the installation that Chadwick designated as 'the showroom'. The cushions reflect a particular intrigue with folds of flesh and the junctions at which parts of the body converge, such as the axilla and the glutes. Chadwick also incorporated fabric derived from underwear (such as the adjustable bra strap on *Armpit* and the gusset on *Buttocks*), nylon stockings, appliqué and tufts of blonde and brown hair in an allusion to pubic and armpit hair. Unlike the outsized soft sculptures of Claes Oldenburg (1929–2022), for example, Chadwick's comparably diminutive objects might be considered within the aesthetic realm of the cute. As theorized by Sianne Ngai, the affect produced by the cute object is dual, 'evoking tenderness for "small things" but also, sometimes, a desire to belittle or diminish them further...cute things evoke a desire in us not just to lovingly molest but also to aggressively protect them'.[5] As a simultaneously decorative and functional item, Chadwick's cushions present a version of the body that is both an eroticized object and a commodifiable product. A comparison to the work of Sarah Lucas (who Chadwick taught during her undergraduate degree at Goldsmiths College, University of London) is irresistible here, specifically her original *Bunny* sculpture from 1997, which was crudely constructed from tights similarly stuffed with kapok and wire. Like *Bunny*, Chadwick's 'Body Cushions' demonstrate the potential for inexpensive everyday fabrics to be transformed into a phantasmatic illusion of animate personhood. Chadwick also referred to the cushions as 'Body Amputations', a name that evokes Ngai's twinning of love and aggression, with the associations with trauma and injury troubling their material pliability. There is also a parallel to be made with the disturbing and often grotesque *poupees* of Hans Bellmer (1902–1975), initiated in the 1930s, which he assembled from various dismembered doll and mannequin parts. Seen through the lens of potential sadism, there is an implicit violence contained within Chadwick's rendering of the body in pieces, in which the stitching of thread might be compared to the suturing of a wound.

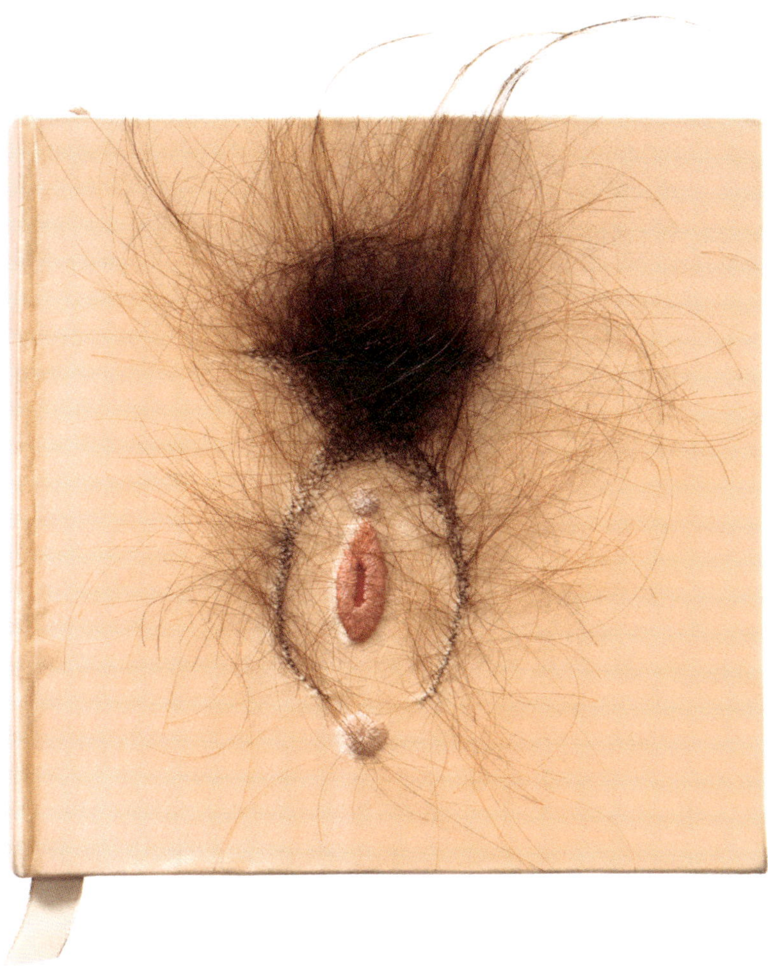

Helen Chadwick, *Satin Fanny Book*, *c.* 1974. Handmade book with satin and human hair, 15.5 × 16 cm (6 1/8 × 6 3/8 in.)

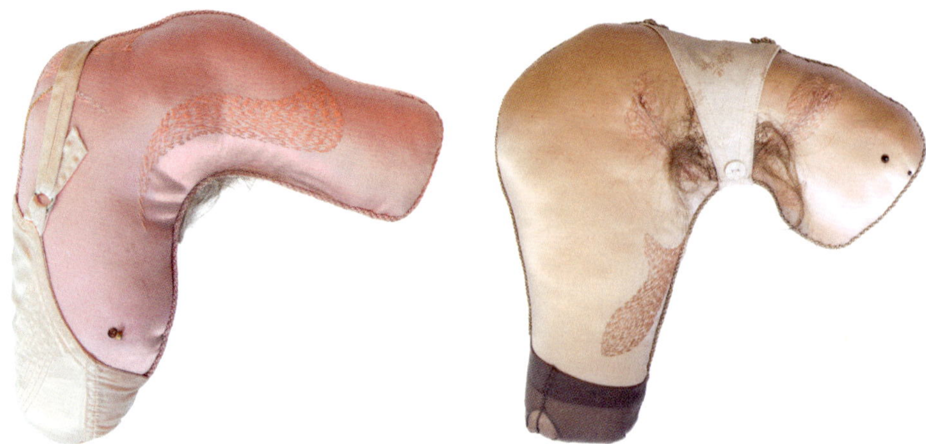

Following Bellmer, it is productive to consider Chadwick's early work in critical relation to the tradition of the surrealist fetish object, particularly as it pertains to questions of desire and sexuality. In his writing on fetishism, William Pietz has suggested that 'the surrealistic object was often constructed to be a material thing that resonated throughout all the registers (ethnographic, Marxist, psychoanalytic, and modernist) of fetish discourse...appearing as a perversely anthropomorphized or sexualized thing'.[6] In 1927 Freud redefined fetishism as being an exclusively masculine perversion, functioning as a psychic traumatic defence against the castration complex.[7] However, Chadwick's appropriation and exploitation of fetishism can be framed as a feminist revisioning of this androcentric deficiency within the theory. As Emily Apter has argued, the lack of a stable phallic referent within the structure of fetishism combined with the notion that any object can 'become a candidate for fetishisation once it is placed on the great metonymic chain of phallic substitutions ultimately undermines the presupposition of a phallic *ur*-form'.[8] Within the logic of sexual fetishism, certain objects or body parts become enchanted with a special erotic power. Pietz refers to these as having the 'quality of synecdochic fragmentedness'.[9] Across cognate forms of fetishism, most notably in commodity fetishism, the object is equally endowed with such a force. Chadwick's multifarious use of human hair, latex, velvet, satin and fur carries numerous predetermined fetishistic associations,

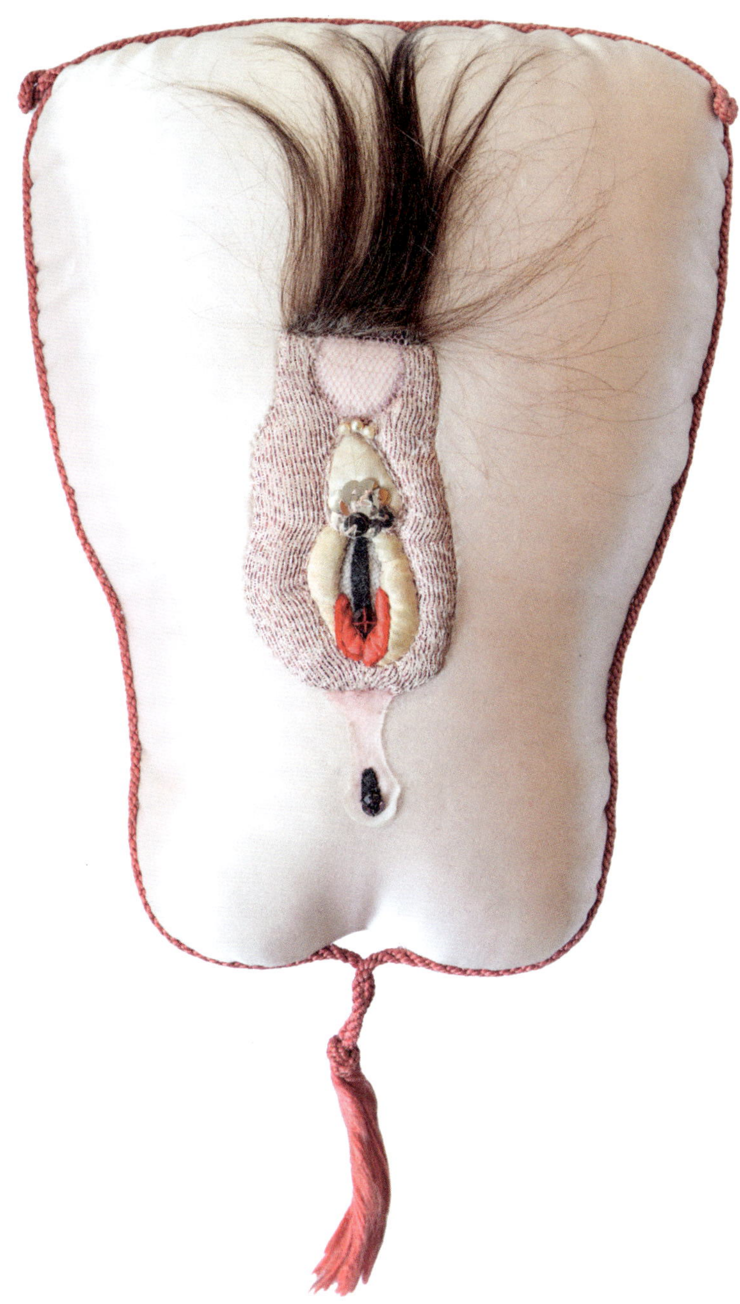

OPPOSITE AND ABOVE **Helen Chadwick, works from the series *Body Cushions*, also referred to as *Body Amputations*, 1973.** OPPOSITE, LEFT ***Armpit*, 1973. Satin, hair and kapok, 24 × 26 × 8 cm (9½ × 10¼ × 3⅛ in.).** OPPOSITE, RIGHT ***Buttocks/Thigh*, 1973. Satin, hair, nylon and kapok, 30 × 30 × 10 cm (11⅞ × 11⅞ × 4 in.).** ABOVE ***Fanny*, 1973. Satin, fabric appliqué, hair and kapok, 28 × 21 cm (11 × 8¼ in.)**

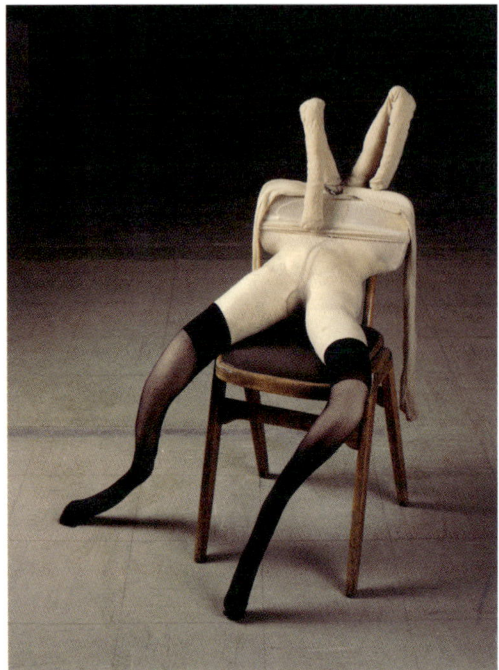

due to the materials' status as metonymic substitutes. Discussing her own fabric sculpture *Pincushion to Serve as Fetish* (1965) - for which an eclectic combination of velvet, metal pins, wool and a plastic funnel were amalgamated to form the curious shape of an animal - Dorothea Tanning (1910-2012) remarked, 'A fetish is something not exactly or always desirable in sculpture, being a superstitious if not actually shamanistic object; and yet, to my mind it's not so far from a pincushion - after all, pins are routinely stuck in both.'[10]

The fetishistic potential of the pincushion was readily exploited by Chadwick in her *Fancy Dress and Sculptures Photograph Book* (1974). The book comprises twelve printed photographs staged by Chadwick, who is dressed in a satin corset and shorts, sheer black stockings, spiked black patent stilettos and fishnet gloves, with clusters of feathers arranged in her hair, at her crotch and stuffed into the edges of the corset near her armpits. Four identical soft sculptures in the material guise of the 'Body Cushions' are tied to her wrists and calves, while a fifth is hung around her neck with a thick ribbon. Unlike the 'Body Cushions', which

Sarah Lucas, *Bunny*, 1997. Tan tights, stockings, plywood chair, clamp, kapok and wire, 101.6 × 90.17 × 63.5 cm (40 × 35½ × 25 in.)

replicated particular parts of the body, the shape of these sculptures - their ambiguous complication of phallic and vaginal forms - is more akin to her early drawings. While the curved phallus is left unadorned, the vulvic part is brusquely studded with numerous pins. The repetitive fervour of their pierced multiplication recalls Yayoi Kusuma's (b. 1929) own turn to soft sculpture in the early 1960s, wherein she covered furniture, shoes and other domestic items with accumulations of large phallic protuberances sewn and stuffed with cotton batting. Chadwick's parallel emphasis on repetition and replication also signifies an erotics of fixation and compulsion.

The literal use of pins conjures an association with the seductive trope of the 'pin-up', specifically in Chadwick's assumption of the contrived and titillating poses associated with such imagery. The deliberate choice of the phrase 'fancy dress' in the naming of the work is also suggestive, perhaps an admission of the theatrical artifice at play in her evocation of the feminine masquerade through her styling and chosen accoutrements. The construction of the book similarly makes use of such materials, from the hand-stitched fuchsia-pink quilted cover made from satin to the fishnet material used in lieu of a title page, which functions as a veil over the first photograph. Equivalent to the process of fetishistic substitution, the masquerade is understood to be a performance of femininity that attempts to conceal phallic lack through the subterfuge of erotic spectacle, with

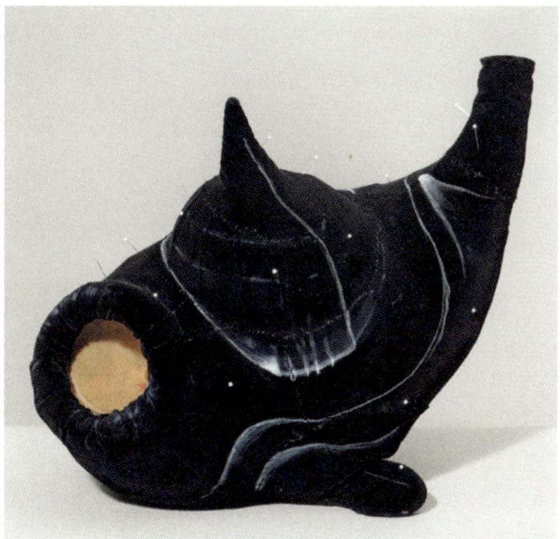

Dorothea Tanning, *Pincushion to Serve as a Fetish*, 1965. Velvet, plastic funnel, metal pins, sawdust and wool, 37.2 × 37 × 45.5 cm (14 5/8 × 14 5/8 × 17 7/8 in.)

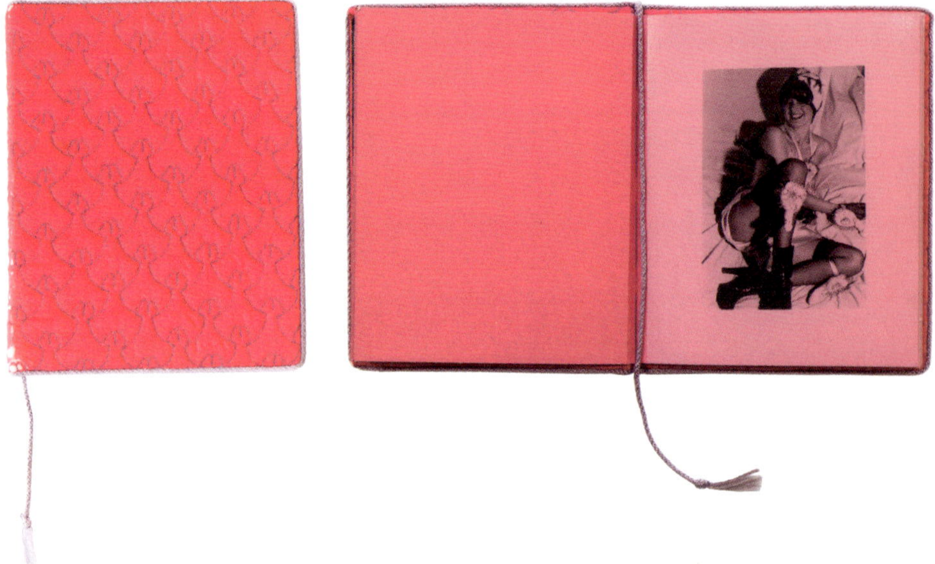

women often perceived as being interchangeable with their adornments. This logic facilitates their cosmetic construction as an image 'to-be-looked at', to borrow a term utilized by Laura Mulvey.[11] Chadwick's preparatory notes for her photographic series *Female Fetishisms* lists the surfeit of items associated with the apparatus of the masquerade available within the department store: perfumery, lipsticks, eyelashes, nail polishes, bras and tights. She also exhibited her *Domestic Sanitation* costumes in the art school's street-facing windows along Brighton's Grand Parade, appropriating the dynamics of the shop display and its place within the spectacle of consumption. Chadwick's 1975 photographs of wax models in the storeroom at Madame Tussauds at Wookey Hole, Somerset, various polythene-wrapped mannequins in a shopfront in Bath and pairs of shoes in the window of 'Harry's' in Brixton comparably demonstrate an interest in the body as being both fabricated and inscribed by consumerist desire. However, her punkish perversion of glamour and the erotic demonstrates how the sartorial tropes of the masquerade can be manipulated and subverted. This gesture invokes Dick Hebdige's appraisal of subculture and style, notably how style can operate as a form of refusal. He writes that commodities are open 'to "illegitimate" as well as "legitimate" uses', able to 'be magically appropriated; "stolen" by subordinate groups and made

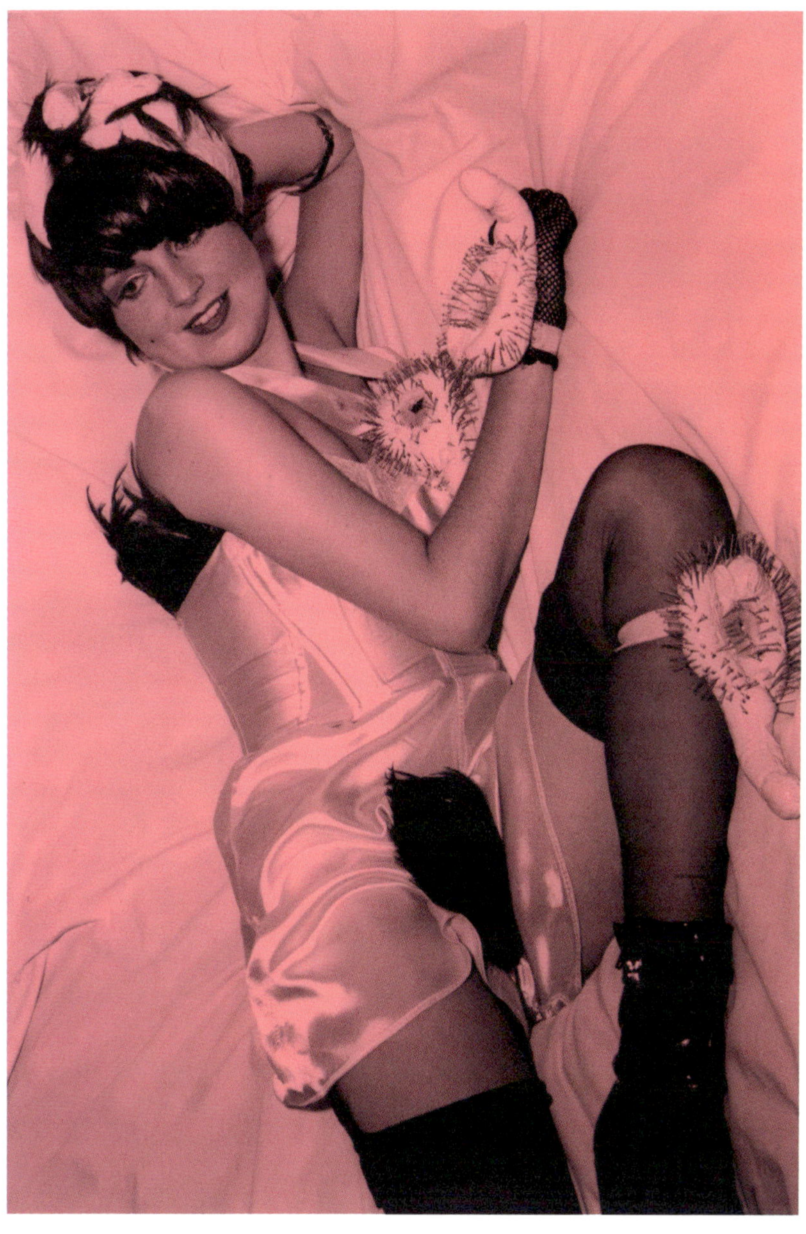

OPPOSITE AND ABOVE **Helen Chadwick, *Fancy Dress and Sculptures Photograph Book*, 1974. Pink satin quilted cover, photographic prints, in twelve parts: 24 × 19 cm (9½ × 7½ in.)**

to carry "secret" meanings: meanings which express, in code, a form of resistance to the order which guarantees their continued subordination'.[12]

○

In Chadwick's self-portrait *Vanity* (1986), her naked body is framed by sumptuous drapery, including white broderie anglaise, pink velvet and ostrich feathers, while she observes herself reflected in a large convex security mirror. The photograph was made as a companion piece to her solo exhibition 'Of Mutability' at the Institute of Contemporary Arts (ICA), London, in 1986. Although it wasn't exhibited, the portrait was staged in the Institute's Upper Galleries, and parts of the exhibition can be seen in view behind her. Chadwick declared in an interview with Iain Gale in 1994 that she was 'nearly massacred in the mid-80s for presenting the female body naked'.[13] In conversation with Emma Cocker two years later, she continued to defend the exhibition, arguing that she had wanted to use 'the body to explode ideology'. She continued, 'Feminism was arguing that you shouldn't see a naked female body. I disagreed with that...I was looking for a way to create a vocabulary for desire where I was the subject, the object and the author...I broke down the normal situation of the viewer as a kind of voyeur....The only way to enter the work was through a kind of mirror identification. Rather than trying to see the female as a desired object, you had to feel yourself as a desiring subject.'[14] By becoming the producer and consumer of her own image, Chadwick rejected the morality of the traditional *vanitas* genre by instead portraying the deviance and erotic enjoyment inchoate within the act of narcissism.

The 'vocabulary of desire' utilized in 'Of Mutability' most significantly referenced neo-classicism, notably the frothy and fanciful indulgence of the Baroque and Rococo periods, with Chadwick reconfiguring certain decorative and architectural emblems. As Naomi Schor has examined, these specific aesthetics have been 'imbued with the residues of the rhetorical imaginary, a sexist imaginary where the ornamental is inevitably bound up with the feminine'.[15] Chadwick wished to redeem these claims of frivolity, by reconfiguring the senses and finding a perverse and indulgent

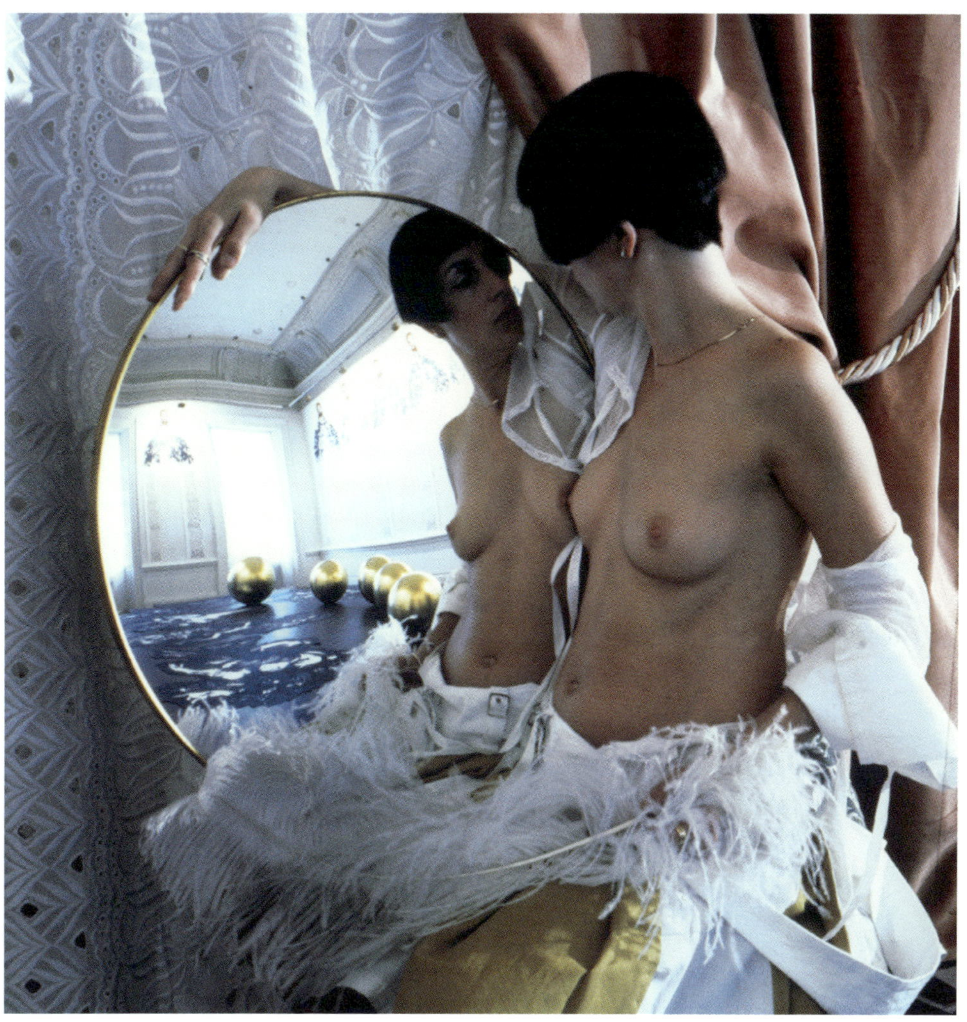

Helen Chadwick, *Vanity*, 1986. Cibachrome photograph, convex mirror, 87 × 87 × 3 cm (34$\frac{1}{4}$ × 34$\frac{1}{4}$ × 1$\frac{1}{8}$ in.)

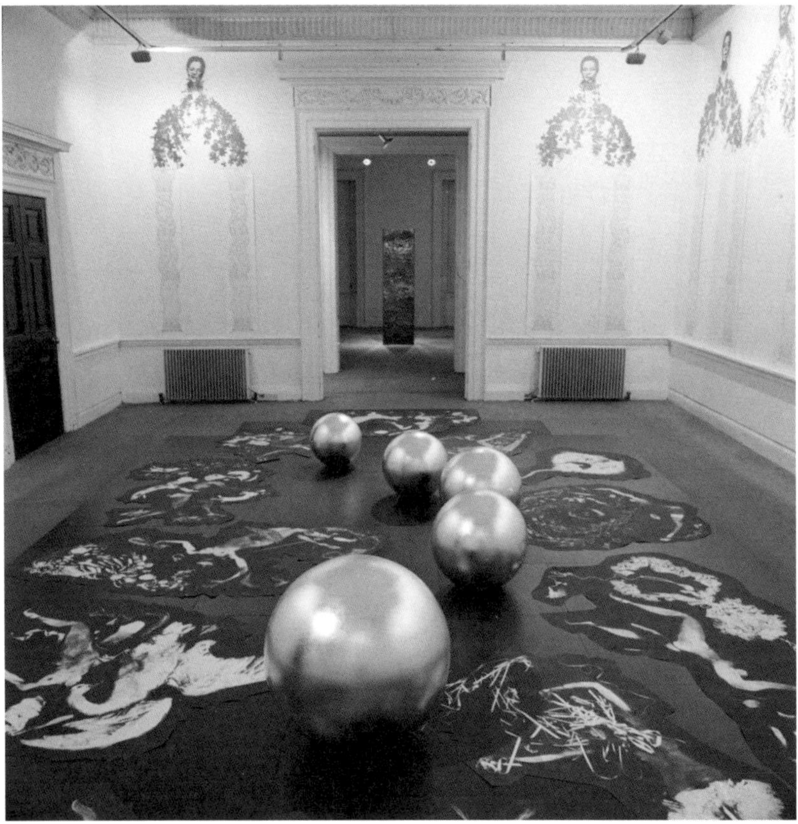

pleasure in them. *Vanity* provoked much debate, as did the numerous photocopied images of her naked body that were utilized within the twelve photographic tableaux that comprised the large-scale installation *The Oval Court* (1984–86). Marina Warner has suggested that feminist critics were disturbed by Chadwick's 'embrace of luxurious beauty in the idiom of the eighteenth century' as they were her 'exultant' eroticism, which they felt demonstrated an uncritical and 'suspect affinity with the *ancient regime* [sic], its inequalities, its sexual exploitation of women'.[16] However, rococo décor particularly appealed to Chadwick due to its exuberant and intoxicating celebration of artifice and excess, wanting to infuse these derided categories with a provocative virility and libidinal charge. The Chadwick Archive contains an extensive album of colour photographs and postcards of baroque architecture in palaces, churches, museums

Helen Chadwick, *The Oval Court* with *Carcass* visible through the door, in the exhibition 'Of Mutability' at the Institute of Contemporary Arts, London, 1986

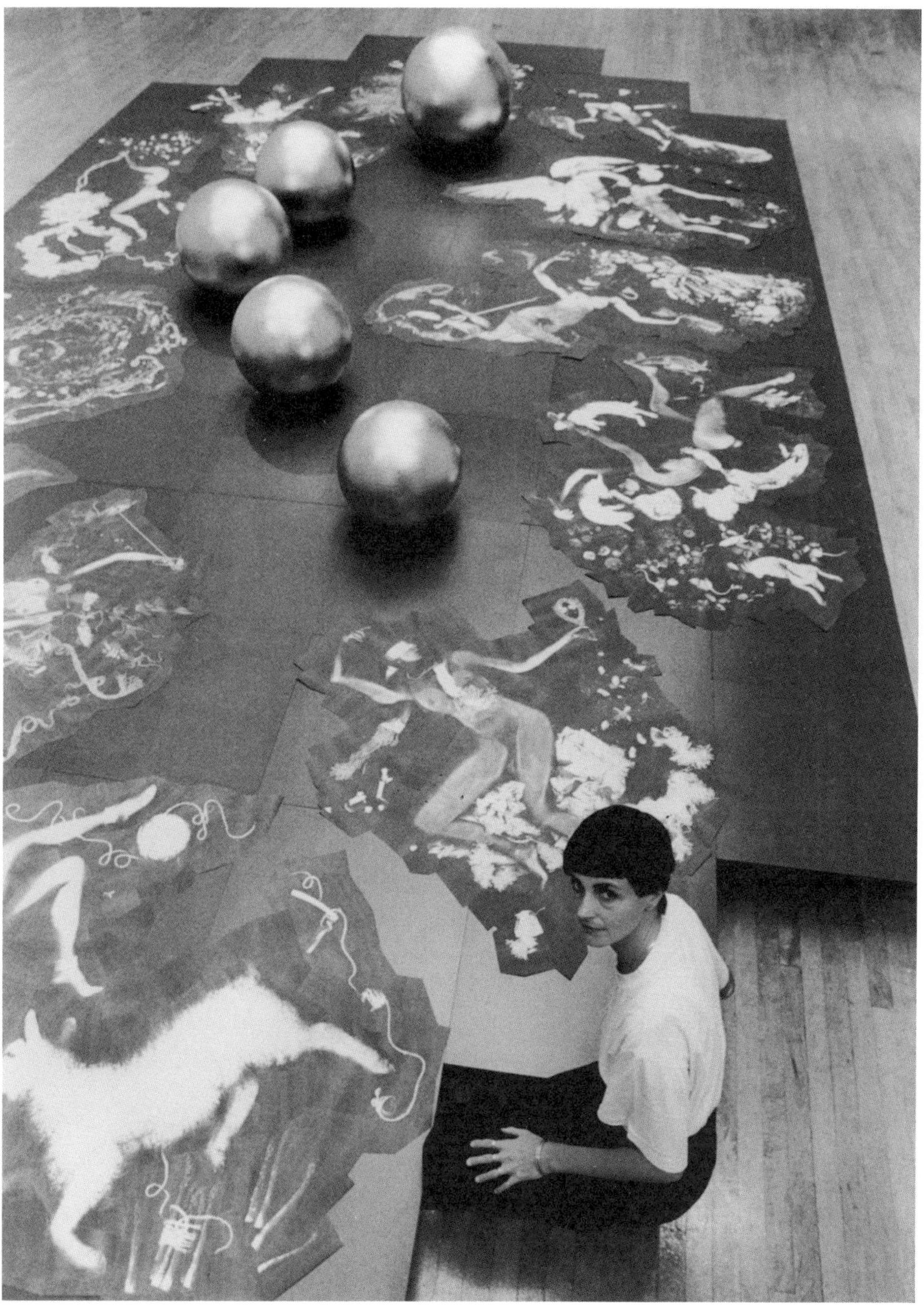

Helen Chadwick with *The Oval Court*, 1984–86

and other historical sites that she captured during a formative trip across Germany and Austria. In a reversal of Adolf Loos's infamous declaration that 'ornament is crime', Chadwick noted, 'I respect modernism...but there is a repression there.' Rather, the 'constructed fantasies' of the rococo churches are 'pleasurable space, sensual space': 'I admire the dynamism of these spaces, and this brings us back to the organic, and the organic as something that encompasses the corporeal and the imaginary.'[17]

The concepts of mutability and liminality that Chadwick was ambitiously exploring in her exhibition were also reflected by the numerous notes she made on Naomi Miller's 1982 book *Heavenly Caves: Reflections on the Garden Grotto*, penning the formula 'Nature+Artifice=Grotto' in one of her notebooks. Miller discussed the grotto as an architectural vehicle where perversion could be sanctioned due to its status as a boundary state, much like the festival or the theatre.[18] Similarly, *The Oval Court* established a synthetic landscape of somatic fluidity and carnivalesque contagion between species, recalling the 'perverse biological ikebana' of Chadwick's childhood play. Her body was positioned in various poses influenced by historical artworks, from Boucher to Bernini, and arranged within a spectacular array of dead animals, food and fruit. There was a lamb, a goose, rabbits, monkfish, skate and other fish and crustaceans, combined with various decorative trimmings and accessories: white socks and ribbons, lace and fishnet tights. In her accompanying text, Warner also identified how these accoutrements had a sadomasochistic edge, particularly noting the inclusion of the noose and hood in addition to the small axe placed at Chadwick's pubis.[19]

Returning to the Freudian paradigm of polymorphous perversity provides a frame in which to examine the ways that the infantile drives of narcissism, orality and sadism are latent within the tableaux. Akin to those early sketches of composite erogenous organs, Chadwick's vast collaged assemblage complicated animal, mineral and sexual dichotomies, conjuring what Jo Anna Isaak has defined as 'the jouissance of the polymorphic, orgasmic body'.[20] For Isaak, jouissance is a revolutionary strategy, indicating the enjoyment and sexual pleasure derived from the body, and conjuring associations with fantasies of desirous disruption. 'I wanted to catch the physical sensations passing across the

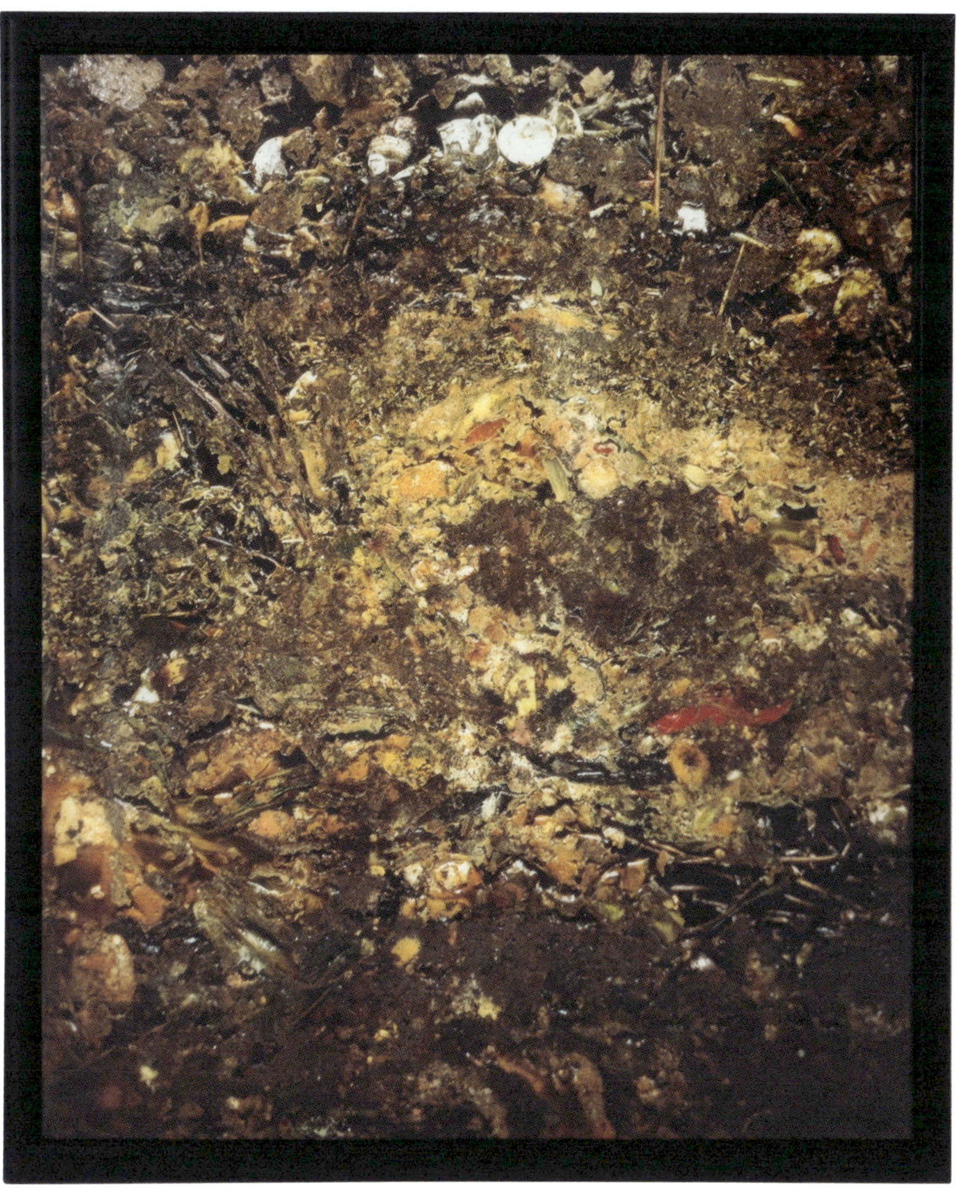

Helen Chadwick, *Carcass (Photograph)*, 1986. Cibachrome photograph, 63 × 60 cm (24 3/4 × 23 5/8 in.)

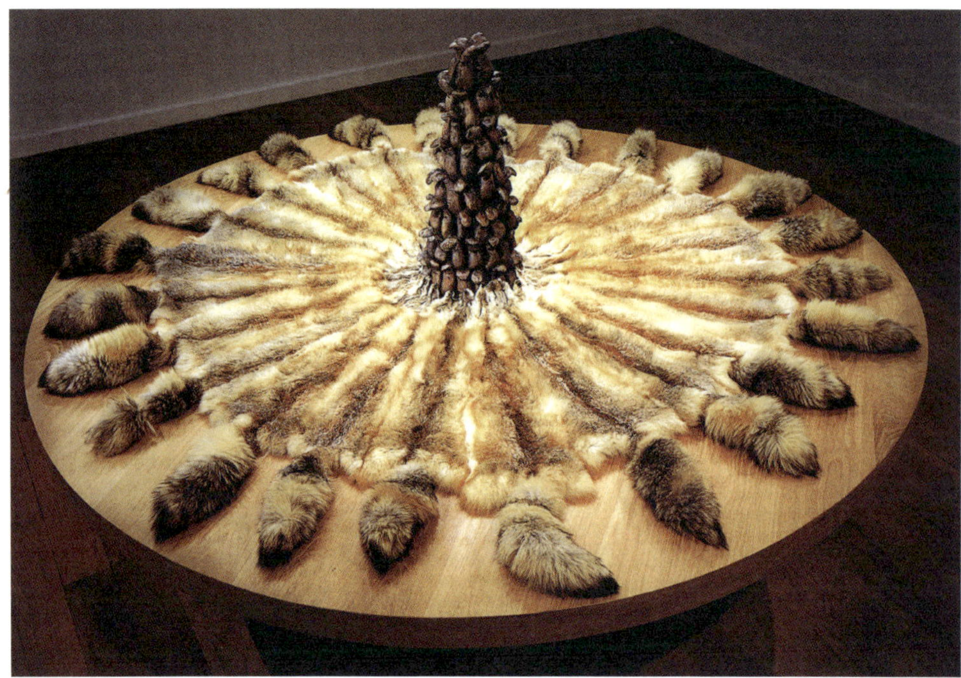

body – sensations of gasping, yearning, breathing, fullness,' Chadwick told Warner. 'Each of them is completely swollen up with pleasure.'[21] She also refers to them as 'gagging' and 'bursting', suggesting a garden of earthly delights precariously brimming with carnal appetite and overabundance, one that might warrant a comparison with the erotic and violent excesses of *The Cook, the Thief, his Wife and her Lover* (1989) by Peter Greenaway (b. 1942), notably the film's varied interactions and slippages between coitus and carcass, and its own resonances with art historical references. *The Oval Court* can most productively be interpreted through Mikhail Bakhtin's analysis of the 'grotesque body' within the Rabelaisian carnival sphere, a protean corporeality with porous thresholds that can blend with animals and objects: 'an open, protruding, extended, secreting body...of becoming, process, and change...opposed to the classical body, which is monumental, static, closed, and sleek'.[22] Chadwick's own appetite – as subject, object, author – is inferred through her recollections about the production of the work, which took place in her home studio in Beck Road, London: gutting the fish and the goose herself, manipulating

Helen Chadwick, *Glossolalia*, 1993. Patinated bronze, fur, oak and glass, 85 × 152 × 60 cm (33½ × 59⅞ × 23⅝ in.)

the flexible limbs of the lamb once the rigor mortis phase had subsided, even wryly noting that working with 'the monkfish was great because we ate it afterwards. And the skate too, that was gorgeous with capers and black butter.'[23]

Carcass (1986), a 2-metre-tall (6½ ft) glass tower filled with rotting organic matter, was exhibited in an adjoining room at the ICA. Viewed in relation to the vital ecstasy of *The Oval Court*, this putrid sculpture was designed to represent death and decay. The multitudinous organic contents within fermented over time, seeping, fizzing and bubbling, until the final fatal leak, which resulted in the installation's infamous destruction. Chadwick continued to play with her food into the 1990s. In the eight photographs that comprise the *Meat Abstract* (1989) series, captured using a large-format Polaroid camera, she arranged her specimens (including tripe, heart, liver, entrails, steak and tongues) in stylized configurations on various jewel-coloured fabric backgrounds, including silk, hide and suede. Combining the conventions associated with still-life painting with the set dressing of a luxurious window display, the gleaming and glistening surfaces of the offal and entrails were enhanced by the harsh electric lightbulbs, rendering them both compelling and yet entirely disagreeable images. They are crudely anonymous, degendered, uncanny, yet somehow still sickeningly retain the imprint of human association, being of the body, albeit human, animal or other. In *Loop my Loop* (1991–92), the borders between species continued to be transgressed, with Chadwick braiding artificial blonde hair together with a sow's intestines. Hair has long been interpreted as a synecdoche for female sexuality across literature and visual art, with the coveting of locks and plaits of hair recurrent in early analyses of fetishistic desire. *Loop my Loop* also mirrors the Victorian convention of using hair as sentimental keepsakes and mourning jewellery, a cherished substitute for the absent body. Chadwick's plans for the work in her notebook included the phrases 'lovelock' and 'lover's knot', likely referring to the sixteenth-century 'lovelock' hairstyle (a plaited tendril of hair tied with a ribbon bow) that male courtiers used to symbolize that they were romantically attached. There was also a fetishistic use of fur in *Glossolalia* (1993), an elaborate sculpture in which an array of fox pelts was stitched together, surrounding a central cone of lambs' tongues cast in bronze. Here, the tongue was made monumental and obscene, a cipher for the male sexual organ. Chadwick's highly allusive use of substitution and dissolution of the corporeal can also be identified in the temptations of *Eat Me* (1991), with its plump, sexually suggestive oyster set in an overlay of buttercups, along with the series *Wreaths to Pleasure* (1992–93). In addition to their cliched associations with romance and the sentimental, Chadwick spoke of hijacking 'the obscenely sexual component' of flowers, mixing them with food items and products from the supermarket, from edible jellies, syrups, jams and purees to toxic chemicals and cleaning detergents, in a perverse appropriation of fertilization.[24]

Towards the end of her career, Chadwick's enduring interests in hybridization and mutability were crystallized in her examination of sexual indeterminacy and inherent bisexuality. The irreverent *Piss Flowers* (1991–92), made in collaboration with her partner, David Notarius, by pissing into flower-shaped moulds placed in the snow of Banff National Park, explored gender ambiguity through an erotic and playful commingling of bodily waste. While Notarius's more diffused stream created the petals, it was Chadwick's concentrated jet of urine that formed the elongated phallic stamens. Her description of the process as a 'penis envy farce' in her corresponding 'Piss Posy' poem might also be construed as a rejection of the Freudian paradigm of Oedipal sexuality, and therefore the castration complex that produces fetishism.[25] Rather, Chadwick can be seen to repeatedly work within the frame of pre-Oedipal sexuality, where the drives are partial and fluid, indeterminate and roving. In his analysis of *Piss Flowers* as being in a Duchampian mode, David Hopkins highlights its 'Rabelaisian spirit', with the body celebrated for its 'metamorphic and polymorphous possibilities'.[26] These possibilities reached their zenith in the production of *Cacao* (1994), the large-scale chocolate fountain made for 'Effluvia', Chadwick's solo exhibition at the Serpentine Gallery, London, in 1994. Oozing, bubbling, gurgling. Excessive, sensual, orgasmic. Fetishistic, exquisite, troubling. 'My libido demanded it,' she maintained, 'a pool of primal matter...in a perpetual state of flux'.[27]

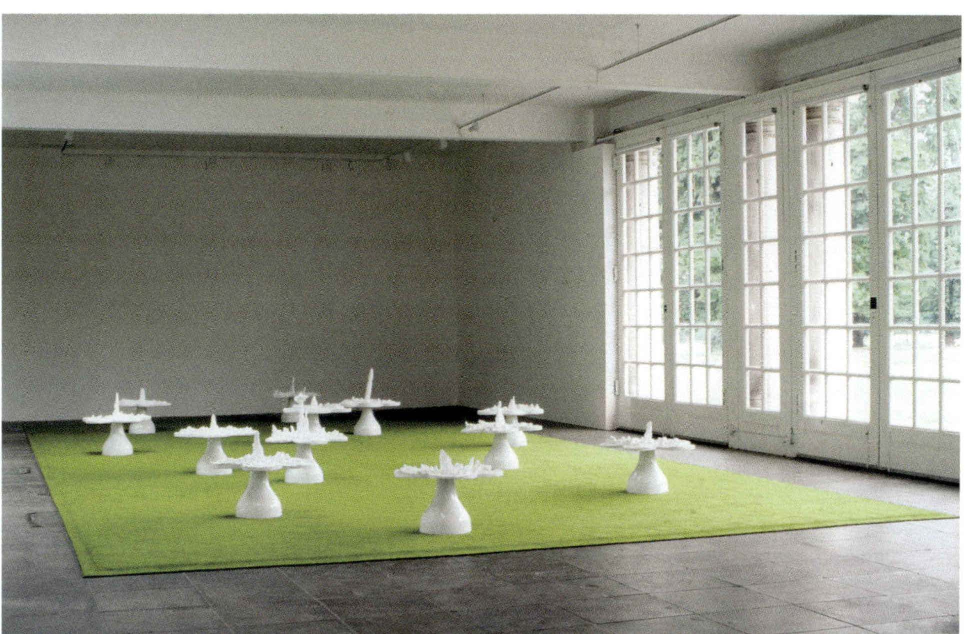

Installation view of *Piss Flowers* in the exhibition 'Helen Chadwick: Effluvia', Serpentine Gallery, London, 1994

Piss Posy

Helen Chadwick

Drink me harder, my delight,
swell to my bursting pretty sluice
And piss a posy
deeper, dear,
here – into my snow white.

rain rogue about my pistil shot
hot juice, as if a bumblebee
would like my petals,
pollinate me

for centre stage's a golden crown,
ring-a-ring a dandelion
molten amber
falls down

calciferous, how Nature's art
does freeze our bold Indifference,
void now volume
daggled plume,
bespattered all around love's spume

locked together, you and I,
bird a hybrid daisy chain,
organs doubled
two a bed and
a floral rhyming wed

Linnaeus what would you say,
how define such wanton play?
vaginal towers
with male skirt,
gender-bending water sport?

each other's measure wear
bared inside-up
contrariwise,
as if chromosome could dare
to host such inverse pleasures, squared

Come sit on me, my mandrill's arse
cast priapic,
former fold,
suck my penis envy farce
like old Venus de Lespugue.

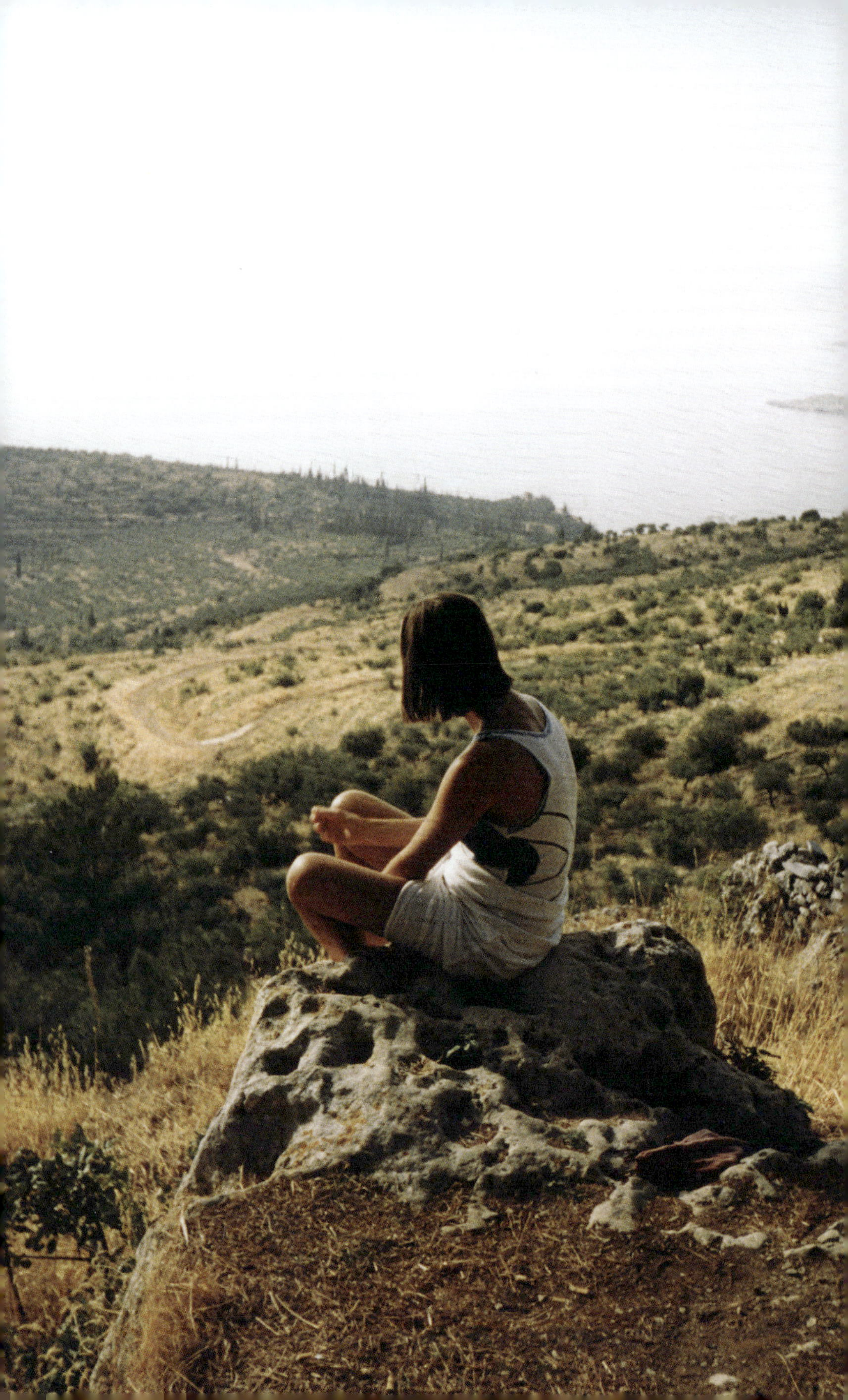

CHAPTER 3

Let the Monuments be Eroticized

Maria Christoforidou

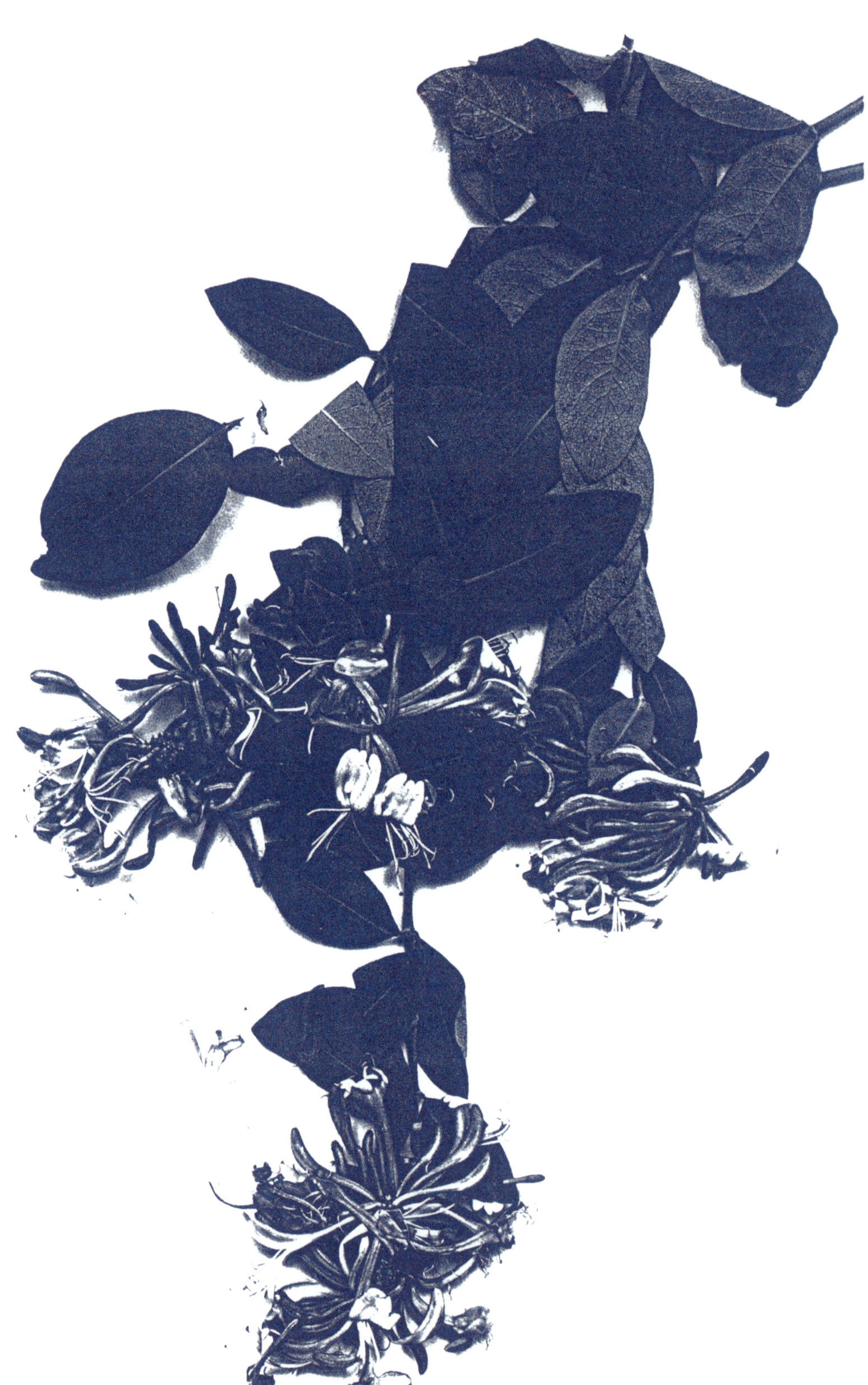

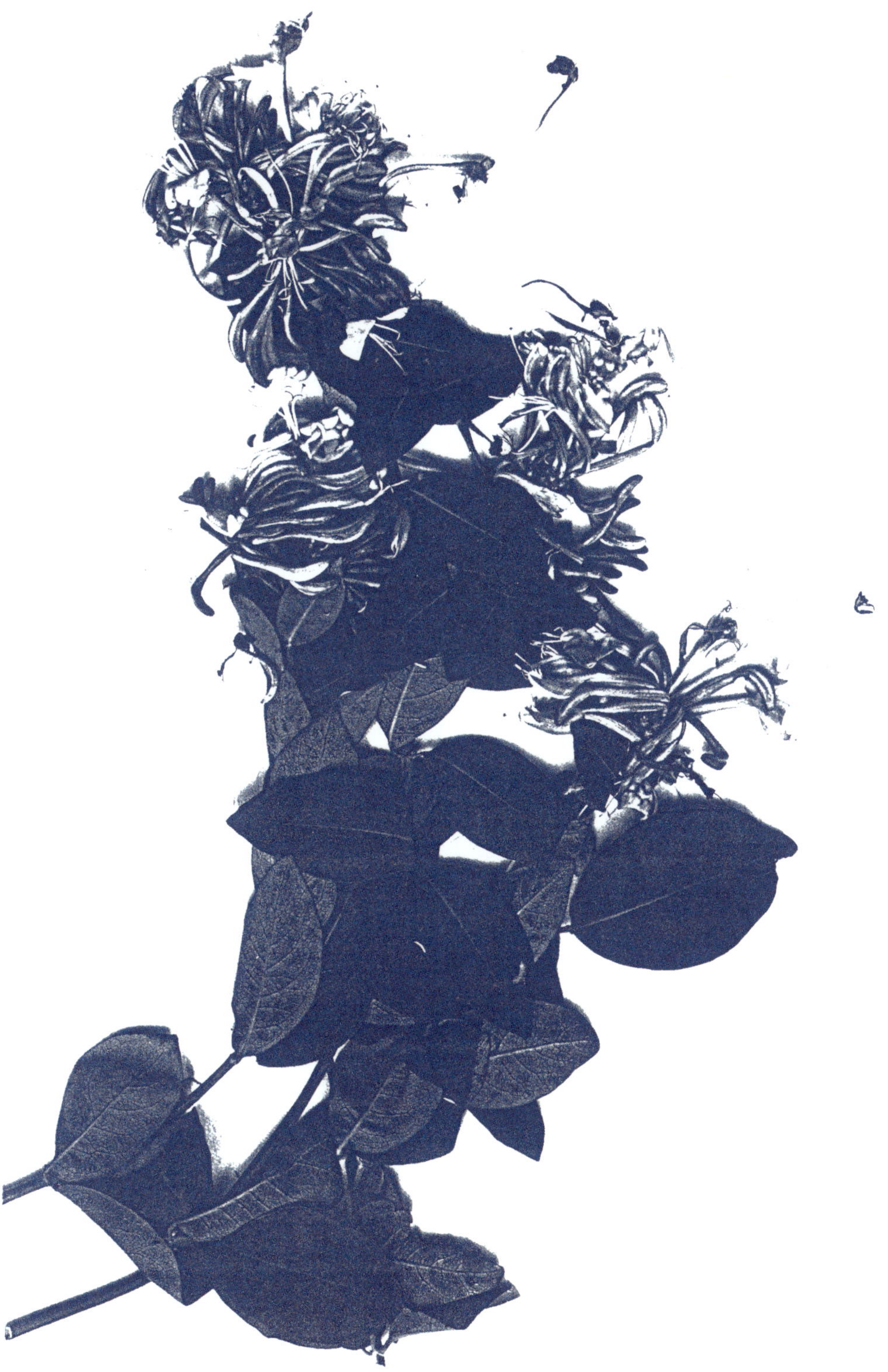

Test prints of honeysuckle as part of the work *The Oval Court,* 1984–86

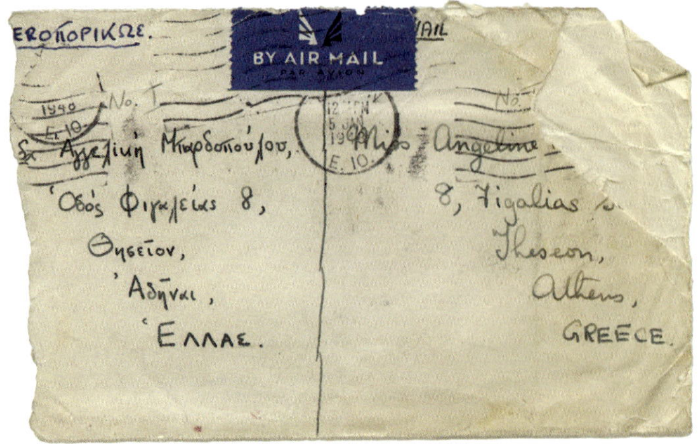

3.

When we reached the boat there was a long, high ladder to climb up. I had those two kit-bags (very heavy), a small pack and my overcoat and it nearly broke my back. There were many soldiers going home and so we found it very crowded inside; so much so that Sergeants have to sleep sit and eat with the soldiers. We sleep in hammocks tied to the ceiling, these things: and overlapping like this: so you can guess that it is pretty hot at night. However, this is a good boat and it is fast. It left Piraeus at 7 p.m. last night, will stay a few hours at Malta and Gibralta, and will probably arrive at Southampton on the 30th or 31st. She can travel 500 miles (700 Kilometres) in 24 hours.

Last night, there was a piano on the upper deck so we had some Xmas carol singing; the same carols that we sang together in Church last Sunday

ABOVE **Letter from William Chadwick to Miss Aggeliki Barthopoulou, 1948**

PAGE 164 **Helen Chadwick in Platsa, Greece, summer of 1995**

1
Opening

It's 1948, in Athens Miss Aggeliki Barthopoulou receives a letter from William Chadwick. He signs the letter Bill, and below, an inordinate number of kisses. Miss Barthopoulou tears it open, reads it and keeps it forever. Mr Chadwick describes a journey on ship. He pens a tiny drawing of hammocks on the lower deck packed tightly like the scales of a fish. Many years later a similar decoration appears on wavy Ionian columns beneath their daughter's lachrymose face.

It's 1997, the aspiring mystic/art student I am is obsessed with *Loop my Loop* (1991–92). I write in unbroken streams of consciousness – 'yes, the erotic union of external and internal, dead and alive, growing and static, always already erotic, she eaten by worms, she eating intestines, hallucination and truth, the inside of the body as pearly and sacred as the bottom of the sea'. I am pleased to learn she is half Athenian; I hold on to that, I am too. I don't look it. I am unaware of her recent and sudden departure.

It's 2024, sitting on the steps of the National Archaeological Museum in Athens *stress eating cherries* I think about Helen Chadwick's connection to a place called by most, Greece. It occurs to me (again) that *we* in 'Greece' don't call ourselves Greek, we say Ellinides/Ellines/Ellas, without the H of Latinization.[1] The Homeric epics refer to different tribes occupying this curly patch of the Mediterranean.[2] One tribe in Thessaly is called Ellines. The meaning assigned to Elenos (masc.) / Elenē (fem.) is 'the bright one', or torch, light, shining, warming. Or burning. Where did the H come from? *That last cherry was very sour.* Where does Helen come from? From a spark of moonlight, from a drop of sun. Anyway, let's accept the H and let's call this nationality Hellenic. The connection between the proper nouns, Helen and Hellenic is undeniable. *This Helen is incandescent in every photo*. Helen in Hellenic tragedies is 'the face that launched a thousand ships', wife of Menelaus, mistress of Paris, but who was her mother? It was Leda, who was 'seduced' by Zeus in the form of a swan. Leda bore Helen and Polydeuces, children of Zeus.[3] That Helen, half immortal, hatched from an egg.[4]

It's 1925, the artist Claude Cahun (1894–1954) writes *Heroines*,[5] where she reimagines the lives of fifteen female figures from biblical history, classical mythology and fairy tales; the Virgin Mary, Sappho, Cinderella and more. Cahun gives a vituperative version of their stories and astute unforgiving appellations as titles – 'Penelope the Irresolute', 'Eve the Too Credulous', 'Helen the Rebel'. This Helen learns how to be beautiful by thinking of nothing at all, and everyone believes her beauty.

Fortified by this rebellious half-ness, light hatching from an egg, I look for evidence of Hellas in the work of Helen Chadwick. Hellas not only as a geographic region but also as a vast mythic area emitting an endless chain of semiosis. Hellas as a concept. The Hellenic is an ermaphrodite[6] nymph running through the work disturbing *everyone* with the help of Eros. Looking for the Hellenic, we cross paths with tenets, cycles, relations, actions and relevancies that point toward the ritual of a mystic. A mystic, she who believes spiritual apprehension of truths is beyond the intellect and she who aims to attain absorption into the Deity. *Helen the Mystic.*

The Hellenic comes to us ancient, Dionysian full of Venus, it comes religious, Orthodox dressed in black, with a cross, an egg, a triangle. The Hellenic in its diaspora[7] becomes a portal and a voracious appetite for other cultures, it comes in the summer. The Hellenic bears medieval astrology, resplendent rococo. The Hellenic is recalcitrant. The Hellenic desires. The Hellenic speaks with its hands.

It's 1992, in Mexico Helen Chadwick is searching for Frida Kahlo,[8] she talks to her students, friends, her hands relish the squelching of cut fruit while making a *tableau vivant* in tribute to Kahlo's still lifes. A full circle, life, stillness, life.

It's 2024, I'm on a pilgrimage to the archive where the papery remains of the artist are held – 100 boxes, Henry Moore Institute, Leeds. Looking for the Hellenic in Helen, looking for her source of power, looking for the relevance to me, a Zambian Hellenic, diasporic, mixed heritage, double consciousness, private eye. The overall effect of the visit is a communion with the erotic as described by Audre Lorde: 'The erotic is a resource within each of us that lies in a deeply female and spiritual plane, firmly rooted in the power of our unexpressed or unrecognized feeling.'[9] Lorde names the erotic as a 'nursemaid of our deepest knowledge' and 'a lens through which we scrutinize all aspects of our existence'.[10] I get to know Chadwick and Lorde decades after their death. In my imagination we become stalwart friends.

2

The hand as symbol of Hellenic culture

What does it mean to be Hellenic? One thing it can mean is to boast an affinity with the Hellenic language. Parallel to the philosophical and medical, Hellenic is a gestural language. In formal recordings, Chadwick, with a BBC English accent, doesn't sound Hellenic - however in her work she speaks with her hands like any Hellenic subject. The Hellenic is two fingers crossed behind your back, any allegiance is nulled. It is a rolled r in your mother's accent; when your mother has an accent, perfect singularity departs through the window, you are always both, or 'neither/nor'.[11] The Hellenic is a portal that allows an exit from the unbending freeway of a monolithic identity.

The wise (or desperate) caught in the doublings of a diasporic existence, embrace this imperfect multiplicity. Helen Chadwick in her text *Lines that Sever, Bind* expresses this multiplicity referring to her mother's birthplace: 'Let the monuments be eroticised and the very gender of the city called into question. Athens, appropriated by western civilisation to legitimise, its own structures, is always offered up as our cradle. But the model preferred is masculine, its female body politic, its African and archaic roots denied.'[12] Let, Call, Question...gender, civilization, roots, body and other queer-facing thoughts - this is an incantation.

○

Noumera/Noumena

In and around Chadwick's two prominent installations *Ego Geometria Sum* (1983) and *The Oval Court* (1984-86), and in the introverted *One Flesh* (1985) and *Lofos Nymphon* (1987), we find thousands of hands, doing 'bits', and none of them showing guilt. As examples accrue, the conspicuous attention lent to the hand points upwards to Chadwick's third-year dissertation – *The hand as a symbol in medieval art* (1973). We hold on to etymology and move through gesture:

> *The sister science to chiromancy (palmistry) is that of chironomy, the art of gesticulation. The heroic ages of Greece, invented gestures for manual numeration, a complex system of positions, indicating figures up to 90, with the fingers of the left hand, and into the thousands with the right hand. In this system design for 30 made with the left hand in number lore is associated with marriage, and is that is nicknamed la nozze...*[13]

La nozze...a gesture that launches 1,000 thoughts.

The scale of elements in *The Oval Court* is determined by Chadwick's own body, the central pool related to the proportions of her hand, and the five golden spheres proportionate to the size of Chadwick's thumb and fingertips.[14]

In the preparatory drawings of *Ego Geometria Sum*, we see how the measurements of the Platonic solids correspond to the average

Helen Chadwick's traced drawings from her dissertation, 'The Hand as a Symbol in Medieval Art', 1973

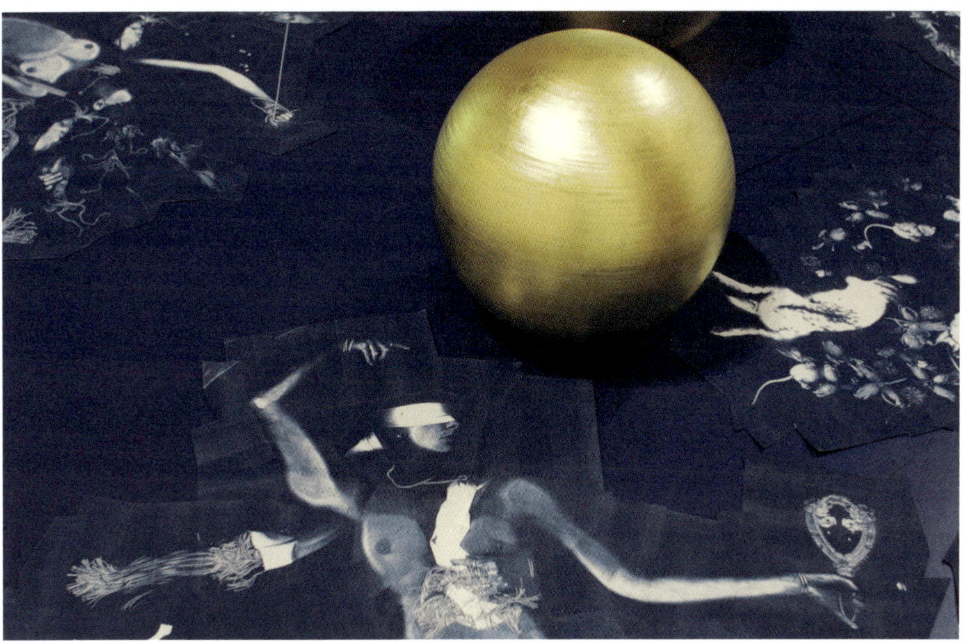

size of a child of the respective age on the national child-measurement percentile scale. In her copy of Susan Griffith's book *Woman and Nature* (held in the Chadwick Library at the Henry Moore Institute), Chadwick has underlined the following lines: 'The cause of the universe lies in mathematical harmony which exists in the mind of the creator.'[15]

The appearance of Hellenic mathematical order often heralds Apollonian reason, perfection, cold hard control, but this is...warmer. The attention to numbers narrates the sequencing of a mystic, a numerologist creator who weighs up her body against 'the cause of the universe'. Not in the mind but in her growing body. Mathematical harmony is characteristic to Chadwick, her attention to numbers carefully and affectionately applies the body to the cosmos.

More underlined Griffith: 'And it is decided that although the celestial substance is *mutable*, yet immutable laws govern all *mutability*, and that the invariability of God's will can be deduced from the perfection of His laws which rule the natural world.'[16]

Contrary to this precept, Chadwick's process in *Ego Geometria Sum* inserts bodily mutability to the stable perfection of the Platonic

Helen Chadwick, *The Oval Court*, 1984–86 (detail)

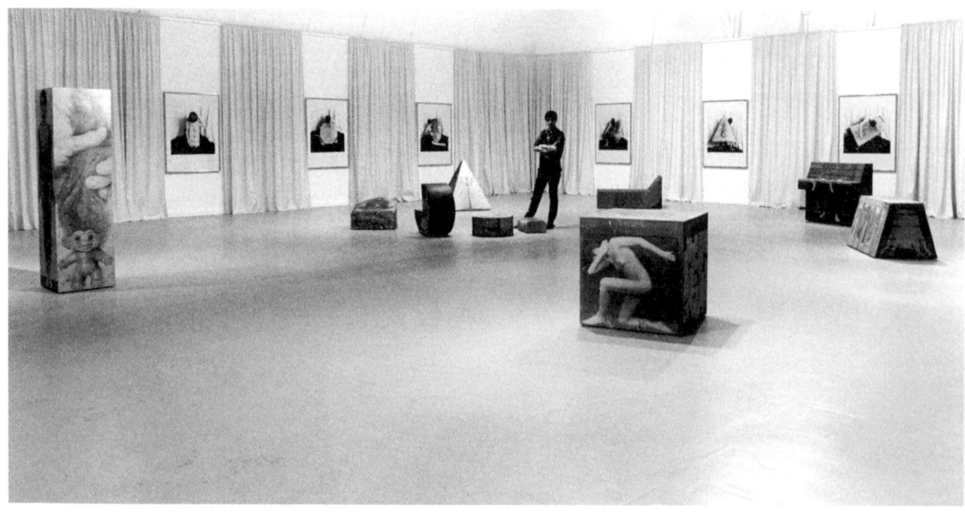

solids, softness of flesh on the hardness of object. This transforms stable geometric formula into invocation, a brazen attempt to investigate the structure of the universe through the body.

Some words are simple, direct, then there are words like infinite monuments that never give up. There, their walls growing taller, here their moats deepening. I am such a word, thousands of millions of atoms make a single I.

In some of her notes we hear Chadwick declare her singular multiplicity in the universal order: 'I am a particle. Cannot present myself as a thing or an image, but only in the dynamic of space. I am a specific amount of something that comes in bits passing through, a particle which is an intermediate state in a network of interactions.'[17]

Seeing the hand write *Hele...*on the side of *Ego Geometria Sum*'s solid cube, we move from the anonymous to the eponymous, everyone and one. This one is named, but not quite. There is a suggestion but no certainty. *Ego Geometria Sum* unfolds the singular *ego* in a 'network of iterations in a dynamic of space'. Chadwick's wordplay in the title unties Descartes's dictum *cogito, ergo sum*[18] and flows from the *I*, thinking its existence, to dexterous hands feeling their way in alignment with a divine realm of

Helen Chadwick, *Ego Geometria Sum*, 1983. Installed at Aspex Gallery, Portsmouth, 1984

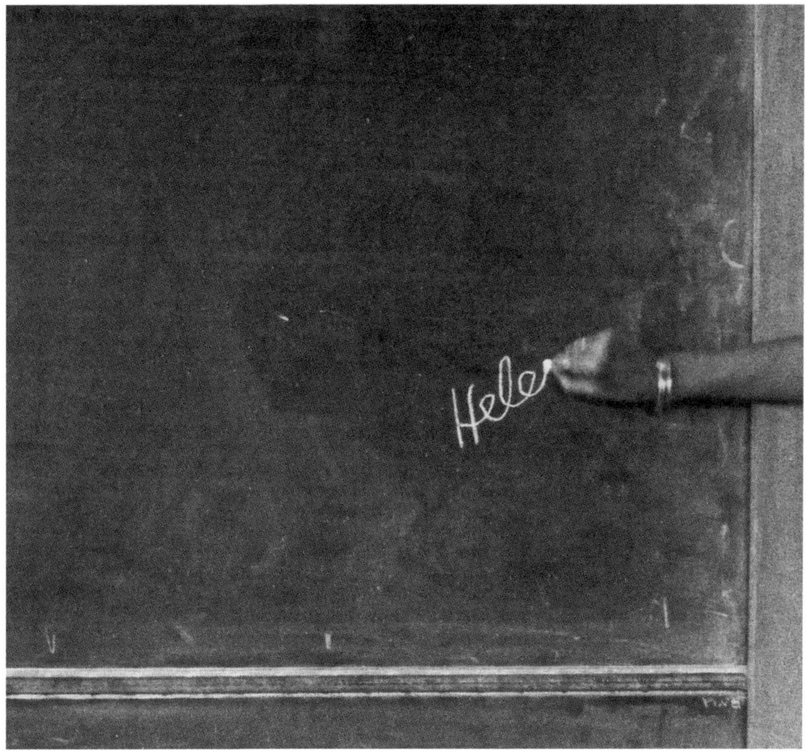

existence, holding on to looped links the mind might be too slow for. The other iterations of *Ego Geometria Sum*, *The Labours* (1983-84) and *The Juggler's Table* (1984) bring us closer to a mystic sleight of hand with a nod to a tarot card, The Magician, I: 'it is like the original point from which the whole universe emerges...an androgynous individual playing with light and shadow, juggling from the unconscious to the super conscious'.[19] Helen the Mystic, who plays with all the inexhaustible bits and specific amounts available to her.

Orthodoxia

I read, in the meticulous script of Chadwick's dissertation, about *Dextera Domini*, Latin for right hand of the Lord. A hand appearing in the sky,

Detail of the inscription 'hele' on the side of Helen Chadwick's *Ego Geometria Sum IX: High School – Age 13 Years*, 1983

often surrounded by a cloud, symbolizes God, who points to the figures of a religious scene. *The hand does not imply gender, but we know.* The illustrations of the dissertation are traced by hand from books, themselves divine. This text is a codex of the elements that take root in Chadwick's practice, then bloom, then fruit, then return to seed. A minute hand, a broach, pinned onto Helen Chadwick's chest, points beyond her face to the sky. She writes, 'the hand more important than the face'.[20] She writes the hand 'is not secondary to language but an accompaniment'.[21] She writes apart from being a 'supplement to language', the hands create their own vocabulary of gestures. She writes how a gesture combined with an object held in the hand 'complements the quality of this gesture and amplifies it's supposed meaning'.[22] *Listen to the hands.*

In the archive there are hundreds of photocopies of Chadwick's hands testing various hand positions for the twelve figures, seasons, star signs, scenes, poems in *The Oval Court*, each an allegory to slowly sink in. Chadwick years after her dissertation still meditates on 'the absorption of pagan images into Christianity'.[23]

Christian saints of the Hellenic Orthodox Church, perhaps evolving from yogic mudras, piously position their hands to denote different sentiments and virtues. An open palm is the absence of evil, an index finger pointing to the sky - pay attention, Jesus joins the ring finger with the thumb to signify a sermon, two hands crossed at the chest of the saint signify bearing a test of faith. In Chadwick's iconography the meaning of gesture is a matter of *hermeneutic* work for the viewer. Chadwick alerts us to the fact that there is 'a demand to give something of yourself when you look at an artwork...it's not easy or quick'.[24]

Each figure in *The Oval Court* has at least three hands pinching, pulling, stroking, choking, squeezing, releasing handfuls of maggots, simultaneously. In the wheat-holding, double-headed figure, we can see the *corna* (horns): 'a Roman protective gesture to ward off the curse of the evil eye. The index and the little finger jab downwards as though to banish the evil into the earth.'[25] *Into the earth.*

The Oval Court is a movable feast where hands show us what is precious, perform important acts of exorcism or reunion. Chadwick's study taught her a vocabulary of symbolic gestures that reveal the nature

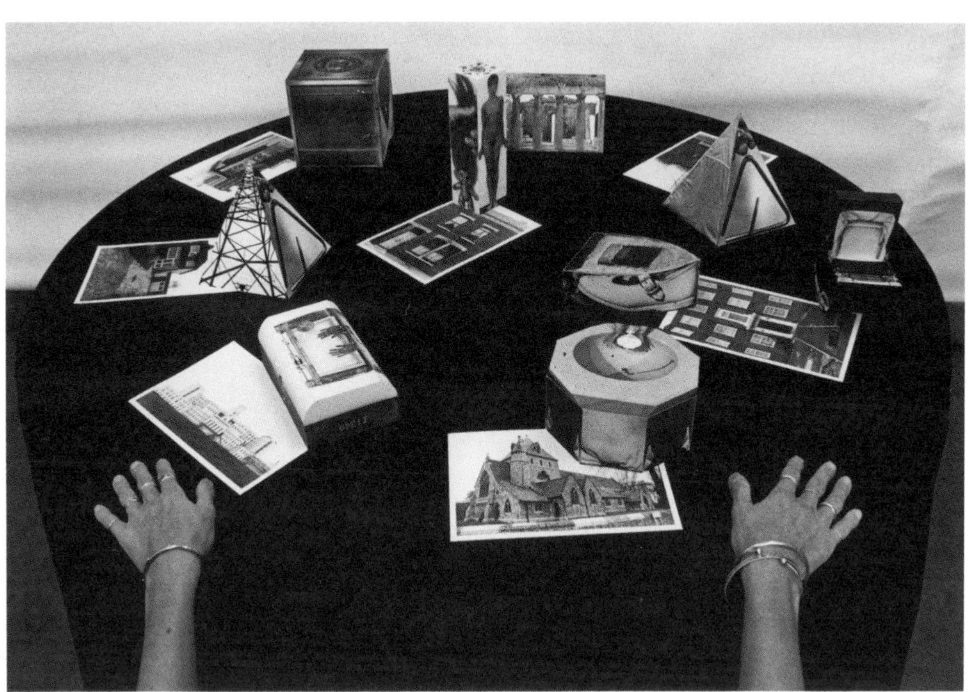

Helen Chadwick, *The Jugglers Table*, 1984. Photographs on table employing preparatory material for *Ego Geometria Sum*, 1983; 10 maquettes: 50 × 50 × 50 cm (19$\frac{3}{4}$ × 19$\frac{3}{4}$ × 19$\frac{3}{4}$ in.)

that pervades inner experience.[26] As the hands point to something outside the normative order of things, looking at the work summons a numinous experience. In mysticism the initiate's task is to be attentive, to empty and allow inner illumination. No linguistic divisions, no adjectives, no nouns, no syntax, only one verb - touch. Give what it asks for. We feel with your eyes, we imagine the touch. This deferral of feeling creates desire. 'A territory for desire.'[27]

O

Since visiting the archive and opening an envelope of photos labelled *Lesvos* - my father's birthplace and home of all my childhood summers - I've been thinking about Sappho:

> *eros dēute m'o lisimelis doni,*
> *glikipikron amachanon orpeton*[28]
> *Eros the solvent of limbs (now again) shakes me*
> *Sweetbitter undefeated who slithers in*[29]

In *If Not, Winter*, a meditation on Sappho's poetic fragments, Anne Carson translates the word *amachanon* as 'unmanageable', relating it to the word *machan*, meaning 'device instrument, technique'. Eros is a creature against whom no technology avails.[30]

Eros, infant god of sensual love, is a fundamental principle of the universe that through desire moves us, an instinct opposite to death (Thanatos). Nevertheless, the technologies of both Eros and Thanatos dissolve our limbs.

Chadwick lays on the magician's table, a life and death switch. *The Oval Court* summons erotic dissolution and does not deny us Mother Earth imagery, but these images are firmly fixed in the artifice of technological repetition, a *nekri fisi* (dead nature/still life). On the other hand, a few feet away, the rotting *Carcass* in its glass coffin, nine months in the making, is fizzing with fertile possibility.

Sappho uses the word *dēute* (now again) after Eros. Carson pays special attention to this temporal adverb of repetition. The composition

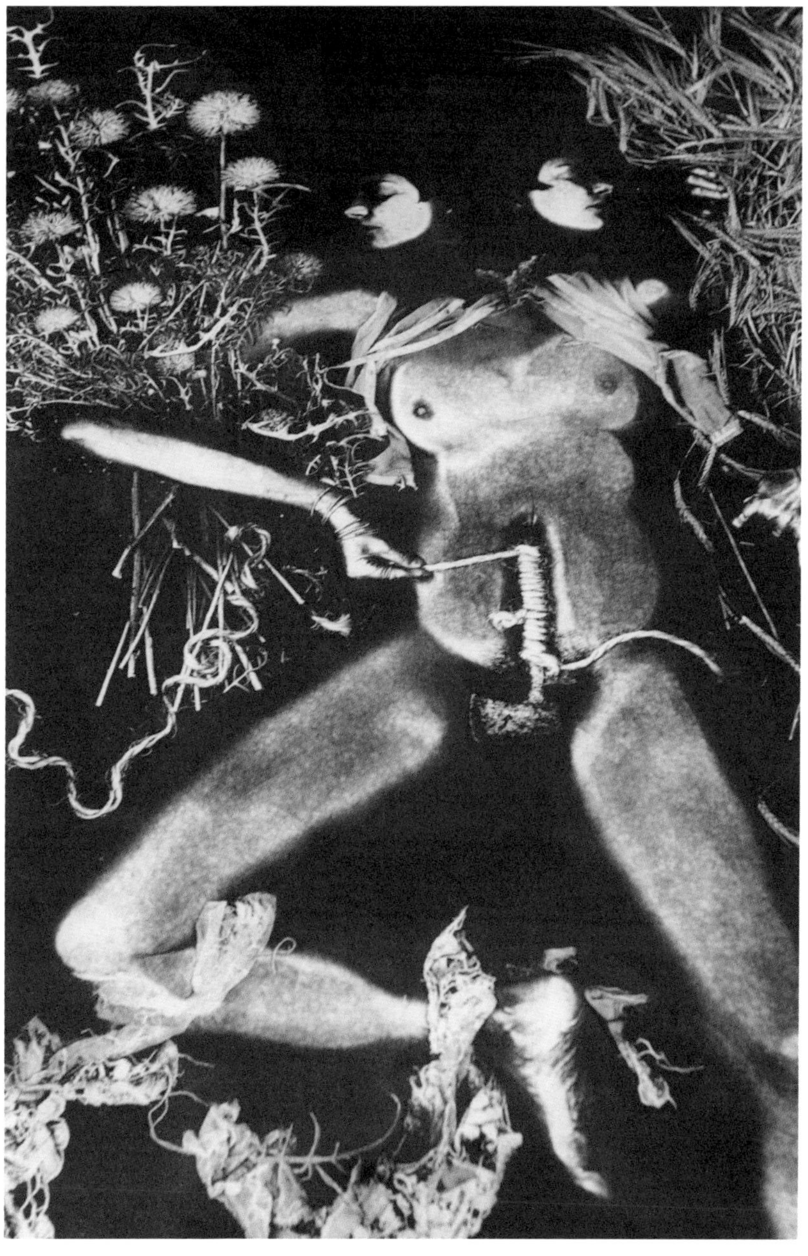

Helen Chadwick, *The Oval Court*, 1984–86 (detail)

of the word brings the present moment and a series of past moments together, meaning 'not for the first time', denoting the cyclical patterns of erotic experience.[31] The photocopy, purposefully a thing of lesser value,[32] is a 'now again'. Its mechanical multiplication nominates an erotic act of abundance, manipulating, reproducing, melting the limbs among flora, fauna, objects, stirred by the in turns violent and tender slithering. The photocopier spoke to Chadwick in an advert on the London Underground and she used it to 'have all the power at my disposal'.[33] This machinic independence brings out the sculptural aspect of her photographic practice, 'the idea of photography as potentially a three-dimensional medium.'[34] The limbs are repeated to manufacture the image like any building. The self-built, sculpted or demolished with mythic tools powered by electrical currents. So, then we enter the mechanically reproduced images as buildings, institutions to educate us in emotional and sensual responses behind the seeing, to learn 'a seeing that encourages feeling'.[35]

The Oval Court asks us to witness the aim of a mystical ceremony, the stepping into helplessness against the forces of nature, the liberation into joyous abandonment. In its dissolution and multiplication of limbs, the figures and their associates dance in the simultaneously primordial and technological blue.

What do you remember? I remember quite clearly her, taking off her clothes and climbing onto the photocopier, her naked derrière pressed against the cold glass. I remember her bending at the waist over the machine, pressing her face against the plate, arranging the cross again around her neck to be visible. Her face pinched, holding her breath under imaginary water, the cross and chain float, a stealthy light captures it and spits it out.

The photocopies are all blue, maybe by chance, but for us Hellenics, in blue we can't help but feel the colour chosen for the flag of the newly nascent Hellenic nation in 1822. Blue for the sea and freedom, white for death and waves.

many barefoot thoughts go astray in some unattainable fluid

A traced image from the dissertation, the pharaoh (A)Khuenaten receives a blessing from the sun, rays like many hands.[36] Chadwick writes how for prehistoric people, the hand was seen as 'a talisman against the evil eye'.[37] In her somewhat mysterious work *The Wall of the City of Palms*, Chadwick's photocopied left and right palms are repeated to create a brick-wall pattern in pale brown.[38] With elastic mental agility we are presented with another 'neither/nor'. The hand, signifier of will and activity, is used as a building block. Builder and Brick. In repetition the hand is restored to the monumental proportions of *Dextera Domini*. The artwork as a grand gesture of protection.

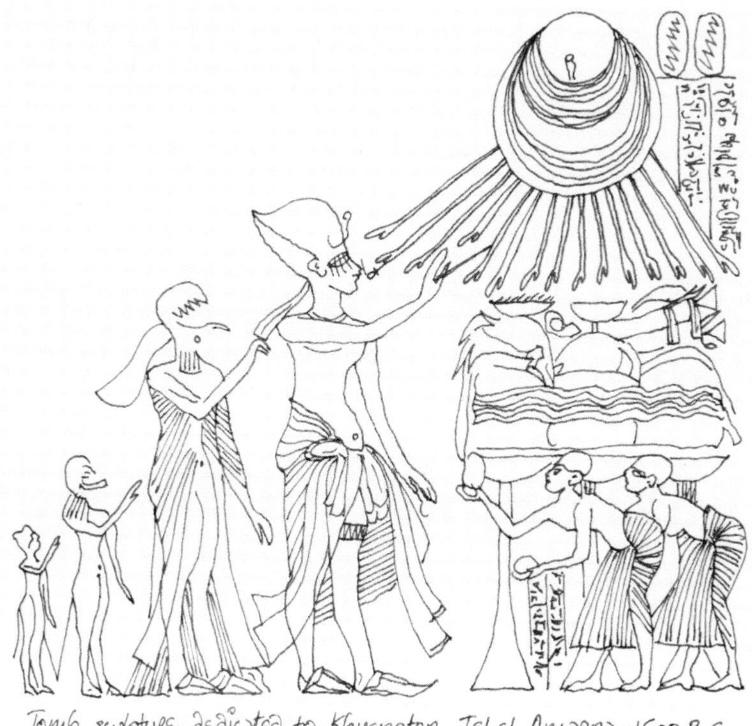

Helen Chadwick's traced drawing of Pharod A-Khuenaten from her dissertation, 'The Hand as a Symbol in Medieval Art', 1973

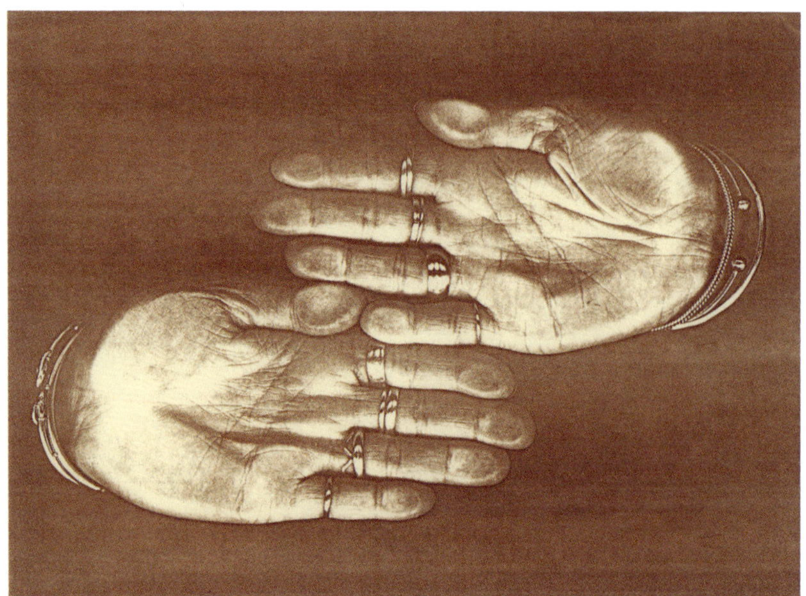

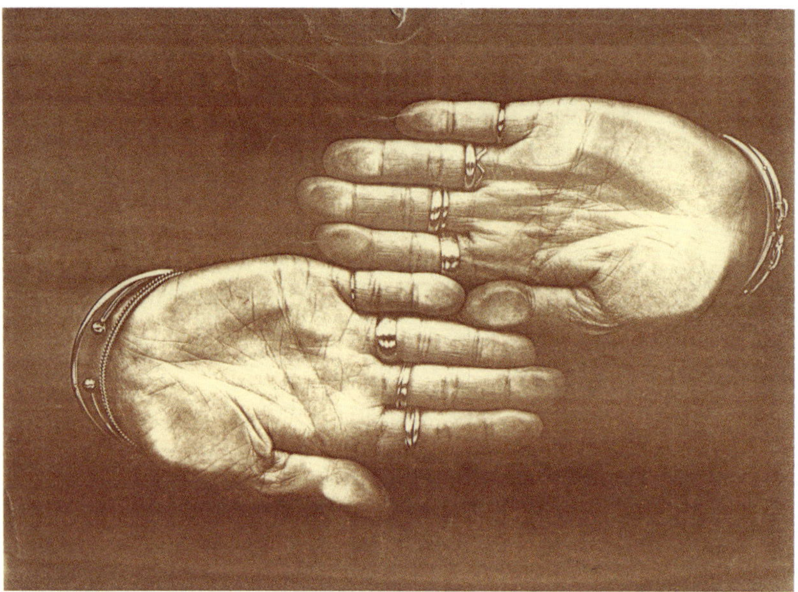

ABOVE AND OPPOSITE **Helen Chadwick, *The Wall of the City of Palms*, n.d.**
Photocopies, dimensions unknown

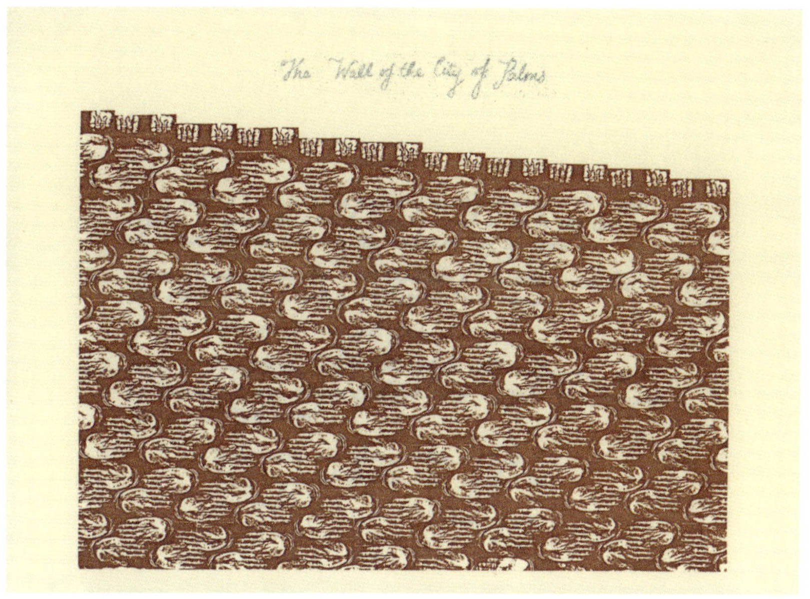

The repetition of hands has a cascade of consequences. In an active disruption of visible reality, repetition reveals an alternative temporality and narrative. The acquisitive hands of *The Oval Court* herald a desire to appropriate, to unite with the all the variegated elements of life - the face cries at the loss of this paradise. Observe a union, as Lorde encourages in *Uses of the Erotic* between the spiritual (psychic and emotional) to the political, to create the erotic 'poetic revolutionary'.[39] Trying to attain a spiritual union with the cosmos, the mystic can inadvertently embody a rebel. Rococo - florid proliferation, wild excess and golden balls - is also a rolling revolution in its own time against the simplification of Catholicism and within the minimalist tendencies of the 1980s art world.[40]

Measured actions bring balance to protect against hybrids of reasonable minds and evil eyes. The hands tell another story that subverts pious Christian denial and singularity of identity, be it human or divine. The hands tear through and wipe clean what Ursula K. Le Guin describes as 'the killer story': 'It sometimes seems that, that story is approaching its end. Lest there be no more telling of stories at all, some of us out here in the wild oats, amid the alien corn, think we'd better start telling another one, which maybe people can go on with when the old one's finished.

Maybe.'[41] Le Guin wisely reminds that the story is not an untold one. Helen the Mystic pays attention to quiet voices and bodily knowledges, narrates 'the life story': 'People have been telling the life story for ages, in all sorts of words and ways. Myths of creation and transformation, trickster stories, folktales, jokes, novels.'[42]

We stand above a lake of *apocalypse* (unveiling). Cosmogony takes many hands. An awakening of social imagination to possibility requires many influences. Punk, Orthodoxy, rococo whisper past the rebellion of many hands, Eros allows the hands to do other work on another sphere of sensual perception. The hands protect, undo and build, undo and build, dissolve, bond, protect, all at the same time. And thus, in kinaesthetic empathy,[43] they loosen *our* own limbs. They move, we move, time dissolves, every now connects to every past and future now, polylingual, polydimensional, polysynchronous, polyamorous.

3

Internal monuments, the mother's body

Those moments that it takes over, and you hadn't meant it to go that way or sound that way and you hadn't meant to feel that way, those are the moments we pray for, and we arrive at that place where we know each other and we just talk about this and that and look at photos, then the story comes out whole, not without pain or rushes, it feels like a birth.

Within *Ego Geometria Sum* and *The Oval Court* there are multiple visible and felt texts countervailing each other. Taking it in turns to be engine and fuel. Tina M. Campt, in her book *Listening to Images* (2017), investigates historically dismissed photographs of the Black diaspora and invites us to 'use our sensory register 'to 'listen to' rather than simply 'look at' images', this 'is a conscious decision to challenge the equation of vision with knowledge'.[44] Campt names an 'exquisitely articulate modality of quiet' - a sublimely expressive unsayability that exceeds both words, as well as what we associate with sound and utterance'.[45] The family photographs of the archive are an equal force to the artwork and operate in this lower sonic register. To tune in to the lower frequency we are quiet and we feel. A lot has been said about Chadwick's refusal of sight. The hand as instrument of speech is fluent in 'unsayability', giving an honest look at the inner and outer world beyond vision or sound. Here in the lower frequencies of touching and being touched, Chadwick honours birth, biology and mother.

A triangular wigwam, a small child sits at the entrance, either side a man and a woman, like many other guardians of ancient pyramids. In the photographic silent, the monumental vibrations are palpable.

○

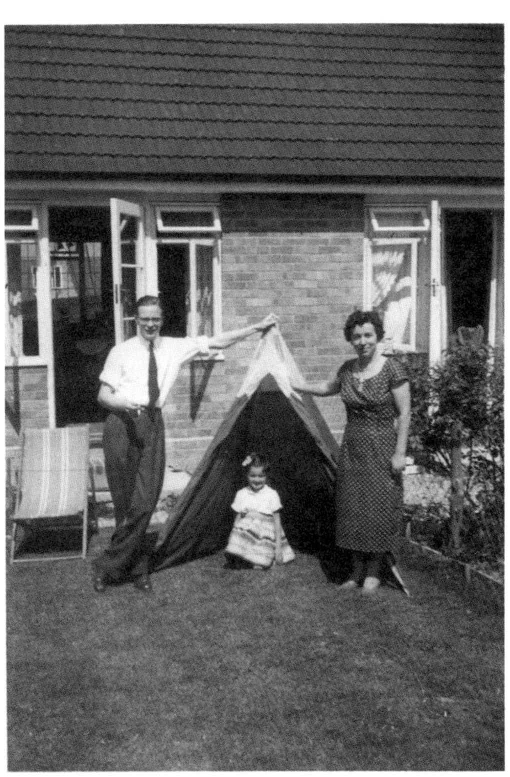

Childhood photograph of Helen Chadwick with her parents, *c.* 1958

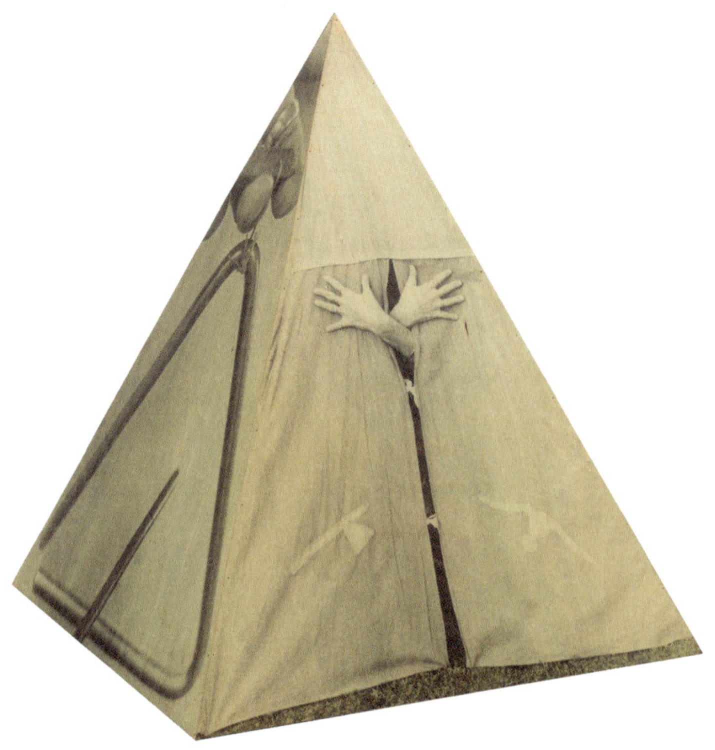

Jacques Derrida once described the book as 'a portable pyramid'.[46] From stone to papyrus to page, the monument is there to be read. In *Ego Geometria Sum* we read the pyramid (wigwam, 5 years) as a longing for protection. Two resolute adult hands emerge out of the dome of childhood. The hands transform the tent into a hidden ceremonial figure. Whoever is inside can see us behind the thin white fabric, they silently project their hands. The pyramid is a mask, 'the monument is eroticized' as a body animates its insides, the way a hand animates the cloth body of a puppet. However, this puppetry runs in reverse; everything is hidden apart from the hands. Either side of the entrance to *Ego Geometria Sum*'s pyramid, two symbols from the 'wild west' resurrect Minoan symbology, a bull and an axe. What are the hands saying? Fingers stretched open, crossed at the wrists. The hands perhaps say 'Stop, I resist, I become monument, I protect my heart,' or 'I carry the past as a feat of repentance.'[47]

Helen Chadwick, *Ego Geometria Sum V: Wigwam – 5 Years*, 1983.
Photographic emulsion on plywood, 89 × 79 × 79 cm (35 1/8 × 31 1/8 × 31 1/8 in.)

On the other face of the pyramid, a hand curls two fingers around a bit of wood that holds a wire, from which a musical triangle is suspended. A golden ring around one finger says 'Helen'. I recognized this instrument from my Hellenic childhood, going from door to door in the neighbourhood on the twenty-fourth of every December, announcing the birth of Christ for a few coins. We can see the tip of the metal 'beater' striking the triangle. The visual doubling, triangle in a triangle, echoes and inspires an engagement with inaudible vibrations. Sinking in lower frequencies helps us interact with Chadwick's work, eyes are not enough. We are transported, through an imaginary metallic sound, to a seminal day for most European children.

Here we find tenderly held Hellenic traditions within a British childhood, we imagine the quotidian celebration of the divine in another diasporic community with its own troubled history. The hand grows as a symbol of the psychological weight of small things: the diasporic social body, indeed spread like seeds, holds on to a root still tapped in the mother land.

The other face of the pyramid is crisscrossed by a triangular technological monument, a pylon you come across at the top of a mountain, its malevolent electrical hum as terrifying as Zeus.

○

This ritual starts with the hands over the incubator, that artificial womb, her thirty-year-old body curled up within it. Manifesting multiple facets of the history of one body, not a splintering, only a returning. Not just an image but an act, doing it and watching yourself doing it, awake, cohabit, seek haptic knowledge of your birth – *will she be possessed by the spirit of her infant self?* Lie here and call forth biological memory, how the cells divided, the transparent skin thickened, kept the light. What secrets lie in the double helix? Why so small? Why the hands? Why the gold? Revisiting her premature birth, I now see bathed in tragic irony the low, symmetrical hum of her premature death.

○

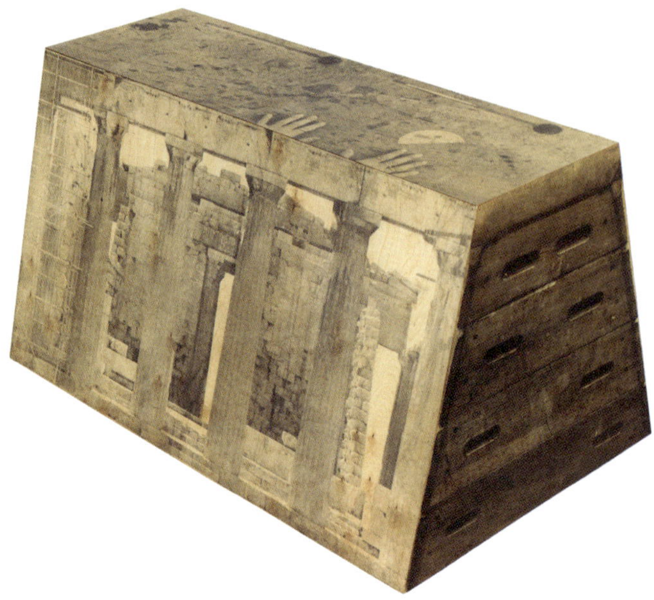

Here in this body are the sacred rivers: here are the sun and moon, as well as all the pilgrimage places. I have not encountered another temple as blissful as my own body.[48]

On the gym vault (horse, 11 years) we see the columns of the Athenian Parthenon sprout a pair of ringed hands that hold on to a school desk for dear life. The body is transformed into the temple of the golden age of Pericles. In 'the progressive angularities of growing up' there is the Hellenic.[49] Stability or immobility? Neither/nor. Helen Chadwick's work creates its audience, the Hellenic diasporic people, the women dreaming of a new story for their bodies, their predicaments. Sliding from past to present and back again, traversing synchronous timelines and modalities of gain and loss.

Her nudity is a matter of practicality in this series of jumps, entrances and exits. Like any well-considered time traveller, she strips down to her skin, to enter a temporal warp that fabric molecules could not withstand. In most fiction, time travellers avoid encountering themselves so as to not disturb the space-time continuum. Not Helen Chadwick, she jumps

Helen Chadwick, *Ego Geometria Sum VIII: Horse – 11 Years*, 1983. Photographic emulsion on plywood, 57.5 × 101.9 × 61.9 cm (22 5/8 × 40 1/8 × 24 3/8 in.)

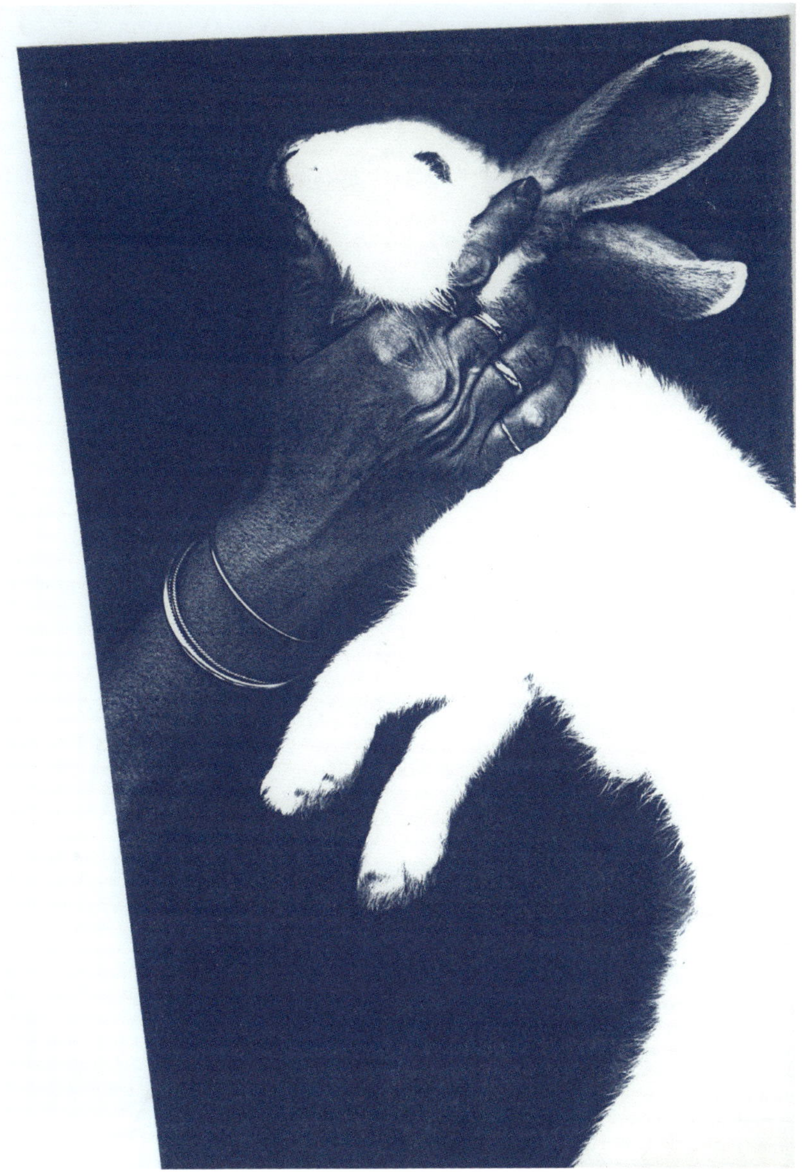

Helen Chadwick, *The Oval Court*, 1984–86 (detail)

straight into herself in this ghost kingdom, cherishing the Hellenic as a holiday, a monument, a faith. The cross glowing above a white M&S bra speaks with persistent attention to Hellenic Orthodox customs and the divine within everyday life. The Hellenic is literally the cross around her neck, and it is burning hot, I am sure of it.

I drink celery juice and lime water. Foxglove and bluebell, pharmakon, cure and poison. Neither/nor. Let all shackles be loosened, let all hands be free.

Upon seeing the hand, rings and all, around the neck of the rabbit, a Hellenic phrase slides out of the cold mud of memory. *Pnigi to kouneli* (choking the rabbit): old fashioned and not so common, this phrase is used to refer to being sexually promiscuous with disturbing regularity. The hand could be benign, but the rabbit's blind upward gaze says it's not. The hand is evidence of forces unseen that tear us apart. Like Eros. Is it unkind? In patriarchal industrialized militarized societies with rigid hyperarchies that sever us from our birthright of desire, here, knowing the cyclical fullness of Eros's blade, knowing the body in life and death, exploring its viscera, here it can be a kindness.

○

The air is different on the hill of nymphs. Do myths lie? Do hills lie?

The Hellenic in the works of Chadwick can be sought at its origin, her mother. Another monument, the mother's body unfastened by metaphors and symbols. The egg, the womb, the birth, the Holy Mary. In *Lofos Nymphon* there are several eggs. In one, Helen Chadwick kneels and hugs her mother, Aggeliki Chadwick nee Barthopoulou, face to breast, both placid inside the oval shape. In the background the Christian Orthodox *mitrópoli* (mother city) in Athens. In yet another egg, the mother faces us holding her grown daughter like a baby, her back turned to us. One of few titles in Hellenic, 'Lofos Nymphon' translates to Hill of Nymphs; this was her mother's address in Athens, before the name of the street was modernized. In this transcendental re-enactment of infant intimacy,

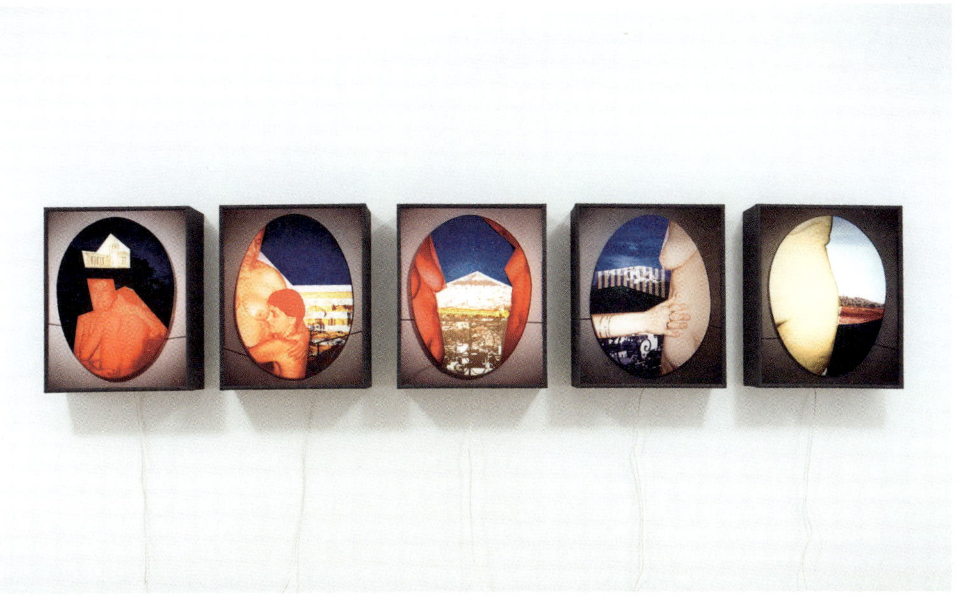

Chadwick asks 'as a modern, with no centre, no core of belief, it is possible to encounter the void of Origin, to give it form and a body, and so return to the site of beginning'.[50] Some other untranslated Hellenic titles are *Agape*, *Filoxenia* (love, hospitality) and *Anatoli* (sunrise), which doubles as both a watercolour and a 'meat abstract' of a biological image, perhaps an egg, the rising of the self/sun.

Under the protection of the egg-shaped cartouche, mother and daughter, breasts and navels, face each other. In the background the tip of Lycavittos,[51] like another breast, points to the sky.

Choosing holy places of divination as the title and background image, the work gathers several strata of long-dead familial peoples and rituals in one place. Another egg within the black cartouche, Chadwick's hand rests on her mother's stomach, the navel within reach. The Parthenon and her mother's breast look down on the scene. *Lofos Nymphon* is an unnerving, intuitive somatic enquiry connecting the mother's breast, womb and navel to ancient Hellenic rituals of the mythological concept of the *omphalos* (navel), *axis mundi*, centre of the cosmos, positioned in the inner sanctum of the temple at the sacred site of Delphi, the omphalos was represented by a large marble monument covered in wool, and

Helen Chadwick, *Lofos Nymphon*, 1987. Oil on linen mounted on plywood, slide projection, in five parts, each oval: 160 × 122 × 7 cm (63 × 48⅛ × 2⅞ in.)

umbilical cords were laced over it in protective of divinizing ritual. In the sacred dark of the temple, the oracle reads and gives the prophecy. In the Hellenic Orthodox Church, the centre of the temple retains its pagan name, *omphalos*. Some things persist.

Reaching out to Mother as *axis mundi*, both bodies become 'nexus of desires', a marvelling at the machinery of life that protects the growing embryo, a desire to return. The I, the first-person singular, is complicated with the mother's flesh. In the centre of the known and unknown world a wish for Protection and Union from a city, a mother, a time long before birth. Once upon a brief time, mother and daughter were held in the same ancestral body.

You mean to stay hidden. You insist to grow. Yet to learn difference, touched by unabating sounds of fluid motion, the name of God is not spoken, you never need, it comes, she makes the sign of the cross over your diminutive body. Inside your mother, you can breathe the water.

Birth is an *enfleshing* of the psyche, this is how we arrive from myth to meat, we dive deeper into cells and molecules and evasive electrons. Listening to the images draws forth minute physical sensations, into a form that is versatile enough to tempt imagination.

Let's listen to the image of Helen Chadwick and her brother. Easter in front of the St John the Baptist Greek Orthodox church, London. Eggs dyed red duel each other, the one that breaks loses, the one that stays intact wins. Another diasporic celebration, a precious scene worth persevering. The children are dressed in traditional Hellenic costume, white cloth skirt (*fustanella*), shirt, embroidered vest, hat and shoes (*tsarouchia*) with pompoms. Note that young Helen is wearing the male version of the national attire. Was this androgynous performance her idea? She smiles, gallant and happy. Her posing skills intact.

The holding of a body with/within a body is ignited in *The Labours* (1983-84). In *Labour X*, Chadwick, in an athletic stance and with bare posterior, looks away as she carries a rectangular image of her upright naked body, the triangle of her pubis never seen by the sun, her face a blurred spectre of speed (see page 66). *How does it feel?* Only the haptic

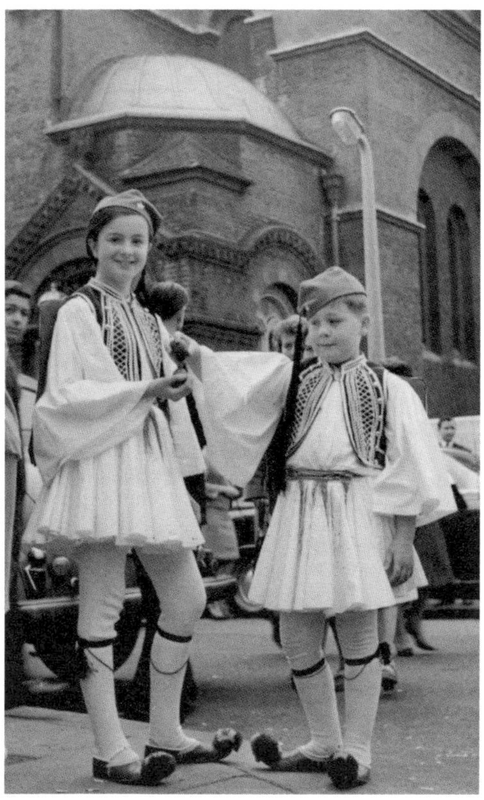

will do in dealing with these doubling matters. How heavy is an effigy of yourself? Margaret Atwood ponders this sort of thing when thinking about orphans, snails and homes in the collection of fictional essays *The Tent*: 'A home filled with nothing but yourself. It's heavy, that lightness. It's crushing, that emptiness.'[52]

References to the home also point towards our first home, the womb. Gaston Bachelard's phenomenology links the human imagination to its surroundings, specifically the domestic space: 'The house protects the dreamer.'[53] As we dream ourselves into existence, a treasure hidden in the corners of the intimate architecture of our mother's body, genial secrets are passed on to us. 'A house that has been experienced is not an inert box. Inhabited space transcends geometrical space.'[54] What is left of us in our mother's womb? A body inscribed on a box of any sort awakens the Egyptian sarcophagus. Thanatos *now again* murmurs too.

Helen Chadwick and her brother dressed in traditional Greek dress, in front of St John the Baptist Greek Orthodox church, London, n.d.

Horrified and impotent against the bombing of Palestinian people, I search, I listen to anything but the news, I come across a poem by Palestinian poet Hala Alyan, 'Interactive :: House Saints' – she says: 'My favourite house is my mother.' That loosens my limbs and I remember Eros stirring in labours and births.

Do we need to look at the origins of the word 'architecture'? Search engines and dictionaries avail - *architectoniki* (αρχιτεκτονική), *archi* (beginning, government) and *tektoniki* (making by hand, creation and birthing, the proto-Indo-European root *tek*-, connecting it to *tekno* (child), *tekne* (art) and *teknologia* (technology) - the Hellenic coalescence of words needs no introduction.

O

One Flesh (1985) combines the mothering preoccupation of *Lofos Nymphon* and *The Oval Court*'s love of photocopied flesh and woven cloth. A mother and her child. The red cloth, the hands, announce the mother as Holy Mary, sweet mother of Christ. Mother Mary is of paramount importance in the Hellenic Church and culture. If you are Hellenic you call out to her in fear or awe several times a day - *Panagia mou!*[55] In medieval paintings the scene forms a pyramid. In the pyramid of *One Flesh*, a vagina and a placenta above her head replace the Holy Spirit and *Dextera Domini*.

One hand points to the infant's genitals - no penis, it's a girl! Christ as a female. The lack of a penis reverses *Ostentatio genitalium* (display of genitals) - some obscure Renaissance painting tradition attributes formal, thematic and theological significance to Jesus' penis.[56] *Helen the Mystic*. Which work does not deconstruct? Does not find shameless, naked antediluvian Eros *within* the piety of dominant orthodoxies? Following the direction of the pointing finger we arrive at an umbilical cord, and then the other hand of the *One Flesh* holy mother. And this, the last hand of which we shall speak, considers cutting the cord still attached to the infant, but not yet.

The umbilical cord (*omphalios loros*) is our connection to the body where we were born.[57] The connection, now again, comes through stories

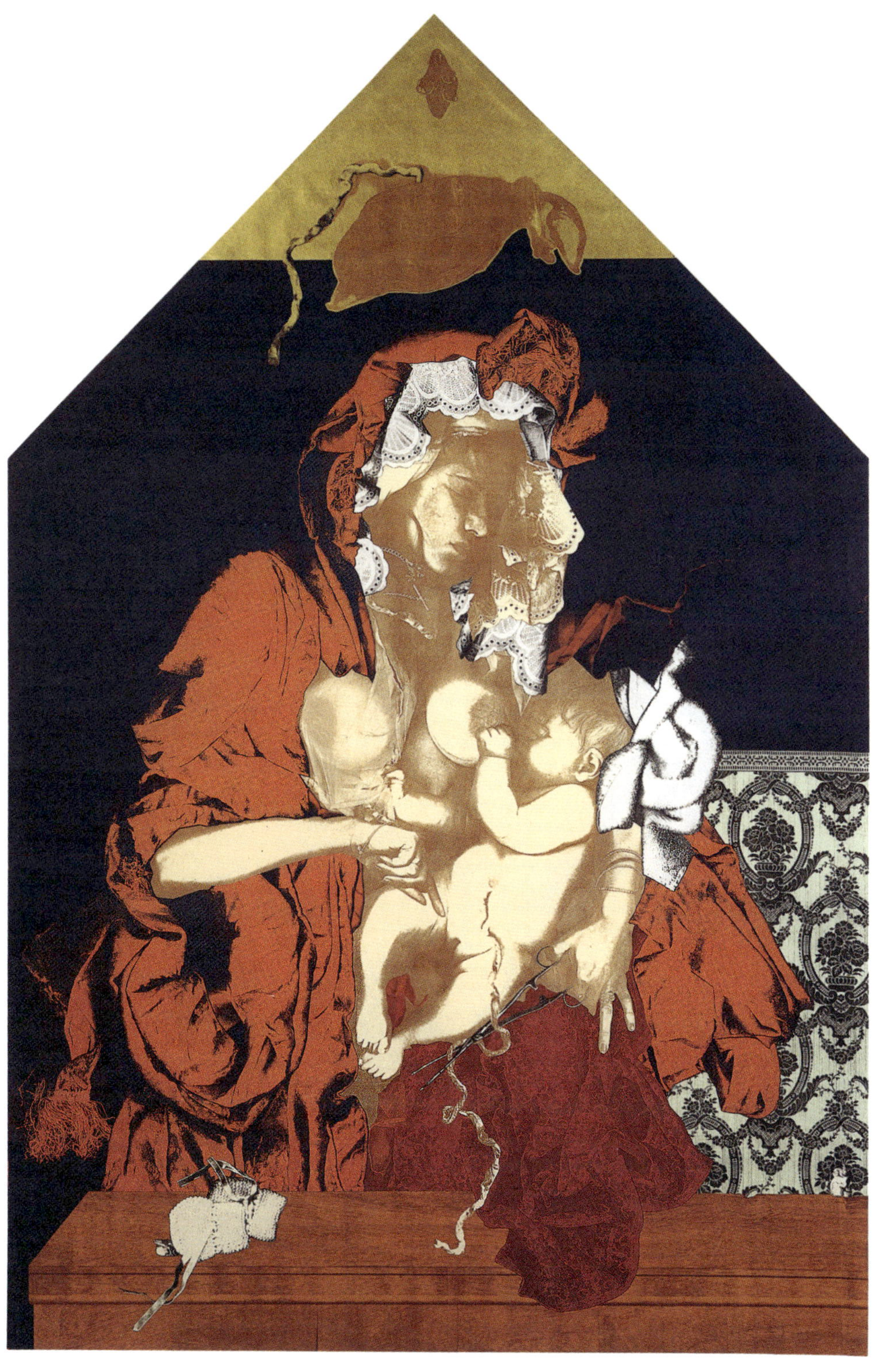

Helen Chadwick, *One Flesh*, 1985. Photocopies, 160 × 107 cm (63 × 42⅛ in.)

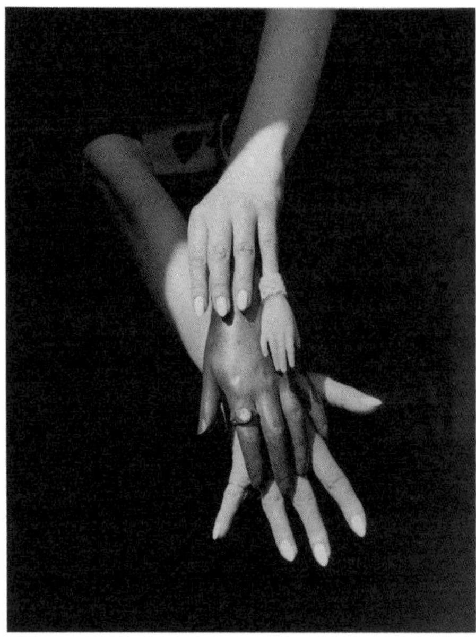

and rituals. In her dissertation codex Chadwick states emphatically in language beyond her years that 'primitives perceived the transfer and passage of power between individuals as a complex system of rituals, depended upon the latent forces inherent upon their personal animal magnetism'.[58] Let's not forget, we are magnetic animals.

Maybe this is what the hands were saying all along. Look at the string, the circular path to the cosmic mother. Painted like so many dancing figures around a vase, photocopied in laser, the line, the light, the path, the cord appear immaterial and heavy. A cord of incessant activity around solid, gold, undivided essence. The Hellenic deep in the cells opens a double door. We are invited to travel tenderly back and forth through the monuments, hands pointing the way. Helen Chadwick's 'complex rituals' embroider the anatomy of a wish, a desire.[59] For connection between abject and beautiful, past and present, this body and that body, this is seduction. The erotic, sweet and supple, allows us to bare the pain of life and reconcile with the unborn void we all return to. There is no closing – only more opening.

It's here and now, in this body, let all monuments be eroticized and be known.

Claude Cahun, *Untitled (Surrealist Hands)*, 1935.
Silver gelatin print, 25.1 × 19.6 cm (10 × 7¾ in.)

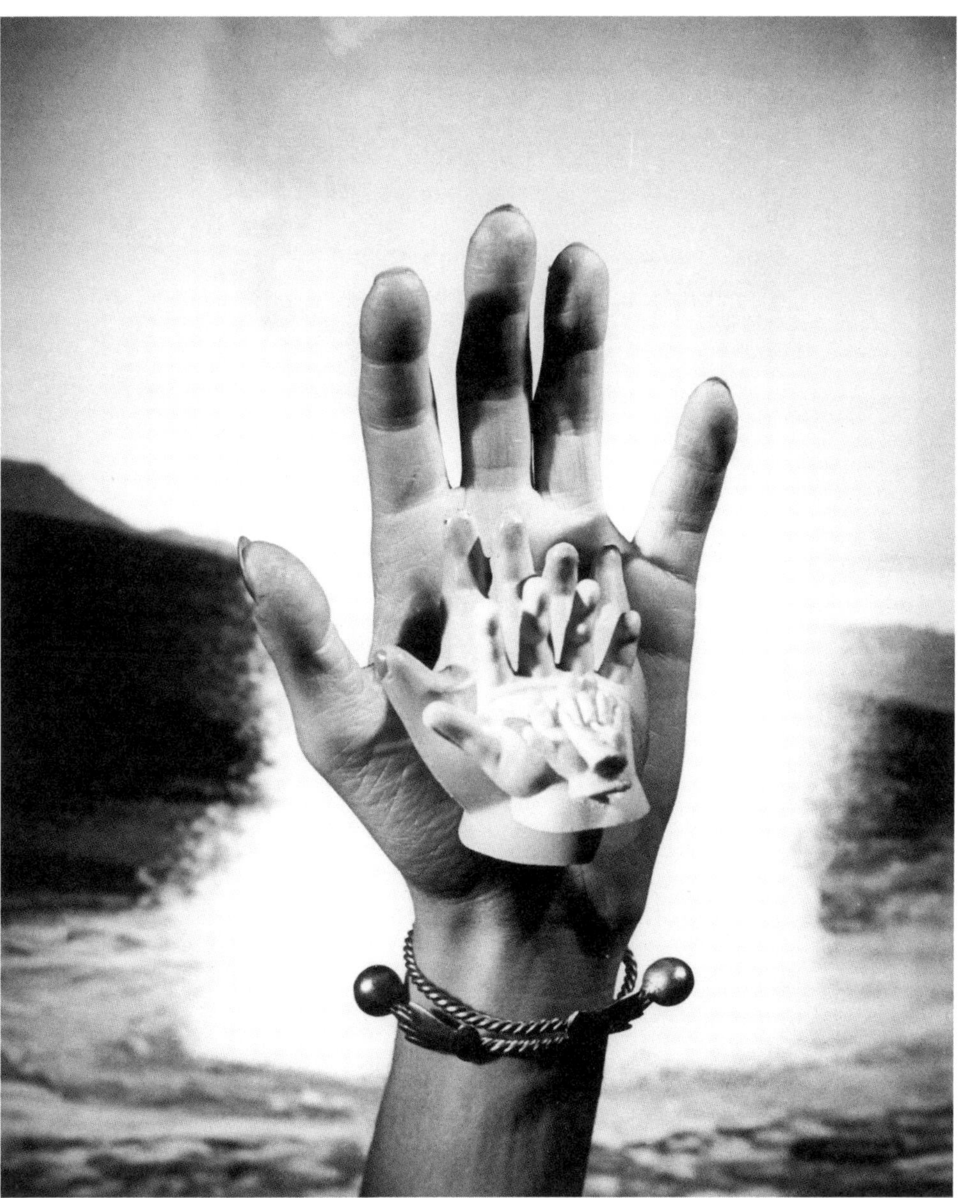

Helen Chadwick's hand portrait, n.d.

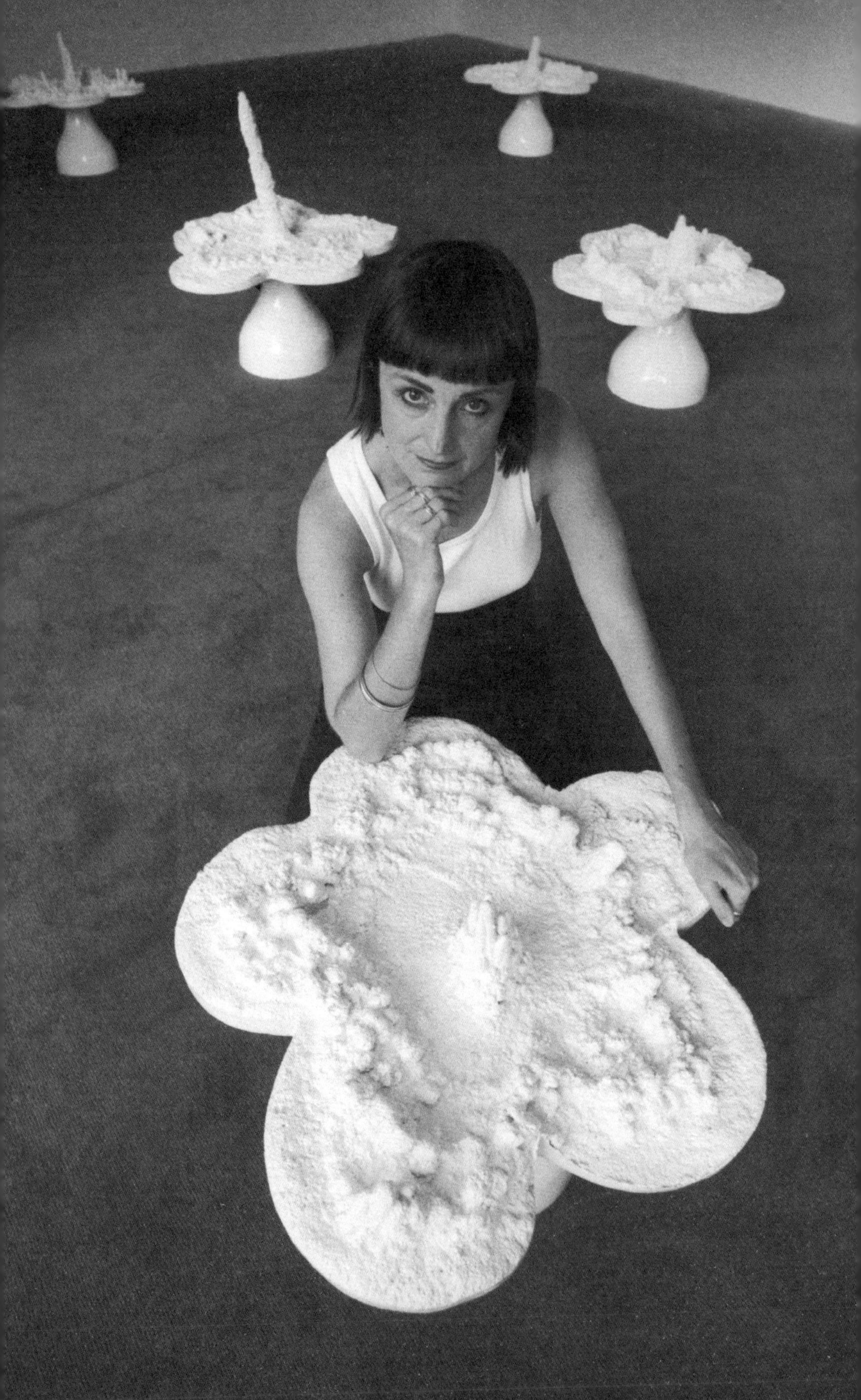

CHAPTER 4

Bad Blooms & Fluid Taxonomies

Katrin Bucher Trantow

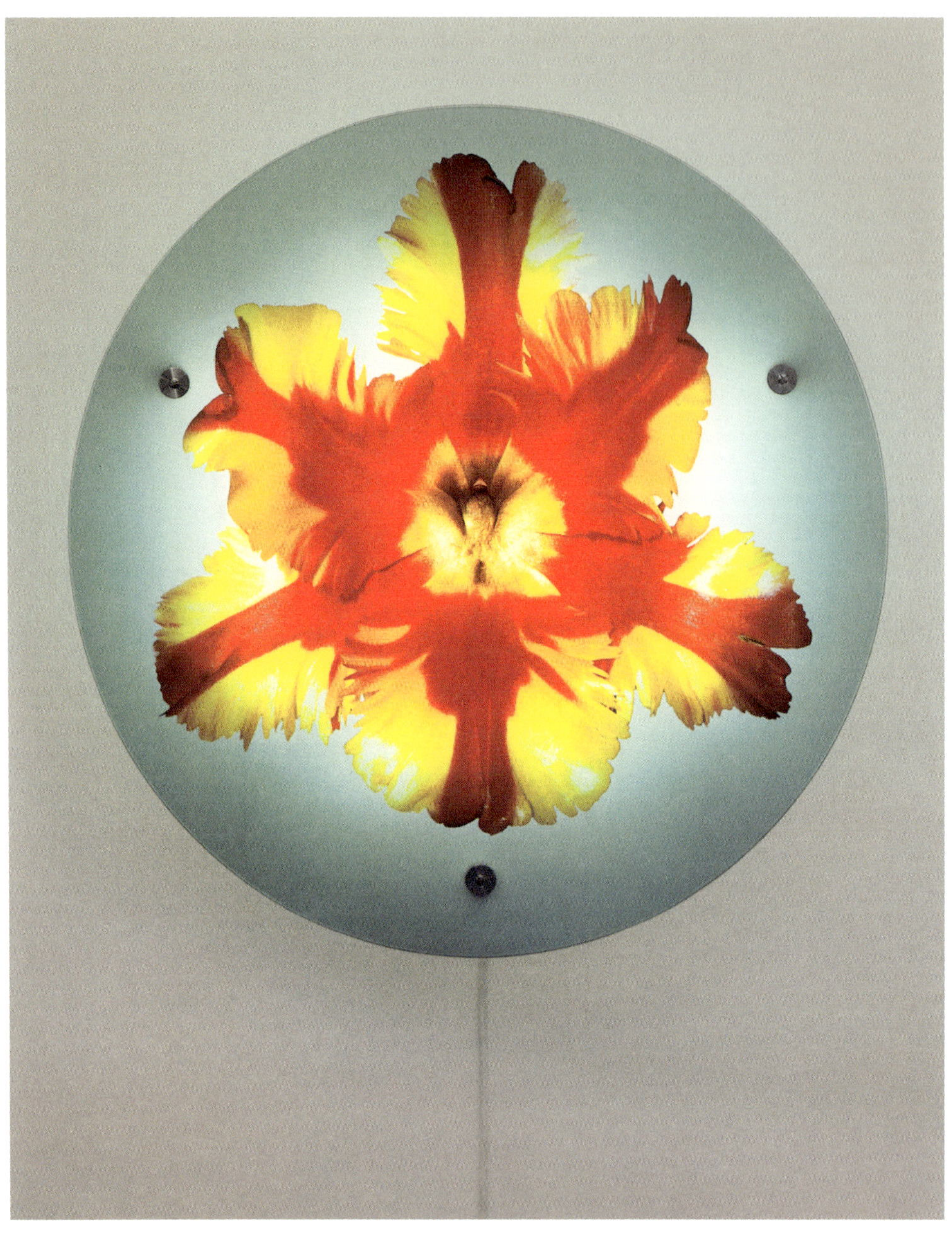

ABOVE **Helen Chadwick, *Billy Budd*, 1994. Cibachrome transparency, glass, aluminium, electrical apparatus, 86 × 14 cm (33 7/8 × 5 1/2 in.)**

PAGE 198 **Helen Chadwick with *Piss Flowers*, 1994**

Ahead of her time, Helen Chadwick created a whole series of works in which flowers play an essential role as props, as protagonists or as metaphors. In each one of them she challenges the singularity and specificity of binary gender roles by inverting and entangling their conceptions. From her hermaphroditic *Piss Flowers* (1991–92), for which she borrowed the outlines of their simple petal forms from Warholian Pop art flowers, to *The Oval Court* (1984–86), where flowers are draped around her naked body, seemingly floating in liquid; from the seductively shiny photographic work *Billy Budd* (1994) to the equally brilliant giant *Wreaths to Pleasure* (1992–93), and the series of paintings *Philoxenia* (1994–95), flowers play a central role. In reference to Charles Baudelaire's *Les Fleurs du mal* (1857), Chadwick titled the exhibition in which she first presented her *Wreaths to Pleasure* to the USA, at Museum of Modern Art (MoMA), New York, in 1995, 'Bad Blooms'. Chadwick had already used the 'Bad Blooms' reference when she showed *Piss Flowers* and *Philoxenia* at the Salzburger Kunstverein, Austria, in 1994, at which point she said she wanted to 'stage the sexuality of the female body in order to add a new and critical, often ironic level...or to turn traditional models upside down'.[1] *Philoxenia* is one of Chadwick's most political late works. By combining botanical paintings of flowers with the names of a of non-Western women that she knew personally, the work creates an alternative botanical taxonomy that 'brings the fear of the foreign and the fear of sexuality directly together. The foreign is represented by the erotic woman.'[2] Such an assimilation of references could allude to the walled Garden of Eden: 'Can we imagine an alternative starting point to the garden of Eden? After all, doesn't every culture have its own Eden?', asks Laurie Cluitmans in her book *On the Necessity of Gardening* (2021).[3]

The etymology of the word 'paradise', from *paradeisos* (an ancient Greek word that derives from the Persian for park or enclosed garden), points to a multitude of paradises or mythological places. The Garden of Eden of the Old Testament – in Western art the place where everything blossoms and flourishes – is the place where the division of the sexes is established like no other. Man is Adam. Woman is Eve. Both are created by God in his image; as masculine in the first instance, and feminine in the second. Amid the fertile, flourishing plant and animal world, they are valued as the stronger and the weaker sex, respectively; nevertheless, both are considered the crown of creation and the most highly developed organism.

Chadwick's complex exhibition 'Of Mutability' explored the conditions of reproduction and reproductivity, and is based on the structure of a formal walled garden. First designed for the Institute of Contemporary Arts (ICA), London, in 1986, it consisted of two interconnected elements: a central pool and surrounding arcades titled *The Oval Court* (1984-86), and *Carcass* (1986), visible in the adjacent room, which consisted of a huge glass tower filled with composting waste, serving as a timely reminder of the constant processes of becoming and passing. According to Chadwick, *The Oval Court* implied both an architectural space and a place of courtship, where a revival of the Garden of Eden and a 'new Eve' would be unveiled, where female sexuality would be evident as a blessing rather than a disgrace. The press release stated that 'Of Mutability' was a 'paradisical landscape in which nature and artificiality are united in an allegory of love'.[4]

Flowers are frequently understood as objects deserving of attention from women artists over centuries.[5] Flowers can become a code; they can be symbolic, or signals of recognition, and they have been used in various protest movements throughout history. In the nineteenth century, the art of floriography led to elaborate floral messages that could be read in their own lexicons. Various queer movements have developed floral codes since then, including the use of the pansy, carnation and lavender as specific symbols. Interestingly, plants and flowers are botanically less binary in terms of female and male elements than the duality of language, or the oversimplified plant taxonomy and hierarchization system developed by Carl Linnaeus (an eighteenth-century Swedish biologist and botanist) would have us believe. For example, the apple blossom - the tree of paradise - has hermaphrodite flowers, i.e. it has male stamens and female carpels, where the pollen reaches the stigma of the carpel mostly through the movement of a third element, the attracted insects.

In 1991, artist and filmmaker Derek Jarman (1942-1994) wrote: 'I intend to celebrate our corner of paradise, the part of the garden the Lord forgot to mention.'[6] His words were penned in resistance to growing

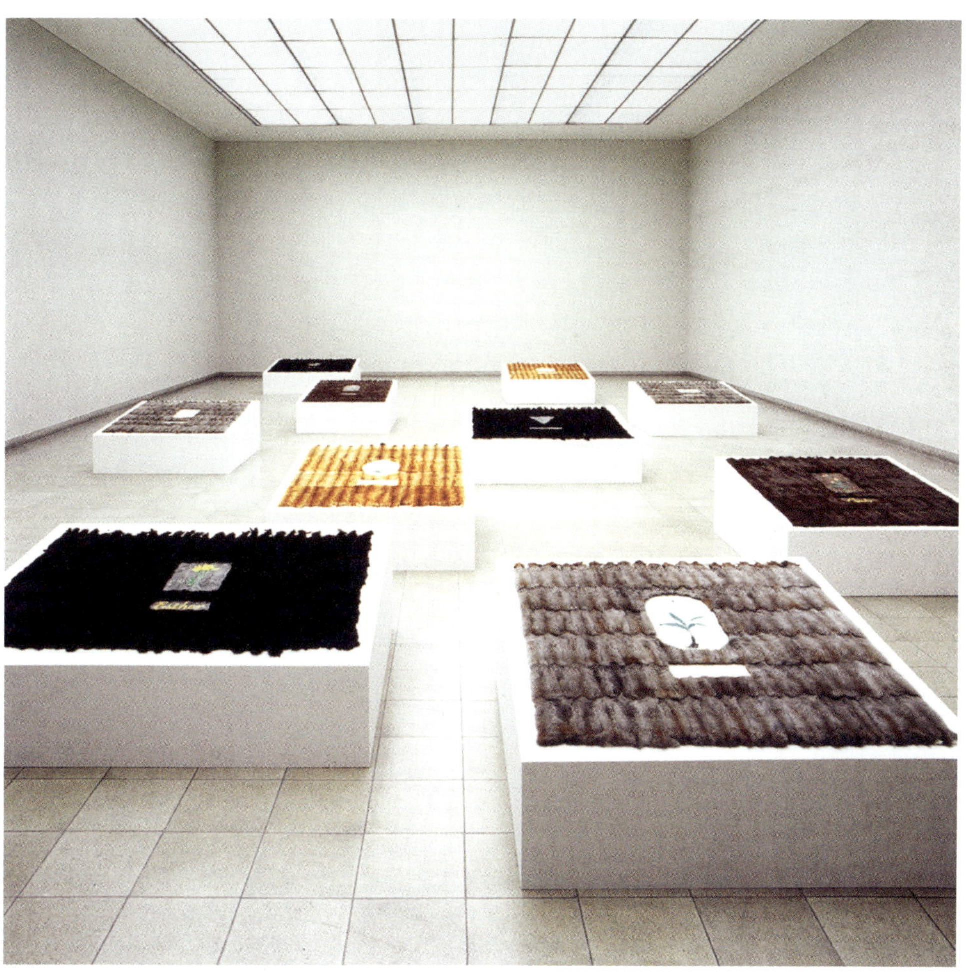

Helen Chadwick, *Philoxenia*, 1994–95. Fur and oil, dimensions unknown. Installed at Kunsthaus Glarus, Switzerland, 1995

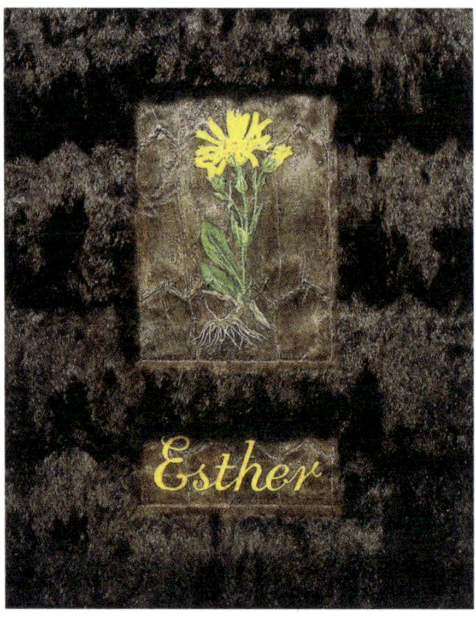

homophobia around the AIDS crisis, as well as a direct reference to his pioneering medicinal private garden at Prospect Cottage on the coast in Kent, where he grew inconspicuous ruderal plants alongside protective (against wind and the effects of the sea) found objects. In the same year Chadwick created her *Piss Flowers*, with 'vaginal towers with male skirt[s]', as a strong statement against binary gender determination. Also in 1991, Chadwick stated in a lecture that 'in language dual structures are defined as oppositional: where we have self, there must be other; gender is male or female, and most problematic and absurd of all is the split between mind and body'.[7] Referencing philosopher Michel Foucault, she systematically designed works to counter rigid categorization, questioning the cultural and societal gender norms that she saw as controlling and which she recognized as manifest across architecture, fashion, art, language and the sciences. For Chadwick, the motif of the flower as a symbol of blossoming gender fluidity thereby appears as a reminder of the fluidity and viscerality of the body. To quote Chadwick from her poem 'Piss Posy' (written as an accompaniment to *Piss Flowers*):

> *Linnaeus what would you say,*
> *how define such wanton play?*[8]

Helen Chadwick, *Philoxenia*, 1994–95 (detail)

In his *Systema naturae* (1735), Linnaeus - on whose research Charles Darwin's theories were later based - presented classes and orders (primarily for identification purposes) of plants in accordance with his *Systema sexuale*. This influential system, linguistically orientated towards male sexual organs, is based on the number and arrangement of male (stamens) and female (pistils) reproductive organs.[9] Flowering plants are at the centre of this resplendent vision of plant sexuality. If legal heterosexual marriage was at the heart of eighteenth-century cultural life, then Linnaeus was thorough in placing 'sex' at the heart of plant taxonomy (plants that reproduced through vegetative and clonal means were deemed asexual).[10] It should be added that this circumstance placed them in a lower developmental category in Linnaeus' hierarchy of taxonomies.

Chadwick's *Wreaths to Pleasure* (1992–93) reveal her strong interest in the combination of science and art. Flower arrangements in the shape of sexual organs or cell structures lie on top of rich, glossy liquids (oils, foods, bubble bath etc.). Erotic attraction and a revulsion of the

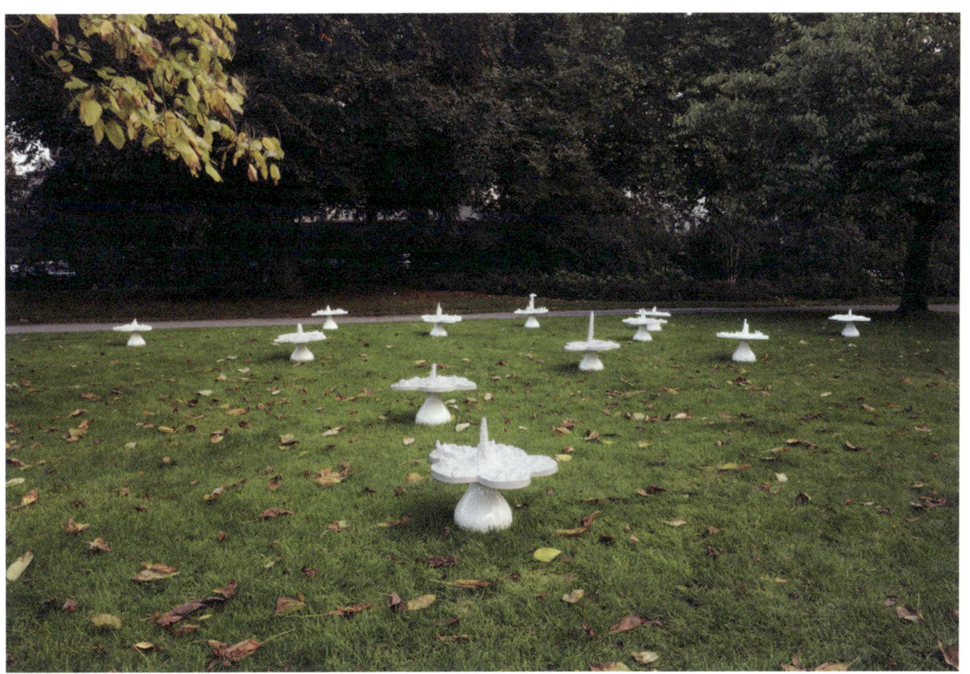

Helen Chadwick, *Piss Flowers*, 1991–92. Bronze and cellulose lacquer, in twelve parts, each 70 × 65 × 65 cm (27½ × 25⅝ × 25⅝ in.). Installation at Frieze London, 2013

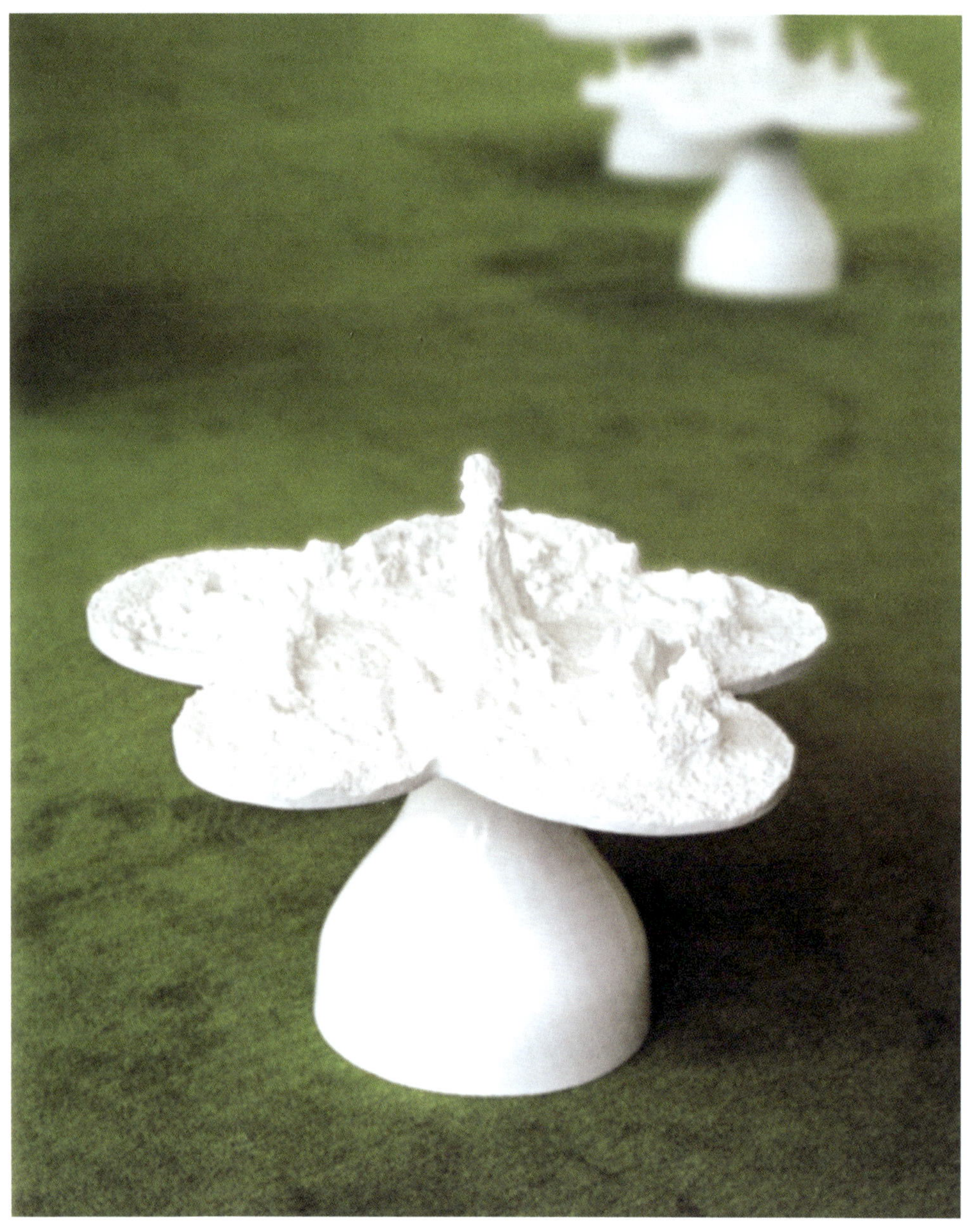

ABOVE AND OPPOSITE **Helen Chadwick, *Piss Flowers*, 1991–92 (details)**

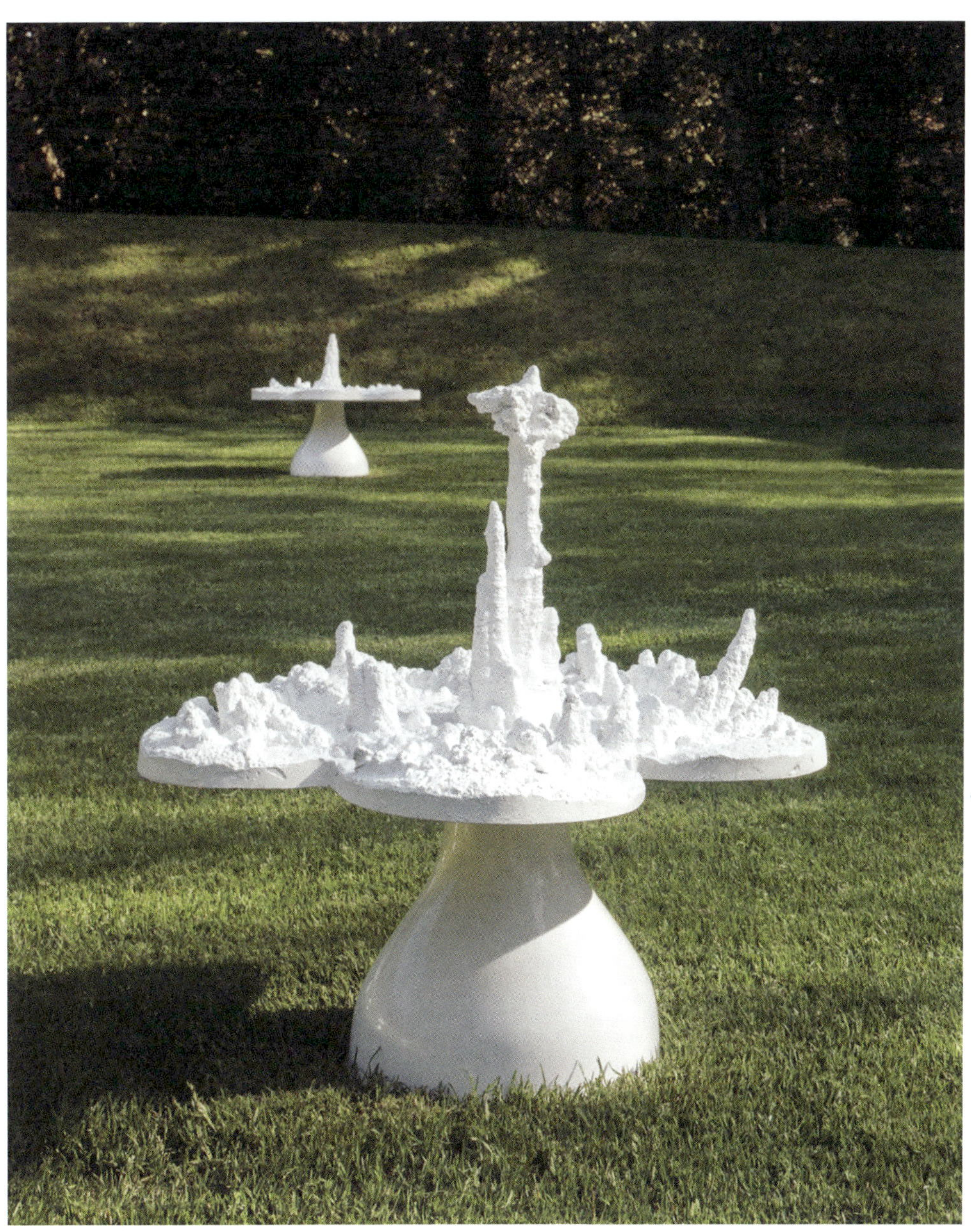

physical merge in fluid images. Reminiscent of oversized petri dishes, here magical mitosis seems to take place in shimmering nutrient solutions. The *Wreaths* are pastel glossy photographs in metal frames that reflect the liquidity of life and the ambiguity of eroticism. Chadwick draws on the 'tondo', a term used to describe a circular work of art that since the Renaissance and Baroque periods has focused on the sublime and the heavenly. In this way, she skilfully plays with the accepted languages of cultural imagery while referencing experiences of eating, devouring, washing and cleaning, science and the toilet bowl.

The form of the flower returns in Chadwick's *Glossolalia* (1993), with its silky fur petals and its stamen of bronze lambs' tongues, and again in *Cacao* (1994), with its bubbling chocolate fountain. Using scent and touch, both works again challenge a multitude of senses and focus on the subconscious and the immediately visceral. Concepts of desire and seduction – so often demonized as feminine – reintroduce themselves as essential parts of everyday life: 'I'm trying to make images of a kind of physical identification of the self through exploring physical matter – and by implication mortality, desire, all those kinds of words, all that kind of vague region – because it's a kind of space that none of us can really know for ourselves and because, for many people, it's a troubled terrain.'[11]

Chadwick uses the flower as a metaphor for the beautiful intensity of the sensual in life, as well as its constant change. Her floral taxonomy is not only fluid on its surface level but also generally malleable and highly inclusive. Chadwick's efforts to disrupt fixed axioms and liquefy cultural imagery embody the senses while undoing the categorization of the human as solely masculine or feminine. Her activities against the cultural division between the animal and plant worlds, and especially between body and mind, still resonate today. In *Liquid Modernity*, philosopher Zygmunt Bauman characterized the twenty-first century as being marked by the dissolution of the ideological superstructures that had long organised and dominated the Western world. 'Liquids', he wrote, 'neither hold space nor bind time. Fluids do not retain a form for long and are constantly ready (and prone) to change.'[12]

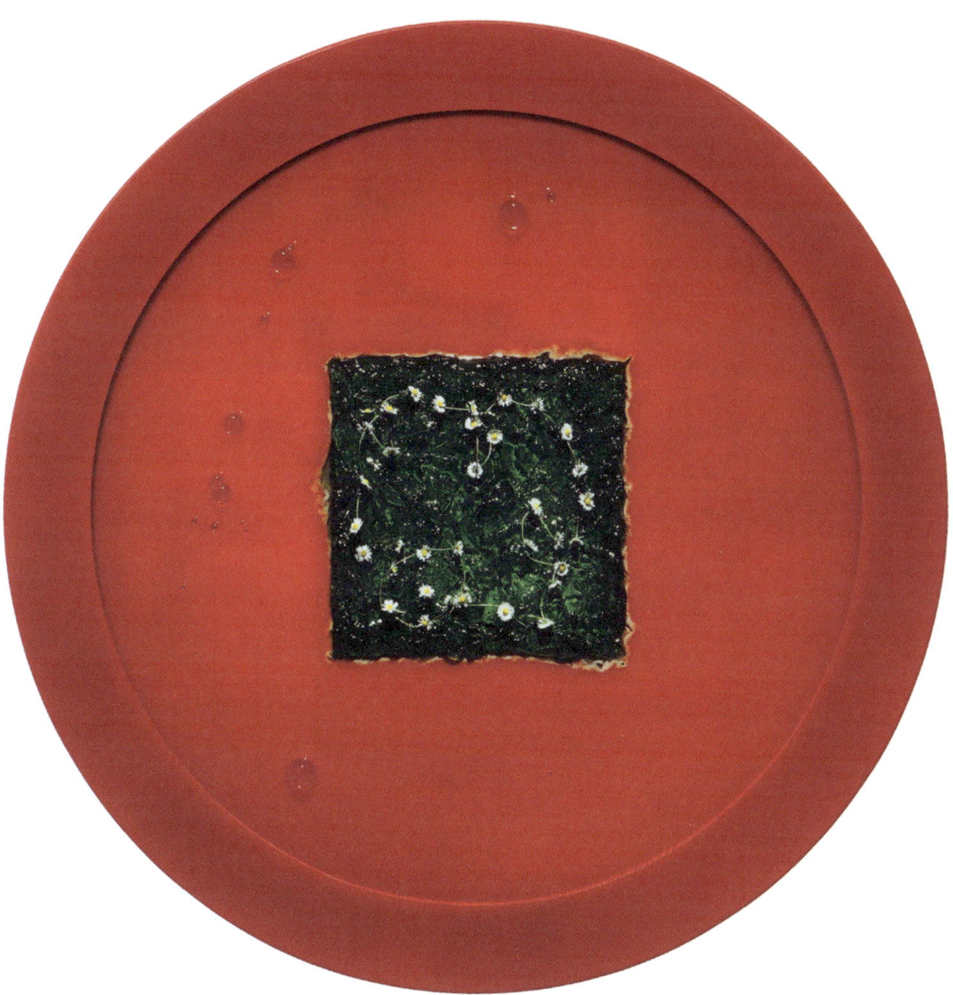

Helen Chadwick, *Wreath to Pleasure, No. 7 (Daisies, Swarfega, Tomato Juice)*, 1992–93. Cibachrome prints, aluminium-faced MDF, glazed and powder-coated steel frame, diameter 110 cm (43¼ in.)

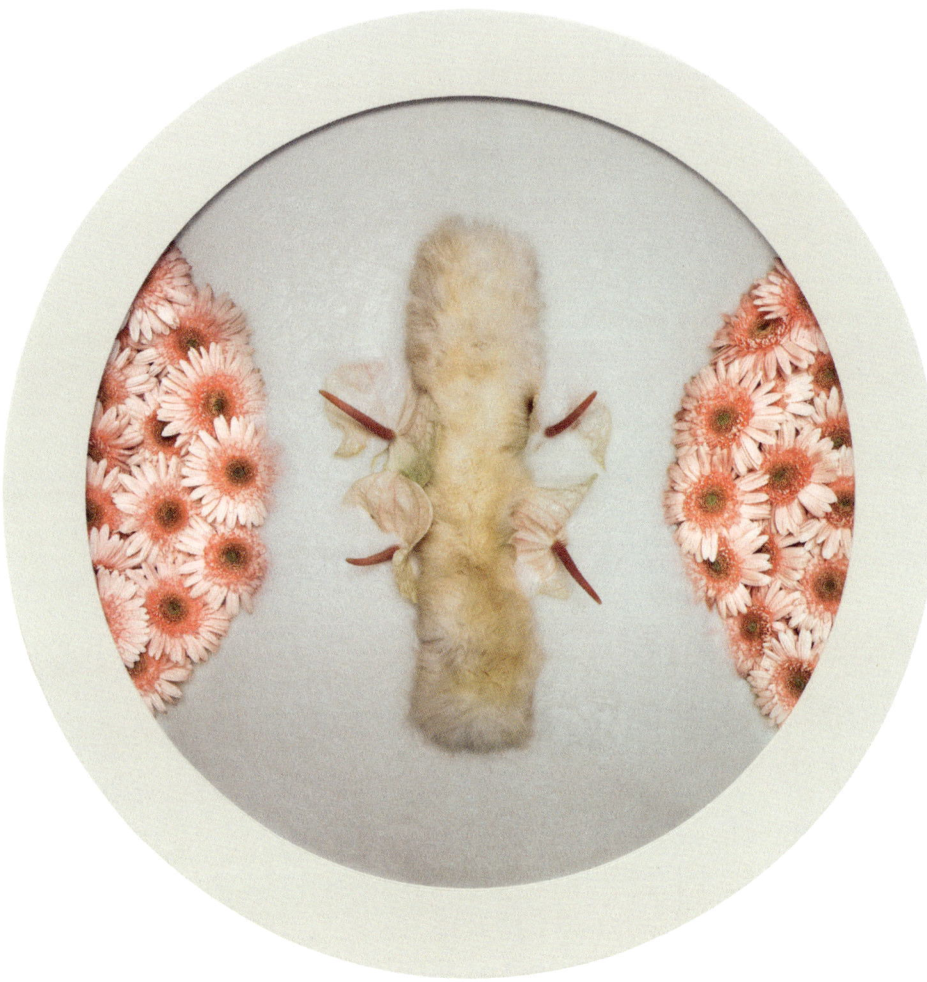

Helen Chadwick, *Wreath to Pleasure, No. 8 (Gerberas, Fur, Lard)*, 1992–93.
Cibachrome prints, aluminium-faced MDF, glazed and powder-coated steel frame, diameter 110 cm (43¼ in.)

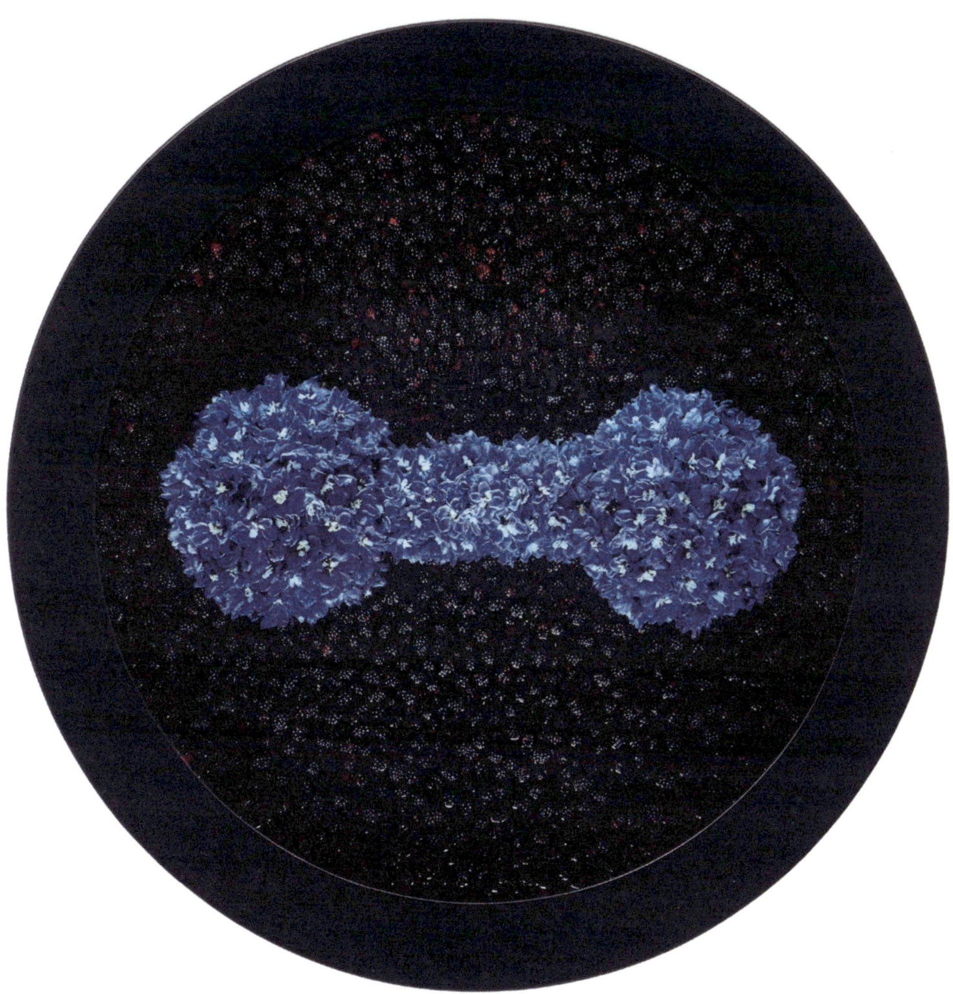

Helen Chadwick, *Wreath to Pleasure, No. 9 (Blue Delphiniums, Blackberries)*, 1992–93. Cibachrome prints, aluminium-faced MDF, glazed and powder-coated steel frame, diameter 110 cm (43¼ in.)

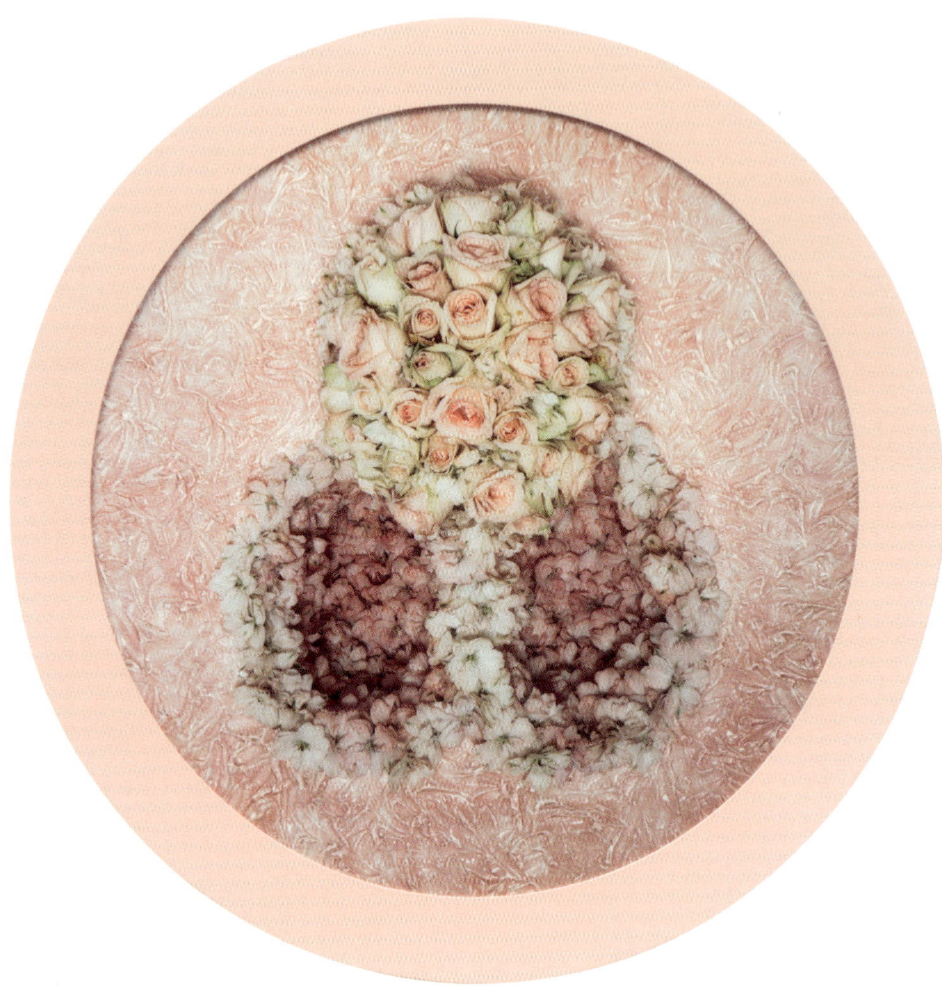

Helen Chadwick, *Wreath to Pleasure, No. 10 (Pink Roses, Germolene)*, 1992–93. Cibachrome prints, aluminium-faced MDF, glazed and powder-coated steel frame, diameter 110 cm (43¼ in.)

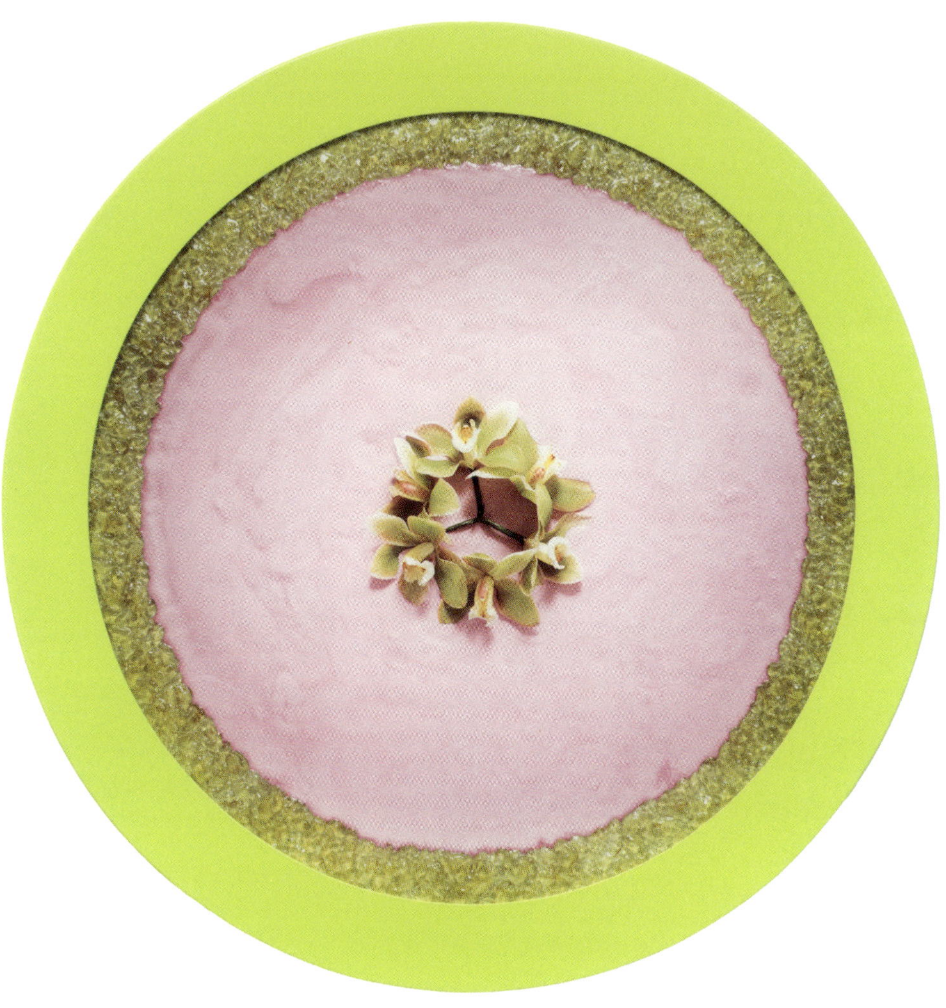

Helen Chadwick, *Wreath to Pleasure, No. 11 (Orchids, Windolene)*, 1992–93. Cibachrome prints, aluminium-faced MDF, glazed and powder-coated steel frame, diameter 110 cm (43¼ in.)

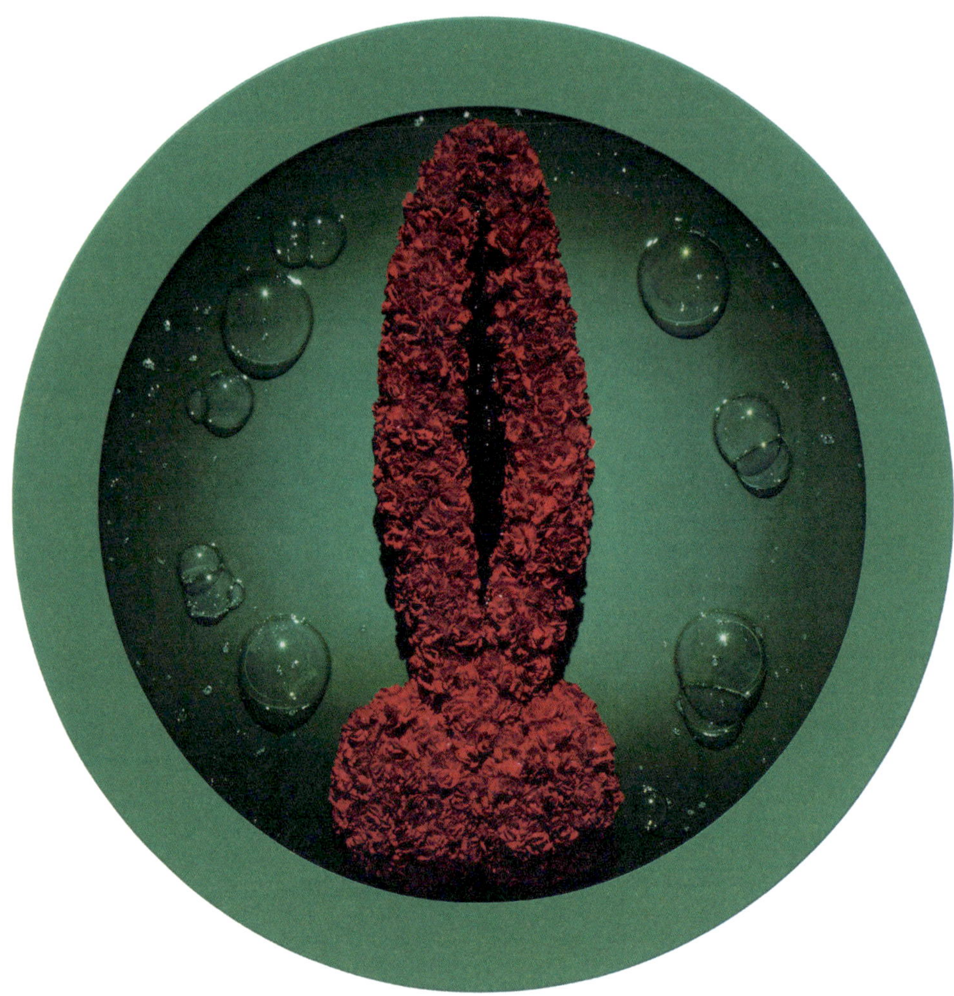

Helen Chadwick, *Wreath to Pleasure, No. 12 (Carnations, Fairy Liquid)*, 1992–93. Cibachrome prints, aluminium-faced MDF, glazed and powder-coated steel frame, diameter 110 cm (43¼ in.)

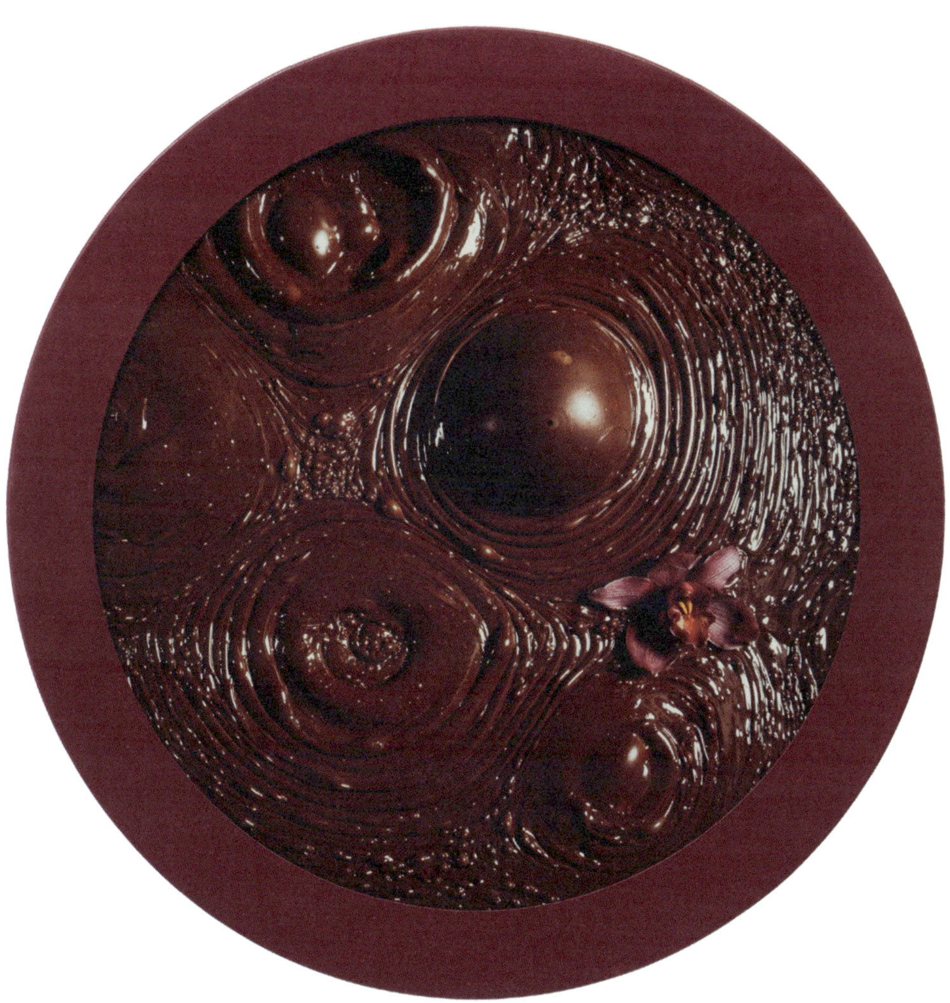

Helen Chadwick, *Wreath to Pleasure, No. 13 (Orchid, Chocolate)*, 1992–93. Cibachrome prints, aluminium-faced MDF, glazed and powder-coated steel frame, diameter 110 cm (43¼ in.)

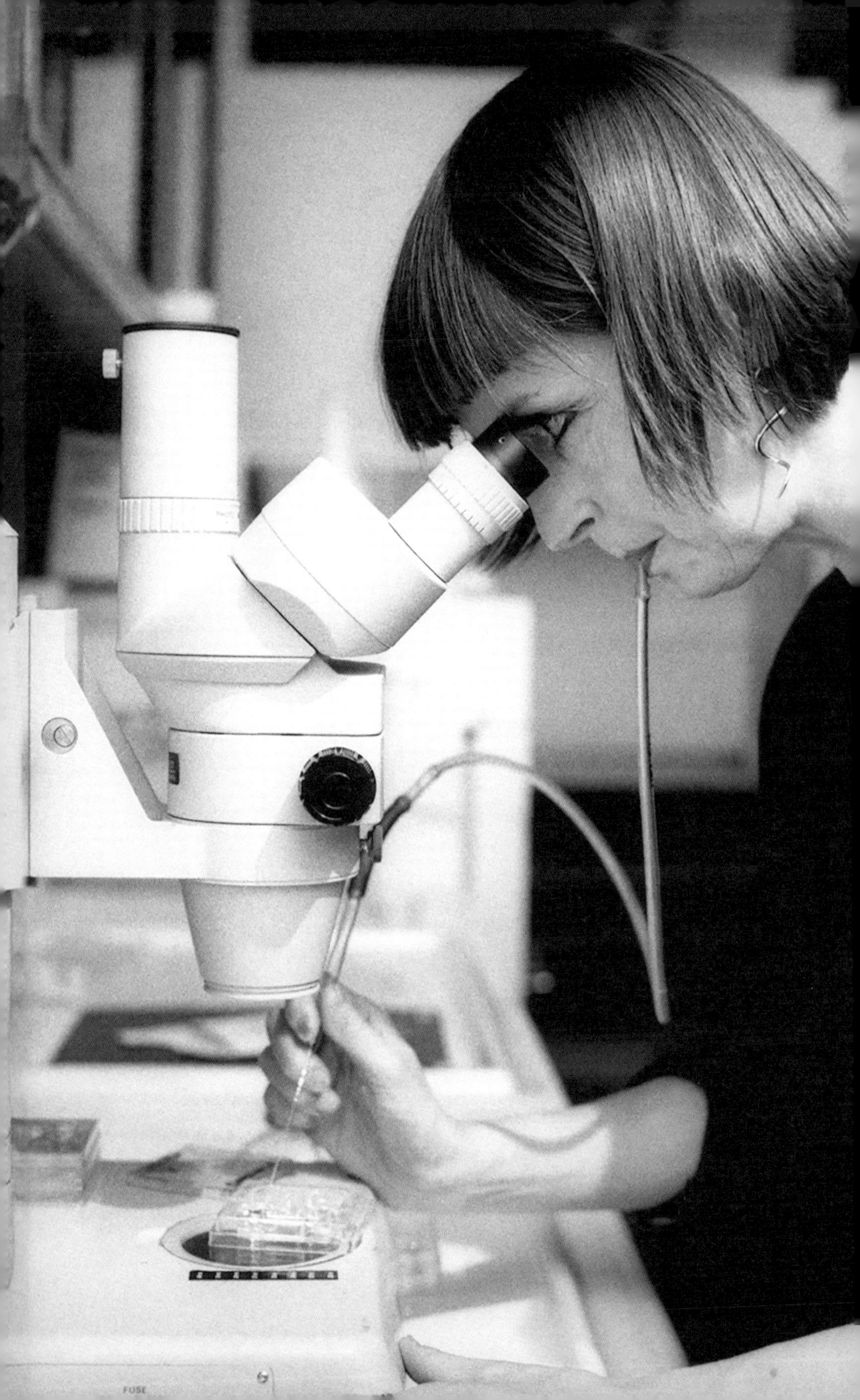
FUSE

CHAPTER 5

Louisa Buck & Laura Smith in Conversation

Laura Smith How did you meet Helen Chadwick?

Louisa Buck I've been thinking long and hard about when and where I first met Helen. And I can't exactly remember. I had seen the extraordinary exhibition 'Of Mutability' at the Institute of Contemporary Arts (ICA), London, in 1986, and it just blew me away. What was this incredible environment made up of photocopies of twelve incarnations of the same female form floating among beasts, plants and food? Who was this artist whose adorned naked body was frolicking with all these creatures? And what was this bizarre great pillar of stinking decomposing weirdness, *Carcass* (1986) - thank God I got to see it before it broke and the ICA took it away! So, before I met her properly I was certainly aware of Helen as this exceptional presence. I do remember seeing her around, at various openings and events. She was unmistakable with that black bob and she always looked super stylish. And a little bit scary, to me. I was still in my twenties and had just finished [studying] at the Courtauld Institute in London - I was just dipping my toe into the London art scene, working for (the now defunct) *City Limits* magazine, writing visual arts reviews. Coming from an art history background, I was still learning about contemporary art, but even from a distance I could see that Helen was a force.

I remember in 1989 I went to Beck Road to Maureen Paley's gallery, Interim Art, and saw Helen's *Enfleshings* (1989) series there: immaculate but disquieting photographic images including a lightbulb nestling in fleshy folds of red meat and a giant illuminated ear, its whorls echoed by a rococo curlicue that was nursing another sphere of light. I was completely astonished. Some artists like Edward Allington (1951-2017) were playing around with architectural ornamentation, but no one I'd encountered was mashing up nature and culture in such a lush, transgressively visceral way. Shortly afterwards I did my first interview with Helen - for *Tatler* magazine of all places - and this took place in her house, also on Beck Road, a few doors down from Maureen. Those Beck Road houses are tiny, but inside Helen's house there was an almost Tardis-like sense of space and order. In the leafy little garden at the back I seem to remember there was either a grape vine or a fig tree, but maybe this is a romantic memory. Helen loved to serve figs, sexily split in half, with a dribble of honey.

PAGE 216 **Helen Chadwick in residence at King's College Hospital Assisted Conception Unit, London, 1995**

It was around this time, in late 1989, that I got to know Helen better. She was a friend of Marina Warner, and I was living with Tom, the brother of Marina's then husband, Johnny Dewe Mathews (b. 1946). Once I stopped being daunted by her fierce intelligence, Helen and I became good friends. I think we bonded over a shared love of the bawdy, and having a good time. She was from Croydon and I'd grown up in Essex, and neither of us shocked easily. Under her pristine exterior she was fantastically earthy and sexy: she could ricochet from the cerebral to the profane in half a sentence, which I adored.

LS What was she like as a friend?

LB My abiding memory of Helen is her mischievousness and her megawatt smile. Both she and her work were an utterly compelling mixture of hardcore rigour and playfulness. She had a distinctive natural style - whatever the occasion she was always beautifully turned out in amazing, quite androgynous clothes - practical, not flamboyant but fabulous. Much to my envy she was small enough to fit into Junior Gautier. Her small knobbly fingers were always covered in gold rings and sometimes she wore a small brooch of a fist clasping an arrow. She also had an ex-voto of a pair of breasts that she would wear as a brooch. She was an intellectual Titan, she really had an incredible reach, an extraordinary brain and vast knowledge across science, art, popular culture - and when you were with her, this just bubbled up. She was such fun to be around, I mourn her daily. She was also a fantastic and loyal friend, and she loved my children too. My baby daughter Nancy, born in 1995, had a mad quiff of blonde hair, and Helen immediately christened her 'The Saxon Queen'.

LS It's lovely to hear you talk about her and her work, and how compelling it was; what do you think has endured about it? Because for me, it's as relevant now as it was when she made it. Where does that come from?

LB Today it's become almost common currency, but it's important to stress that in the UK art world at that time it was really outrageous to be using a language that fused ornamentation, fleshy-ness and the abject. The so-called New British Sculpture by artists largely represented by the

Lisson Gallery still held sway, and the overall vibe was a kind of post-Pop, post-minimal fusion, with a bit of quirky but emphatically blokey irony thrown in. Decorative was a dirty word, and any reference to beauty had to be put firmly in parentheses. Into all this came Helen, with her sexy, erudite, gorgeously irreverent work that took the gentle piss out of the boys and their ponderous use of bits of metal and building materials.

Back to your question, I would agree that yes, her work is totally relevant to our world now. Whatever form it takes, at its core Helen's work is an exploration of selfhood and identity before identity politics became widely foregrounded. Even if she wasn't specifically depicting herself, her work was always intensely personal. She was investigating what it means to exist as a multifaceted sexual, sensory being, and she was doing so by using the immediately physical and experiential to Trojan Horse in a wealth of cultural, political and scientific references.

With Helen the word 'fluid' applies in every possible way. One thinks about the *Viral Landscapes* (1988–89) or indeed *Enfleshings*; they're genderless, or rather they're gender-full. They are nonbinary in every sense. Throughout her work, Helen wanted to explore the fluidity of identity, literally and metaphorically. Her *Viral Landscapes* are a brilliant expression of the porosity and permeability of all boundaries, whether geographical or bodily. At the time, the AIDS and HIV crisis was devastating so many of our communities; it was a very present, horrific threat. The *Viral Landscapes* addressed this, but they also went beyond a specific situation to interrogate where, how and what we understand as a beginning and an end. On a shoreline, where does the sea stop and the beach start? As human bodies ingesting oxygen and food, playing host to bacteria and viruses, where does the outside end and the inside begin? For as long as we exist as a species, these remain basic human concerns, and they were core concerns of Helen's. So whether in this way, or with her hermaphroditic *Piss Flowers*, or really in all that she made, Helen's work remains current because it is really about who and what we are: physically, intellectually and materially.

LS One of the things that I have found quite difficult in my reading about her is that lots of people talk about her as very invested in binaries: male/female, dark/light, grotesque/fetish, and I just don't see that at all. I don't see this kind of polarization; rather, exactly as you said, I see fluidity.

LB I think when people talk about binaries they are perhaps saying more about themselves than they are about Helen. Again and again she rejected any vacuum-packed readings of her work. She liked the word 'polymorphous' and talked about the 'problematic' as something not necessarily negative, but a means of stirring up more possibilities. People - and especially a number of the art world's Alpha Males - had a problem with the way in which she embraced the ambiguous and the seductive. Because it is so much a personal matter when something tips from being seductive to being repulsive. Helen delighted in pushing such distinctions and ramping up these paradoxes whilst complicating and playing with notions of beauty and acceptability. For example, massed flower petals can be construed as smotheringly claustrophobic, or sublimely exquisite. My grotesque could be your gorgeous and vice-versa. Now notions of the nonbinary, and fluidity about identity, are made manifest in multifarious ways. But Helen was there already, doing it then, in a highly personal but also very universal way. You can't talk about her work in simple two-liners. Every comment you make about it, there's always a corollary, there's always an opposite, there's always a 'no but...' or an 'at the same time, it's exactly the opposite'. This is what makes her work so fascinating and so enduring, because it's in a constant state of fluidity: nothing is finite, nothing is fixed, nothing is certain.

LS I want to talk a bit more about the use of her own body from a feminist perspective, but there's also something interesting about using her body and her own waste products - her urine, for example, which is indexical - so that between her and the work, there's no interference of media, the work is not mediated.

LB In the late eighties Helen was often castigated for using her own naked body in her work. Especially in *The Oval Court* (1984-86), where she's cavorting in ribbons, beads and bows alongside the dead animals. Or in *Vanity* (1986), where she's looking at herself in the mirror, swathed in pearls and ostrich feathers and looking divine. Some in the previous generation of feminists disapproved of her using her body and accused her of objectifying herself. Too much frivolity! Too much playfulness! What they didn't realize was that this was Helen in fact very seriously exploring her selfhood. And celebrating herself. Helen was her own model, and because of this she could do whatever she wanted, like Rembrandt with his tronie self-portraits. But then, in part due to these responses to her work, Helen moved away from using the specificity of her body. Although Helen was a feminist, she didn't want her work to be solely tied into gender politics.

It is interesting to look at Helen's *Viral Landscapes* alongside *Corps Étranger* by Mona Hatoum (b. 1952), made five years later in 1994. In both works, what was then cutting-edge science is used to present this intimate bodily specificity as the absolute epitome of physical self. You can't get more personal than the cells from - or in Hatoum's case, an endoscopic view of - the inside of your vagina. But in both these works this view is also made universal, because unless the viewer is a medical expert, these magnified cells and endoscopically viewed viscera could be male or female, or indeed monkey, pig or dog. So, Helen's *Viral Landcapes* are fantastically personal, her body is her material, but they are also abstracted to become a metaphor and a symbol of something else altogether. Whether she was using her own naked body or her cells or using meat, viscera, flowers or urine cast in snow, Helen was celebrating her - and our - physicality and the glory of sensuousness that we can all experience.

LS There's a lovely quote about that work, where she says: 'I was looking at a vocabulary for desire where I was the subject and the object and the author.' She's trying to embody those three things, which I think she could only do by being naked.

LB Yes all these elements come into play. And the word 'play' is very important, as another thing that is crucial about Helen is how incredibly playful she was, and playful in all senses. Just look at her titles! There's a lovely quote where she talks about how making art is playful in the same way that children's games can be violent and horrible, but at the same time both can also be delicious, sensual and full of pleasure and joy. And again, these things are not mutually exclusive, there are no binaries there. They are enmeshed, intertwined. Helen knew she was being provocative, making sex, death, danger and beauty all co-exist, and especially in the 1980s and the beginning of the 1990s. And the art world remains suspicious of humour and playfulness.

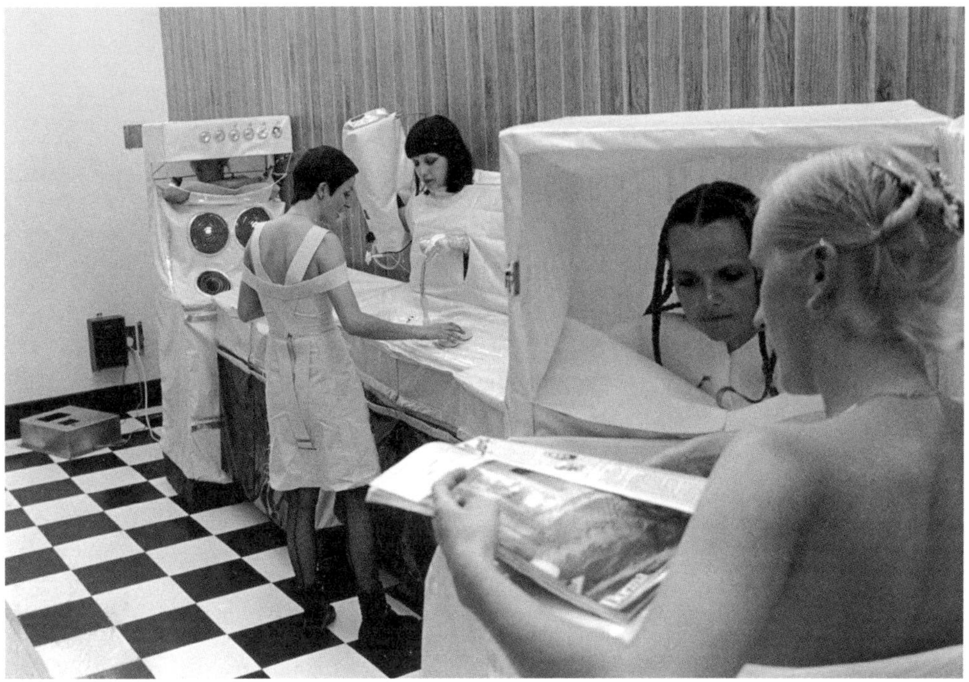

LS What do you think was important to her? What drove her to make the work that she did?

LB I think all true artists are compelled to make work. It's not a career choice, it's a life choice. And I think the C word, the 'career', is a parallel consideration. Having said that, Helen was very aware and exacting about how and where her work was presented, and the context in which it was shown. And always, her production values were second to none. She had to make work, and she had to make work in a certain way. Right from the earliest *In the Kitchen* (1977) performances, her work was intentionally, often hilariously, provocative. She was responding to the patriarchal, sexist world around her, responding with vigour and rigour, and a sense of fun. But she didn't only make art to make mischief. There was a strong desire in her to change things. She was also a wonderful teacher. All the artists I know that were taught by her say she was the best teacher they had. She was incredibly generous, and happy to share her erudition, her knowledge and her enthusiasms. She made her art to investigate, to communicate, to celebrate, to provoke, to change, to express herself and to put wonderful things into the world.

Helen Chadwick, *In the Kitchen*, 1977.
Performance at Chelsea College of Art, London

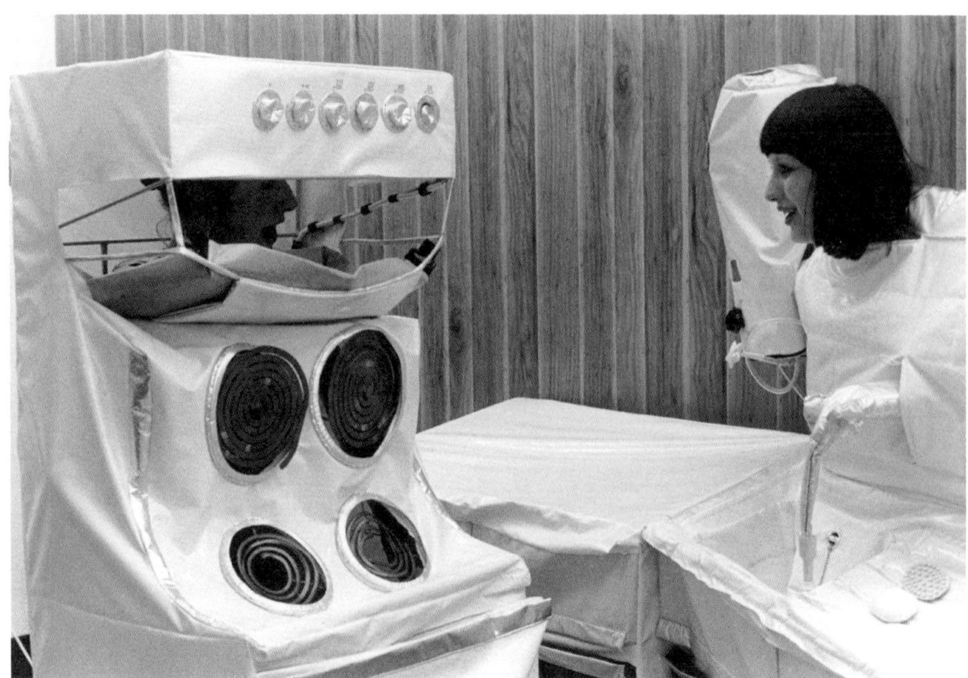

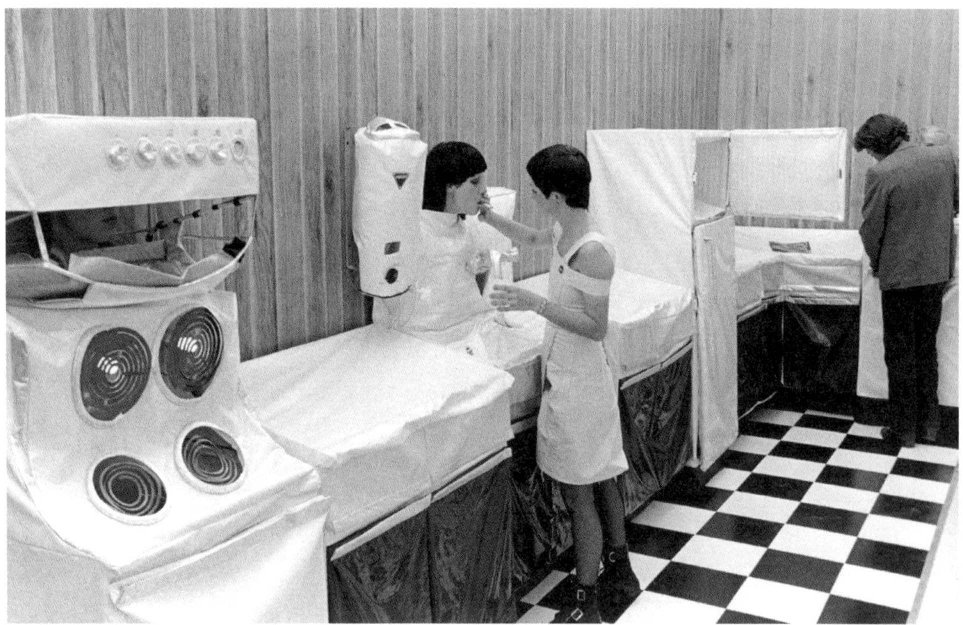

Helen Chadwick, *In the Kitchen*, 1977.
Performance at Chelsea College of Art, London

LS I'm interested in the influence that you think she's had on generations of artists since. I know from everyone I've spoken to how much of an important teacher she was. Nearly every artist of a certain generation that I speak to was taught by her, whether at the Royal College of Art, the Slade, Goldsmith's, Chelsea or St Martin's. I think you can clearly see the impact of that teaching on many of the Young British Artists (YBAs) such as Tracy Emin, Sarah Lucas and Damien Hirst.

LB It's very obvious how much of Helen's materials and attitude reverberated through the next generation of artists, the so-called YBAs, even if it wasn't - and still hasn't been - much acknowledged. If you think about one of Helen's earliest works being a jelly mould of her own face - that people could eat! - and then think about Mark Quinn (b. 1964) and the cast of his head in his own frozen blood! Helen was playing with the *vanitas* tradition right from the word go. Or consider Damien Hirst's use of animal matter - Helen's dead lamb in *The Oval Court* predates his *Away from the Flock* (1994) by ten years! Then of course there's Anya Gallaccio's use of decaying massed flowers and chocolate. While there's nothing new in the art of the last century using low-grade materials, there's no doubt that the chutzpah with which Helen embraced organic, sometimes unstable and often unlikely materials - whether cleaning fluids, oil, ointment, fur or chocolate - for both metaphorical and visual purposes was hugely influential. This revelling in and fusing of the physical, the visceral, the organic and the synthetic continues to resonate today.

LS And her use of excess?

LB Oh yes, excess was so important! And so difficult for so many in the art world to stomach! Massing, grouping, theatricality, Helen could make spectacular works out of the most mundane substances. A love of spectacle was something that other artists were taking on board as well. But the intense physicality of her work, the use of matter as material, and her taking nature and framing it in ways that were exquisite and repellent at the same time was, I feel, truly innovative. The way she tenderly arranged meat, intestines, fur and fabric into stunning and unholy alliances remains unique. She gave the next generation of artists the licence to be provocative, to be funny and to make mischievous mock of macho minimalism. Helen's *Wreaths to Pleasure* (1992–93), or *Cacao* (1994), used a framing geometry, but with all this crazy stuff going on inside. I am sure that Damien Hirst took note of this with his later vitrines. Helen's work was always so meticulously framed and presented, containing and restraining and thus amplifying the impact of the organic matter, or weird cleaning fluids, or whatever it was she was using. One of the *Wreaths to Pleasure* combines tomato juice and green Swarfega cleaning gel, and you can actually see them chemically reacting, fizzing at the edges.

LS And you can kind of smell it when you look at it, it's almost synaesthetic?

LB Absolutely. That's a really important point. I think the fact that her work puts all the senses into overdrive is something that subsequent generations of artists have run with. Obviously Carcass and Cacao were genuinely odoriferous. But with the *Meat Abstracts* (1989) or *Wreaths to Pleasure* and other works, their physical presence is so throat-grabbing that you can smell them by association. They conjure up pungent and often uncomfortable memories. Helen really took the vanitas tradition and the idea of sensory assault and rebooted it in a way that a lot of younger artists took note of, whether it's Quinn, Hirst, Gallaccio or Sarah Lucas: think *Two Fried Eggs and a Kebab* (1992).

LS I'm interested in hearing from you about Helen's incredible attention to detail and the mastery of so many skills that are indeed difficult to master, from sewing to bookbinding, from photography to sculpture. The first time I went to her archive, I guess I was expecting something much more punky and raw, but to open her notebooks was to discover her tiny, beautiful, precise handwriting, all her incredible handbound books with beautiful stitching, the costumes she made, all sewn by hand with flawless stitching. That fascinated me, because although spirit of the work is quite punky, its creation is pristine.

LB The spirit can be punky, but it achieves its impact by being so beautifully resolved. When you look at a Helen Chadwick, you don't think 'oh, look at that exquisite stitchwork' – because it's so beautifully rendered, the ideas are set free. It's very much her rigour of presentation that allows the maximum communication of what she wants to say. The lightbox had to be absolutely the right shape; the casting of piss holes in the snow is an incredible technical feat - achieving the right consistency of plaster so that it was delicate enough to produce her required knobbly finish but not melt into lumps; or to get the right viscosity of *Cacao*, so that the chocolate wasn't so liquid that it would splash, but it was thick and viscous and sexy. It would make bubbles the right shape, with the right kind of 'fart'. Her production values were exacting. She was also very good at delegating and getting top specialists to help realize her work when she needed to. Edward Woodman (b. 1943) took immaculate photographs. She also worked with the best fabricator that she could possibly find, Mike Smith. And with *The Oval Court* she chatted up Xerox to get the latest top-of-the-range Xerox machine that was then available, to be able to bring all these creatures, amazing sea animals, and locks of hair, and a goose, and a skate - and put them directly onto the photocopier. Helen's rigour, her amazing attention to detail was there right from the word go, the soft 'white goods' costumes that she made herself for *In the Kitchen* are so beautifully rendered, so you actually believe: 'ha-ha, those two hot plates are breasts'. She was so skilled in enabling viewers to make trompe l'oeil visual leaps without them even knowing it.

LS So that you're not looking at all at how it's fabricated and you just go with it?

LB Exactly. You don't think 'ooh, how did she make those?' You just think 'ah! What the hell is that?' Her work makes you think strange, disquieting thoughts: thoughts you feel like you shouldn't really be having, but that are also pleasurable. You might be slightly turned on in a way that you think you shouldn't be! This comes through her formidable technique, but without waving a 'craft' flag. The fact that she could find beauty in - for example - a load of intestines and a lock of fake blonde hair (*Loop my Loop*, 1991), or make a lump of steak into something cosmic by the mere addition of a lightbulb, was almost alchemical. And always unexpected. Often the flowers were the least beautiful thing she worked with. The masses of petals could sometimes border on too excessive, too smothering. She was always challenging stereotypes and confounding expectations.

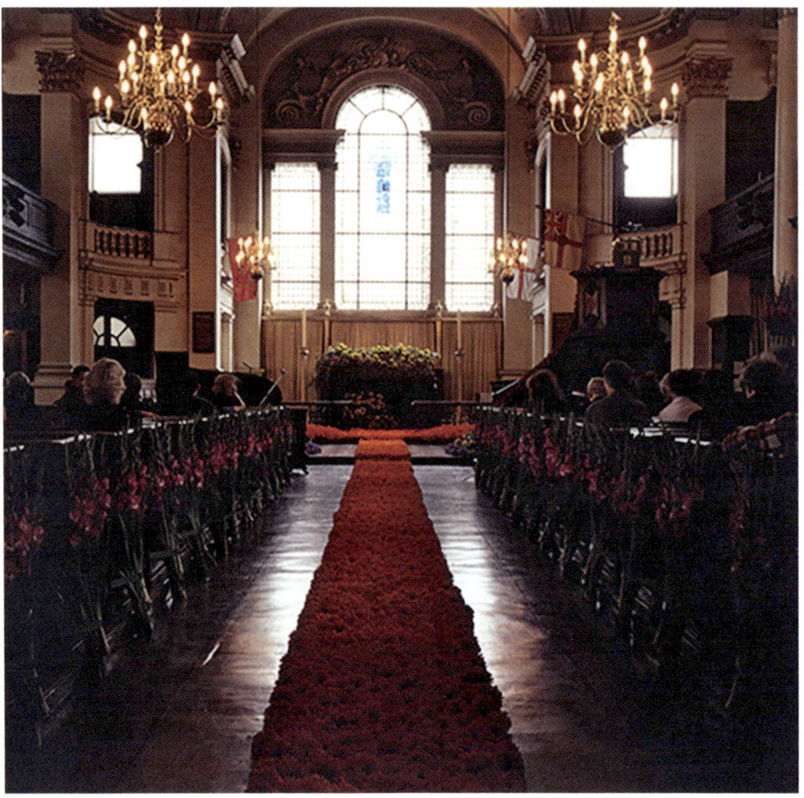

LS Can you talk a bit about her Greek heritage, or how important it was to her?

LB I'm really sad that I never got to stay at her little house in Greece - we had plans but she died before they were realized. I know she loved the fact that she was half-Greek. She made that great work with her mum, *Lofos Nymphon* (1987), where she's like a baby in her mother's arms with the Parthenon in the background. She adored the Mediterranean, her genetic link to the classical and especially the Dionysian. Also being mixed heritage, not being one nationality, was another way of complicating things. So her nationality and ethnicity were important to her. She'd always say, 'I'm Greek, I love gold,' and hold out her hands, with gold rings on practically every finger - even, as I recall, on her thumbs.

LS Could you tell us about the memorial service that you arranged after Helen died?

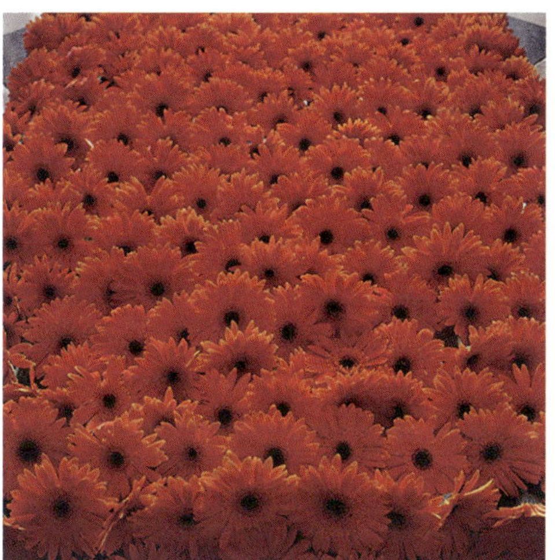

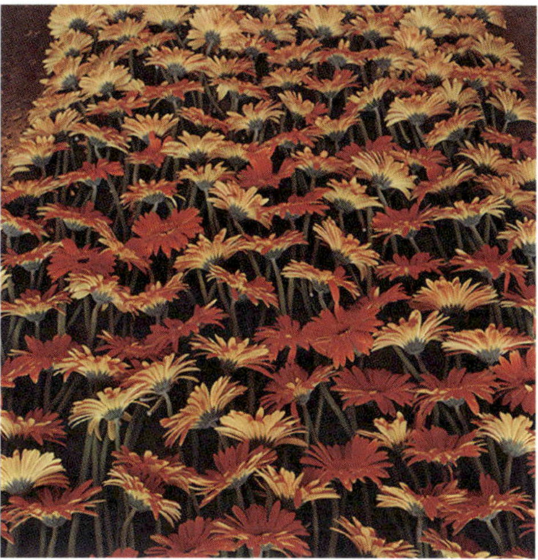

LB When Davey rang up and told me Helen had died, it was a devastating shock, as it was for all of us. There was a funeral - which fell on the day of Nancy The Saxon Queen's first birthday - but we all realized very quickly that we needed to do something much bigger for all the people that Helen had touched. Helen died on 15 March 1996, and the memorial was on 21 September that year. A group of us, including Zelda Cheatle (b. 1957), who was working with Helen when she died; the artist Cathy de Monchaux (b. 1960); Marjorie Allthorpe-Guyton, who was then Head of Visual Arts at the Arts Council; and various other people, all got involved in making sure that it was absolutely the best it could be. Because we loved Helen. But we also knew how bloody exacting she was, and that she would be looking down from her cloud in absolute horror if we didn't get it right! We were blessed with St Martin-in-the-Fields and its Curate, the wonderful Reverend Bernhard Schünemann. I will thank him to my dying day because he gave us free rein to do whatever we wanted in that beautiful church overlooking Trafalgar Square. We fundraised about £7,000 for flowers, which was a hell of a lot back in 1996. But while flowers were crucial, we also wanted at all costs to avoid any wobbly pastiche of Helen's work. So I left it to Cathy [de Monchaux] because I knew she'd get it right, and she did, with interest. She and the collector Eric Franck hired a van and went off at dawn to Covent Garden Market on the day of the memorial and came back with an abundance of flowers.

There were densely massed orange gerberas up the aisle like a wonderful flaming carpet and - because the undersides of the petals

ABOVE AND OPPOSITE
Helen Chadwick's Memorial Service at St-Martin-in-the-Fields, London, 1996

were a darker pink - it had a kind of velvety pile, and the whole thing was shimmering. At the end of each pew there were purple gladioli, fanned out like heraldic spears and strapped together with broad bands of black elastic, which had a rather kinky fetishistic vibe that I'm sure Helen would have appreciated. Up the beautiful early eighteenth-century wooden pulpit, Cathy used massed ranks of dark blackish-red roses, which were lined up like arrows all the way up its sweeping staircase. Then behind the altar, there was an explosion of sunflowers. It looked amazing. It had the spirit and spectacle of Helen's work and its sense of excess, but also the correct formal rigour and restraint. Cathy did her proud. There were great addresses from a terrific array of people including Marina Warner, Mark Hayworth-Booth and Peter Gabriel, who was a big fan of her work. There was beautiful music, including 'It's Raining' (originally by Irma Thomas), sung by Sarah Jane Morris, which was intensely moving, and Peter Gabriel performed his 'Here Comes the Flood'. At the end, in honour of Helen's heritage, we also had a pair of Greek balalaika musicians - the Two Costas: Costa Realice and Costa Savides - up in the gallery. They played traditional Greek music, which drifted down as all the flowers were dismantled and distributed to the congregation as they left.

In true Helen style this was done very correctly, with designated helpers wrapping up bunches of flowers in proper florist's paper so that people could take armfuls of flowers away with them. And off they went across London, some of them went to France, these vivid floral elements just dispersed. It was as if Helen's fantastic spirit just went out everywhere. Then we had a good old knees-up at the ICA, with Greek food, of course. I'm very proud of the memorial service. We had Helen's beautiful dandelion head from her great *Nebula* (1996) work, on the front of the order of service. All her work was about the fact that life is but a transient bubble, we are meat, we will rot; our intellect lights us up, but in the end we all vanish. So it was especially poignant that she herself died so young. When you look at her work, it seems in some strange way as if it was leading up to this untimely end. Among the last great works that she made, with the human embryos and plant matter, the *Monstrance* (1996) memorial ring and the *Nebula* necklace were themselves *memento mori* and also partly inspired by Victorian memorial mourning jewellery. Death was always there in her work.

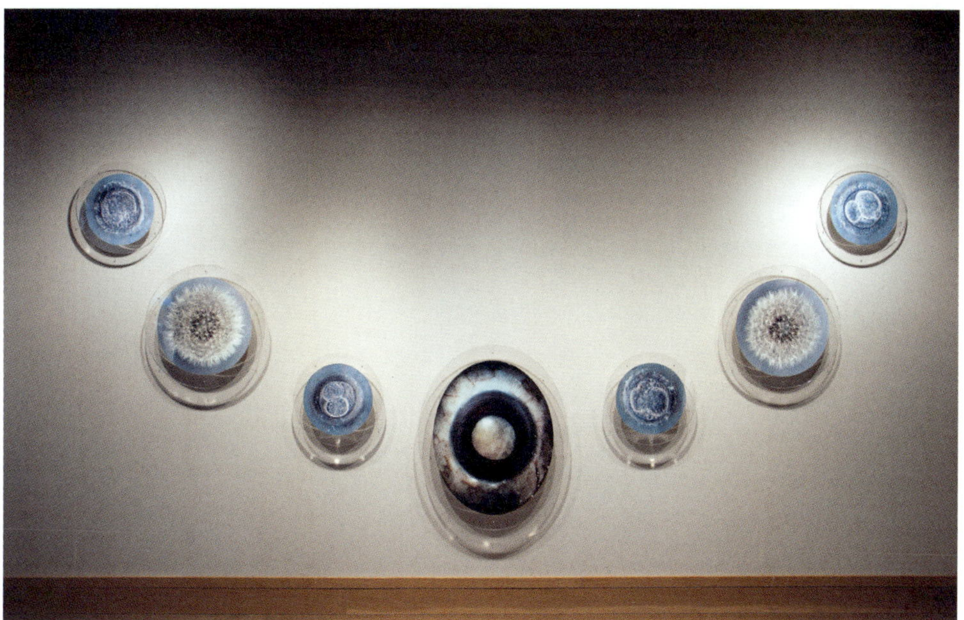

LS What should we do? What is the responsibility of curators and writers? What should we do with her legacy?

LB We need to show her work as much as possible, and that's why this exhibition is so important. Keep it out there and allow other artists respond to it, to mix it up, to put it with the work of the present, the work of the past, the work of the future. And to write about it in different contexts. Her work was of its time and it's also beyond its time, it lives on in ours. It needs to be spread, dispersed, exhibited, responded to and put in a dialogue with work from all periods and all cultures. Although so much of what Helen made was in direct dialogue with art historical traditions, it also transcends the limits of Western art history and culture because it's so much about physical presence. I'd like to see it with work from artists of all different cultures and different art worlds and art histories. I think its possibilities are endless.

This interview took place on 17 May 2024

Helen Chadwick, *Nebula*, 1996. Cibachrome photographs, Perspex, four parts 46 × 7 cm (18$\frac{1}{8}$ × 2$\frac{3}{4}$ in.), two parts 60 × 7 cm (23$\frac{5}{8}$ × 2$\frac{3}{4}$ in.), one part 90 × 76 × 7 cm (35$\frac{1}{2}$ × 30 × 2$\frac{3}{4}$ in.)

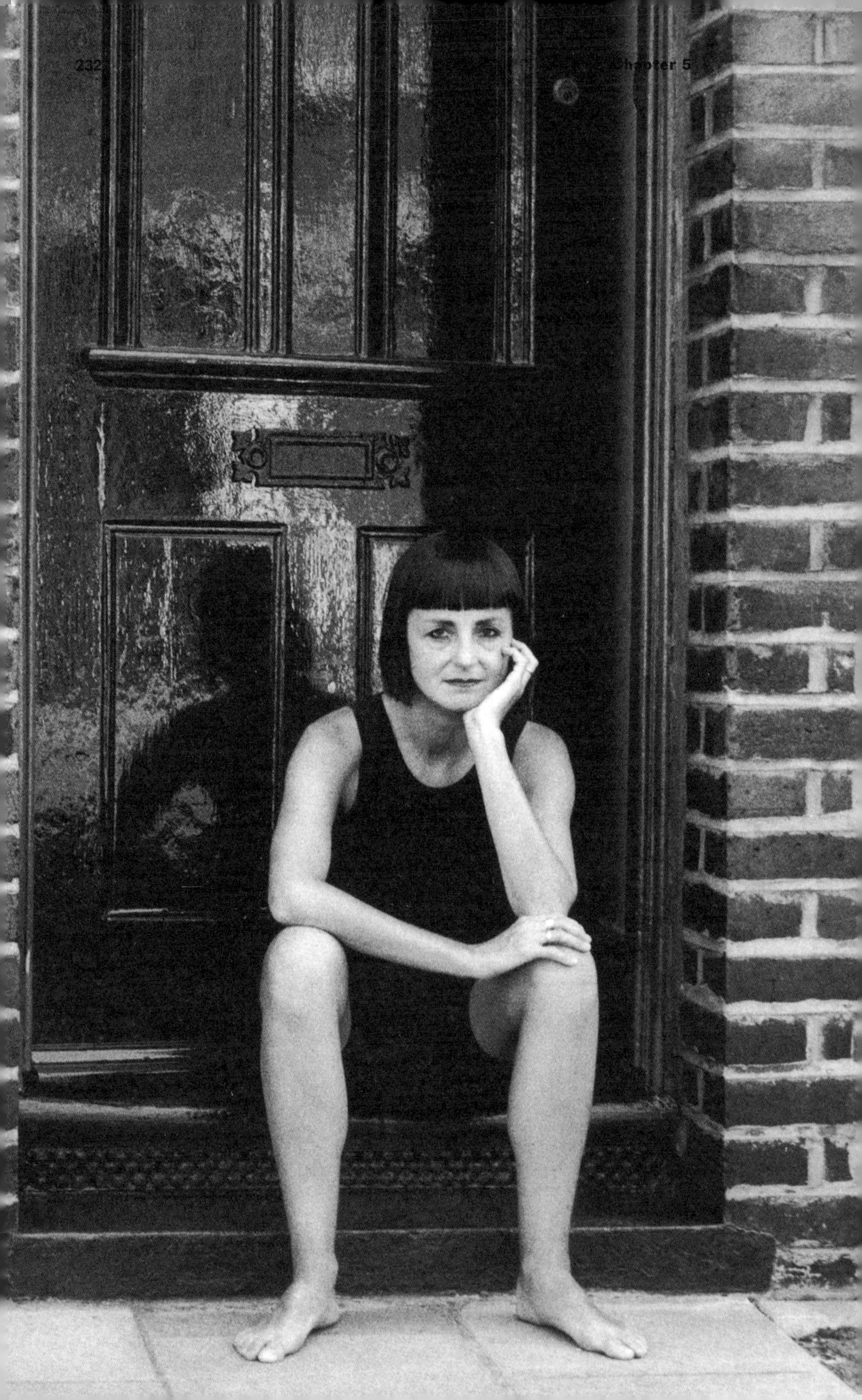

CHAPTER 6

David Notarius & Laura Smith in Conversation

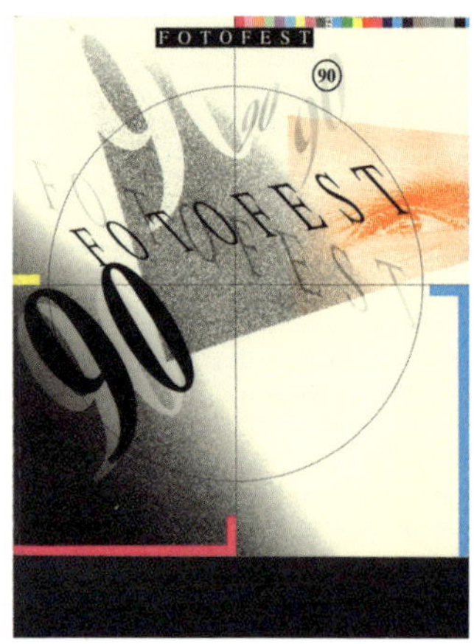

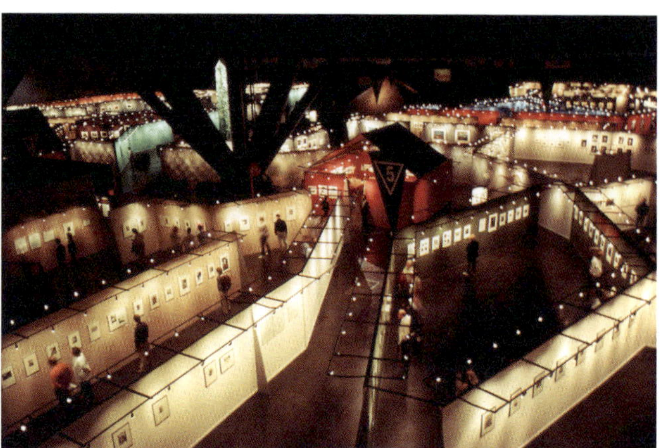

Laura Smith When and how did you first meet Helen?

David Notarius I met Helen in 1990 at the 'Fotofest' photography exhibition in Houston, Texas. She was one of several artists exhibiting and I was part of the team who built the walls to hang their photographs on.

LS Can you remember what was she exhibiting?

DN Yes, Helen was exhibiting works from her *Enfleshings* (1989) series.

LS And how were they received in Texas?

DN Well, this was an exhibition of a few hundred photographers; it was in a convention hall and there were photographers there from all over the world. There was a lot to see. But Helen's works were received very well.

LS How then did you eventually come to move in with Helen, in Beck Road, London?

DN Well after the exhibition, Helen went back to the UK. We kept in touch, Helen came to back to America for an exhibition, I then travelled to England. After a few trips back and forth, I eventually moved to London in 1991.

LS Can you tell me about Beck Road at that time?

ABOVE *Fotofest* exhibition catalogue (left) and installation view of 'Fotofest', Houston, Texas, 1990 (right). Page 232: Helen Chadwick outside her home on Beck Road, London, 1995 (detail). Bromide fibre print, 18.5 × 28 cm ($7\frac{1}{4}$ × 11 in.)

DN I would say about 80 per cent of the street was artists and everyone sort-of knew each other. It was a very lively place. It wasn't like a typical London street. Helen and her previous partner [Philip Stanley (b. 1950)] had been quite instrumental in creating the Beck Road community. He [Philip] had started the Beck Road Residents Association. Some of the artists were originally there as squatters when the street was derelict, and then many of the houses were provided as short-term leases from Acme (who still provide artists' studios or artists' spaces today). It was the Association and Acme who fought to keep the houses, because the council was going to tear them down.

LS So you moved into a really vibrant community?

DN Yeah. Everyone owned their own houses by the timc I arrived, or most people did. And they were artists, writers, painters, sculptors, photographers, plus there was one gallery on the street.

LS Can you tell me what Helen was like? What was important to her? What drove her?

DN It's hard to say, but she was very driven. Helen would have an idea and would tenaciously bring it to fruition. For each new idea she would figure out what she needed to learn or do, and she would work and work and work on it, and research and speak to anyone she needed advice from. She was compelled to get these things done.

LS What do you think is enduring about her work now?

DN A lot of it is very timeless. I think a lot of her work has a universal appeal. It speaks to everybody in some respect. Her work always evokes reactions from people, which is, I think, the primary thing that any artist wants: a reaction. Whether that is good or bad, positive or negative. And the works are very emotional to look at, you can feel her love emanating from them.

LS I guess that's what makes them timeless: they connect to feelings rather than to something merely cognitive.

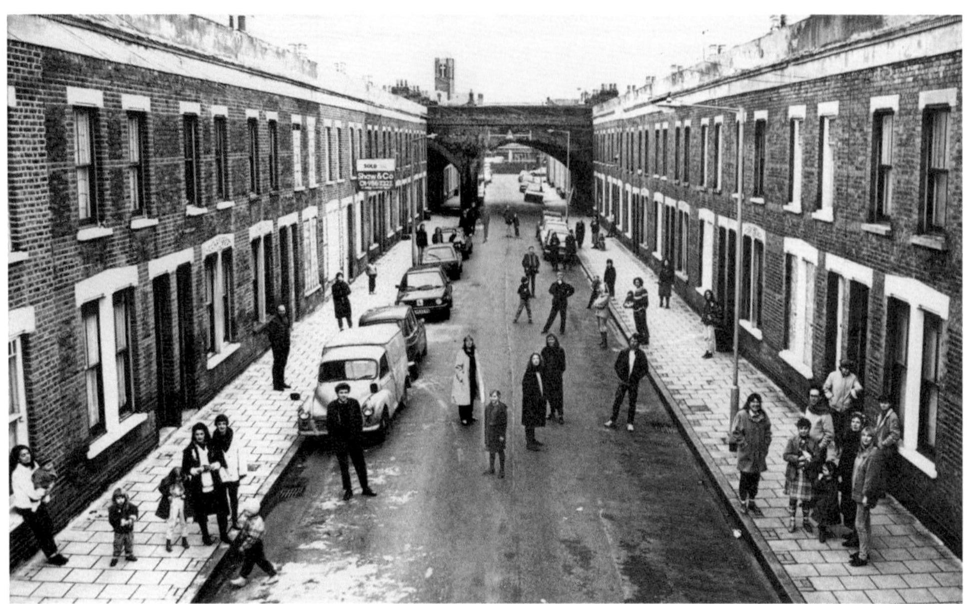

DN Yeah.

LS You said that she was very driven. How did she approach making a work? Because I know that she was incredibly talented across so many different mediums and so many different skill sets and techniques. I'm interested in how, if she had an idea, how that took form, how she decided to make a chocolate fountain, or to photograph flowers smothered in engine oil or a lamp buried inside a piece of meat.

DN Well, the lightboxes and the meat works were part of a whole Frankenstein thing that Helen had going on. She was very influenced by the filmmaker David Cronenberg at that time. She was keen to find a way of taking something inanimate and bringing it to life. So the idea was to reanimate the meat, to bring it to life with electricity and light but in a way that was beautiful, not monstrous. Helen also loved the whole play of juxtaposing different materials, especially materials that you wouldn't normally see together. All the different textures working together and the sort of feelings that they would invoke through their combinations.

LS And did she teach herself to use the different materials or to learn new skills?

Photograph of the residents of Beck Road, London, n.d

DN Often she did. Other times she would talk to workmen/women and get advice. For example, Helen (often) talked to architects, and she talked regularly to a carpenter that she used for fabrication. So, she was always learning from other people.

LS And were you quite involved with a lot of the work?

DN Yeah, I think it's more that I was assisting.

LS But you did collaborate on her seminal work *Piss Flowers* (1991-92). Can you talk about that?

DN Well, Helen was doing a residency at the Walter Phillips Gallery at the Banff Centre in Alberta, Canada. She was playing around with different ideas to do with snow and casting, creating form from negative space, as well as a sort of ongoing exploration for her into reversing genders. That's how the *Piss Flowers* came about.

LS So, what was the process of making them?

DN Basically, peeing in the snow! Helen had some moulds made from sheet metal that were shaped like a flower, or the outline of a flower. The moulds were like giant cookie cutters. The process was that we'd form a mound of dense, heavily packed snow, patted down with a shovel, and we'd push the mould into the top of it. Then we would take turns peeing into the mould before filling up the holes with plaster.

LS And how did you then extract the plaster, because I guess getting the right consistency of plaster, so that it wouldn't crush the snow, was tricky?

DN Well it was freezing where we were making them; Canada in the middle of January is very, very cold, especially up in the Rockies. But that is also why we packed the snow down so densely, so that the plaster didn't have anywhere to run. It would set within 15-20 minutes in the cold, we'd leave it for about a half hour, just be safe, then we'd just lift it out. The plaster would heat up a bit as it set and melt the snow.

LS How long did it take to make the full set?

DN We were up there for about three or four weeks, and we'd generally make two or three a day, depending on how cold we were. Some of them just ended up being trash though, so we got rid of those.

LS And how did she make those decisions around which to keep and which to trash?

DN I think it has to do with the different textures and surfaces that the piss created, basically the ones that appealed to her the most had more depth or more contrast.

LS Were there other pieces that you worked on together?

DN There was a piece called *Philoxenia* that Helen made in 1994. It came about because I had a friend who was cleaning out an old tannery building in east London. I brought home a bag of old furs for Helen. She started playing around with them and that's how a lot of her fur pieces really started. *Philoxenia* became the starting point for a whole project that Helen worked on that dealt with racism and the treatment of women at the time. It consisted of ten fur panels. Helen shaved a square into the middle of each and then painted flowers and the names of ten women that she knew into the squares. The women were all of ethnic origins with non-traditional Western names. Each flower represented the person whose name was painted on the panel, so it became a kind of tribute. Unfortunately, the work burned in the Momart [warehouse] fire in 2004, so it doesn't exist anymore.

We were working on the evolution of this work when Helen died. It was going to be a railway carriage, for a travelling exhibition on the Belgian railways. The work was inspired by an essay that Helen had been planning to use in the exhibition catalogue, which is about the Nazi occupation of Greece. It includes an account from a Greek train driver who was forced to take Greek Jews to the concentration camps in Germany. The work was going to consist of a carpet for the train carriage with the Star of David woven into it, as well as the names of all these

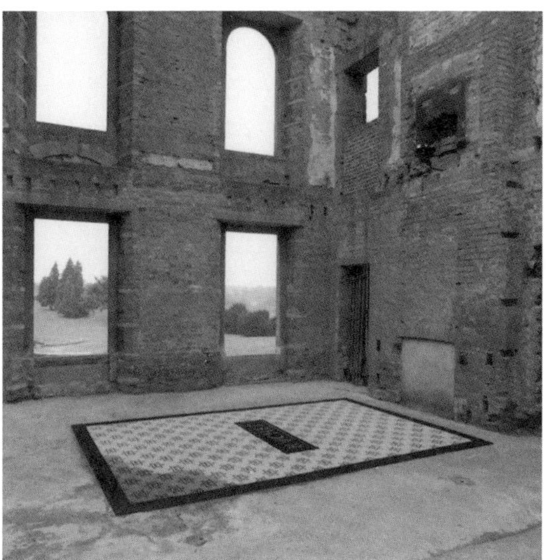

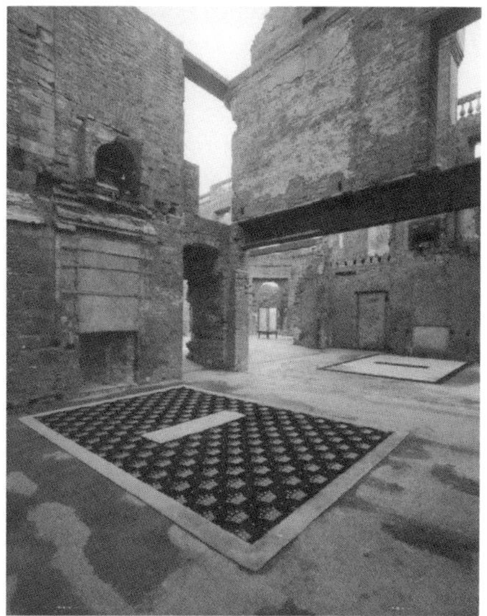

different women printed onto the inside walls of the carriage. Sadly we never completed it.

LS I wanted to ask you about the influence that she might have had on the next generations of artists, because I know she was such a prolific teacher. And I guess you were there with her when she was teaching every day. She taught at all the key London art schools, and so she taught some of the most important contemporary artists of the next generation. I don't think contemporary art would exist in Britain in the same way without Helen.

DN I think one of the central things that she taught her students was not to be conventional, to look outside of the box, to use different materials. Helen was a champion of using materials that most artists wouldn't even think about using.

LS Her use of unusual materials allowed her to explore different sensations like pleasure and desire, and the grotesque and the transgressive. Do you have an idea of where her interest in these contrasts came from?

DN Well, Helen was a prolific reader. She was always interested in things that are visceral, or things that are beneath the surface. As I said, she

Helen Chadwick, *Rachel*, 1995. Metal and wool, 457.2 × 304.8 cm (180 × 120 in.). Installed at Witley Court, Worcester, as part of exhibition 'England's Glory', organised by Ikon Gallery, Birmingham

liked the works of Cronenberg, for example, but she also liked some old Hammer films. She was always fascinated by the mechanics of how the gore and materiality in those films were made. Helen wanted to really look at the body, think about what is inside the body. What diseases look like, to think about sex and violence and death, as well as beauty.

LS Can you talk a little bit about the work that she was making when she died?

DN Helen was working on a number of IVF pieces using unviable embryos and foetuses. Her idea was to take these things that had been discarded and to make them into something beloved or beautiful. She was also working with images from the Wellcome Trust that document the head of a human foetus with one eye, for example, or a chimpanzee foetus. Helen wanted to take things that people thought were ugly and make them beautiful. It had a lot to do with how we look at the body, how we look at reproduction, how we look at what is unviable, what we throw away, what's been rejected, and make something precious out of all these things that had not been considered precious.

LS A final question I would like to ask you: how do you think we should honour Helen's legacy and ensure her continued relevance?

DN I think there are two ways to honour Helen's legacy. First, by making her work available to be seen, where people can witness it and experience it. The work is made to be seen, not be in a warehouse somewhere or a private collection for a few people. It should be available to the public. Second is to remember Helen for her teaching. She loved teaching, helping students learn about art, about their artistic potential. She always looked out for the underdog, too, the people who were not exactly accepted – Helen would always champion them.

This interview took place on 23 May 2024

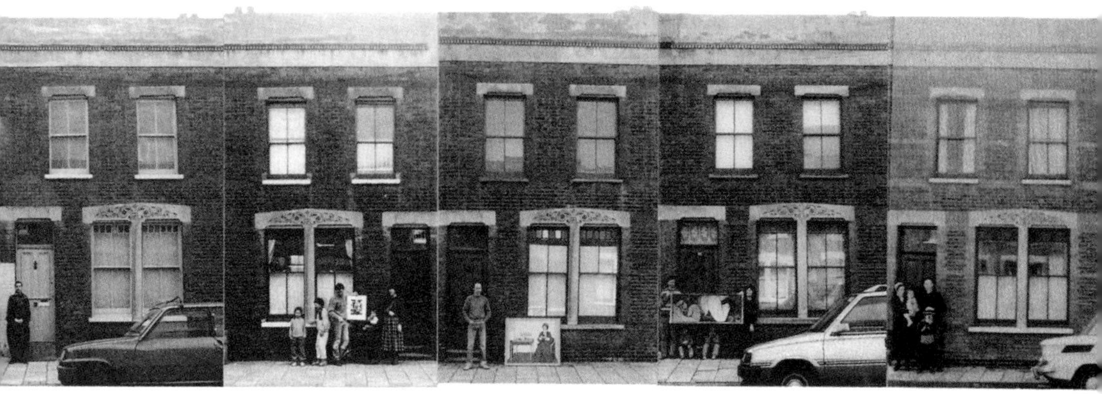

Maureen O. Paley
founder and director of Interim Art

Jeremy Sancha
illustrator

Joanna Sancha
modelmaker and frame-maker

Aragon, Tamsin and Tristan

David Hamilton
artist

Brian Campbell
photographer/ frame-maker

Phyllis Mahon
artist

Matthew, Orla and Uisliu

Peter Bunting
painter

Karen Bunting
painter

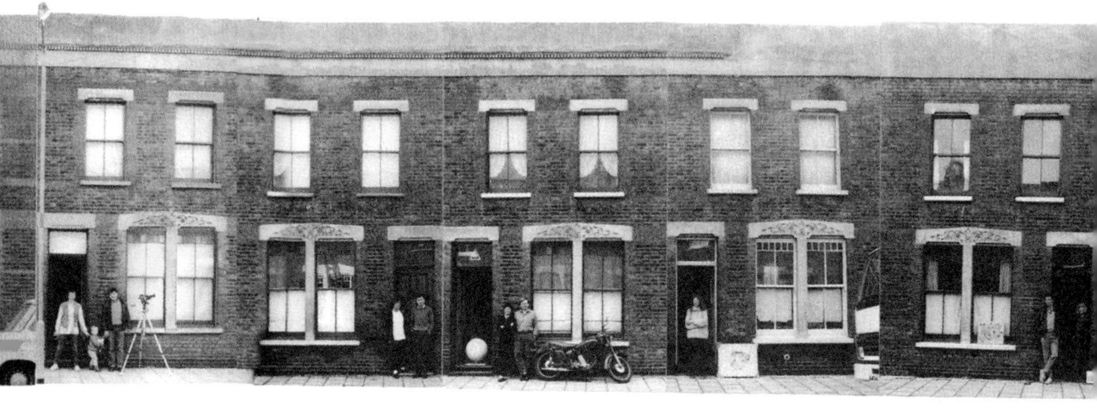

Krystyna Malinowska
film-maker

Tomasz Pobog Malinowski
film-maker

Martin

Alison Turnbull
painter

Trevor Shearer
painter

Helen Chadwick
artist

Philip Stanley
architect

Debbie Duffin
artist

Peter Smith
artist

Jennie Smith
designer/illustrator

Artists' houses on Beck Road, from the Beck Road Arts Trust campaign brochure, published by Acme, 1988

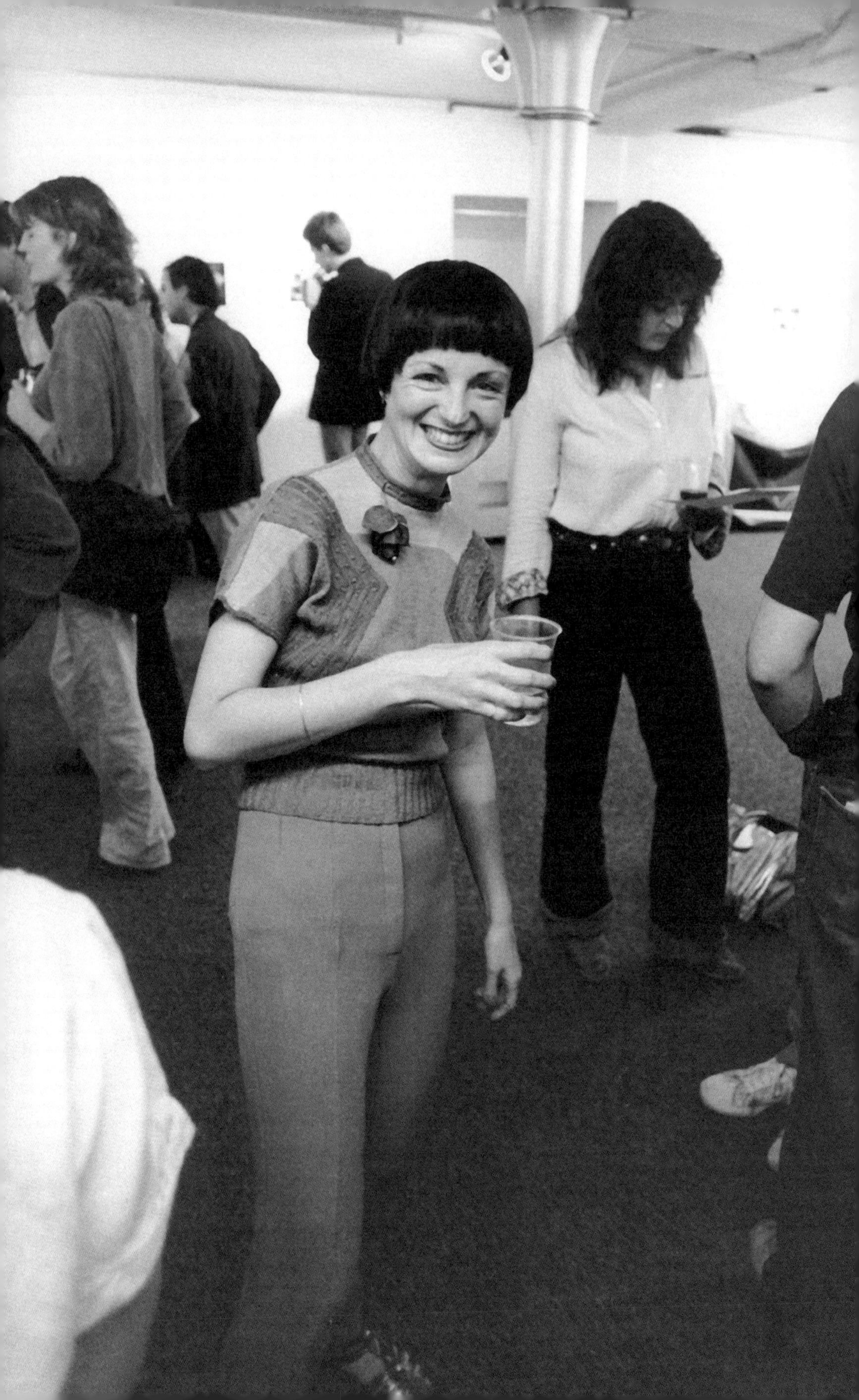

Chadwick's Influence

Maureen Paley
Cosey Fanni Tutti
Mikey Cuddihy
Shelagh Keeley
Anya Gallaccio
Cathy de Monchaux
Nicolas Deshayes
Mark Haworth-Booth
Peter Gabriel

My last memory of Helen Chadwick is her knocking on my door the very day she was to die. She handed me something to fax for her and I waved goodbye as she walked down the street, through the railway arch, on her way to the Architectural Association, where she suddenly passed away that evening. The shock of seeing her one day, never to see her again, has haunted me forever in its finality. So many more things to have said and done. Her life was cut abruptly short, too young, with no warning to anticipate such a loss.

She was a self-invented person and artist. I was always struck by the fact that her mother was Greek, and she was therefore first-generation English on her mother's side. She was incredibly self-possessed and always made a strong impression wherever she went. She told me that it might be better for me to curate and run a gallery than to be an artist. That was in 1981 – the rest is history. She was naturally inventive and experimental in the mediums she chose to make her works with. I was devastated by her death, but I think her *Viral Landscapes* (1988–89) hinted at her understanding of the fragility of life and all matter – the internal body as a landscape – dust to dust.

MAUREEN PALEY

PAGE 242 **Helen Chadwick at an exhibition opening, n.d.**

I first met Helen when she moved into the house opposite me in Beck Road, Hackney. We became friends, and us both being women artists was at the heart of our friendship. I would visit her often. We'd sit and have tea and cake, talking about life and art, discussing ideas about what we were both working on and what was important to us in terms of expressing ourselves. At times we shared similar themes about *self*, using our (naked) bodies, our sensuality. But we worked very differently. My style of practice is free-form, it's based on improvised action and response. The statements Helen made through her art were incredibly well thought out and executed to perfection. I was fascinated by, and in awe of, her meticulous approach. Sitting in her studio and witnessing the construction of *Model Institution* (1981) or *Train of Thought* (1978), seeing her so excited that she'd managed to source the exact materials she needed. Overall I remember Helen for her sense of fun, the positivity she brought to my life, her support artistically and personally – and her smile was utter magic.

COSEY FANNI TUTTI

Helen's light. Her studio was at the front of the house on the ground floor, at street level. When she was home – in her studio, her light was always on. There was something encouraging about that. I worked on the top floor of my house, overlooking the street, along and across the road from Helen. My studio faced south, and I worked by natural light, until it was too dark to see anything. Work-wise, we often shared the same concerns. At one point, she was fitting her naked photographed body into life-sized wooden sculptures, made in the shape of defining objects from her childhood: an incubator, a pram, a bed. At the same time, I was building paper houses in my studio, using my own body outline – as caryatids – to hold up roofs of ersatz brick and stone. (These defining works we showed together at the Riverside Studios in 1985, along with *Chimeres* (1984) by Annette Messager (b. 1943).) Later, a Xerox machine appeared in Helen's front room; it was the size of a cooker – the latest technology at the time; we all came over to admire it. Xerox were sponsoring her for a show at the ICA – the whole upstairs gallery. She lay fish, flowers, offal on the screen, Xeroxed them in blue, and her own naked self, kissing a dead lamb; the effect was beautiful, like everything was floating in a depth of shallow water, just underneath the surface.

When she died, her light went out; the street went dark.
I missed that light so very much.

MIKEY CUDDIHY

Helen was a beautiful genius. I still miss her wicked sense of humour, charm, fun and spirit of generosity.

Helen and I met in Chicago in 1988 doing on-site installations in Japan, and became fast friends. We saw each other a lot in New York, where I lived, showing together in many exhibitions dealing with the body throughout the eighties and nineties. Often we talked about the viscerality and eroticism in our work. She was always so insightful and supportive. I remember us discussing the brilliance of David Cronenberg's film *Dead Ringers* (1988).

In February 1991 Helen and I were invited to the Walter Phillips Gallery at the Banff Centre in Alberta, Canada, to be resident artists together for one month. The gallery was commissioning new work from both of us for an exhibition. This is when Helen made her outstanding work *Piss Flowers* (1991–92). In 1995 Helen had a solo exhibition of her *Wreaths to Pleasure* (1992–93) photographs at MoMA, New York, titled 'Bad Blooms'. I remember how vulnerable she was about the work and at the same time so strong in her belief in it.

I am so thankful for the intense time we shared together. Her work is powerful, fearless, and it was way ahead of its time.

SHELAGH KEELEY

When I was at art college, Helen Chadwick was one of a very few contemporary female-identifying artists whose work I had seen in the flesh. I saw her as a warrior, a foot soldier, recognisable by her black leather tunic, more Joan of Arc than Louise Brooks. Despite her initially severe appearance, she was warm and funny. And, as a woman artist, by being visible, and importantly accessible, she made the idea of being an artist real. Her most direct influence on me was her use of unconventional materials. Her work was initially beautiful, it seduced you into looking closer, but on second view was alienating, ambiguous. Her work presented the actual stuff of a body, making visible the mutability of life. Her huge glass tank of vegetable waste at the ICA, *Carcass* (1986), which began as distinct layers of material, coloured bands that blurred and dissolved into each other, was significant for me. Seemingly made as a stable, formal composition, it exploded, which I guess was technically a disaster, but from my perspective – by releasing the foul smell of decay, staining the space – it took the work from an image of mutability to an actual body. Later, *Piss Flowers* used process and gender, literally by pissing in the snow, to generate positive and negative forms. In hardware terminology, male and female parts are made to join or connect. A simple, playful – or to some, taboo – gesture, literally marking space, and a moment in time, and in so doing directly casting reality.

ANYA GALLACCIO

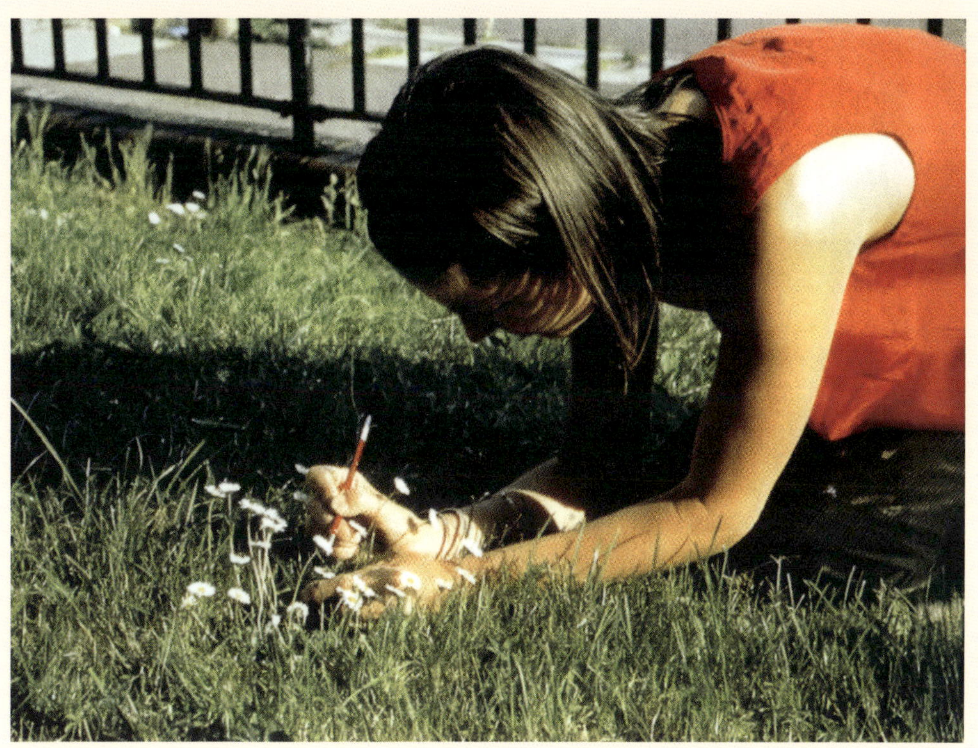

Helen Chadwick making *All Flesh is Grass*, 1991, at the Serpentine Gallery, London

There was no doubt in Helen's mind that in another time she would have been burned at the stake as a witch. We concurred on this fact one day in 1995, sitting by the pool of a very creepy abandoned ambassadors' residence in Buenos Aires, Argentina. We had been driven to this house as a 'rest afternoon' after Helen had lost her temper the day before during a meal that consisted entirely of steak. We had been on the go relentlessly for days, having been ludicrously overscheduled to give tutorials to local artists along with hanging an exhibition of our own work. Our British Council minder implied that she shouldn't complain because we were being paid a per diem to be there. At which point, Helen slapped her hands together and said, 'if I want to be paid, I teach in London, and if I want a holiday I will pay for one. I'm here to hang an exhibition and to meet local artists, not to give them tutorials.' The Greek hand slap/clap really hurts, so you have to mean it. Helen was never a pushover. She was really lovely, kind and generous with her time and her thoughts, but she had clear boundaries and was never afraid to stand up for herself or her work.

The next day we were duly delivered to this deserted house to 'rest'. Pigeon feathers were everywhere, which she said was a voodoo thing, as the ambassador had obviously done something to offend the local community. Helen always knew everything about any given situation. She was a mine of information and knowledge. Every country we showed in she would have learnt a few words and studied the culture. The spirit of the house was very unsettling to our witchy minds, so we sat outside by the pool, naked, because we had no costumes, and spent the afternoon discussing our witchcraft, life, the art world and relationships. I will never forget that day.

A few months later we were in Helsinki, Finland, for another group show. Helen described our spooky pool afternoon to artist Lawrence Weiner (1942–2021), so he decided to go one better and found a sauna hut beside the Baltic Sea for us all. Another naked afternoon for Helen, Lawrence, Juan Muñoz (1953–2001) and myself! Sweating and drinking brandy, gazing out at the frozen Baltic. Talking of life, art, travelling and relationships.

Helen commented then that no one understands how hard all of the travelling, and showing work, and being 'on' – far from the studio and home – is. But we agreed that this day was pretty special, and another one to always be remembered. Unbelievably they have all gone now, it's just me left remembering…

Next stop was St Petersburg, Russia. On our last day we went to a natural history museum, the basement full of glass jars containing foetuses who had been born prematurely due to 'birth defects'. You could hear the thoughts crackling in the air as a roomful of artists gazed at these fantastical creatures. But none more than Helen; the air above her was practically on fire with creative thoughts, which turned into action as soon as she got back to the studio. She was developing this body of work when she died.

Some months later, it was my privilege to arrange the flowers for her memorial service at St Martin-in-the-Fields. It was incredible to try to channel Helen's spirit and her relationship with flowers. As people left the service, we filled their arms with flowers, Trafalgar Square was awash with a stream of bouquets waving in the breeze. I like to think I did her proud.

CATHY DE MONCHAUX

Helen Chadwick printed depictions of the body onto various supports with light, liquid and chemical processes, producing desire-inducing imagery that draws the viewer into the darker realities of passing time. Made with forensic precision, her works exist in vitro. They propose a view of bodies pressed behind glass and confined within frames, offering us visceral *natures mortes* in high definition.

In *Piss Flowers* – a body of work that has shaped me significantly as a sculptor – Chadwick imprints her and her partner's body into material. Abandoning figuration, the sculptures are nonetheless wholly corporeal by their means of making: using their own urine as the acid etch in blocks of snow, trickles and jets carve into the material like a hot knife in butter. In a form of molybdomancy, as if divining the future by flinging molten metal into cold water, they are cast into plaster and then bronze. The mould is broken away to reveal a detailed topography of the urine's course; deep ravines, crests and valleys turn into erect calcified stalagmites, moments frozen in time. In an emulsion of yonic and phallic, they are sexually charged but without assigned gender. The use of bronze recalls bubbling terrestrial magma, pushing through the Earth's crust in an efflorescence of rock, but the white enamelled coating reminds me of sanitaryware, I want to lick it and sit on it, but it might hurt.

In these works, there is no real measure of scale. Their precise arrangement at once carries the reverence of gonshi, Chinese scholar's stones placed upon their lacquered pedestals, the allure of melting meringues left out in the rain and a *parterre* of flowers on a manicured lawn.

As a viewer I feel disembodied, tiny, like I'm high up looking down onto a solar system, surveying a dissection, a landscape, a pattern of cells. Suddenly I am a bumblebee, gliding through a corolla, sitting upon a pistil. Drunk on pollen I delve down into the bacterial flora, deep into the cloaca, elbowing my way through heavy corridors of flesh with my headlights on. Then I am inside my own body, following a course mapped by a photosensitive dye, it's internal contours bulbous and glossy under infrared light. I feel like I've been turned inside out, the inner walls of my termite mound exposed for all to see, my extremities fizzing like polystyrene doused in white spirit. As I come to, emerging back into the world, I rub my eyes – phosphenes of colour float over my retinas and merge with the landscape beyond.

NICOLAS DESHAYES

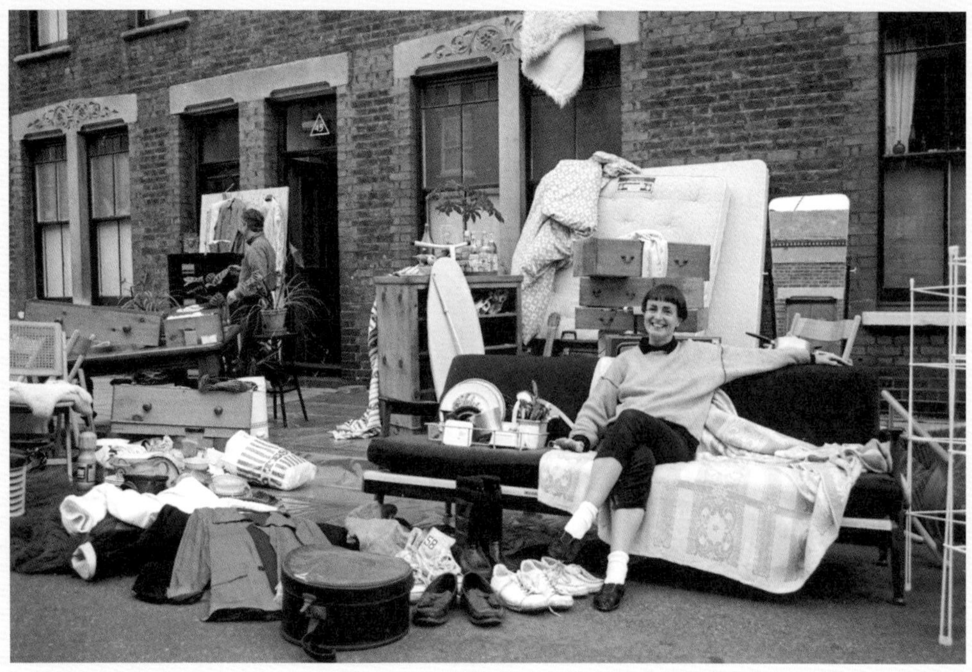

The private view card for Helen's exhibition 'Of Mutability' at the Institute of Contemporary Arts, London, in spring 1986 was so beautiful that I went the next morning, instead of to the opening, and had the grand upstairs rooms to myself. I was enchanted and sent Helen a fan letter. We had lunch and the V&A (where I was then Senior Curator of Photographs) bought her earlier work *One Flesh* (1985). Later, *The Oval Court* (1984–86) from 'Of Mutability' became my largest and most expensive acquisition for the museum. I showed it in 'PHOTOGRAPHY NOW' in 1989. Helen also made her *Meat Lamps* for the occasion, with a large Polaroid camera that came over from Germany.

When the 'Oral History of British Photography' was set up by the British Library in the 1990s, I trained as an interviewer one afternoon at the National Sound Archive in Exhibition Road. I wanted to interview Helen. As I walked back to the V&A,

Helen Chadwick outside her home in Beck Road, Hackney, London, 1987

we fell in step. I asked if she would be willing. 'As my greatest patron during the 1980s, I can refuse you nothing,' she said. When I travelled by tube to Beck Road with the Marantz tape recorder a few weeks later, I felt nervous, but Helen alighted from the same train and we walked to her house together. We completed the life story interviews over two sessions of several hours.

With other friends, I organised Helen's memorial service at St Martin's-in-the-Fields on 21 September 1996. The artist Cathy de Monchaux came up with the idea of laying hundreds of yellow and orange gerbera flowers down the nave, continuing into the sanctuary and onto the altar. Mourners took flowers away at the end. As they stepped into the sunshine in Trafalgar Square, they seemed to float and glide. A few days later I showed Helen's mother the figures from *The Oval Court* in their custom-made green metal press at the V&A – Helen's extraordinary form now mortal and immortal.

MARK HAWORTH-BOOTH

I first met Helen in the early nineties when I was looking for artists to work with on various projects. Artists Mike Coulson (b. 1952) and Nichola Bruce (b. 1953) had been directing film and video for us, and they researched and recommended well over a hundred artists. From them, I picked the most interesting for what I had in mind.

The *EVE* project (1997) was a CD-ROM, at a time when computers were very dry, male, sci-fi environments in primary colours. We wanted *EVE* to represent nature and be more 'feminine' and mysterious, and we chose the artist accordingly. Helen's work was truly innovative, sensual and sexual and fitted perfectly. We also wanted artwork that would have elements that could be moved – animated – within the CD-ROM, for which Helen's work was ideal.

Helen's work continues to bring me pleasure; we have two of my favourite *Wreaths to Pleasure* hanging in the room in my house where the grand piano lives and I continue to look at them while playing. We've also had a revamp in Real World Studios and put two other beautiful wreaths in the dining room; they have changed the whole atmosphere of the place…for the better.

Helen was an extraordinary artist whose work and influence is under-acknowledged. She pioneered themes of life and death that Damien Hirst later became well known for. She is getting more recognition nowadays from many of the artists (and many of her students) who she influenced, and who are now better known than she was at the time.

Her memorial service at St Martin-in-the-Fields in Trafalgar Square was a very special event. The church was packed with people and flowers and at the end of the service we were all invited to take the flowers home. At first people were grabbing one or two blooms, but very quickly they began leaving the church with as many as they could carry. Trafalgar Square was filled with people going in every direction with sad faces and armfuls of beautiful flowers. What a wonderful way to remember Helen.

PETER GABRIEL

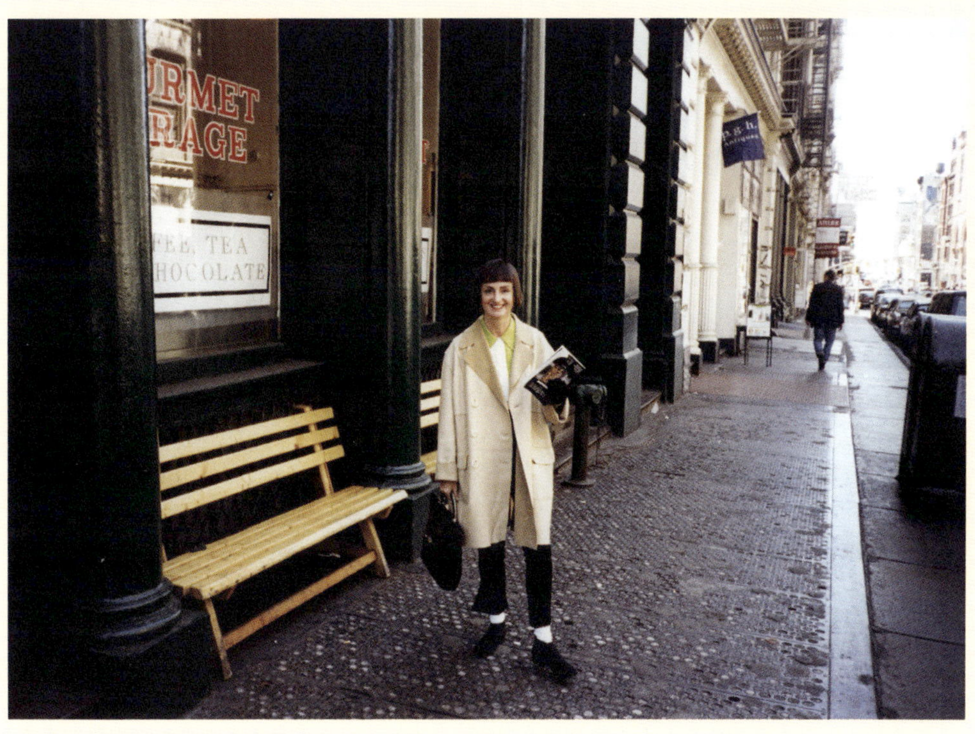

Helen Chadwick in Soho, New York, after her opening at MoMA, 1995

Notes

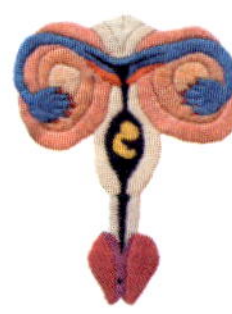

Chapter One

1 Helen Chadwick quoted in Mary Horlock, 'Between a Rock and a Soft Place', in *Helen Chadwick*, Barbican Centre exh. cat. (Berlin: Hatje Cantz, 2004), p. 33.
2 Helen Chadwick regularly returned to this quote from Angela Carter's *Sadeian Woman* (1979), even printing it as a prologue to her exhibition catalogue *Helen Chadwick: Delight* (Philadelphia, PA: Institute of Contemporary Art, University of Pennsylvania, 1991).
3 *Memento mori* is an artistic trope that serves to remind the viewer of the inevitability of death. The concept is rooted in classical philosophy and Christianity, and examples can be seen in funerary art and architecture from the medieval period onwards. The *vanitas* tradition is a little more complicated; a *vanitas* painting also contains objects symbolic of the inevitability of death but also the transience and vanity of earthly achievements and pleasures; it thus exhorts the viewer to consider mortality and to repent.
4 Chadwick quoted in Niclas Östlind, 'Notes on the art of Helen Chadwick, especially the early works', in *Helen Chadwick*, exh. cat. (Stockholm: Liljevalchs Konsthall, 2005), p. 9.
5 Marina Warner, 'Helen Chadwick', in *Helen Chadwick*, exh. cat. (London: Richard Saltoun Gallery, 2018), p. 3.
6 Warner quoted in Horlock, 'Between a Rock and a Soft Place', p. 40.
7 Warner, 'Preface', in *Helen Chadwick* (2004), p. 9.
8 Archive material referenced in *Helen Chadwick's 'Ego Geometria Sum': A Biography*, Henry Moore Institute Essays on Sculpture No. 64 (Leeds: Henry Moore Institute, 2012), p. 4.
9 Chadwick quoted in Mark Sladen, 'A Red Mirror', in *Helen Chadwick* (2004), p. 13.
10 Chadwick quoted in Östlind, 'Notes on the art of Helen Chadwick, especially the early works', p. 5.
11 Chadwick quoted in '#17 Beck Road', *50 stories from The Acme Archive*, acme.org.uk, accessed 10 June 2024.
12 Chadwick quoted in Östlind, 'Notes on the art of Helen Chadwick, especially the early works', p. 17.
13 Chadwick quoted in Horlock, 'Between a Rock and a Soft Place', p. 33.
14 Chadwick quoted ibid., p. 34.
15 Chadwick quoted in Waldemar Januszczak, 'Invading your space', *The Guardian*, 18 November 1987.
16 Chadwick quoted in Eva Martichnig, 'Getting Inside the Artist's Head', in *Helen Chadwick* (2004), p. 47.
17 Chadwick quoted in Januszczak, 'Invading your space'.
18 Chadwick quoted in Martichnig, 'Getting Inside the Artist's Head', p. 48.
19 Ibid.
20 Chadwick quoted in Sladen, 'A Red Mirror', p. 9.
21 Ibid., p. 17.
22 Chadwick quoted in Martichnig, 'Getting Inside the Artist's Head', p. 49.
23 Warner, 'Preface', p. 10.
24 Chadwick quoted in Warner, 'Helen Chadwick', p. 4.
25 Warner, 'In the Garden of Delights', *Enfleshings* (New York: Aperture, 1989), p. 47.
26 Warner quoted in Sladen, 'A Red Mirror', p. 17.
27 Chadwick quoted ibid., p. 19.
28 Chadwick quoted in 'Interview with Mark Haworth-Booth', Portfolio Gallery pamphlet (1996), n.p.
29 Julia Kristeva, *Powers of Horror: An Essay on Abjection* (New York: Columbia University Press, 1982), p. 65.
30 Chadwick quoted in Horlock, 'Between a Rock and a Soft Place', p. 37.
31 Chadwick quoted in Sladen, 'A Red Mirror', p. 20.
32 James Elkins, *On the Strange Place of Religion in Contemporary Art* (London: Routledge, 2004), p. 90.
33 Chadwick quoted in Sarah Kent, 'Border Territory', in *Lifelines: Four British Artists*, exh. cat. (Liverpool: Tate, 1990), p. 32.
34 Chadwick quoted in Emma Cocker, 'Interview with Helen Chadwick', in *Helen Chadwick*, exh. cat. (Hull: Ferens Art Gallery, 1998), p. 2.
35 Chadwick quoted in Susan de Muth, 'My dreams seep into an unprocessed soup: In Bed with Helen Chadwick', *The Independent*, 19 July 1994.
36 'Helen Chadwick', www.theartstory.org/artist/chadwick-helen.
37 Chadwick quoted in Januszczak, 'Invading your space'.
38 'Helen Chadwick', op. cit.
39 David Notarius quoted in Andy Beckett, 'What a swell party it was', *The Independent*, 1 June 1996.
40 Chadwick quoted in James Hall, 'Golden Flowers', *The Guardian*, 25 January 1994.
41 Chadwick quoted in *Helen Chadwick* (2018), p. 17.
42 Andrea Schlieker, *Effluvia* (London: Serpentine Gallery, 1994), p. 18.
43 Chadwick quoted in Sladen, 'A Red Mirror', p. 26.
44 Richard Saltoun quoted in *Helen Chadwick* (2018), p. 19.
45 Chadwick quoted in Horlock, 'Between a Rock and a Soft Place', p. 35.
46 Warner, 'Helen Chadwick', p. 3.
47 Ibid., p. 2.
48 Ibid., p. 3.

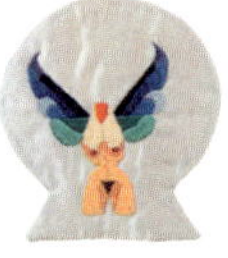

Chapter Two

1 Helen Chadwick in Judith Collins, 'An Opera for Milly Mudd: Artist Helen Chadwick in Conversation with Judith Collins', in *From Marble to Chocolate: The Conservation of Modern Sculpture*, ed. Jackie

Heuman (London: Archetype Publications, 1995), p. 152.
2 Helen Chadwick quoted in 'Interview with Mark Haworth-Booth', in *Stilled Lives*, exh. cat. (Edinburgh: Portfolio Gallery, 1996), n.p.
3 Sigmund Freud, 'The Sexual Aberrations', in *Three Essays on the Theory of Sexuality: The 1905 Edition*, ed. Philippe Van Haute and Herman Westerink, trans. Ulrike Kistner (London: Verso Books, 2016), pp. 16–17.
4 Sigmund Freud, 'The Transformations of Puberty', in *Three Essays on the Theory of Sexuality*, p. 82.
5 Sianne Ngai, 'Introduction', in *Our Aesthetic Categories: Zany, Cute, Interesting* (Cambridge, MA, and London: Harvard University Press, 2015), pp. 3–4.
6 William Pietz, 'The Problem of the Fetish, I', *RES: Anthropology and Aesthetics*, no. 9 (Spring 1985), p. 10.
7 Sigmund Freud, 'Fetishism', in *The Penguin Freud Reader*, ed. Adam Phillips (London: Penguin Modern Classics, 2006), pp. 90–95.
8 Emily Apter, 'Introduction', in *Fetishism as Cultural Discourse*, ed. Emily Apter and William Pietz (Ithaca, NY: Cornell University Press, 1993), p. 4.
9 Pietz, 'The Problem of the Fetish, I', p. 14.
10 Dorothea Tanning quoted in Alyce Mahon, 'Life is Something Else: Chambre 202, Hotel du Pavot', in *Dorothea Tanning*, exh. cat. (London: Tate Publishing, 2018), p. 53.
11 Laura Mulvey, 'Visual Pleasure and Narrative Cinema', *Screen*, vol. 16, no. 3 (Autumn 1975), pp. 6–18.
12 Dick Hebdige, 'One', in *Subculture: The Meaning of Style* (London and New York: Routledge, Taylor & Francis e-Library, 2002), p. 18.
13 Helen Chadwick in Iain Gale, 'Helen Chadwick talking to Iain Gale', *Modern Painters*, vol. 7, no. 3 (October 1994), pp. 106–7.
14 Helen Chadwick in Emma Cocker, 'Indifference in difference: an interview with Helen Chadwick', *MAKE*, no. 71 (1996), p. 22.
15 Naomi Schor, 'Decadence: Wey, Loos, Lukács', in *Reading in Detail: Aesthetics and the Feminine* (New York and London: Methuen, 1987), p. 45.
16 Marina Warner, 'The nude, the gaze, and the self', in *Helen Chadwick: The Oval Court* (London: Afterall Books, 2022), p. 59.
17 Chadwick in Collins, 'An Opera for Milly Mudd', p. 160.
18 Stephen Walker, 'The grotto and architectural conceit', in *Helen Chadwick: Constructing Identities Between Art and Architecture* (London: I.B. Tauris & Co. Ltd, 2013), pp. 100, 119.
19 Marina Warner, 'In the Garden of Delights: Helen Chadwick's "Of Mutability"', in *Of Mutability: Helen Chadwick*, exh. cat. (London: Institute of Contemporary Arts, 1986), n.p.
20 Jo Anna Isaak, 'Introduction', in *Feminism and Contemporary Art: The Revolutionary Power of Women's Laughter* (London: Routledge, 1996), p. 3.
21 Chadwick in Warner, 'In the Garden of Delights', n.p.
22 Mary Russo, 'Female Grotesques: Carnival and Theory', in *Feminist Studies/Critical Studies*, ed. Teresa Lauretis (London: Macmillan Press, 1986), p. 219.
23 Chadwick in Collins, 'An Opera for Milly Mudd', p. 154.
24 Ibid., p. 158.
25 Helen Chadwick, 'Piss Posy', in *Stilled Lives*, n.p.
26 David Hopkins, 'Spinsters: Post-Duchampian Women', in *Dada's Boys: Masculinity after Duchamp* (New Haven, CT, and London: Yale University Press, 2007), p. 177.
27 Chadwick in Collins, 'An Opera for Milly Mudd', p. 159.

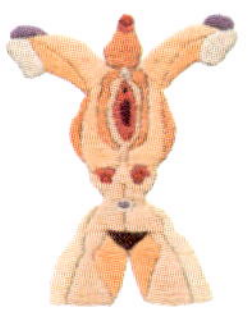

Chapter Three

1 Ellinides: Hellenic fem.; Ellines: Hellenic masc.; Ellas: Hellas (fem.), aka Greece.
2 Aeolians, Achaeans, Dorians, Ionians.
3 Leda at the same time bore Castor and Clytemnestra, children of her husband, Tyndareus.
4 In other myths, Helen comes from an egg left by the goddess Nemesis, www.worldhistory.org/Helen_of_Troy/
5 Claude Cahun, *Héroïnes* [1924], translated by Norman MacAfee in Shelley Rice (ed.), *Inverted Odysseys: Claude Cahun, Maya Deren, and Cindy Sherman* (Cambridge, MA: The MIT Press, 1999), p. 59.
6 The H was removed by the author.
7 'Diaspora' from the Greek diaspeirein (disperse): dia (across) and speirein (scatter, seed).
8 Helen Chadwick, *Artists' Journeys: Helen Chadwick on Frida Kahlo* (London: BBC, 1992).
9 Audre Lorde, *Uses of the Erotic: The Erotic as Power* [1978], in *Your silence will not protect you* (London: Silver Press, 2017), p. 22.
10 Ibid.
11 Here I am returning and referring to Jacques Derrida's thinking about the pharmakon (the Hellenic word for drug poison and/or medicine mentioned in Plato's Phaedrus (370 BCE) in relation to writing), neither remedy nor poison, simultaneously a liminal either/or and both. The term reappears in several instances Derrida's work, developed in his essay 'Plato's Pharmacy' (1968), where he discusses the word as an example of polysemy: the existence of multiple meanings in a single word, in this case contradictory. The diasporic condition invites polysemy in subjectivity, creating an ambivalent, undecidable I. The essay was published in English in *Jacques Derrida, Dissemination* (Chicago, IL: University of Chicago Press, 1982), pp. 65–182.
12 Helen Chadwick, *Lines that Severed, Bind* (1986), typed text with handwritten annotation, Helen Chadwick Archive, Henry Moore Institute,

Leeds. Also published in *Lofos Nymphon*, exh. cat. (Sheffield: Mappin Art Gallery, 1987), n.p.

13 Helen Chadwick, *The hand as a symbol in medieval art*, handwritten text, Helen Chadwick Archive, Henry Moore Institute, Leeds.

14 Tom Evans, 'A Mirror to Yourself: Helen Chadwick interview by Tom Evans' [June 1986], in David Brittain (ed.), *Creative Camera: Thirty Years of Writing* (Manchester: Manchester University Press, 1999), pp. 145-49.

15 Susan Griffin, *Woman and Nature: The Roaring Inside Her* (London: The Women's Press, 1984), p. 10.

16 Ibid.

17 Helen Chadwick, handwritten notes, Helen Chadwick Archive, Henry Moore Institute, Leeds.

18 René Descartes, *Discourse on the Method of Rightly Conducting the Reason, and Searching for Truth in the Sciences* (Edinburgh: Sutherland and Knox, 1637).

19 Alejandro Jodorowsky and Marianne Costa, *The Way of Tarot: The Spiritual Teacher in the Cards* (Vermont: Inner Traditions/Bear & Company, 2009), p. 127.

20 Chadwick, *The hand as a symbol in medieval art*.

21 Ibid.

22 Ibid.

23 Chadwick, *The hand as a symbol in medieval art*.

24 Helen Chadwick quoted in 'Interview with Mark Haworth Booth', in *Stilled Lives*, exh. cat. (Edinburgh: Portfolio Gallery, 1996), n.p.

25 Bruno Munari, *Supplement to the Italian Dictionary* (Mantova: Corraini Editore, 1963), p. 26.

26 In Helen Chadwick's library (also held at the Henry Moore Institute, Leeds) there is a variety of books on the artistic, religious, scientific, phycological, history and iconography of the body and the cosmos. These titles read like a poem written about Chadwick's work.

27 Chadwick quoted in 'Interview with Mark Haworth Booth'.

28 Anne Carson, *If Not, Winter: Fragments of Sappho* (London: Virago Vintage, 2003), p. 264.

29 Sappho, frg. 130. My translation here alters Carson's translation of the fragment, which reads: 'Eros the melter of limbs (now again) stirs me, sweetbitter unmanageable creature who steals in.' Ibid., p. 265.

30 Carson, *If Not, Winter*, p. 375.

31 Ibid.

32 Chadwick quoted in 'Interview with Mark Haworth Booth'.

33 Ibid.

34 Ibid.

35 Ibid.

36 Chadwick, *The hand as a symbol in medieval art*.

37 Ibid.

38 Helen Chadwick Archive, Henry Moore Institute, Leeds.

39 Lorde, *Uses of the Erotic*, p. 24.

40 Ideas developing from Édouard Glissant's 'Baroque as a World Philosophy', *The UNESCO Courier*, vol. XL, no. 9 (1987), p. 18, about artificial reproduction of nature and knowledge of it, reality, rules and so on.

41 Ursula K Le Guin, *The Carrier Bag Theory of Fiction* [1986], in *Women of Vision*, ed. Denise du Pont (New York: St. Martin's Press, 1988), p. 6.

42 Ibid., p. 7.

43 Kinaesthetic empathy is derived from the Greek words *kinisi* (movement) and *aesthesis* (sensation). Kinaesthetic empathy is the capacity to participate in somebody's movement, or their sensory experience of movement. Thank you to Dr Ruth Pethybridge for introducing me to this notion, which I had been looking to name for years.

44 Tina M. Campt, *Listening to Images* (Durham, NC: Duke University Press, 2017), p. 4.

45 Ibid.

46 See Derrida's text 'The Pit and the Pyramid: Introduction to Hegel's Semiology', in *Margins of Philosophy* (Chicago, IL: University of Chicago Press, 1982), pp. 69-108, and the discussions around it, for example Miriam Leonard's essay 'Derrida between "Greek" and "Jew"', in *Derrida and Antiquity* (Oxford: Oxford University Press, 2010), pp. 135-38, grinds down ideas about interiority and exteriority to traditions of the Jewish archive, Greek philosophy, *galut* (exile), liminality, Egypt, monolingualism and the Other.

47 The Christian Orthodox saint Mary of Egypt, a desert ascetic of the Middle Ages who repented of a life of debauchery, is often depicted in this gesture. Sometimes in iconography she is depicted as a deeply tanned old woman, her body covered by hair.

48 Attributed to Saraha, an early Buddhist Tantric sage, via the meditation teacher and psychologist Tara Brach, 'Planting Ourselves in the Universe', http://blog.tarabrach.com/2012/10/planting-ourselves-in-universe.html, 17 October 2012.

49 Chadwick quoted in 'Interview with Mark Haworth Booth'.

50 Chadwick, *Lines that Severed, Bind*.

51 Modern Hellenic suggests a possible origin of the name as a place 'run by wolves': *lykos* (wolf) and *vatos* (accessible, walkable). Another etymology suggests a Pelasgian, pre-Mycenean, origin: (Lucabetu = mastoid hill).

52 Margaret Atwood, *The Tent* (London: Bloomsbury, 2006), p. 30.

53 Gaston Bachelard, *The Poetics of Space* [1958] (Boston, MA: Beacon Press, 1994), p. 6.

54 Ibid.

55 *Panagia mou* is Hellenic for 'My Mother Mary'. Panagia (Παναγία), fem., *pan-*, and *hágia* (the All-Holy, the Most Holy); one of the titles of Mary, mother of God, used especially in Eastern Orthodox Christianity.

56 The last of Chadwick's books I picked up in the archive was Caroline Walker-Bynum, *Fragmentation and Redemption: Essays on Gender and the Human Body in Medieval Religion* (New York: Zone Books, 1991), which then led me to Leo Steinberg, *The Sexuality of Christ in Renaissance Art and*

in Modern Oblivion (Chicago, IL: University of Chicago, 1983).

57 This is inspired by the last verse in Allen Ginsberg's poem 'Song' (1954): 'yes, yes, that's what I wanted, I always wanted, I always wanted, to return to the body where I was born'.

58 Chadwick, The hand as a symbol in medieval art.

59 I read somewhere that a kabbalistic scripture describes desire as 'your destiny hidden in you by the gods'. Unsure of the veracity of its origin, I cherish the sentiment of Eros moving us from within.

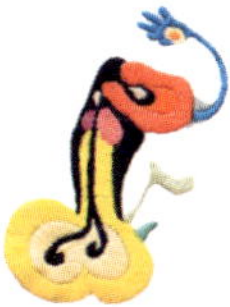

Chapter Four

1 Silvia Eiblmayr, *Helen Chadwick: POESIES* (Austria: Salzburger Kunstverein, 1994), p. 6.

2 Ibid., p. 4.

3 Laurie Cluitmans, *On the Necessity of Gardening: An ABC of Art, Botany and Cultivation* (Amsterdam: Valiz, 2021), p. 112.

4 Imogen Racz, 'Helen Chadwick's *Of Mutability*: Process and Postmodernism', *Journal of Visual Art Practice*, vol. 16, no. 1 (2016), https://pure.coventry.ac.uk/ws/portalfiles/portal/13186304/JVAP_Racz_Of_Mutability_for_Coventry.pdf, accessed 19 June 2024.

5 For centuries, flowers have been closely associated with the image of women. Flowers and still lifes belong to the most accessible field of artistic research and depictions of women. In the age of enlightenment and colonial conquest, pioneering painters such as Rachel Ruysch and Maria Sybille Merian, who have been rediscovered in recent exhibitions all over the Western world, perfected flower still lifes as a form of high art, as well as painting and researching depictions of flowers for biological and scientific reasons - in order to identify them as well as study their methods of pollination.

6 Derek Jarman, *Modern Nature* (Minneapolis, MN: University of Minnesota Press, 1992), p. 23.

7 Mark Sladen, 'A Red Mirror', in *Helen Chadwick*, Barbican Centre exh. cat. (Berlin: Hatje Cantz, 2004), pp. 13-32.

8 Helen Chadwick, *PISS POSY* (1992), in *Stilled Lives*, exh. cat. (Edinburgh: Portfolio Gallery, 1996), n.p., reprinted here pp. 162-63.

9 Birgitta Bremer, 'Linnaeus' sexual system and flowering plant phylogeny', *Nordic Journal of Botany*, vol. 25, nos 1-2 (April 2007), pp. 5-6.

10 Madelaine Bartlett and Banu Subramaniam, 'Re-imagining Reproduction: The Queer Possibilities of Plants', *Integrative and Comparative Biology*, vol. 63, no. 4 (October 2023), p. 949, https://doi.org/10.1093/icb/icad012, accessed 19 June 2024.

11 Helen Chadwick quoted in Waldemar Januszczak, 'Interview with Helen Chadwick', *The Guardian*, 18 November 1987, www.theguardian.com/artanddesign/1987/nov/18/20yearsoftheturnerprize.turnerprize, accessed 17 June 2024.

12 The wider quote reads: 'liquids, unlike solids, cannot easily hold their shape. Fluids, so to speak, neither fix space nor bind time. While solids have clear spatial dimensions but neutralize the impact, and thus downgrade the significance, of time (effectively resist its flow or render it irrelevant), fluids do not keep to any shape for long and are constantly ready (and prone) to change.' Zygmunt Bauman, *Liquid Modernity* (Cambridge: Polity Press, 2000), cf. S.2ff.

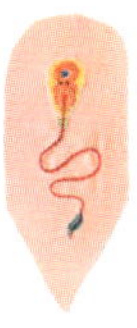

PAGES 258–61
Helen Chadwick, embroidered satin pendants, *c.* 1974

Timeline

1953 Helen Chadwick was born in Croydon, London. Her parents met in Athens during the Second World War and moved to Croydon in 1946.

1972 Fine Art Foundation course at Croydon College

1973–76 BA Fine Art course at Brighton Polytechnic (now the University of Brighton). Though officially a sculpture student, Chadwick recalled that 'traditional media were never dynamic enough...right from early on in art school, I wanted to use the body to create a set of interrelationships with the audience'. This culminated in her 1976 BA degree show, *Domestic Sanitation*.

1976–77 MA Fine Art course at Chelsea College of Art, London, ending in her career-launching MA degree show, *In The Kitchen*. This was also shown at Art Net, London after Chelsea College of Art.

1977 Moved to Beck Road, London.

- *New Contemporaries*, London Filmmakers Co-op, London
- *Northern Contemporaries*, Whitworth Art Gallery, Manchester

1978–79 *Train of Thought* exhibition at Acme Gallery, London; touring to Spectro Gallery, Newcastle; Ikon Gallery, Birmingham

1979 Selector and organiser of mixed media art for Hayward Annual, London.

- *British Art Show: Old Allegiances and New Directions*, City of Birmingham Museum and Art Gallery and Ikon Gallery, Birmingham; touring until 1984 to Royal Scottish Academy, Edinburgh; Mappin Art Gallery, Sheffield; Southampton Art Gallery
- *Furniture/Sculpture*, Ikon Gallery, Birmingham

1980 Recipient of the Arts Council of Great Britain's Film Distribution Award.

- *Whitechapel Open*, Whitechapel Gallery, London
- *Events*, London Filmmakers' Co-op, London

1981 Recipient of Greater London Arts Association Visual Arts Major Award.

- *Six Artists in Industry*, City Art Gallery and Museum, Bradford

1981–84 Another part of Chadwick's MA degree show, *Model Institution*, an installation and audio piece of a recreation of an office cubicle, toured to Newcastle Polytechnic Gallery; Sheffield Polytechnic Gallery; Architectural Association; Chalmers Art Gallery; Cockpit Gallery; Oval House and Battersea Arts Centre, London; Brighton Polytechnic; Orchard Gallery, Derry.

1982
- *Fine Art/Fine Ale*, Sheffield Polytechnic Gallery
- *Live to Art*, Tate Gallery, London
- *Small Works V*, Newcastle Polytechnic Gallery
- *Women Live*, London Filmmakers' Co-op
- *Alternative Tate Show*, Paton Gallery, London

1983
- *Growing Up*, National Portrait Gallery, London and Cockpit Gallery, London
- *Portraits Out of Placements*, Spectro Gallery, Newcastle
- *Ego Geometria Sum* was first exhibited at Serpentine Gallery's group exhibition, *Summer Show I*, and was originally entitled *Growing Pains*. It was exhibited later the same year at Art and Research Exchange, Belfast
- *New Perspectives on the Nude*, Ffotogallery, Cardiff
- *Summer Show I*, Serpentine Gallery, London
- *Some Sculpture Now*, Brighton Polytechnic

1984 Recipient of London Arts Grant Aperto '84, 41st Venice Biennale, Venice.

- *Ego Geometria Sum*, Aspex Gallery, Portsmouth
- *Self-Expressed*, Plymouth Arts Centre, Plymouth and Spacex Gallery, Exeter
- *Expanded Media Show*, Sheffield Polytechnic Art Gallery
- *Dog Work*, Interim Art, London
- *Rationalisierung 1984*, Staatlichen Berliner Kunsthalle

1985 Chadwick began an active teaching career as a visiting lecturer across a number of London art schools. Her posts at Goldsmiths (1985-90), Chelsea College of Arts (1985-95), Central Saint Martins (1987-95) and the Royal College of Art (1990-94), ensured an important influence on contemporary British Art in the late 1980s and '90s.

- *Ego Geometria Sum*, Riverside Studios, London
- *Re-visions*, Cambridge Darkroom and John Hansard Gallery, Southampton
- *Hand Signals*, Ikon Gallery, Birmingham; touring to Milton Keynes Gallery and Chapter, Cardiff
- *Four Walls*, Camerawork, London
- *Out of Hand*, The Warehouse, London
- *Performance Art*, Tate, London
- *Human Interest*, Cornerhouse, Manchester
- *Kunst mit Eigen-Sinn*, Museum of Modern Art, Vienna
- *Figures & Myths*, Aberystwyth Arts Centre
- *Image & Exploration*, The Photographers' Gallery, London
- *Imposters*, Interim Art, London

1986–87 Artist in residence at Birmingham City Museum and Art Gallery. This is where Chadwick created her work *Allegory of Misrule*, recreating an 18th-century oil painting of the same title in the museum's collection by Johann Georg Platzer (1704-1761), and using the taxidermied animals in the museum's Natural History department. Her solo exhibition, *Allegory of Misrule*, followed in 1987.

Chadwick's first major institutional exhibition, *Of Mutability*, opened at Institute of Contemporary Arts, London; touring to Ikon Gallery, Birmingham; Harris Museum, Preston; Third Eye Centre, Glasgow; Kunstverein, Freiburg.

1987 Nominated for The Turner Prize for her exhibition, *Of Mutability*.

- *Allegory of Misrule*, Birmingham City Museum and Art Gallery, Birmingham
- *Upon an Oval*, Mappin Art Gallery, Sheffield

1988 Artist in National Parks commission programme organised by the Department of Environment at the Victoria and Albert Museum, London. Exploring the conventions of the landscape, virality, and following the British government's AIDS awareness campaigns in 1987, Chadwick created her *Viral Landscapes* series (1988–89).

- *Blood Hyphen*, Edge '88 International Biennial for Public Art, Woodbridge Chapel, London
- *Cameos*, Torch Gallery, Amsterdam and Torch Onrust Gallery, Cologne

1989 Aperture publish Chadwick's first book, *Enfleshings*.

- *Viral Landscapes*, Museum of Modern Art, Oxford
- *Enfleshings*, Interim Art, London
- *Lumina*, Portfolio Gallery, Edinburgh
- *Lamps*, Marlene Eleini Gallery, London

1990 *Meat Abstracts* and *Enfleshings* series included in the large-scale photography festival, *Fotofest*, held in Houston, Texas. This is where she met a local artist, David Notarius. They married a year later, in 1991.

1990 Recipient of the Bill Brandt Award.

- *Meat Lamps*, Ehlers Caudill Gallery, Chicago and Burden Gallery, Aperture Foundation, New York
- *Viral Landscapes*, 121 Art Gallery, Antwerp and Friedman Guinness Gallery, Frankfurt

1991

- *Lofos Nymphon*, Galerie Oboro, Montreal
- *De Light*, Institute of Contemporary Art, Philadelphia
- *Les couleurs de l'argent*, Musée de la Poste, Paris
- *Physical Relief*, Hunter College Art Galleries, New York
- *Postmodern Prints*, Victoria and Albert Museum, London
- *Le corps vacant*, Musée d'art contemporain de Montréal
- *Exploring the Unknown Self*, Tokyo Metropolitan Museum of Photography
- *Long Live the New Flesh*, Kettle's Yard, Cambridge
- *Real Fake*, Rotunda, Milan; touring to Villa Stuck, Munich
- *Europa 1991*, Baden Kunstverein Karlsruhe
- *Doubles* (with Danny Leriche), Galerie d'Art Contemporain du Centre Saint-Vincent, Herblay
- *De-Composition: Constructed Photography in Britain*, Oriel Mostyn, Llandudno; touring to Chapter, Cardiff; Museo de Arte de São Paulo Assis Chateaubriand, São Paulo; Centro Cultural Recoleta, Buenos Aires; Centro de la Imagen, Mexico City; Instituto Cultural Cabañas, Guadalajara; Palazzo delle Esposizioni, Rome; San Giovanni In Monte, Bologna; Slovak National Gallery, Bratislava; Muzeum Sztuki, Lodz; Ludwig Múzeum, Budapest; Muzeul National de Arta al Romaniei, Bucharest; Art Museum, Constanta; Macedonian Museum of Contemporary Art, Thessaloniki; Ileana Tounta Contemporary Art Center, Athens; Varna Art Museum; International Photography Meeting, Plovdiv

1991–92 Residency at Banff Art Centre, Canada, where Chadwick created *Piss Flowers*. The residency concluded with an exhibition, *In Side Up* (with Shelagh Keeley), at the Walter Phillips Gallery, Banff, which toured to Mercer Union, Toronto.

1992

- *Fruit Rage/Fruit Snatch I & II*, Edge '92 International Biennial for Public Art, Plaza de los Carros and Plaza de la Paja, Madrid, and Spitalfields Market, London
- *Im Fleischgarten & Viral Landscapes*, Galerie Vier-Andreas Weiss, Berlin
- *Meat Lamps*, The British School at Rome
- *Im Fleischgarten*, Friedman Guinness Gallery, Frankfurt and Produzentengalerie, Hamburg
- *BBC Billboard Project*, London
- *The Boundary Rider: 9th Sydney Biennale*, Sydney
- *Home*, Kajaani Art Hall
- *37 Räume*, Staatlichen Berliner Kunsthalle, Berlin
- *Small is Beautiful*, Flowers Gallery, London
- *Twelve Stars*, Arts Council Gallery, Belfast; touring City Art Centre, Edinburgh and Barbican Art Gallery, London
- *Flora Photographica*, Serpentine Gallery, London; touring to The Royal Botanic Gardens, Edinburgh; Manchester City Art Gallery, Manchester; Mead Gallery, Warwick Arts Centre, Coventry
- *Whitechapel Open*, Whitechapel Gallery, London; touring to Butler's Wharf, London
- *Physical Encounter*, The Gardner Arts Centre, Brighton
- *Innocence and Experience*, Manchester City Art Gallery; touring to Ferens Art Gallery, Hull; Nottingham Castle Museum and Art Gallery; Kelvingrove Art Gallery and Museum, Glasgow
- *Traces of the Figure*, City Museum & Art Gallery, Stoke-on-Trent; touring to Cartwright Hall, Bradford

1993

- *Trophies*, Galerie Eugen Lendl, Graz
- *XXY*, Interim Art, London
- *Bronzes*, Angel Row Gallery, Nottingham
- *Time Out Billboard Art Project*, London
- *Summer Exhibition*, Royal Academy of Arts, London
- *The Black & White and Colour Summer Show*, Zelda Cheatle Gallery, London
- *Elective Affinities*, Tate Liverpool, Liverpool
- *Outpost*, Edinburgh Blood Donor Centre, Edinburgh
- *Das Bild de Körpers*, Frankfurter Kunstverein, Frankfurt
- *Public and Private*, Stills Gallery, Edinburgh
- *Schönheit Macht Schamhaft*, Aschenbach Gallery, Amsterdam

- *Bad Girls*, Institute of Contemporary Arts, London

1994
- *Flesh & Flower*, Zelda Cheatle Gallery, London
- *Effluvia*, Serpentine, London; touring to Museum Folkwang, Essen and Fundació 'la Caixa', Barcelona
- *Poesies*, Salzburger Kunstverein, Salzburg and Kunsthaus Glarus
- O2 (with Hermoine Wiltshire), Zone Gallery, Newcastle
- *Artists' Impressions*, Kettle's Yard, Cambridge; touring to Nottingham Castle Museum and Art Gallery, Nottingham and The New Art Gallery Walsall
- *Other Men's Flowers*, Factual Nonsense, London
- *A Positive View*, Saatchi Gallery, London
- *Back to Basics*, Flowers East, London
- *Dialogue with the Other*, Kunsthallen Brandts Klædefabrik, Odense
- *Fluxbritannica: Aspects of the Fluxus Movement 1962–73*, Tate Gallery, London
- *Something the Matter: Helen Chadwick, Cathy de Monchaux, Cornelia Parker*, 22nd *International Biennial of São Paulo*, São Paulo; touring to Museo Municipal de Bellas Artes, Rosario; Centro Cultural Recoleta, Buenos Aires; Museo Nacional de Bellas Artes, Rio de Janeiro; Galeria Athos, Bulcao

1995 First solo exhibition in the United States at The Museum of Modern Art, New York, entitled *Helen Chadwick: Bad Blooms*; touring to Indianapolis Museum of Art; Norrköpings Konstmuseum; Uppsala Kunstmuseum.

Artist residency organised by Arts Catalyst in the assisted conception unit at King's College Hospital, London, photographing IVF embryos rejected for implantation.

- *Blumenstücke: Kunststüke*, Kunsthalle Bielefeld
- *Home and Away*, Tate Liverpool
- *Konrad Lorenz's Duck*, Ex Lanificio Bona, Turin
- *Cabinet Art*, Jason & Rhodes, London
- *Landscape*, Trondhjems Kunstforening, Trondheim
- *England's Glory*, Witley Court and Gardens, Great Witley
- *Féminin-Masculin, le sexe de l'art*, Centre Pompidou, Paris
- *20 Modern British Photographers*, Victoria and Albert Museum, London
- *Identità e Alterità*, 46th Venice Biennale, Venice
- *Decadence*, Trondhjems Kunstforening, Trondheim
- *Wasser & Wine*, Kunsthalle Krems
- *Chocolate!*, Swiss Institute, New York
- *UK Wit & Excess*, Contemporary Art Centre of South Australia, Adelaide; touring to Australian Centre for Contemporary Art, Melbourne; Institute of Modern Art, Brisbane; Ivan Dougherty Gallery, Sydney
- *Kleinplastik*, Galerie HS Steinek, Vienna
- *Private/Public: ARS 95*, Nykytaiteen Museo, Helsinki

1996 Helen Chadwick died, aged 42, in Camden, London.

- *Stilled Lives*, Portfolio Gallery, Edinburgh
- *In Memoriam – Helen Chadwick*, Galerie Eugen Lendl, Graz
- *Zijsporen: Kunst Op Het Spoor*, Gynaika, Antwerp
- *Mai de la photo: Mauvais Genre*, Reims
- *Body Visual*, Barbican Art Gallery, London and King's College Hospital, London
- *Bristol Festival of the Sea 1996*, Bristol
- *2nd Autumn Triennial on Photography*, Graz
- *Love and death and all that*, Galerie HS Steinek, Vienna

1997 The start of the Arts Council England Helen Chadwick Fellowship, organised by the Ruskin School of Art (where she was an advisor) and the British School at Rome (where she was a faculty member), supported by Arts Council. Continued annually until 2010, when Turner Prize winner, Elizabeth Price, was the final recipient.

- *A Changed World*, Hindu Gymkhana, Karachi, Pakistan; touring to The Old Fort, Lahore; Johannesburg Art Gallery; South African National Gallery, Cape Town; National Gallery, Bulawayo; National Gallery of Zimbabwe, Harare; Nicosia Municipal Arts Centre, Nicosia; St James Cavalier Centre for Creativity, Valletta
- *International Electronic Cinema Festival*, Montreux, Switzerland
- *Angel Angel*, Kunsthalle Wien, Vienna; touring to Galerie Rudolfinum, Prague
- *The Quick and the Dead: Artists and Anatomy*, Royal College of Art, London; touring to Mead Gallery, Warwick Arts Centre, Coventry and Leeds Art Gallery, Leeds

1998–99
- *Helen Chadwick*, Ferens Art Gallery, Kingston upon Hull; touring to Nottingham Castle Museum and Art Gallery and Pitshanger Manor Art Gallery, London
- *Is This Art?*, Toyota Municipal Museum of Art, Toyota; touring to Kawamura Memorial DIC Museum of Art, Sakura and Art Tower Mito, Mito
- *Secret Victorians*, Firstsite, Colchester; touring to Arnolfini, Bristol; Ikon Gallery, Birmingham; Middlesbrough Art Gallery; Hammer Museum, Los Angeles

1999
- *Helen Chadwick*, Graves Art Gallery, Sheffield

2000
- *Hair: Obsession and Art*, Museum Bellerive, Zürich
- *Psycho*, Anne Faggionato, London

2001
- *Fluid*, Wolverhampton Art Gallery; touring to Howard Gardens Gallery, University of Wales Institute, Cardiff; Bonington Gallery, Nottingham; Middlesbrough Art Gallery
- *Mirror, Mirror: Self-portraits by Women Artists*, National Portrait Gallery, London; touring to Leeds Art Gallery; Victoria Art Gallery, Bath; Royal Museum and Art Gallery, Canterbury

2002
- *Self Evident: The Artist as the Subject 1969–2002*, Tate Britain, London

2003
- Helen Chadwick; Zelda Cheatle Gallery, London
- Helen Chadwick: 10 Years Later, Galerie Eugen Lendl, Graz
- *A Century of Artists' Films in Britain*, Tate Britain, London
- *And the One Doesn't Stir Without the Other*, Ormeau Baths Gallery, Belfast
- *Other Criteria: Sculpture in 20th Century Britain*, Henry Moore Institute, Leeds

2004
- My Personal Museum: Ego Geometria Sum from the Helen Chadwick Archive, Henry Moore Institute, Leeds
- Helen Chadwick: A Retrospective opens at the Barbican Art Gallery, London; touring until 2005 to Liljevalchs Konsthall, Stockholm; Trapholt Kunstmuseum, Kolding; Manchester Art Gallery.

2005
- *Presence*, Gimpel Fils, London

2006
- *Important Mischief*, Leeds Art Gallery, Leeds

2009
- *Pot Luck: Food and Art*, The New Art Gallery Walsall

2010
- *Childish Things*, Fruitmarket Gallery, Edinburgh

2011
- *Images of the Mind*, German Hygiene Museum, Dresden
- *United Enemies: The Problem of Sculpture in Britain in the 1960s and 1970s*, Henry Moore Institute, Leeds

2012 Wreaths to Pleasure exhibited at the Henry Moore Institute, Leeds.
- *Transformation*, The New School House Gallery, York
- *Self-portrait*, Louisiana Museum of Modern Art, Humlebæk
- *Polychromies: Surface, Light and Colour*, Leeds Art Gallery, Leeds

2013 Works from the Helen Chadwick Estate exhibited at Richard Saltoun Gallery, London.
- Piss Flowers, Frieze Sculpture Park, London
- *Mad, Bad and Sad: Women and the Mind Doctors*, Freud Museum, London
- *In Order to Join*, Museum Abteiberg

2014
- Bad Blooms exhibited at Richard Saltoun Gallery, London.
- *Recital*, Arcadia Misa, London
- *Keywords: Art, Culture and Society in 1980s Britain*, Tate Liverpool

2015
- *In Order to Join: The Political in a Historical Moment*, Gallery MMB & Chhatrapati Shivaji Maharaj Vastu Sangrahalaya, Mumbai

2016
- *The Conformist*, Belmacz, London
- *Piss Flowers*, Jupiter Artland, Edinburgh

2017
- *Bristle: Hair and Hegemony*, Drogheda's Highlanes Gallery
- *Liberties*, Newlyn Art Gallery & The Exchange, Penzance
- *31 Women*, Breese Little, London
- *Dreamers Awake*, White Cube, London
- *Beneath the Pavement, the beach*, S2, Sotheby's Gallery, London
- *(x) A Fantasy*, DRAF, David Roberts Art Foundation, London
- *Eat Me*, Trapholt, Museum of Modern Art and Design, Kolding

2018
- *Women Look at Women*, Richard Saltoun Gallery, London
- *Intimacy, Activism and Aids*, Tate Modern, London
- *Nocturnal Union: A View of the Surreal*, Austin/Desmond Fine Art, London

2019
- *Gigantisme – art et industrie*, FRAC, Grand Large – Hauts-de-France, Dunkerque
- *Desire in Art from the 20th Century to the Digital Age*, IMMA (Irish Museum of Modern Art), Dublin
- *If I Was a Rich Girl*, Kunst Raum Riehen, Riehen
- *This Life is So Everyday: The Home in British Art 1950–1980*, Graves Gallery, Sheffield
- *The Assembled Human*, Museum Folkwang, Essen
- *Part 1: Matrescence*, Richard Saltoun Gallery, London

2020
- *Part 2: Maternality*, Richard Saltoun Gallery, London
- *Bodily Objects*, Arusha Gallery, Edinburgh

2024
- *Sculpture in The Park*, Compton Verney, Warwickshire

2025
- Helen Chadwick: Life Pleasures, The Hepworth Wakefield; touring until 2026 to Museo Novecento, Florence and Kunsthaus Graz

Collections
- Arts Council Collection, London
- British Council, London
- Great Ormond Street Hospital, London
- Harris Museum, Preston
- Henry Moore Institute, Leeds
- Jupiter Artland, Edinburgh
- Leeds Museums & Galleries, Leeds
- LUX Collection, London
- MoMA The Museum of Modern Art, New York
- Museum Moderner Kunst, Vienna
- National Galleries of Scotland, Edinburgh
- National Portrait Gallery, London
- Nottingham City Museums and Galleries, Nottingham
- Sheffield Galleries & Museums Trust, Sheffield
- Tate, UK
- The Hepworth Wakefield, Wakefield
- The Jewish Genealogical Society, London
- The Wellcome Collection, London
- Victoria and Albert Museum, London
- Walker Art Gallery, Liverpool
- York Art Gallery, York
- Zabludowicz Collection, London

Note: Solo exhibitions underlined

Contributors' Biographies

Editor

Laura Smith is Director of Collection and Exhibitions at The Hepworth Wakefield, where she has curated exhibitions of the work of Andrew Cranston (2023) and Sylvia Snowden (2024). She was previously curator at Whitechapel Gallery, London, and Tate. At Whitechapel her exhibitions included: 'Action, Gesture, Paint: Women Artists and Global Abstraction 1940–70' (2023), 'Emma Talbot: The Age' (2022), 'Eileen Agar: Angel of Anarchy' (2021), 'Simone Fattal: Finding a Way' (2021) and 'Helen Cammock: Che si può fare?' (2019). At Tate she curated exhibitions of Claude Cahun, Barbara Hepworth, Linder, Liliane Lijn, France-Lise McGurn, Lucy Stein and Rebecca Warren, and group shows including 'Virginia Woolf: An Exhibition Inspired by her Writings' and the Turner Prize 2016. Smith writes extensively on modern and contemporary art, recently contributing chapters to *Revisiting Modern British Art* (2022) and *The Oxford Handbook of Virginia Woolf* (2021), as well as monographs on Judith Godwin, Pia Arke, Lisa Brice, Lewis Hammond, Sylvia Snowden and Caragh Thuring.

Other Authors

Katrin Bucher Trantow is chief curator and deputy director of the Kunsthaus Graz. She began her curatorial career at the Kunsthalle Basel. As an art historian and historian, her curatorial focus is on interdisciplinary approaches and the re-reading of art history. Such re-readings have been particularly evident in projects such as 'Sol LeWitt's *Wall. Performed*' (2023), 'Faking the Real' (2022), 'Connected. Peter Kogler with...Fernand Léger with Friedrich Kiesler with Hedy Lamarr' (2019), 'Faith Love Hope' and 'Landscape in Motion' (both 2015), and 'Measuring the World' (2011). She has also curated solo exhibitions by the artists Hito Steyerl ('Animal Spirits' 2022) and Katharina Grosse ('Wer ich? wen Du?' 2024). Bucher is a member of the IKT, a juror for various art awards, on the advisory board of Kunst im öffentlichen Raum Graz and also directs the Kunsthalle Burgenland project. She is the editor of various catalogues, and her writing has been published in magazines such as *Camera Austria International*, *Domus* and *Parnass*.

Louisa Buck is a writer and broadcaster on contemporary art. She is a Contributing Editor and London Contemporary Art Correspondent for *The Art Newspaper* and a regular reviewer and commentator on BBC radio and TV. Her articles have appeared in publications ranging from *The Guardian* and *Vogue* to *Frieze* and *Artforum*. She is the author of a number of catalogue essays for institutions including Tate, Whitechapel Gallery, ICA London, MCA Australia and the Stedelijk Museum in Amsterdam. Her books include *Moving Targets 2: A User's Guide to British Art Now* (2000); *Market Matters: The Dynamics of the Contemporary Art Market* (2004); *Owning Art: The Contemporary Art Collector's Handbook* (co-authored with Judith Greer, 2006); *Commissioning Contemporary Art: A Handbook for Curators, Collectors and Artists* (2012), and in 2016, she authored 'The Going Public Report' commissioned by Museums Sheffield. She was a judge for the 2005 Turner Prize and is a founding member of The Gallery Climate Coalition.

Maria Christoforidou is an AfroGreek artist, writer and Fine Art lecturer at Falmouth University. Her work moves in different formats – lectures, performances, workshops, poems, film, photography – by listening to the inner body and 'speaking nearby' to archives or ancestors. Using fiction, academic research and collaboration as tools, her images and words aim to interrogate archives, gently peeling back legacies of colonialism. Her interest in images and stories that shape diasporic identity brought her to co-curate 'Surplus Cinemas', a 3-day film and event programme at Beursschouwburg, Brussels (2022). Her writing has been performed/spoken in different settings including: Theatre Academy, Helsinki; Spike Island, Bristol; Onassis Air, Athens; Trengwainton Gardens, Cornwall and Hordaland Kunstsenter, Bergen. Writings online include texts for exhibitions by Lucy Stein, Hales Gallery, London (2023); Jessica Warboys, Gaudel de Stampa, Paris (2020), and 'The Poem Returns as an Echo', The Contemporary Greek Art Institute, Athens (2024). Her video-poem *Maltha: the thrice burnt archives of unreliable prophecies* commissioned by transmediale for refusal 20/21, almanac, Berlin, has been shown in Beursschouwburg, Cinematek Brussels, MOOOV Film Festival, I Have A Dream Festival, Athens, and MOCA Skopje.

Philomena Epps is a writer and researcher living in London. Her writing and art criticism has appeared in *Artforum*, *ArtReview*, *Art Monthly*, *Flash Art*, *Frieze* and *The White Review*, among others. She has published texts on numerous artists including Heidi Bucher, Mona Hatoum, Nicola L., Ketty La Rocca, Magali Reus and Jo Spence. She is currently a PhD candidate in the History of Art department at University College London. Focused on the work of Rose English, Alina Szapocznikow and Hannah Wilke, her doctoral research examines the relationship between fetishism and sexual difference in multidisciplinary artistic practice across the late twentieth century.

David Notarius grew up in the north New Jersey suburbs, and later, New Hope, Pennsylvania, before moving to Houston, Texas, in 1979. His various careers include working as a railroad brakeman and fireman, merchant seaman, radio programmer, farmer, in film production, as an artist-technician and artist. His background in art comes from his father, Harold Notarius, who was an aerospace engineer and an accomplished sculptor. While living in New Hope, David studied painting under the Surrealist artist John DeMoss, later attending art classes at the University of Houston and the Sir John Cass School of Art, London. In 1990, while working as part of the installation crew at 'Fotofest 90' in Houston, he met Helen Chadwick. They fell in love and after eighteen months of cross-ocean romance, David moved to London. In 1991, they were married. He lived with and assisted Chadwick with her work until her death in 1996. He still lives in London, has since remarried, and has a daughter. He continues to manage Helen Chadwick's estate and is involved with exhibiting and promoting her work.

Marina Warner is a writer of cultural history, fiction and memoir. She has explored myths and fairy tales in *Alone of All Her Sex: The Myth and the Cult of the Virgin Mary* (1976), *From the Beast to the Blonde: On Fairy Tales and Their Tellers* (1994) and *Stranger Magic: Charmed States & the Arabian Nights* (2011). Her essays are collected in *Signs & Wonders* (1994), *Forms of Enchantment: Writings on Art and Artists* (2018) and *Myths, Magic and Marvels* (forthcoming, 2026). *Inventory of a Life Mislaid* (2021) tells the story of her childhood in Egypt. She has curated many shows, including 'Only Make Believe: Ways of Playing; The Shelter of Stories', which will open at Compton Verney in October 2025. She is Professor of English and Creative Writing at Birkbeck College, a Distinguished Fellow of All Souls College, Oxford, and a Fellow of the British Academy. In 2015, she received the Holberg Prize in the Arts. She contributes regularly to the *New York Review of Books* and the *London Review of Books*, and her book *Sanctuary: Ways of Dwelling, Ways of Telling* will be published in 2025. She is author of *Helen Chadwick: The Oval Court* (2023).

Acknowledgments

Given the impact and influence that Helen Chadwick's work and teaching have had on the development of contemporary art in Britain, it is astonishing that it has taken until now, nearly thirty years since her premature death, for her work to be recognised with a monographic publication. Our thanks go to The Estate of Helen Chadwick and Richard Saltoun Gallery for all their invaluable assistance, as well as to the contributing authors Katrin Bucher Trantow, Louisa Buck, Maria Christoforidou, Philomena Epps, David Notarius, Laura Smith and Marina Warner, for providing such compelling insights into Chadwick's remarkable life and work. Thanks too to the artists, writers, creatives and musicians who have provided personal reflections on Chadwick's friendship and influence. We are grateful to Thames & Hudson, particularly Roger Thorp, Rosalind Horne and Sadie Brookes, for their belief in the project and attention to detail in producing this striking book, and to Farah Dailami at The Hepworth Wakefield for her editorial talents. We are also deeply grateful to the Paul Mellon Centre for Studies in British Art for supporting its production.

I would also like to thank the supporters of the largest retrospective exhibition to date of Chadwick's work at The Hepworth Wakefield, timed to coincide with the publication of this book. The exhibition would not have been possible without the generous support of The Estate of Helen Chadwick and Richard Saltoun Gallery, who have worked tirelessly to promote and champion Chadwick's artistic legacy. We are grateful to the public lenders who have supported the exhibition: significantly Leeds Museums and Galleries and The Archive of Sculptors' Papers at the Henry Moore Institute who, as the keepers of Chadwick's archive, have provided substantial backing, loans and guidance. We would also like to thank: Tate; York Art Gallery; Museums Sheffield; Arts Council England; Nottingham City Museums and Galleries; The Victoria and Albert Museum, London; Birmingham Museums; Walker Art Gallery, Liverpool; Harris Museum, Preston and Jupiter Artland for their generous loans, as well as all of the private lenders who have so kindly lent precious works of art from their homes and collections. We are delighted that the exhibition is touring to Museo Novecento in Florence and Kunsthaus Graz, and we extend our gratitude and friendship to our collaborative touring partners. Finally, we would like to thank The Henry Moore Foundation, Tony's Chocolonely, Atelier Ellis and the Helen Chadwick Exhibition Supporters' Circle for helping enable the realisation of this ambitious exhibition at The Hepworth Wakefield.

Simon Wallis, Director, The Hepworth Wakefield

Illustration Credits

Works by Helen Chadwick
© Estate of Helen Chadwick

2, **15–19**, **22**, **100**, **105**, **139**, **145–7**, **150–51**, **172**, **258–9**, **261** Leeds Museums and Galleries (Henry Moore Institute Archive of Sculptors' Papers). Photo: Anya Fiáine-Fox **7**, **30–38** The Estate of Helen Chadwick. Courtesy of Richard Saltoun Gallery, London, Rome and New York **10**, **12**, **23**, **25–8**, **40**, **42–3**, **74**, **98–9**, **134**, **136–8**, **140**, **155**, **166–8**, **174–5**, **177**, **181–3**, **185**, **189**, **193**, **197**, **223–4**, **239**, **242**, **257** Leeds Museums and Galleries (Henry Moore Institute Archive of Sculptors' Papers **21** Leeds Museums and Galleries (Henry Moore Institute Archive of Sculptors' Papers). Photo: Tate **24** Courtesy the Estate of Helen Chadwick and LUX Collection, London. © LUX 2024 **45**, **254** Leeds Museums and Galleries (Henry Moore Institute Archive of Sculptors' Papers). Photo: Edward Woodman **46–8**, **50**, **51**, **186** Private Collection of Marguerite Steed Hoffman Photo: Jeff McLane **49** York Museums Trust (York Art Gallery). Presented by the Art Fund and the Esmee Fairbairn Foundation, 2013. Photo: York Museums Trust **52** Sheffield Museums - Graves Art Gallery. Photo: Sheffield Museums **53**, **188** Arts Council Collection, Southbank Centre, London **54** Nottingham City Museums and Galleries. Photo: Leeds Museums and Galleries (Henry Moore Institute Archive of Sculptors' Papers) **57–66** Private Collection. Photo:Mark Pilkington, courtesy of Tate **69–73**, **132**, **173**, **179**, **195** Victoria and Albert Museum, London. © Estate of Helen Chadwick; Victoria and Albert Museum, London **75** Tate: Purchased 2018. Photo courtesy of Richard Saltoun Gallery, London, Rome and New York **76** The Estate of Helen Chadwick. Photo: Edward Woodman **79–84** The Estate of Helen Chadwick. Courtesy Richard Saltoun Gallery, London, Rome and New York. Photo courtesy of Tate **85** © Edward Woodman. All Rights Reserved, DACS. Photo: Edward Woodman **86**, **107**, **118**, **120–22**, **126**, **129**, **130–31**, **157**, **191**, **200**, **209–11**, **213**, **214** The Estate of Helen Chadwick, Courtesy Richard Saltoun Gallery, London, Rome and New York. Photo courtesy of Richard Saltoun Gallery **88–9, 90–1**, **92–3**, **94–5**, **96–7** Courtesy National Museums Liverpool, Walker Art Gallery **102–3** Tate. Photo: Edward Woodman **104**, **158** The Estate of Helen Chadwick, Courtesy Richard Saltoun Gallery, London, Rome and New York. Photo: Edward Woodman **106** Harris Museum, Preston. Photo courtesy of Richard Saltoun Gallery, London, Rome and New York **108** Jupiter Artland Foundation. Photo courtesy of Richard Saltoun Gallery, London, Rome and New York **109 (above)** Leeds Museums and Galleries (Leeds Art Gallery). Purchased with the aid of grants from the National Art Collections Fund and the MLA / V&A Purchase Grant Fund, 2003. © Leeds Museums and Galleries, UK / Bridgeman Images **109 (below)** Private Collection. © Marlena Eleini / Bridgeman Images **113** The Estate of Helen Chadwick; Courtesy Richard Saltoun Gallery, London, Rome and New York. Photo courtesy of Banff Art Centre, Canada **114–15** Photo courtesy of Banff Art Centre, Canada **117** Private Collection. Photo courtesy Richard Saltoun Gallery, London, Rome and New York **119** Private Collection. Photo courtesy Richard Saltoun Gallery, London, Rome and New York **123** © Edward Woodman. All Rights Reserved, DACS. Photo: Edward Woodman **125** The Estate of Helen Chadwick; Courtesy Richard Saltoun Gallery, London, Rome and New York **127**, **161**, **206** The Estate of Helen Chadwick; Courtesy Richard Saltoun Gallery, London, Rome and New York. © 1994 Helen Chadwick. Photo courtesy of Serpentine Gallery London **128** Private Collection of Heloisa Ganesh. Photo courtesy Richard Saltoun Gallery, London, Rome and New York **142** Metropolitan Museum of Art, New York, USA. © The Metropolitan Museum of Art / Art Resource / Scala, Florence **143** © Northwestern University / © The Easton Foundation. Licensed by DACS, UK and VAGA at Artist Rights Society (ARS), NY. Photo: Peter Moore **148** Courtesy the Artist and Sadie Coles HQ, London. © Sarah Lucas **149** Tate: Purchased, 2003. © DACS, 2024 **153** Loaned by Birmingham Museums Trust on behalf of Birmingham City Council. © Edward Woodman. All Rights Reserved, DACS. Photo: Edward Woodman **154** Victoria and Albert Museum, London; Tate. © Edward Woodman. All Rights Reserved, DACS. Photo: Edward Woodman **196** Paris, Musée d'Art Moderne. © 2008 Christie's Images Limited. Photo: Christie's **164** Leeds Museums and Galleries (Henry Moore Institute Archive of Sculptors' Papers). Photo: David Notarius **198** Courtesy Richard Saltoun Gallery, London, Rome and New York. © Kippa Matthews. Photo: Kippa Matthews **203–4** Photo: Edward Woodman **205** The Estate of Helen Chadwick; Courtesy of Richard Saltoun Gallery, London, Rome and New York. Photo: Peter White **207** The Estate of Helen Chadwick; Courtesy of Richard Saltoun Gallery, London, Rome and New York. Photo: Jupiter Artland **212** Private Collection. Photo courtesy of Richard Saltoun Gallery, London, Rome and New York **215** Private Collection. Photo courtesy of Richard Saltoun Gallery, London, Rome and New York **216, 228–9** © Edward Woodman. All Rights Reserved, DACS. Photo: Edward Woodman **231** Yale Center for British Art, Gift of Joy of Giving Something, Inc. **232** Purchase for Photographs Collection, National Portrait Gallery, 1988.© Gautier Deblonde. Photo: Gautier Deblonde **234 (left and right)** Courtesy FotoFest. © FotoFest. **236** Courtesy Beck Road Arts Trust. © Edward Woodman. Photo: Edward Woodman **241** Courtesy Beck Road Arts Trust. Photo: Tomasz Pobog Malinowski **249** Courtesy the Estate of Helen Chadwick

Index